VOLTAIRE ALMIGHTY

VOLTAIRE ALMIGHTY

A Life in Pursuit of Freedom

Roger Pearson

BLOOMSBURY

Published by Bloomsbury Publishing, New York and London
Distributed to the trade by Holtzbrinck Publishers

All papers used by Bloomsbury Publishing are natural, recyclable
products made from wood grown in well-managed forests. The
manufacturing processes conform to the environmental
regulations of the country of origin.

Library of Congress Cataloging-in-Publication Data has been applied for.

Endpapers: Plan de Turgot © Giraudon/Bridgeman Art Library

ISBN 1-58234-630-5
ISBN-13 978-1-58234-630-4

First U.S. Edition 2005

1 3 5 7 9 10 8 6 4 2

Typeset by Hewer Text UK Ltd, Edinburgh
Printed in the United States of America by Quebecor World Fairfield

For Vivienne

I have always valued freedom above everything else.

Mémoires pour servir à la vie de M. de Voltaire

CONTENTS

ENDINGS (1768–1778):
FROM GARDEN TO GRAVE

Dramatis Personae

(being a list of the principal personages appearing in the action)

ADAM, PÈRE: Jesuit priest and for many years a house-guest of Voltaire at Ferney.

ALEMBERT, JEAN LE ROND D' (1717–83): illegitimate son of Mme de Tencin (q.v.), who abandoned him as a baby on the steps of Saint-Jean-le-Rond church; celebrated mathematician and scientist who collaborated with Denis Diderot (q.v.) on the *Encyclopédie* (until he resigned in 1758) and wrote its *Discours préliminaire* (1751), was elected a member of the Académie des Sciences at a young age and later of the Académie Française (1754).

ALGAROTTI, COUNT FRANCESCO (1712–64): noted for his popularization of Newtonian science in *Il Newtonianismo per le dame* (1737); subsequently a member of Frederick the Great's court, where he numbered among the king's lovers.

ARGENS, JEAN-BAPTISTE DE BOYER, MARQUIS D' (1704–71): radical deist and *philosophe*.

ARGENSON, MARC-PIERRE DE VOYER, COMTE D' (1696–1764): brother of the marquis d'Argenson (q.v.) and also lifelong schoolfriend of Voltaire; after a period as the senior official in charge of censorship and book publication, became Minister of War and founded the École Militaire. A supporter of the *philosophes*, he was the dedicatee of the first volumes of the *Encyclopédie*.

ARGENSON, RENÉ-LOUIS DE VOYER, MARQUIS D' (1694–1757): lifelong schoolfriend of Voltaire, supporter of the *philosophes*, noted political theorist, and Minister of Foreign Affairs (1744–7).

ARGENTAL, CHARLES-AUGUSTIN FERIOL, COMTE D' (1700–88): nephew of Mme de Tencin (q.v.), magistrate, diplomat at Versailles (representing the Duke of Parma), lifelong schoolfriend of Voltaire, whom he advised on his plays and for whom he acted as intermediary with the Comédie-Française during Voltaire's long absence from Paris.

ARGENTAL, JEANNE GRÂCE BOSC DU BOUCHET, COMTESSE D': wife of the above, who also advised on Voltaire's plays.

AROUET, ARMAND (1685–1745): elder brother of Voltaire, lawyer and public administrator.

AROUET, FRANÇOIS (1649–1722): father of Voltaire, lawyer, public administrator and businessman.

AROUET, MARGUERITE-CATHERINE: see Mignot.

AROUET, MARIE-MARGUERITE, née DAUMARD (?1661–1701): mother of Voltaire.

BACULARD D'ARNAUD, FRANÇOIS-THOMAS-MARIE DE (1718–1805): poet, dramatist and writer of romances; once a protégé of Voltaire but later scorned by him; sometime lover of Mme Denis (q.v.).

BEAUMARCHAIS, PIERRE-AUGUSTIN CARON DE (1732–99): dramatist, entrepreneur and adventurer, editor of Voltaire's Complete Works in the Kehl edition.

BENTINCK, CHARLOTTE-SOPHIE D'ALDENBURG, COUNTESS (1715–1800): married William, third son of John William Bentinck, the first Earl of Portland, from whom she separated in 1740, friend and probably mistress of Voltaire.

BERNIÈRES, GILLES-HENRI-MAIGNART, MARQUIS DE: senior judge in the Rouen *parlement*.

BERNIÈRES, MARGUERITE-MAGDELEINE DU MOUTIER, MARQUISE DE: wife of the above, mistress of Voltaire.

BOILEAU(-DESPRÉAUX), NICOLAS (1636–1711): formerly a lawyer, then poet and author of *L'Art poétique* (1674); neighbour of Arouet family in the Palais de Justice.

BOLINGBROKE, HENRY ST JOHN, VISCOUNT (1678–1751): thinker and Tory statesman, exiled to France after death of Queen Anne, and again from 1736 to 1744. Author of *Letters on the Study and Use of History* (1752).

BOUFFLERS, MARIE-CATHERINE DE BEAUVAU, MARQUISE DE (1711–?): abandoned by her husband, she took up residence at Lunéville in Lorraine at the court of Stanislas (q.v.), the deposed King of Poland, and became his mistress.

BRETEUIL, LOUIS-NICOLAS LE TONNELIER, BARON DE: father of Mme du Châtelet (q.v.).

CALAS, JEAN (1698–1762): Protestant merchant in Toulouse, executed on false charge of having murdered his son. Finally exonerated in 1765.

CHAMPBONIN, ANNE ANTOINETTE FRANÇOISE PAULIN, MME DU RAGET DE: neighbour and frequent house-guest of Voltaire and Mme du Châtelet at Cirey. Her son worked for a time as Voltaire's secretary.

CHARLES IX (1550–74): King of France, son of Catherine de Médicis, who acted as regent during his minority and at whose behest he instigated the Saint Bartholomew's Day massacre of French Protestants on 23–4 August 1572.

CHARLES XII (1682–1718): King of Sweden and subject of Voltaire's first prose history.

CHÂTEAUNEUF, ABBÉ FRANÇOIS DE CASTAGNÈRE DE (?–1708): Voltaire's godfather.

CHÂTELET, GABRIELLE-ÉMILIE LE TONNELIER DE BRETEUIL, MARQUISE DU (1706–49): mathematician and scientist; Voltaire's lover and companion from 1733 until her death.

CHOISEUL, ÉTIENNE-FRANÇOIS, COMTE DE STAINVILLE and DUC DE (1719–85): after a brilliant military career, became a diplomat, as a protégé of Mme de Pompadour (q.v.), and then (as Minister of Foreign Affairs) effectively prime minister from 1758 until his fall from power in 1770.

CIDEVILLE, PIERRE-ROBERT LE CORNIER DE: lifelong schoolfriend of Voltaire, magistrate in the Rouen *parlement* and supporter of the *philosophes*.

CLAIRON, MLLE, pseudonym of CLAIRE-JOSÈPHE LERIS DE LATUDE (1723–1803): leading tragic actress with the Comédie-Française from 1743 to 1765; with Lekain (q.v.) introduced more natural style of acting.

COLLINI, COSIMO ALESSANDRO (1727–1806): Voltaire's secretary (1752–6); from 1759 employed by the Elector Palatine, Prince Karl-Theodor, and became the first Keeper of the Mannheim Natural History Collection.

CONDORCET, MARIE-JEAN-ANTOINE-NICOLAS DE CARITAT, MARQUIS DE (1743–94): mathematician, elected to the Académie des Sciences at the age of twenty-six, pupil of d'Alembert (q.v.), *philosophe*, politician during the Revolution, and early biographer of Voltaire.

CORNEILLE, MARIE-FRANÇOISE: see Dupuits.

CRAMER, GABRIEL (1723–93): Genevan publisher.

CRAMER, PHILIBERT (1727–79): Genevan publisher and member of Geneva's ruling council.

CRÉBILLON, PROSPER JOLYOT, SIEUR DE (1674–1762): leading dramatist, official censor, and member of the Académie Française.

DAMILAVILLE, ÉTIENNE NOËL (1723–68): friend of Voltaire, supporter of the *philosophes*.

DEFFAND, MARIE DE VICHY-CHAMROND, MARQUISE DU (1697–1780): former mistress of the Regent, Philippe d'Orléans (q.v.); distinguished salon hostess and contemporary of Voltaire, whom she had met at the court of the duchesse du Maine (q.v.) and with whom she remained in contact for the rest of her life.

DENIS, MARIE-LOUISE, née MIGNOT (1712–90): Voltaire's niece, mistress (from 1745) and companion (1754–78).

DESFONTAINES, ABBÉ PIERRE-FRANÇOIS GUYOT (1685–1745): ex-Jesuit priest, journalist, translator and critic, and Voltaire's most reviled enemy.

DIDEROT, DENIS (1713–84): innovative thinker and atheist *philosophe*, editor of the *Encyclopédie*, dramatist, novelist, art critic; many of his more controversial works were published only posthumously.

DOMPIERRE D'HORNOY, ALEXANDRE: see Hornoy.

DU BARRY, MARIE-JEANNE BÉCU, COMTESSE (1743–93): mistress of Louis XV following the death of Mme de Pompadour (q.v.); executed during the Terror.

DUCLOS, MARIE-ANNE DE CHÂTEAUNEUF (MLLE DUCLOS) (*c*. 1670–1748): leading actress at the Comédie-Française.

DUFRESNE: see Quinault.

DUNOYER, CATHERINE OLYMPE (PIMPETTE): Voltaire's first love.

DUPLESSIS-VILLETTE, CHARLES MICHEL, MARQUIS DE: friend and host of Voltaire in the last days of his life.

DUPLESSIS-VILLETTE, REINE-PHILIBERTE ROUPH DE VARICOURT, MARQUISE DE (BELLE ET BONNE): wife of the above, protégée of Voltaire during the last years of his life.

DUPUITS, MARIE-FRANÇOISE, née CORNEILLE: descendant of the dramatist Pierre Corneille (1606–84), and protégé of Voltaire and Mme Denis (q.v.).

ÉTALLONDE, JACQUES-MARIE-BERTRAND GAILLARD D': an associate of the chevalier de La Barre (q.v.) and tried *in absentia*, having fled from France to become an officer in the Prussian army. Eventually exonerated after Voltaire's death.

FAWKENER, SIR EVERARD: merchant and later diplomat; became British ambassador to Constantinople (present-day Istanbul); close friend of Voltaire during the latter's stay in England (1726–8).

FLEURY, ANDRÉ HERCULE, CARDINAL DE (1653–1743): chief minister under Louis XV.

FLORIAN, MARIE-ELISABETH DE DOMPIERRE DE FONTAINE, née MIGNOT, MARQUISE DE: younger daughter of Voltaire's sister, Marguerite-Catherine Mignot (q.v.).

FONTAINE, MME DE: see Florian.

FONTAINE-MARTEL, ANTOINETTE-MADELEINE DE BORDEAUX, COMTESSE or BARONNE DE: Voltaire lodged with her from 1731–3.

FORMEY, SAMUEL (1711–98): born in Berlin, the son of Huguenot refugees; became Perpetual Secretary of the Berlin Academy.

FRANCIS I (1708–65): Duke of Lorraine (1727–35), Grand Duke of Tuscany (from 1737), Holy Roman Emperor (from 1745), husband of Maria Theresa (from 1736).

FRANKLIN, BENJAMIN (1706–90): American physicist and statesman, and one of the founding fathers of the United States.

FREDERICK II, or FREDERICK THE GREAT (1712–86): King of Prussia from 1740; first wrote to Voltaire in 1736, and the two men corresponded until Voltaire's death.

FRÉRON, ÉLIE-CATHERINE (1718–76): journalist, opponent of Voltaire and the *philosophes*.

FREYTAG, BARON FRANZ VON: Frederick II's representative in Frankfurt, who 'arrested' Voltaire after his departure from Berlin.

FYOT DE LA MARCHE, CLAUDE-PHILIPPE: schoolfriend of Voltaire, senior judge in the Dijon *parlement*.

GOUVERNET, SUZANNE-CATHERINE GRAVET DE CORSEMBLEU DE LIVRY, MARQUISE DE: Voltaire's mistress in 1716 and perhaps subsequently.

GRAFFIGNY, FRANÇOISE D'ISSEMBOURG D'HAPPONCOURT DE (1695–1758): impoverished aristocrat and battered wife, she became famous for her novel *Lettres d'une péruvienne* (1747) and her play *Cénie* (1750). Wrote several lengthy letters recording life at Cirey.

HELVÉTIUS, CLAUDE-ADRIEN (1715–71): extremely rich tax-farmer, *philosophe* and author of *De l'esprit* (1758), which was banned by the Paris *parlement* and the Pope.

HENRI III (1551–89): King of France (from 1574).

HENRI IV (1553–1610): King of France (from 1589).

HERVEY, LORD FREDERICK (1730–1803): son of Lord John Hervey (q.v.), Bishop of Derry and later (1779) fourth Earl of Bristol; visited Voltaire at Ferney.

HERVEY, LORD JOHN (1693–1743): friend of Voltaire during his stay in England.

HERVEY, LADY MARY (1700–68): wife of the above; a noted beauty and member of the Prince and Princess of Wales's circle.

HOLBACH, PAUL-HENRY THIRY, BARON D' (1723–89): German-born atheist *philosophe*, author of *Le Système de la nature* (1770), in which he propounds his materialist philosophy.

HORNOY, ALEXANDRE-MARIE-FRANÇOIS DE PAULE DE DOMPIERRE D': son of Voltaire's younger niece, Marie-Élisabeth Mignot, by her first marriage (to Nicolas-Joseph de Dompierre de Fontaine), who then added the name of Hornoy, the family seat of his mother's second husband, the marquis de Florian (q.v.).

HOUDON, JEAN-ANTOINE (*c.* 1741–1828): sculptor noted for his busts and statues of Voltaire and other contemporaries: Diderot (q.v.), Rousseau (q.v.), Buffon, Washington, Franklin (q.v.).

HUBER, JEAN (1721–86): a native of Savoy, painter and sketch-artist known for his depictions of Voltaire.

JORE, CLAUDE-FRANÇOIS: Rouen publisher of the *Lettres philosophiques*.

KÖNIG, SAMUEL (1712–57): German mathematician who tutored Mme du Châtelet and was supported by Voltaire in his dispute with Maupertuis (q.v.).

LA BARRE, JEAN-FRANÇOIS LEFEBVRE, CHEVALIER DE (1745–66): young aristocrat executed for sacrilege and impious behaviour; subsequently championed by Voltaire.

LA CONDAMINE, CHARLES-MARIE DE (1701–74): mathematician who helped Voltaire win substantial amounts in a national lottery before undertaking an expedition to South America to take measurements of the earth at the equator.

LA HARPE, JEAN-FRANÇOIS DE (1739–1803): dramatist, journalist and critic. Protégé of Voltaire.

LALLY, THOMAS ARTHUR, BARON OF TOLLENDAL and COMTE DE (1702–66): brilliant soldier of Irish Jacobite descent who fought with distinction at the battle of Fontenoy (1745); executed in 1766 for alleged treason during his service to the French crown in India.

LALLY-TOLLENDAL, TROPHIME-GÉRARD, CHEVALIER (later marquis) DE: son of the above.

LA METTRIE, JULIEN OFFROY DE (1709–51): physician and materialist philosopher; author of *L'Homme machine* (1748) and *L'Homme plante* (1749); sought refuge from the French authorities at the court of Frederick the Great.

LA NEUVILLE, JEANNE CHARLOTTE DE VIART D'ATTIGNEVILLE, COMTESSE DE: neighbour of Voltaire and Mme du Châtelet at Cirey.

LA VALLIÈRE, ANNE-JULIE-FRANÇOISE DE CRUSSOL, DUCHESSE DE (1713–93): wife of the duc de La Vallière (q.v.); a famous beauty and a match for her husband's libertinage.

LA VALLIÈRE, LOUIS-CÉSAR DE LA BAUME LE BLANC, DUC DE (1708–80): grandson of Louis XIV's famous mistress, the duchesse de La Vallière (1644–1710), who became a nun at the age of thirty; celebrated for his library, his amours and his generosity as a host. Charged with organizing private entertainments for Louis XV.

LECOUVREUR, ADRIENNE (1692–1730): made her début with the Comédie-Française in 1717 and became the leading actress of her time.

LEKAIN (stage name of HENRI-LOUIS CAIN) (1729–78): leading actor in the Comédie-Française and creator of many of Voltaire's most successful male roles.

LENCLOS, NINON DE (1620–1705): legendary courtesan and society hostess, noted for her freethinking and unconventional morals.

LESZCZYNSKA, MARIE (1703–68): daughter of Stanislas I, King of Poland (q.v.), and wife of Louis XV, by whom she had ten children (none of whom survived to succeed him).

LINANT, MICHEL: tutor to Mme du Châtelet's son at Cirey.

LIVRY, SUZANNE DE: see Gouvernet.

LONGCHAMP, SÉBASTIEN: Voltaire's secretary.

LOUIS XIII (1601–43): son of Henri IV, King of France from 1610.

LOUIS XIV (1638–1715): son and successor of Louis XIII.

LOUIS XV (1710–74): great-grandson and successor of Louis XIV.

LOUIS XVI (1754–93): grandson and successor of Louis XV; deposed in 1792 and executed the following year.

MAINE, LOUIS-AUGUSTE DE BOURBON, DUC DU (1676–1736): legitimated son of Louis XIV and Mme de Montespan, who might have succeeded his father but for the deal struck between Philippe d'Orléans (q.v.) and the Paris *parlement* under which Philippe d'Orléans became Regent.

MAINE, LOUISE-BÉNÉDICTE DE BOURBON-CONDÉ, DUCHESSE DE (1676–1753): wife of the above (from 1692), and presided over her own court at Sceaux and Anet.

MAISONS, JEAN-RENÉ DE LONGUEIL, MARQUIS DE: schoolfriend of Voltaire at whose house he fell ill with smallpox.

MARIA THERESA (1717–1780): Archduchess of Austria, Queen of Hungary and Bohemia, wife of Emperor Francis I (q.v.).

MARIE-ANTOINETTE (1755–93): Austrian princess, daughter of Francis I (q.v.) and Maria Theresa (q.v.), and wife of Louis XVI (q.v.); executed during the Terror.

MARIVAUX, PIERRE DE (1688–1763): novelist, comic dramatist, and journalist. Elected to the Académie Française (in preference to Voltaire) in 1742.

MARMONTEL, JEAN-FRANÇOIS (1723–99): contributor to the *Encyclopédie*, writer of short stories, plays, and historical romances with philosophical content; editor of the *Mercure de France* from 1758; a protégé of Voltaire and sometime lover of Mme Denis; elected to the Académie Française in 1763 and succeeded d'Alembert (q.v.) as Perpetual Secretary in 1783.

MAUPEOU, RENÉ-NICOLAS DE (1714–92): chancellor under Louis XV, who (temporarily) reformed the *parlements*.

MAUPERTUIS, PIERRE-LOUIS MOREAU DE (1698–1759): geometer and scientist, elected to the Académie des Sciences at the age of twenty-five, and the first Frenchman to be elected to the Royal Society in London; President of the Academy of Science in Berlin from 1740; early advocate of Newtonian science, travelled to Lapland to measure a degree of the meridian (1736); tutor and lover of Mme du Châtelet; ridiculed by Voltaire during his dispute with König (q.v.).

MAUREPAS, JEAN-FRÉDÉRIC PHÉLYPEAUX, COMTE DE (1701–81): minister under Louis XV until exiled in 1749 for an epigram mocking Mme de Pompadour (q.v.); recalled to office by Louis XVI.

MIGNOT, ABBÉ ALEXANDRE JEAN: son of Marguerite-Catherine Mignot (q.v.) and Voltaire's nephew, who played a key role in securing a Christian burial for him.

MIGNOT, MARGUERITE-CATHERINE, née AROUET (1686–1726): Voltaire's sister, and mother of Mme Denis (q.v.) and Mme de Fontaine (later marquise de Florian (q.v.)).

MIGNOT, PIERRE-FRANÇOIS (?–1737): husband of the above.

MIRABEAU, HONORÉ-GABRIEL DE RIQUETI, COMTE DE (1749–91): leading Revolutionary statesman and orator; advocate of constitutional monarchy; buried in the Panthéon and later removed.

NECKER, JACQUES (1732–1804): Genevan banker who settled in Paris and directed French finances from 1776 until 1781, and again from 1788–90.

NECKER, SUZANNE CURCHOD (1739–94): daughter of a Genevan pastor and wife of the above (from 1765: the future Mme de Staël was their daughter); leading salon hostess in Paris, numbering many Huguenots and *philosophes* among her guests.

NONNOTTE, ABBÉ CLAUDE-FRANÇOIS (1711–93): Jesuit author of *Les Erreurs de Voltaire* (1762) and thereafter one of Voltaire's favourite bugbears.

PALISSOT DE MONTENOY, CHARLES (1730–1814): dramatist, opponent of the *philosophes* but admirer of Voltaire, author of the satirical comedy *Les Philosophes* (1760).

PANCKOUCKE, CHARLES-JOSEPH (1736–98): celebrated publisher who initiated production of the first Complete Works of Voltaire.

PÂRIS, JOSEPH (known as PARIS-DUVERNEY) (1684–1770): one of four brothers, sons of an innkeeper, who became leading financiers under the Regency and during the reign of Louis XV. With his brother Jean (Pâris-Montmartel), facilitated many investment opportunities for Voltaire, and later enriched Beaumarchais (q.v.), enabling the latter to take on the Kehl edition of Voltaire's complete works.

PASCAL, BLAISE (1623–62): Jansenist mathematician, physicist and philosopher, author of the *Lettres Provinciales* (1656–7) and the *Pensées* (published posthumously).

PHILIPPE D'ORLÉANS (1674–1723): son of Louis XIV's only brother, and Regent during Louis XV's minority.

POMPADOUR, JEANNE-ANTOINETTE POISSON LE NORMAND D'ETIOLES, MARQUISE DE (1721–64): born into the *haute bourgeoisie*, she became Louis XV's mistress in 1745; intelligent and cultivated patroness of the arts, and highly influential in political affairs.

QUINAULT, ABRAHAM-ALEXIS (DUFRESNE): celebrated actor at the Comédie-Française and creator of Voltaire's earliest leading roles.

QUINAULT-DUFRESNE, JEANNE-FRANÇOISE (MLLE QUINAULT) (*c.* 1700–83): stage-director and leading actress at the Comédie-Française; noted salon hostess.

RICHELIEU, ARMAND DU PLESSIS, CARDINAL DE (1585–1642): chief minister under Louis XIII (from 1624).

RICHELIEU, LOUIS-FRANÇOIS-ARMAND VIGNEROT DU PLESSIS, DUC DE (1696–1788): great-nephew of the above, led a highly successful military career and became a *maréchal de France*. Lifelong schoolfriend of Voltaire, who masterminded his marriage to Elisabeth de Guise.

ROCHEBRUNE (? ROQUEBRUNE), GUÉRIN DE (?–1719): writer of popular verse; Voltaire's probable biological father.

ROHAN-CHABOT, GUY-AUGUSTE, CHEVALIER (later COMTE) DE (1683–1760): undistinguished aristocrat who hired men to beat up Voltaire.

ROUSSEAU, JEAN-BAPTISTE (1671–1741): poet and satirist, exiled from France in 1707.

ROUSSEAU, JEAN-JACQUES (1712–78): Genevan-born *philosophe* (and critic of the *philosophes*), author of the *Discours sur l'inégalité* (1754), a radical political theorist in *Du contrat social* and pioneering educationalist in *Émile* (both 1762), a bestselling novelist with *Julie, ou la Nouvelle Héloïse* (1761), and innovative autobiographer with his *Confessions* (written 1764–70; published posthumously in 1781 (books 1–6) and 1788 (books 7–12)) and his *Rêveries du promeneur solitaire* (written towards the end of his life and published in 1782).

RUPELMONDE, MARIE-MARGUERITE D'ALIGRE DE (1688–1752): widow and briefly Voltaire's mistress.

SAINT-ANGE, LOUIS URBAIN LEFÈVRE DE CAUMARTIN, MARQUIS DE (1653–1720): former member of Louis XIV's ruling council and an important source of Voltaire's interest in, and knowledge of, French history.

SAINT-LAMBERT, JEAN-FRANÇOIS DE (1716–1803): soldier and poet, author of *Les Saisons*, ally of the *encyclopédistes*, member of the Académie Française, and lover of Mme du Châtelet.

SAUSSURE, HORACE-BÉNÉDICT DE (1740–99): leading Genevan physicist, and son of a professor of physics.

SAUSSURE, JUDITH DE (1745–?): sister of the above.

SAXE-GOTHA, LOUISA DOROTHEA VON MEININGEN, DUCHESS OF: friend and correspondent of Voltaire.

STANISLAS I (1677–1766): former King of Poland, father of Marie Leszczynska (q.v.), and ruler of Lorraine.

TENCIN, CLAUDINE-ALEXANDRINE GUÉRIN, MARQUISE DE (1682–1749): defrocked nun, briefly the mistress of Philippe d'Orléans (q.v.), mother of d'Alembert (q.v.), whom she abandoned as a baby, distinguished salon hostess, and author of romances.

TENCIN, PIERRE GUÉRIN, CARDINAL DE (1679–1758): brother of the above, Archbishop of Lyon, opponent of the Jansenists, and for a time an influential minister of state under Cardinal Fleury (q.v.).

THIRIOT (OR THIERIOT), NICOLAS-CLAUDE (1697–1772): lifelong friend of Voltaire whose amiability was not matched by his loyalty.

TRONCHIN, FRANÇOIS (1704–98): lawyer and playwright, member of Geneva's ruling council, and an influential friend of Voltaire during his period of residence in Geneva. Occupied Les Délices after Voltaire.

TRONCHIN, JEAN-ROBERT (1702–88): brother of the above, lawyer and banker (in Lyon), and later a tax-farmer in Paris. From 1754 acted as banker to Voltaire, who held the property of Les Délices in his name (1755–65).

TRONCHIN, THÉODORE (1709–81): leading physician in Geneva and then Paris (from 1766), who attended Voltaire at various times, including during his last illness.

TURGOT, ANNE-ROBERT-JACQUES (1727–81): economist and administrator, Controller-General of finance (1774–6) who pursued a policy of liberalization.

VADÉ, JEAN-JOSEPH (1720–57): parodist and author of popular comedies, notorious for his use of the dialect of Paris markets in his plays.

VERNES, JACOB (1728–91): Genevan pastor.

VERNET, JACOB (1698–1789): Genevan pastor and professor of theology.

VILLETTE, MARQUIS DE: see Duplessis-Villette.

WAGNIÈRE, JEAN-LOUIS (1739–?): Voltaire's secretary.

WILHELMINE, MARGRAVE OF BAYREUTH (1709–58): sister of Frederick the Great, friend and regular correspondent of Voltaire until her death.

WÜRTTEMBERG, FREDERIKA SOPHIA, DUCHESS OF: daughter of the above and wife of the Duke of Württemberg (q.v.), from whom she separated in 1756 after eight years of marriage.

WÜRTTEMBERG, KARL EUGENE, DUKE OF (1728–?): funded the extravagance of his court at Stuttgart in part by selling annuities to Voltaire (and being constantly late with the quarterly payments).

France, Europe and America 1643–1799

1643   Accession of Louis XIV (b.1638) to the French throne. His mother, Anne of Austria, appointed Regent (until 1651)

1660   Marriage of Louis XIV and Maria Theresa, Infanta of Spain

1661   Louis XIV assumes full control of government following the death of his chief minister, Cardinal Mazarin

1683   Death of Queen Maria Theresa

1684   Secret marriage of Louis XIV to Mme de Maintenon (1635–1719), governess to his two illegitimate sons by Mme de Montespan (1640–1707): the duc du Maine (1670–1736) and the comte de Toulouse (1678–1737)

1685   Revocation of the Edict of Nantes by which in 1598 Henri IV had granted religious toleration to French Huguenots (Protestants): some 50,000 Huguenot families flee abroad, notably to Prussia, the city state of Geneva, Switzerland, the United Provinces (i.e. Holland) and their colony in southern Africa, England and British North America

1687   Isaac Newton, *Principia mathematica*

1689   Bill of Rights in England

1690   John Locke, *Essay Concerning Human Understanding* (trans. into French, 1700) and *Second Treatise on Government*

1694   **Birth of François-Marie Arouet, later known as Voltaire**

1697–1718   Reign of Charles XII of Sweden

1701–1713   War of the Spanish Succession, during which England, Holland and the Holy Roman Empire (i.e. Austria, Hungary and some German states) joined forces to prevent a union of France and Spain following the accession of Philip V to the Spanish throne (which he occupied until 1746)

1710   Gottfried Leibniz, *Essais de théodicée*

1711   Death from smallpox of Louis de France (b.1661), the Grand Dauphin (also known as Monseigneur), only son of Louis XIV and Queen Maria Theresa

1712   Death from scarlet fever of Louis, duc de Bourgogne (b.1682), the Dauphin (and elder son of Louis de France), and of his wife, the duchesse de Bourgogne, and his eldest son, the four-year-old duc de Bretagne, during the same epidemic. The duc de Berry, younger son of Louis de France, is killed shortly afterwards in a riding accident

1713   Papal bull *Unigenitus* issued in Rome, condemning Jansenism

1714   The duc du Maine and the comte de Toulouse legitimated. The duc du Maine declared heir to the throne

1715   Death of Louis XIV. Accession of Louis XIV's great-grandson Louis XV (b.1710), the younger brother of the duc de Bretagne. The duc du Maine's claim to the throne set aside, and Philippe, duc d'Orléans (b.1674) appointed Regent, being the son of Louis XIV's only brother and thus first Prince of the Blood

1721   Montesquieu, *Lettres persanes*. Robert Walpole appointed first Prime Minister of Great Britain

1723   Death of Philippe d'Orléans

1725   Marriage of Louis XV to Marie Leszczynska (b.1703), daughter of the deposed King of Poland, Stanislas (1677–1766), and subsequent mother to Louis XV's ten children, none of whom survived him. Death of Peter the Great of Russia (acceded 1682)

1726 Cardinal Fleury appointed as Louis XV's chief minister (having been his tutor), and governs France until his death in 1743

1733–1735 War of the Polish Succession. Following the death of the reigning king, Augustus II of Saxony, Austria and Russia press the claims of his son, while France seeks to promote the candidacy of Stanislas Leszczynski, the Queen's father, who had ruled Poland from 1704–9. Austria and Russia succeed in having Augustus III enthroned while France secures the duchy of Lorraine for Stanislas, on the understanding that it will pass into French hands after his death

1740 Accession of Frederick (b.1716) to the throne of Prussia

1741–1748 War of the Austrian Succession. Precipitated by the death of the Emperor Charles VI in 1740 and the refusal by the Elector of Bavaria and Frederick of Prussia to recognize the Pragmatic Sanction under which the Habsburg dominions passed to the late emperor's daughter, Maria Theresa (who, as a woman, could not succeed her father as ruler of the Empire). France, together with its Bourbon ally, Spain, enters an alliance with Prussia and Bavaria and opposes its traditional Habsburg enemy in Vienna. Britain, already engaged in the so-called War of Jenkins's Ear with Spain over colonial claims in South America, sides with Austria, as do Holland and Russia. Prussia seizes Silesia from the Austrians

1745 Maria Theresa's husband, Francis, former Duke of Lorraine, elected emperor. Battle of Fontenoy, near Tournai in the Austrian Netherlands (now in modern Belgium), where the French under Maurice de Saxe and the duc de Richelieu win a famous victory against Austria and its British, Hanoverian and Dutch allies

1748 Peace treaty signed at Aix-la-Chapelle in 1748. Publication of Montesquieu, *De l'esprit des lois*

1755   Lisbon earthquake

1756–1763   Seven Years War. After the so-called Diplomatic Revolution, the alliances of the War of Austrian Succession are reversed but the causes of war remain the same: territorial claims in Europe and colonial ambitions in North and South America and the Indies. Britain and Hanover now side with Prussia, as does Denmark. To oppose them France enters a grand alliance with its age-old Habsburg enemy in Vienna, and is joined by Saxony, Sweden and Russia

1758   Duc de Choiseul becomes Louis XV's Foreign Minister and effectively prime minister (until 1770)

1762   Trial and execution of the Protestant merchant, Jean Calas, in Toulouse. Accession of Catherine (later the Great) to the Russian throne (until 1796). Rousseau, *Du contrat social*

1762–1764   Expulsion of the Jesuits from France

1763   Peace of Paris. France cedes control of Canada, Mississippi and India to Great Britain

1766   Lorraine becomes part of France on the death of Stanislas

1770   Maupeou's temporary reform of the French *parlements*. Marriage of the Dauphin, Louis XV's eldest grandson and heir, to Marie-Antoinette of Austria (b.1755), daughter of Francis I, Holy Roman Emperor, and Maria Theresa of Austria

1774   Death from smallpox of Louis XV. Accession of Louis XVI (b.1754; executed 1793)

1774–1776   Ministry of Turgot, who liberalized tax laws and commercial regulations

1775   American War of Independence begins

1776   American Declaration of Independence at Philadelphia (4 July)

1776–1781   Jacques Necker, a Genevan-born Protestant, succeeds Turgot at the Ministry of Finance

1778   Franco-American treaty. **Death of Voltaire**

1783   Peace of Versailles marks the end of the American War of Independence

1786   Death of Frederick the Great

1789   Storming of the Bastille (14 July). Beginning of the French Revolution. King accepts the legality of the *Assemblée constituante* (15 July) and the adoption of the *tricolore* (red and blue from the arms of the City of Paris, white for the Bourbon monarchy). Declaration of the Rights of Man (26 August). A Parisian crowd, led by and largely comprised of women, march on Versailles and force the return of the royal family to the Tuileries palace in Paris

1791   Louis XVI attempts to flee the country and is captured at Varennes in north-eastern France (June). Death of Mirabeau, the revolutionary leader. **Voltaire's remains transferred to the Panthéon in Paris (July).** *Assemblée législative* succeeds the *Assemblée constituante* (October)

1792   *Assemblée législative* declares war on Austria, to forestall Austro-Prussian attack intended to restore the King to power. Tuileries palace stormed and Louis XVI deposed (10 August). *Convention (nationale)* replaces the *Assemblée législative* in September, and under the leadership of Danton proposes the abolition of the monarchy. Louis XVI stands trial (11 December, until 20 January 1793)

1793   Louis XVI executed (21 January). Marat assassinated (13 July) and Robespierre comes to power. Reign of Terror begins on 17 September (and ends with the execution of Robespierre on 28 July 1794). Execution of Queen Marie-Antoinette (16 October)

1795   Beginning of the rule of the Directoire

1799   The brilliantly successful Corsican army general Napoleon
            Bonaparte (1769–1821) seizes power in a *coup d'état* on 9 No-
            vember (le 18 brumaire)

Curtain Rise

I MAGINE YOURSELF IN Paris, on the Left Bank of the Seine. Your stroll began in the formal gardens of the Palais du Luxembourg, and now you have come down the hill, in a long, gentle arc, past the Sorbonne and the Lycée Louis-le-Grand, to the river. In front of you, across the Pont Saint-Michel, lies the Île de la Cité, with the spire of the Sainte-Chapelle soaring up from the courtyard of the Palais de Justice. Over to your right the cathedral of Notre-Dame sits foursquare at the end of the island, like squat cargo at the stern of a ship. On your left, stretching back at an angle, runs the rue Saint-André-des-Arts, while on the opposite bank the tidy ranges of the Louvre march west to the Tuileries gardens and north to the Palais Royal.

Today such a walk might have brought you down the Boulevard Saint-Michel. At the end of the seventeenth century, long before Baron Haussmann carved his broad, mob-exposing boulevards through the cluttered masonry of the medieval city, you could nevertheless have made a similar journey and noted these self-same landmarks. Your route would have been more tortuous, and the hazards would have been different: slops from above, after a maliciously brief warning, or filth underfoot. Indeed had you been well-born you would not have been walking at all.

Moreover, without the modern thoroughfare, you might have thought it rather a long way. For you would in fact have been proceeding from the perimeter of the city to its centre. At the end of the 1600s the capital of France numbered about half a million inhabitants, a quarter of its present total. The city boundaries extended from the Palais du Luxembourg in the south to the imposing gateways of the Porte Saint-Denis (recently built in 1672) and the Porte Saint-Martin (1674) in the north, and from the Arsenal and the Bastille in the east to the Tuileries palace in the west. Outside these boundaries lay the nascent 'faubourgs', or false burgs, the forerunner of the modern suburb. And beyond the Tuileries lay the Champs-Elysées with its bucolic but not notably Elysian fields.

For over 500 years Paris had been the largest city in Europe, though now it was being overtaken by London. With so many people crammed together into such a small area, space was at a premium and living conditions were primitive. As in London, the bridges – with the two exceptions of the Pont Neuf and the Pont Royal – bore houses and shops. The Pont Neuf, begun in 1578 and completed in 1606, spanned – and still spans – the entire river by setting foot on the western tip of the Île de la Cité. Further west, down-stream, the Pont Royal has no need of an island: completed in 1689, it allowed its first users to avoid city-centre congestion by proceeding directly across the Seine from the Tuileries to the rue du Beaune, and thence to all roads south.

Sanitation, where it existed, was rudimentary; fresh water was often in short supply; and accommodation for the majority was cramped and uncomfortable. Fire and epidemic were constant hazards. Public order was not guaranteed: for gentlemen a pistol or sword were pertinent accessories, while for ladies the most valuable accessory was a gentleman. A carriage was essential, if you could afford it. The streets were mostly narrow and unsalubrious, without pavements: little light penetrated between their tall façades, especially to the lower floors. Many had an open drain coursing down the middle, running with the sewage that was released from innumerable privies at dead of night or with the blood of daylight slaughter from a butcher's shop. It clotted on your shoes and turned them a ruddy brown. Sometimes the beast escaped the cleaver and fled, spattering terrified pedestrians in its panicked flight. The broader streets were strewn with horse dung as countless carts and some 10,000 carriages, private or for hire, pursued their frenzied course around the capital (though generally not all at once). Axle-grease posed a constant threat to clean stockings.

Smoke curled from thousands upon thousands of chimneys, in every season. Tanners and dyers, fishmongers and blacksmiths, churches with their rotting dead and hospitals with their purulent quick, all contributed to the pestilential fug. From tallow-factories rose the nauseous stench that was the price Parisians paid for their candlelight. There were no trees, save on the outer 'boulevards' – those former bulwarks, or ramparts, of the city's defensive walls that Louis XIV had turned into airy, tree-lined promenades in the 1670s. Within these walls the atmosphere was foul and dank, lingering like congestion in the strangulated airways of the medieval city. Even along the Seine the wind found its passage impeded by the bridge-borne tenements, and the effluvia of this river-sewer wafted uncertainly on the breeze. Only on the houseless Pont Neuf did the air seem a little better: for it offered a large space in which to breathe (28 metres wide by 278 metres long) and a vantage-point from which to look up and catch a glimpse of the firmament, not just a tiny patch of sky or a dripping gutter. Here were the first pavements in Paris. Tucked away in the semicircular bays above each of the bridge's supports were small shops or stalls, nicely positioned to lure the leisured or to tempt the needy. And there was water, from the Samaritaine: Paris's first public water-fountain, pumping water up from the river and proclaiming its dubious generosity with a sculpture of the Good Samaritan.[1] But even here the well-to-do who came to stroll or watch the fireworks and the river-jousts found it advisable to have a perfume bottle and a handkerchief at the ready to keep the fetid fumes at bay. No wonder the terrors of Hell retained such a powerful grip on the popular imagination: smoking fire and sulphurous brimstone were all around.

And the noise! The clatter of wheel on cobble, the crack of whip and driver's curse, the hawker's cry and the policeman's halloo, the urgent pleas of flower-girl and pamphlet-seller, the knowledgeable mutterings of the *bouquinistes* whose stock of second-hand books might conceal a bibliophile's dream, the proud boasts of tooth-pullers and the screams of their grateful victims,[2] street entertainers singing for their supper, or charlatans promising everything from a wrinkle-free forehead to a cure for all your ills. And army men hailing prospective young recruits, luring tomorrow's cannon-fodder with the offer of jam today: a drink, a girl, a good square meal.

Hellish as Paris was, most people just had to get used to it. But some moved out, like Louis XIV in 1683. At the end of the seventeenth century the Parisians' king was living at the magnificent palace of Versailles fourteen miles away (some three hours by carriage). Louis XIII had built a hunting-lodge there in 1624, and his son later decided to make it his principal royal

residence in preference to the reek and bustle of Paris. Following marriage to
the Infanta Maria Theresa of Spain in 1660 the 22-year-old Louis XIV had
initiated an ambitious and costly programme of building and garden design.
Now, like Apollo, the Sun King dwelt at a mysterious, awe-inducing distance
from his capital, ruling over a court of opulent splendour and a nation of
some twenty million subjects.

During his reign and that of his predecessor, who had been ably guided by
Cardinal Richelieu, France had overtaken Spain as the most powerful
country in Europe. Once riven by sectarian strife – in the Wars of Religion
that dominated French history in the second half of the sixteenth century – it
had then found itself free to concentrate on its territorial ambitions. Over the
period between Richelieu's rise to power in 1624 and Louis XIV's death in
1715, France was at war for on average two years out of every three. The
periods 1635–59 and 1689–1713 were particularly bellicose. And expensive. At
the end of the century the nation's coffers were virtually empty, and much
administrative effort was going into devising and levying taxes. The King's
fighting days were nearly over, and French military superiority would end
with the Battle of Blenheim in 1704.

But, for the moment, glory shone all around: in royal pomp and
circumstance, in architecture, in the theatre, in poetry and painting. If
you had been standing on the Pont Neuf in the 1690s, you could have
thought you were at the centre of the world. A Gallic *omphalos*. For here you
were in the capital of the greatest kingdom on earth. Parisian clothes,
furniture and other luxury items were exported all over the world and
regarded as the height of fashion. Yet you had only to travel ten minutes in
any direction to purchase them direct. The French language was similarly
exported. Throughout educated, upper-class Europe it had become the
lingua franca of well-bred civility. It was the language of diplomacy, and the
hallmark of sophisticated elegance in most European courts. For this was the
Grand Siècle, the great age of French history and culture, and you were part of
it. The acme of civilization.

At least so it seemed if you were one of the people fortunate enough to
belong to the Parisian élite. In a country where some four-fifths of the
population eked a miserable existence from the land and barely a quarter of
the male population – and significantly fewer women – could read, Parisian

power and prestige lay with a tiny and very privileged minority of some two to three thousand people. Beneath them a much larger, prosperous and well-educated middle class aspired to join them. Their shared world was a small one, and – apart from Versailles itself – the centres of polite society were select and few: the theatre, the opera, the salon, or the gardens of the Tuileries, the Palais Royal, and the Luxembourg. In these beautiful places anyone who was anyone could be sure to meet a somebody. And at the heart of their political and professional world stood the *parlement*, not a parliament but courts and administrative offices that ruled over Paris and its environs in the name of the King. The law was a growth industry (by the 1760s the city would count one legal official to every eighty-five Parisians), and for its magistrates the *parlement* in its myriad manifestations was the surest ladder from bourgeois commonership to aristocratic bliss.

These were the places where people met and talked and strived. But communication in late-seventeenth-century France was severely circumscribed by a limited technology, the constraints of good manners and the watchful eye of the censor. This was a world with no telegraph or telephone. Travel was expensive or arduous, and often both. Law courts and academies may have brought the men together, but for women an evening at the Opéra, the Comédie-Italienne, or the Comédie-Française was a vital opportunity for social intercourse, which is no doubt why so many members of the audience – male *and* female – conversed during the performances. Supper-parties and balls, salon receptions and theatre visits, these were the privileged channels for the live exchange of information and opinion, while the circulating manuscript and the printed word offered the sole equivalent of the recording and the action replay. It was a small world in which appearances counted for everything and reputation was all.

But even a small world can have dark corners. The day-to-day running of the city was essentially in the hands of the Lieutenant of Police, a post created in 1667. Not only were the police there to ensure obedience to the law, they also played a key role in regulating and supervising food supplies, public health, street lighting, fire prevention, and the city's industries. They therefore constituted the executive arm of the Châtelet, the assembly of lower courts that were located on the Right Bank just north of the Palais de Justice and the *parlement*. The maintenance of public order was paramount. This meant ensuring that everyone had enough to eat (the provision of bread was subsidized), limiting firearm use, suppressing begging, and controlling gambling and prostitution. It also meant enforcing religious observance and suppressing potential subversion. The Lieutenant and his police governed the dark corners of Paris with the help of a spy network drawn from the ranks of the pious or the impecunious, and its members stood ready to inform on anyone thought to be a danger to religion or the monarchy. For within and without the pale of the Establishment there existed a city-wide web of clandestine publication and whispered conversation. Beyond the theatre and the opera lay fairground, coffee-house, and tavern, potential seedbeds of subversion and market-places for the exchange of satire, tract and pamphlet. Louis XIV's Paris may have been short on privacy, but it was long on subterfuge.

And so imagine, too, that you were present in the vicinity of the rue Saint-André-des-Arts on Monday, 22 November 1694. For there you might have witnessed an intriguing scene at the local church. A small group of well-dressed persons arrives at the entrance: a woman is carrying a babe-in-arms. After a short ceremony the priest signs a certificate stating that the baby, 'born on the previous day' and now named François-Marie, has been duly baptized into the Church of Rome. The godfather is wearing clerical garb, and the godmother has an almost aristocratic air. What could be more respectable? But wait . . . 'born on the previous day'? Little François-Marie looks as though he has been around much longer than that. Perhaps even nine months longer. No, this baby certainly wasn't born yesterday.

In all likelihood the greatest French dramatist after Corneille and Racine had just performed in his first starring role; and the future scourge of the Roman Catholic Church had just taken his first, irreverent bow. His death, some eighty-three years on, would be no less theatrical and no less irreverent. Then, on the Left Bank of the Seine, in the fine residence of his friends the marquis and marquise de Villette, he would defy the priests with a simulated incapacity to confess his sins and then proudly breathe his last. Eleven years later the street in which he died would be renamed the quai Voltaire. For by then the squealing infant had become a hero and a god.

Beginnings
(1694–1733)

From Cradle to Champagne

Voltaire aged thirty. Oil painting by Nicolas de Largillière, 1728.

CHAPTER ONE

Of Uncertain Birth (1694–1704)

*How Zozo came to live in a beautiful courtyard,
and how he was kicked out of the same*

Once upon a time in Paris, in the courtyard of the Palais de Justice,
there lived a young boy whom nature had endowed with the quickest
of wits and the most wilful of dispositions. His soul – if he had one –
was written upon his countenance. He was quite sound in his judgement, and he
had the most straightforward of minds. His family nicknamed him Zozo: he
later called himself Voltaire. While he believed in God Almighty, he none the
less considered that there was still work to be done. 'God created man free,' he
wrote at the age of seventy-three: 'and that is what I have become.'[1] This is the
story of his extraordinary life, the story of a search for freedom.

Zozo was probably a bastard. Like Candide, the hero of his most famous
work. Officially little François-Marie was born in Paris on Sunday, 21
November 1694, the second surviving son of François Arouet, a lawyer, and
his wife Marie-Marguerite (née Daumard). Unofficially – but according to
Voltaire himself, on several occasions – he entered the best of all possible
worlds on Friday, 20 February 1694, the son of the chevalier Guérin de
Rochebrune (or Roquebrune), a writer of popular songs. This was certainly
his preferred paternal origin, and he defended his mother's honour by
claiming that it lay in her preference for 'a man of wit and intelligence' – 'a
musketeer, officer, and author' – over 'Monsieur his father who, in the matter
of genius, was a very mediocre man'.[2]

Little is known about Rochebrune except that he was descended from an ancient, aristocratic family from the Haute Auvergne and died of 'dropsy' in 1719. Though he wrote the libretto for a cantata on the subject of Orpheus, he appears mostly to have written songs of a rather more facetious and ephemeral kind. Curiously Voltaire includes a reference to him in a short verse tale he wrote in 1716, *Le Cadenas* (*The Padlock*), in which a sixty-year-old husband seeks to ensure his beautiful young wife's fidelity by the imposition of a chastity belt. Was the son paying tribute to his father by imitating his bawdy? Quite possibly. Voltaire may even have met Rochebrune, because the chevalier is known to have been living in the close vicinity of the Arouet family in 1707. But when did young François-Marie learn that he was his real father? Was there perhaps a physical resemblance? We do not know.

But we do know that Rochebrune was a client of Zozo's ostensible father, and it is likely that this is how the musketeer-lyricist first attracted his mother's attention. Marie-Marguerite Arouet came from a good Parisian family. Her father held an important position in the Paris *parlement* and stood one rung beneath that of noble on the ladder of social status — reflected in heraldic quartering — which was then so important. Accordingly, when she married François Arouet on 7 June 1683, she represented a step up for him (and he a handsome purse for her). In the marriage certificate her age is stated as 'about 22' — clearly this family were not sticklers for birthdays — and so she was about twenty-three when her first child, Armand-François, was born on 18 March the following year. He died soon afterwards — as did approximately 50 per cent of infants born at that time — and he was followed almost exactly a year later by Armand, on 22 March 1685, who survived to become Zozo's elder 'brother'. On 28 December 1686 came Marguerite-Catherine, subsequent mother of three — including the eldest, Marie-Louise, whom Voltaire would later take as his mistress and companion for the last thirty years of his life. Robert Arouet, born on 18 July 1689, fared no better than Armand-François. Thereafter Marie-Marguerite Arouet appears to have favoured a rest — or practised birth control — before the happy event of five years later that brought the future hero of the Enlightenment into being.

Was it a happy event? Without being quite a Madame Bovary, Marie-Marguerite Arouet would seem to have been unwilling to forgo some of the legitimate if illegal pleasures of adultery. She had done her maternal duty with scrupulous statistical exactitude – two dead, two alive, one boy, one girl – and it was time for some fun, especially as wet-nurses and nannies did all the hard work. Her husband was eleven years older and somewhat suspicious of pleasure. She began to mix with another of his clients, the legendary courtesan Ninon de Lenclos, who had been one of the most celebrated salon hostesses of the century, at once a great intellect and a full-blooded proponent of free love and freethinking. And she began to meet some of the young and not-so-young men who gathered like moths round Ninon's ageing but still beguiling flame, men of wit and talent and amorous designs . . .

On the basis of the limited available information the likeliest scenario is that Marie-Marguerite fell for Rochebrune and became pregnant by him in the course of 1693. When the child was born on 20 February 1694 (discreetly, at Chatenay, then a country village some five miles north of the centre of Paris), it was sickly and not expected to live – which might, in the circumstances, have been helpful. The baby was duly 'ondoyé', the French term for the unofficial baptisms performed even to this day in bidet, bath, or kitchen sink by doting Catholic parents (or nervous, interfering grand-parents) just in case some accident should befall their treasured offspring before its day in church and so deprive it of eternal bliss. Indeed something similar had happened four years earlier with young Armand, who had arrived in such a precarious state of health that eleven days elapsed before he could be properly baptized. Perhaps Marie-Marguerite's poor record in producing viable male heirs would allow her highly respectable husband to avoid the necessity of legitimating a poetaster's bastard son as his own. For how else does one explain the enormous gap of nine months that elapsed before the official baptism in November? And why nine months? Was that the deal? If baby François-Marie could survive for the same time outside the womb as he had within, then François Arouet would do the decent thing? For the long delay suggests that he knew the child was not his own. At any rate the sickly baby did survive, and so began a life of stubborn insistence that would inconvenience many more people than just his parents.

But how, in the small world of Paris, does one publicly baptize a bastard child of nine months without setting tongues wagging? The godparents of Zozo's elder brother Armand had been the answer to a parvenu's prayers. His godmother was the duchesse de Saint-Simon, whose husband had been a member of the *conseil d'état* – the highest council of ministers – under Louis XIV.[3] The godfather was the duc de Richelieu, father of Voltaire's lifelong friend, and nephew of the great Armand du Plessis, Cardinal de Richelieu, who had become prime minister under Louis XIII at the age of thirty-nine and more or less single-handedly governed France until his death eighteen years later in 1642. Like François Arouet's family the Richelieus originally came from the Poitou region in the west of France, which may explain the connection. But compare baby François-Marie's godparents, whose Christian names not only became his own but were – oh so coincidentally – also those of his mother and supposed father. The godmother, Marie Daumart (née Parent) was the wife of a cousin on his mother's side, Symphorien (or Sébastien) Daumard, a highly placed official in the royal constabulary whose title of *écuyer* or squire placed him on the bottom rung of the aristocratic ladder (entitling him to one heraldic quarter). This godmother therefore constituted the best the Arouets could do in social terms while also guaranteeing discretion by being a member of the family.

The godfather was François de Castagnère, abbé de Châteauneuf. As an 'abbé' he had – like so many male offspring of the French aristocracy in the eighteenth century who had the misfortune not to be first-born – received a theological training and assumed a quasi-ecclesiastical status without being fully ordained. Often this meant being able to derive an income from a benefice, or living, without having to work, itself such an unaristocratic thing to do. In this capacity the abbé could lend an air of religious propriety to the proceedings. Moreover he was well connected: his brother was a senior diplomat. He was also a friend of the family and so could be relied on for his discretion. Such religious scruples as he might have had at becoming godfather to a nine-month-old bastard would have been offset by the freethinking spirit in which he, too, frequented the circle of Ninon de Lenclos. (He later boasted that it was to his own handsome person that the ageing beauty had granted her last favours – as a sixtieth-birthday present to herself.) Moreover he doted on the child and visited the wet-nurse daily to advise on the best means of ensuring its survival. Were it not for Voltaire's own testimony about Rochebrune, one might even suspect the abbé of having been his father. But perhaps he was a close friend of Rochebrune – as

well as Marie-Marguerite — and saw it as his duty to take his godfatherly role
seriously on their behalf. Indeed in 1751 Voltaire would write that it was
entirely thanks to Châteauneuf that he had been properly baptized at all.[4] As
we shall see, this godfatherly solicitude would also extend to ensuring that
young François was introduced to Ninon de Lenclos in the autumn of 1704.
He was ten (or nine), and she was eighty-three: their meeting would represent
a further baptism of sorts, and it would transpire that her favours extended
beyond the sexual.

And so, on Monday, 22 November 1694, Zozo officially became the son
of François Arouet. This man whom we must henceforth call his father had
been born in Paris on 19 August 1649. He was the son of another François
(born c.1605), who, in very early adulthood, had come from the village of
Saint-Loup near Airvault in the Poitou to settle in Paris as a silk and cloth
merchant. The family had been in the tanning business originally, and
Voltaire's father and grandfather could trace their solid merchant heritage
back to Hélénus Arouet at the end of the fifteenth century. From tanning, the
business had evolved over the generations into one that traded also in wool
and cloth, but grandfather Arouet's move to Paris and into the luxury
commodity of silk represented a definite step upmarket. He married a certain
Marie Mallepart in 1636, who bore him seven children (and lived till 1688).
Voltaire's father was the youngest of these and clearly decided to raise the
family's status still further by studying law. On 19 February 1675, at the age of
twenty-five, he bought a practice as a notary and worked hard to better
himself before marrying somewhat above his station eight years later.

But real social advancement came from working for the king. If one had
the money and the right credentials it was possible to buy a position in the
administration, a royal office. Such offices had been created and sold by the
crown in large numbers since the early sixteenth century. They were an
excellent source of capital. The king would create a new court or tribunal to
exercise judicial or administrative functions in a particular area — taxation, for
example — and the consequent new offices would be offered for sale: a small
salary was attached, plus various privileges, exemptions and fee-generating
opportunities that made them highly remunerative. Such offices could then
be sold on or bequeathed like franchises, and — as in the case of the husband
of Voltaire's godmother — they sometimes brought entitlement to hereditary

noble rank. Accordingly, on 16 December 1692, François Arouet sold his notary's practice in the Châtelet, and on 10 September 1696 – having now acquired his new 'son' – bought a position as 'receveur des épices' in the Chambre des Comptes. The latter was a so-called 'sovereign court', charged with the supervision of royal finances and the receipt of taxes: in François Arouet's case, the taxes levied on the lucrative spice trade. The required expertise was a legal training and a head for figures: the reward was a healthy commission on all tax raised. Not to mention some very prestigious accommodation in the Palais de Justice, the former medieval palace of the kings of France.

For the first five years the new taxman-cum-magistrate had to bide his time as the assistant to his predecessor, but once he had assumed the succession the Arouet family duly departed from their house on the rue Guénégaud, which runs down to the river beside the Hôtel des Monnaies and the Institut de France. From this address in the parish of Saint-André-des-Arts on the Left Bank, they moved into a ten-bedroom house on the Île de la Cité, complete with cellar, attic and stables. On one side the house gave on to their private garden, while on another they looked out on to the central courtyard of the Palais – and the imposing prospect of the Sainte-Chapelle. They lived at the end of the rue Nazareth, near the rue Bethléhem and the rue Jérusalem, and so it was clear that they had arrived in some style at the Holy of Holies: the legal and administrative centre of Paris.

Zozo could hardly have felt more legitimate. Nor more sad. For his mother died soon afterwards, on 13 July 1701, aged 'about 40'. How or why? We do not know. This left François Arouet to finish bringing up his three children, Armand (16), Catherine (14), and François-Marie (7ish) on his own. He certainly had the means to do it. In 1696 he had paid 240,000 *livres* for the post in the Chambre des Comptes – that is to say, over a thousand times the annual pay of a well-paid manual worker. He owned two houses in Paris, one in the rue Saint-Denis (where his grandfather had set up in business on first arriving in Paris, with a shop called 'The Peacock') and the other in the rue Maubué, as well as a sizeable property in the country at Gentilly. This he would sell in 1707 in order to buy another, at Chatenay, with courtyard, garden, and six bedrooms, which he retained until his death on 1 January 1722. In Paris he ran two berlins – a four-wheeled covered carriage with an external seat behind for the footman. On 27 January 1709 he married his daughter off to his own mirror-image: Pierre-François Mignot, the son of a merchant and now – like himself – a *conseiller du Roi* (or King's Counsel) and an important official in the Chambre des Comptes. As a dowry he gave Catherine the house in the rue Maubué, plus 60,000 *livres*, plus a pearl necklace and a diamond, together worth 5,000 *livres*, plus a 'bottom drawer' of conjugal necessities worth a further 1,000. This was the dowry gift of a wealthy man. When he died, his estate was worth 367,845 *livres*, all paid – of which Zozo would get a third. Though he very nearly didn't.

Such wealth did not derive solely from his official post at the Chambre des Comptes. Having sold his notary's practice Voltaire's father had continued to work as a freelance legal consultant to wealthy clients. And he was also a money-lender. In those days of the most rudimentary banking arrangements, it was customary for the rich to make money by lending to the needy, and the posher the needy the better. He had lent the duchesse de Saint-Simon fifty *écus* (the equivalent of 150 *livres*) back in 1689 – for godmotherly services rendered? – but she had proved an unreliable debtor and the IOU was still among his papers when he died. Other debtors, however, must have contributed to the Arouet fortune and paid good rates of interest. And his youngest son would later follow most profitably in his usurious footsteps.

Thus by the summer of 1701 Zozo had moved into a beautiful courtyard at the heart of the best of all possible cities. One of his neighbours was the writer Nicolas Boileau (or Boileau-Despréaux). Born in 1636, the son of an official in the Paris *parlement*, he had studied law at the Sorbonne and become an advocate. But when he inherited on his father's death in 1657 he was then able to devote himself to literature. In 1674 he published his *Art poétique*, a didactic poem in four cantos modelled on Horace's *Ars poetica* and which later achieved comparable status as *the* authoritative statement of neo-classical aesthetics in France. Accordingly Boileau is often seen as the founding father of French literary criticism. He knew the great writers of the seventeenth century as friends – Racine, Molière, La Fontaine, etc. – and his election to the Académie Française in 1684, at the behest of Louis XIV, set the seal on an illustrious career. And there he lived, just across the way: the lawyer who had legislated for poetry. Voltaire's mother knew him, albeit judging him to be rather a silly man for one who had written such a good poem, and there is every reason to suppose that her son, too, met him and was thrilled to rub shoulders with such a celebrity.

Another neighbour was the abbé Nicolas Gédoyn. Appointed a canon of the Sainte-Chapelle at the age of thirty-four, he had moved into the courtyard during the same year as the Arouets. He was a man of considerable talent, devoted to classical literature, and became noted for his translation of Quintillian. He, too, was elected to the Académie Française, in 1719. His writings on antiquity suggest that he took a fairly liberal view in theological matters, and the oft-repeated rumour that it was he, and not Châteauneuf, who had played the leading male role in Ninon de Lenclos's sixtieth-birthday celebrations suggests that he was viewed as not unduly austere in his moral conduct either. But the fact that he was actually thirteen at the time shows just how unreliable rumour can be . . . or that Ninon tended to the economical in the statement of her years . . . or that perhaps her seventieth-birthday party had been no less memorable than her sixtieth.

Such was the ambience in which the young Voltaire lived out his early childhood: a domain of wealth, position, prestige, intellectual and literary distinction — and adult fun. He noted later[5] how his father's connections had brought them both into contact with all the leading literary figures of the day, not only the immortal Boileau but many whose names were soon to be forgotten. But we know almost nothing of the realities of Zozo's early domestic life. A former maid recalled subsequently, in 1744, how she had finally managed to get his elder brother Armand to have some bad teeth extracted by getting him drunk on champagne, but no such anecdotes have survived to illuminate Voltaire's tender years. As to his early education, we can only surmise that an array of private tutors provided him with the rudiments of learning. Châteauneuf continued to look after his interests, teaching him both what he needed to know and perhaps one or two things that he did not. Into the former category fell the writing of verse, in those days an accomplishment as essential to a gentleman as needlework or singing was to a lady. Like a capacity to dance the minuet, it was a sign of being well-bred. From a very young age, it seems, Châteauneuf had the boy reciting poetry — notably the verse fables of La Fontaine, which represented a particularly 'modern' choice for the time — and he was soon teaching him how to write it as well. Legends have sprung up about Zozo's precocious abilities in this domain, in particular how he could recite a seventy-line poem at the age of three (a total of 560 syllables, to be precise). What *is* clear is that he liked to compete as a versifier with his brother, who was nine years older, and was actively encouraged by his family to do so. To compete and win!

What emerges no less clearly is that Châteauneuf – and he an abbé – saw it as his godfatherly role to introduce the boy to religious scepticism at an early age, as though inoculating him against the very doctrines that he himself had had to study. In this respect he was a so-called *libertin*, as free in his theology as he was in his interpretation of Christian morality. The poem which Zozo is supposed to have learnt by heart at the age of three – but which he almost certainly did read and learn some time before he was ten – was called *La Moïsade*, an anonymous mock-epic of satirical intent in which Moses is presented as a shrewd politician founding a false religion purely as a means to hold sway over a credulous people. The poem begins: 'A teaching so irrelevant/Shall not my doubts destroy:/With empty sophism thou shalt not/My reason fool nor try./The human mind wants proof more clear/ Than any priestly platitude.' At the evident risk of considerable over-simplification, the fifteen million words that Voltaire wrote over the ensuing eighty years were an obstinate repetition of those six simple lines. But what matters is that he did not just repeat the message, he also acted on it and exemplified it. 'Jean-Jacques [Rousseau] writes for the sake of writing,' he would comment (unfairly) in 1767. 'Me, I write to get things done.'[6]

One final detail from Zozo's childhood is suggestive in this regard, a story that continues to be handed down from generation to generation by his descendants (through his sister Catherine's branch of the Arouets), the Dompierre d'Hornoy family. According to this tradition,[7] Zozo was also known as 'le petit volontaire', meaning that he was a 'determined little thing'. For them this is why he later called himself 'Voltaire' (though, as we shall see, there are other explanations). Be that as it may, the baby who had refused to die was proving quite a handful, and like many youngest children he had had to learn to fight his corner. And the fame of his emerging talents was such that none other than Ninon de Lenclos asked to see him. Some time in the autumn of 1704 Châteauneuf took Zozo to meet her and to recite a few lines of his own verse. The young boy was appalled by the sight of this shrivelled old lady with black and yellow skin who looked 'like a mummy',[8] but she must have been impressed by him. A few days later she wrote a will that included a bequest of a thousand francs (then synonymous with *livres*, in the feminine) – to be spent on books (or *livres* in the masculine). A very large sum for a very small boy, so large indeed that his father never let him get his hands on it until after he himself had died. And since it took five years for his estate to be wound up, Zozo was in his early thirties before he could spend the money. By which time he had amassed a considerable quantity of his own.

When Châteauneuf took his godson to meet this living legend – just in time, for she died within the year – the life of the youngest Arouet had undergone a radical change. His father had just packed him off to boarding-school, to the Collège Louis-le-Grand, situated near the top of the Montagne Sainte-Geneviève and just across from the Palais du Luxembourg – beside the future Panthéon. François Arouet had decided that it was time to let the professionals deal with 'le petit volontaire'. On his way up the social ladder the ambitious lawyer had registered a coat-of-arms, and the shield – which his family had been sporting unofficially for the past two centuries – comprised three flames ('d'or à flammes de gueules'). For in the local dialect of Poitou 'arrouer' meant 'to burn'. And Voltaire would later adopt this coat-of-arms, no doubt wryly aware that its flames bore some resemblance to the fires of Hell – and, as we learn in *Candide*, to the flames depicted on the headgear worn by victims of the Holy Inquisition. Zozo may have been baptized twice and he may have had an abbé for a godfather, but the devil in him was not so easily to be exorcized. Perhaps the Jesuits at the Collège Louis-le-Grand could do better. For theirs was the best school in France and therefore – as Dr Pangloss might have said – in the whole world.

CHAPTER TWO

Of Priests and Poets (1704–1711)

What became of young Arouet among the Jesuits

Y OUNG FRANÇOIS-MARIE AROUET entered the Collège (now
Lycée) Louis-le-Grand as a boarder in the autumn of 1704, when he
was officially nine and unofficially ten. The former Zozo now
signed himself 'Arouet', which was much more grown-up. The education was
free, but his father had to pay 400 francs (or *livres*) a year for the
accommodation. Not an impossible sum, but enough to ensure a certain
exclusivity. Especially when it went up to 500 francs five years later after a
change of headmaster (or 'Recteur').

But why was he at a Jesuit college at all when his elder brother Armand,
now fifteen, was being educated elsewhere at the Jansenist college of Saint-
Magloire? Jansenism was a religious doctrine derived from the works of St
Augustine by Cornelius Jansen, or Jansenius (1585–1638), Bishop of Ypres
(then in the Spanish Netherlands), and expounded in his *Augustinus*,
published posthumously in 1640. Adherents – among them the tragedian
Jean Racine and the mathematician and thinker Blaise Pascal – had been
attracted to the moral austerity of the doctrine. For Jansenists, human beings
are incapable of discerning what is good without the help of divine grace. To
seek salvation by 'good works' is an illusory pursuit, for in our 'freedom' we
may be sinning further. Self-denial and submission to God's will are key.
This moral austerity found especial favour among the magistrates of the
parlements, including Voltaire's father.

But in 1704 the political tide was running strongly against the Jansenists.

A French theatre in the eighteenth century.

Louis XIV regarded them as subversive, if not republican, and throughout the last twenty years of his reign he persecuted them with the same vigour as French Protestants (the so-called Huguenots). The centre of Jansenist thinking – the Cistercian monastery and convent at Port-Royal, not far from Versailles – was abolished by papal bull in 1708, with the remaining nuns being forcibly evicted by the police in 1709, the buildings razed in 1710, and the bodies in the graveyard provocatively dug up and dispersed in 1711. In 1713, at Louis's behest, a further papal bull, *Unigenitus Dei Filius*, condemned the teaching of the leading Jansenist, Pasquier Quesnel, thus setting the scene for a struggle between *parlements* and crown that lasted until the Revolution of 1789.

In sending his younger son to the Collège Louis-le-Grand, François Arouet had decided to row with the prevailing tide. It may also be, of course, that his elder son was beginning to show signs of the unnerving religious ardour that would later have him roaming round cemeteries in quasi-ecstatic convulsions, and that his father had determined that one Jansenist fanatic was quite enough for any family. Or else he considered himself to have climbed still further up the social ladder since Armand had been dispatched to school and now wanted François-Marie (not to mention himself) to have the benefit of the influential friendships and contacts that attendance at such an illustrious institution would bring. And just how influential these connections were can be inferred from the fact that the change of leadership that led to the introduction of higher fees arose from the departure of the Recteur, Père Le Tellier, to become father confessor to the King at Versailles (succeeding Père La Chaise, of cemetery fame).

The Jesuits were in the political ascendant in France, and a Jesuit education seemed a sure passport to success. Not so much an old-school-tie network as a cassock conspiracy to maintain power and influence through the advancement – and consequent loyalty – of the brightest men in France. And abroad. For at that time the Jesuits directed some 700 schools throughout the world. Founded in 1534 by St Ignatius Loyola, the so-called Society of Jesus was especially noted for its missionary zeal, which meant that its members not only educated the pagan in their own lands but also brought the cleverest back to France for a glimpse of true civilization. Thus at Louis-le-Grand, for example, where about 10 per cent of the pupils were either not French or born of French parents living abroad, Arouet met boys from all over the known world. Many came from the eastern Mediterranean – Greece, Syria, Armenia – to be equipped with an education that would allow them to return and serve the King's (and the Jesuits') interests in the Levant. A few even came from China, baffling their fellow-pupils with their strange way of talking.

But the other 90 per cent were home-grown and, for the most part, bred in the purple. In the French parlance of the day, they belonged either to the *noblesse d'épée* (nobility of the sword), the ancient aristocracy who had gained their titles predominantly in the military service of the king, or to the *noblesse de robe*, those more recently ennobled and who owed their advancement to administrative service on behalf of the king – and thus wore the robes of officialdom and professional qualification. Accordingly, by the time he left school, Arouet was friends for life with boys who would become: a senior official in the Rouen *parlement* (Cideville); the senior judge presiding over the Dijon *parlement* (Fyot de la Marche); the Minister of Foreign Affairs between 1744 and 1747 (the marquis d'Argenson); and the Minister for War between 1743 and 1757 (his younger brother, the comte d'Argenson). The comte d'Argental – who, though only eleven when Arouet eventually left school, turned out to be perhaps his truest friend – became a Parisian lawyer of distinction and a diplomat at the French court. The future duc de Richelieu went on to a glorious military (and amorous) career and became a *maréchal de France*.

Viewed from today's perspective, life at Louis-le-Grand may seem hard, even to those who have attended West Point Military Academy or a British public school. Admittedly those of unimpeachably blue blood could bring their own servants, which saved them having to pick things up, and of course there was a blessed absence of rugby and hockey. But there were prayers and masses and sundry devotions sufficient to test the most hardened of knees and the very highest of boredom thresholds. For seven long years Arouet followed a regime that was designed to lick even the most recalcitrant young lordling into shape. The day began at 5 a.m., with prayers, quiet study and the recitation of material learnt by rote. From 7.30 a.m., lessons. Mass was celebrated at 10, followed by lunch and recreation. Lessons began again at 2 p.m. Supper was at 6 p.m., followed by further recreation. Then came more testing of rote-learning. The day ended with prayers and readings from the

Scriptures before lights out at 9 p.m. And presumably total exhaustion. Sundays were not quite so bad, though Mass was said twice. Confession followed by communion was obligatory at least once a month, but everyone was encouraged to present himself weekly. And all had to take their turn as altar-boys, thereby allowing posterity to entertain the pleasant image of an angelic teenage Voltaire piously attending a priest in the performance of his holy duties. From time to time the boys were obliged to participate in week-long retreats, which must certainly have made normal lessons seem rivetingly exciting. During such retreats they were completely cut off from the outside world and devoted the entirety of their time to religious devotion. After his last one, in May 1711, Arouet informed his close friend Fyot de la Marche (who had had the good fortune to go home early) that he had just sat through fifty sermons.

The boys were supervised with a ceaseless vigilance born of hard-won experience and a healthy respect for the devil and his works. Corporal punishment was extensively administered, and with a degree of vigour that (according to Voltaire's later testimony) varied from the violently cruel to the gently erotic. When not under the attentive eye of the teachers (or 'regents'), the young male élite of France was watched over by 'prefects' at every moment of the day – and night. Divided into smallish groups, the boys slept in dormitories, together with a young priest whose job was as much pastoral as custodial. Needless to say, such pastoral relationships could become intensely intimate, and after a school inspection in 1708 the inspectors felt obliged to recommend to the priests that they refrain from embracing the children – 'at least in public if they are unable to do so in private'.[1] Nevertheless there was certainly some considerable measure of exaggeration, not to say a wicked desire to shock, when Voltaire subsequently told the mother of Alexander Pope at a dinner party in Twickenham that if he suffered such constant ill health (as he then alleged) it was because he had been repeatedly sodomized at school.

But most priests are neither buggers nor sadists, and these pastoral relationships could mutate into adult friendships. One such dormitory prefect, Father Thoulier, later corresponded regularly with Voltaire, though not before he had left the Jesuit order and become a writer, as the abbé d'Olivet. Indeed, in one respect at least, he may even have been a role model.

The letters u and v being identical in Latin, d'Olivet's pseudonym represented an almost anagrammatic version of Thoulier – just as 'Voltaire' is
thought by many to derive from a rearrangement of Arouet l.j., where l.j. is
short for 'le jeune', or the younger. Voltaire never explained the reasons
behind his choice of pseudonym, and this particular name-game is un-
winnable. But some participants – who don't like the 'petit volontaire' theory
either – see in 'Voltaire' a reversal of 'Airvault', the town in Poitou from
which the Arouets hailed.

Latin, of course, played a central part in the syllabus at Louis-le-Grand,
which was the standard Jesuit syllabus then followed throughout France and
its colonies. 'Latin and a lot of nonsense', as the former pupil put it himself
many years later in his *Dictionnaire philosophique* (*Philosophical Dictionary*). For the
Jesuits, Latin was not just the language of Virgil and Cicero and a necessary
part of a gentleman's 'classical' education. It was also the language of the
Mass and the medium in which Christians everywhere – or at least Roman
Catholics – might communicate across national boundaries, the lingua franca
of God's universal church on earth. For this reason Ancient Greek was
neglected, whereas Latin was taught as a living language, to be deployed in
prose and verse and on any number of edifying and often sacred topics. The
results were not necessarily literary masterpieces. Voltaire later recalled a
teacher's own Latin poem about St Francis Xavier calming a raging tempest
by casting his crucifix into the deep only for a god-fearing crab miraculously
to return it. But the idea was to encourage facility of expression and active
language-use rather than the sterile acquisition of endless grammatical rules.
The rest of the syllabus – the 'nonsense' – has a very unenlightened look to
it: endless theology, the barest smattering of history and geography, no
modern languages or natural sciences. Things got better in the pupil's
penultimate year, when there was a strong emphasis on literature and
especially poetry, which young Arouet loved. In the final year they focused
(or not) on 'philosophy' – a mixture of Aristotle and Thomas Aquinas –
which a less young Arouet found futile and uninteresting. Especially as René
Descartes was resolutely refused admission on to the syllabus. For the boys
must be protected against the pernicious example of this Jesuit-educated
philosopher (1596–1650) who had fled France for Protestant Holland in his
early thirties and there devoted himself to the independent pursuit of truth.

Worse, his *Discourse on Method* (1637) proclaimed that his Jesuit education had left him with nothing but doubt.

The lessons at Louis-le-Grand took various forms. Sometimes a 'regent' would lecture to very large groups, numbering well over a hundred. At other times the pupils would be split up into groups of ten, like Roman soldiers (*decuria*), with one pupil being put in charge (a *decurion*); and the groups would compete with each other in debate and tested performance. As in the Arouet household a spirit of competition was strongly fostered, and the gift of the gab was at a premium. It was as though everyone had to grow up to be a silver-tongued barrister. Indeed there were many actual competitions, formal public occasions attended by doting parents and other adults. There was no question of everyone having prizes (except perhaps in Heaven, though even then . . .): only the best would do, and only the best would win. The successful entries were preserved for the school archives. In the realm of literature the objective was thus not only that the boys should come to love and appreciate fine writing but that they should be able to produce it as well, in verse as in prose. In this respect Châteauneuf's earlier efforts as godfather-cum-tutor must have stood his godson in excellent stead as a future competitor.

At the top end of the school the teaching was of a quality to match these ambitions. In addition to regents and prefects the staff included other priests called *scriptores*, a combination of academic scholar and writer-in-residence who would share erudition, enthusiasm and skills with these highly privileged – and fortunate – boys. Young Arouet, who stood out for his quick and enquiring mind, was in close and regular contact with such men, whose additional function was to step outside the official syllabus as and when the pupil in question was intelligent enough – and of sufficiently robust moral character – to be able to cope with the unorthodox. The Jesuits prided themselves on their intellectual acumen and on their ability to situate themselves at the cutting edge of contemporary thinking, in all domains, secure in their faith no matter what reason might throw at them. One *scriptor* to whom Arouet was particular close, Father Tournemine, had made it his business to get to know the leading freethinkers of the day. He mixed and debated with deists (who believed in God but not that God 'revealed' Himself to us, whether in the person of Jesus Christ or the Prophet

Mohammed) and atheist 'materialists' (who believed that matter is eternal and that the universe owes nothing to divine agency). Tournemine was a kind of specialist on freethinking, which was why he was made editor of the Jesuit periodical, the *Mémoires* (or *Journal*) *de Trévoux*. The idea was to engage the 'enemy' on its own intellectual terrain and rout it. One can imagine the effect that conversations with such a man must have had on the young Voltaire, and why he found the standard final-year syllabus so tedious and unconvincing.

France was then engaged in the War of the Spanish Succession, and rather unsuccessfully so. As British schoolchildren used to be taught, these were the years of BROM: the first Duke of Marlborough's stirring victories at Blenheim (1704), Ramillies (1706), Oudenarde (1708) and Malplaquet (1709). The first months of 1709 had brought the severest of winters – rivers were frozen solid, and even the sea turned to ice along the French coast – so that agricultural shortages would follow hard on the heels of military defeat and its crippling economic cost. The population of Paris was reduced by a fifth, and the city itself severely flooded in the ensuing thaw.[2] Autumn-sown crop seed had rotted in the ground, the kingdom had been invaded, Lille was besieged and taken . . . In short, France was in crisis. And fifteen-year-old Arouet would engage in long debates about the military and political issues with another of his teachers, Father Porée, who recalled later how Arouet had 'weighed the mighty interests of Europe in his little scales'.[3] Born in 1676, Charles Porée had been ordained in 1706, and after two years at Rouen (where Tournemine had also taught), he had only recently been posted to Louis-le-Grand. With Father Lejay he was to be one of the two regents in charge of those in their penultimate year. At Louis-le-Grand – and throughout France for at least another two centuries – this year was known as the Classe de Rhétorique. But whereas Lejay was a cantankerous and unpopular teacher, Porée was young, broad-minded and fun.

In May 1709 the nervous and starving people of Paris took to the streets to pay homage to the city's patron saint, Sainte Geneviève, and to enlist her support. The reliquary containing the alleged relics of this sixth-century shepherdess and having the appearance of a miniature church (made of precious metals and considered a masterpiece of thirteenth-century craftsmanship) was paraded along a traditional route from the church that bears her name on the Montagne Sainte-Geneviève (now the site of the Panthéon) down to the cathedral of Notre-Dame. A huge throng – including *parlement* dignitaries and senior churchmen, nobles both local and foreign, and anyone from a merchant to a scoundrel – besought her beneficent intervention in the agricultural and military affairs of the nation, not to mention their own. Just as they had for centuries past. Even Erasmus thought he had been cured by such a procession, at the end of the fifteenth century (though the ceremony then had been brought on by the Seine bursting its banks). There had been forty-four such parades in the course of the sixteenth century, occasioned by more bad weather or the ghastly scourge of the Huguenots. But the custom had then begun to lapse. In the course of the seventeenth century there had been only seven, the last being in the year of Voltaire's birth (which Sainte Geneviève must have had cause to regret). After May 1709 there would be only one more.[4]

As usual this kind of occasion called for some versifying, and Father Lejay set the example to his pupils by composing a Latin ode in honour of the said saint. Perhaps prompted by Father Porée, Arouet decided to write a French version in imitation and completed it during the school year 1709–10. Though quaint to our eyes and not without technical and stylistic blemish, this ode – of eleven ten-line stanzas in octosyllabic metre and a complex rhyme scheme – demonstrates no little verve and ingenuity in deploying the hackneyed rhetoric of the day: the glorious and munificent saint, the humble and penitent poet who has but the gift of his words to offer her, the fervent hope that there might soon be an end to famine and cruel war, and a curious but wholly typical blend of classical mythology and Christian piety. His teachers were so impressed – and so keen to impress the outside world with what their school could produce – that they had it printed and circulated as the work of 'François Arouet, Étudiant en Rhétorique, et Pensionnaire au Collège Louis-le-Grand'. This was Voltaire's first publication. Yet he would never again accept authorship of it: such claptrap could not be acknowledged by the sworn enemy of superstition and mob-bewitching mumbo-jumbo. And, had he lived to see it, he would no doubt have approved heartily when, after the 1789 Revolution (which outlawed Christianity), the reliquary was sent to be melted down at the Mint (recently built in the street, beside where the Arouets used to live) and Sainte Geneviève's alleged body parts were incinerated and scattered on the waters of the river.[5]

Young Arouet was now the star of the school. At the end of his year of 'rhetoric' he was awarded first prize for both Latin discourse and Latin verse composition. His official reward was a sumptuous book on the history of the religious wars in sixteenth-century France. And who should be there in the audience at prize-giving but Jean-Baptiste Rousseau, perhaps the leading poet of the day. Rousseau (no relation of Jean-Jacques) later recalled how he had asked to be introduced to this prodigy and met a boy 'of sixteen or seventeen' – little did he realize how right he was to be so approximate, even though he had overestimated by a year – who had 'rather an unattractive face but a sharp, alert look in his eye'.[6] While the star pupil had won the prize for Latin, the publication of his ode had demonstrated the high regard in which his talent for French verse was also held. And the regard was yet higher after a retired soldier came to the Jesuits to ask their help in composing a poem to petition the Grand Dauphin, Louis de France, the King's only son and heir. This soldier had served in the Grand Dauphin's regiment and was seeking alms to alleviate his destitution. The task was delegated to young Arouet, who promptly provided fourteen enterprisingly rhymed and metrically skilful lines of flattery, humility and erudite allusion. They did the trick. The soldier got his money, and both news and evidence of the schoolboy's rapidly growing reputation had now reached Versailles.

The annual prize-giving at Louis-le-Grand, which took place in August, was the occasion of a school tradition that may have shaped young Arouet's destiny more than anything else, certainly in the literary sphere. For it was customary for the boys to put on a play. Indeed not just one play, but two – and a ballet in between. First would come a tragedy, or at least a serious drama: often in Latin, and sometimes in French. After the 'interval', a comedy, usually in French. The ballet – which had long been a traditional part of any theatrical programme throughout the seventeenth century – allowed those young gentlemen who were nimble on their feet to show their paces and a well-turned calf, especially when professionals from the Opéra were brought in to coach them. The plays were written by the teachers themselves, and each year they would choose from a well-tried repertoire. The school would be turned upside-down for weeks as preparations were made. Occasionally, when some new writing talent joined the staff, further plays would be added to the repertoire – as happened on the arrival of Father Porée, whose new comedy brought the house down. Needless to say, such goings-on were the subject of much slanderous talk about the worldliness and even the immorality of the Jesuits, but their pedagogical purpose was clear: to encourage the boys to feel and understand these literary texts (and attendant moral issues) from the inside and to appreciate their detail and complexity more deeply. Again, the emphasis was on doing and not just on learning and analysing. And for those who took part, the training in deportment and elocution was invaluable, not to mention the boost to their confidence as public speakers and performers.

The event was staged out-of-doors, in the main courtyard of the school, in order to accommodate a large stage and a very large (mixed) audience drawn from the cream of French society and consisting also of many monks and priests for whom such revelry would have provided a welcome contrast to their quotidian routine. The weather in August was usually secure, but at Arouet's last prize-giving (on 5 August 1711) the clouds looked ominous. Father Porée duly prayed to the deity for metereological clemency, only to be answered in mid-prayer by a torrential downpour, much to the amusement of his pupils and sceptics everywhere. We have no evidence about young Arouet's own participation in these schoolboy theatricals, but what is certain is that he came to love the theatre more than almost anything in his life. We know also that in the latter stages of his school career he tried his hand at writing a tragedy, *Amulius et Numitor*, based on the story of Romulus and Remus. He later destroyed the manuscript: the two short fragments that survive suggest that he was probably right to do so. But he would soon manage better. And the boy who had collapsed in helpless mirth on reading Molière's *Amphitryon* at the age of eleven would not restrict himself to tragedies.

François Arouet was now about to leave school. His last year – the 'Classe de Philosophie' – brought no prizes, and indeed in May 1711 he failed the oral examination during which he was supposed to defend his dissertation. Asked to resit the oral, he pleaded a headache, got his father to sign a sick-note, and left the dissertation to defend itself. And so he ceased formally to be a pupil at Louis-le-Grand on 6 August 1711. But it must be said that he had informally been weaning himself off official Jesuit nourishment for some time. As we have seen, his meeting with Ninon de Lenclos – and all that she represented – occurred shortly after he first joined the school in the autumn of 1704. Châteauneuf, his godfather, died in 1708 but not before introducing him to the leading freethinkers who would play such an important role in his early adulthood. And like all schoolboys – especially those who live in Paris during the holidays – he was keen to explore what lay beyond the school walls. To do so, it would seem that he needed more money than his father was prepared to allow him. At the age of thirteen he had borrowed 500 *livres* (more than his father was then paying in fees) from a woman called Thomas and was eventually pursued for the debt when he reached his majority (aged twenty-five), at which point he pleaded unsuccessfully that his innocence (*sic*) had been abused. In his final year at school, Voltaire later claimed,[7] he approached a pawnbroker with a view to borrowing money on the book prize he had won the previous August. It so happened that two crucifixes – people will pawn anything – were positioned on either side of the man, and young Arouet could not resist remarking that it would be more appropriate to have only one and to place it 'between two robbers'. By which, of course, he meant himself and the money-lender. Seeing the latter's anger, he beat a hasty retreat, but was soon caught up by the man, whose business sense had recovered its customary superiority over his emotions. Offered a six-month loan against the book at a punitive rate of 10% interest (the payments to be deducted in advance), François accepted – the prostitute, the gaming-table or some pressing creditor clearly could not wait – and he was very cross six months later when he discovered that the pawnbroker had disappeared. The book was worth four or five times what he had borrowed (the Jesuits gave handsome prizes). Result: an extra-curricular lesson in life.

The schoolboy was evidently clever enough to keep this alternative life sufficiently secret from his father and teachers for there to have been no talk of either disinheritance (yet) or expulsion (ever). He was well respected and even admired by the likes of Father Porée, and he in turn retained considerable affection and respect for them. They had imbued him with a love of literature – and the secrets of how to write it – that would prove to be the most valuable of lifelong gifts. Inevitably the question also arises as to what part his school education played in his subsequent intellectual development. It would be simplistic to argue that it had put him off religion. In fact it seems, perhaps surprisingly, that the kind of Christianity preached and taught by the Jesuits at Louis-le-Grand was not so far removed from the deist beliefs that the mature Voltaire would come to profess and defend. For like the Jesuits he, too, believed in the existence of God – doggedly, and in the teeth of all manner of evidence that pointed to a contrary conclusion. Moreover the catechism everyone learnt at school was of a kind that played down the more supernatural or miraculous aspects of the Christian story. Long before a recent Bishop of Durham caused consternation (and perhaps thunderbolts) by suggesting that biblical accounts of the Virgin Birth and even the Resurrection are not to be taken literally, this particular catechism – the so-called Canisius catechism – makes little mention of original sin or Hell or even of Christ's Passion, let alone the Holy Spirit. Though they belonged to the Society of Jesus, the Jesuits in their teaching laid greater emphasis on God the heavenly Father, a compassionate deity with a broad understanding of human frailty and a limitless capacity to forgive us our sins. Accordingly their faith and pedagogic practice were characterized by an urbane intellectual and moral flexibility that had long since made them the implacable enemies of the Jansenists – and which now left its unmistakable mark on Arouet le jeune.

But we must not overemphasize this debt. During the last few weeks of his stay at the school it was rumoured that he and his friend Fyot de la Marche were thinking of training for the priesthood and becoming Jesuits themselves. If not a joke, the rumour suggests at the very least that Arouet's extramural activities had not become widely known. But in a letter to his absent classmate the future Voltaire is categoric: the pair of them are 'much too clever to do such a stupid thing'.[8] The boys at Louis-le-Grand were educated not only to know but to do. And to do well. Obviously it was hoped that many would be so strengthened in their religious beliefs and so thoroughly persuaded of the merits of being a Jesuit that they would in their turn be ordained and join the Order. But even those who remained unfrocked could serve the cause of God, the King, and the Society of Jesus. Young Arouet learnt to compete, to succeed, to write verse, and to think for himself, but it is doubtful if any member of the aforesaid trinity later benefited from these skills or these talents. 'Devoured by a thirst for celebrity', as his own father confessor put it,[9] Zozo-François was all set to do his own thing.

CHAPTER THREE

White Nights and Early Nights
(1711–1718)

How François fell in love and out of favour

YOUNG FRANÇOIS AROUET now returned to live full time in the beautiful courtyard of the Palais de Justice, at the heart of the French legal establishment. It was time to think of a career, and for his father there was only one: the law. His son, however, wanted to be a poet. As he gazed across the family garden at the figure of Nicolas Boileau, he must have thought: he managed it, so why not I? But Boileau had had to wait for his father to die before he could swap the tedium of the brief for the delights of the rhyming couplet. If only . . . But François was not Oedipus. At least not yet.

Biographers are sometimes criticized for reading their subjects' lives backwards and finding causes and patterns that are the chimerical products of hindsight. But in the case of Voltaire it is difficult to escape the conclusion that the child was father to the man. His probable biological father was a versifier and his official father a lawyer. His godfather taught him poetry, and his family lived in the middle of the Paris *parlement*. He would become the greatest French dramatist and epic poet of his century, and he would later be acclaimed as the first human-rights campaigner of the modern era. Literature and law were the systole and diastole of his vitality, the positive and negative of his seemingly limitless energy as he strove in language and action to flout and reform the status quo. With his fifteen million words, give or take a few, Voltaire would change the rules.

But first he had to contend with his father. A poet? After all that education? Did the boy intend to be a wastrel? To be a burden on his family? To die a pauper? Nowadays a long Romantic tradition has caused us to think of poets as private dreamers, ill-adapted to social intercourse and the horrors of a materialist world but thereby guardians of value and the messengers of our common soul. In 1711 François senior would have viewed a young poet as a modern parent might view an aspirant television celebrity. Where was the job security, the intellectual seriousness, the moral worth? Was his second 'son' going to end up like Rochebrune, a purveyor of ephemeral satires and sundry ditties of ill repute? For that was the likeliest scenario. How plausible is it ever for a parent to imagine that their offspring may become a celebrated writer, fit to be compared with those recent masters, Corneille and Racine, and even with those incomparable ancient models, Sophocles and Virgil?

But for François junior, fresh out of school, oozing with self-confidence, and filled with ambition and teenage hormones that urged him to rebel, the future was there to be conquered, the present to be ridiculed, and the past to be outdone. Verse was as natural a medium then as a radio broadcast is for us, and poems would circulate in manuscript with the elusive ease of sound waves. For any piece of writing to be published in print meant ideally trying to obtain royal permission (the so-called *privilège*), which was granted after due vetting only to the most reputable works. It was still possible to be published without the *privilège* but by 'tacit permission' when the censor found no especial fault with the work but saw no reason of merit or exemplary piety for the king to grant it an imprimatur. This individual, a kind of licensed book-reviewer, was usually an expert in the relevant field and was appointed by the bureau in charge of state censorship. This body saw itself essentially as a standards watchdog, but of course one person's standards are another's oppression. And the oppressed will always find a way. Which is the major reason why approximately half the books published in French during the eighteenth century were published outside France.

Much material – whether in print or manuscript – was clandestine, and circulated under the more or less successful cover of anonymity. Controlling this particular media output was difficult and required a vigilant police force, supported by a network of informers. Just as today a satirical weekly might pride itself on the number of libel actions it attracts, so in early eighteenth-century France a young writer might seek to make a name for himself precisely by daring the authorities to act, sailing close to the wind of retribution before running with the safe breeze of celebrity. Such retribution could take the form of being asked to leave Paris and to endure for a time the relative obscurity and potential tedium of the provinces, or it could take the rather more inhibiting form of imprisonment – without trial – in the Bastille. Sometimes, in such circumstances, it was better to leave the country. And one had to be careful not to be condemned for another's misdemeanours. Like Jean-Baptiste Rousseau, exiled on 7 April 1712 for satirical verses he had not written (though he had written many others). As Rousseau subsequently warned his young admirer and protégé, innocence was no guarantee of justice. And just because you got away with an epigram that you had indeed written, that did not mean you would not be brought down by one you hadn't.

Such were some of the dangers that Arouet *père* could no doubt foresee, and against which he would prove powerless to protect his brilliant, headstrong son, his 'petit volontaire'. If only he would learn a proper profession. At first the school-leaver reluctantly agreed to attend the École de Droit (the Paris law school), with a view to training as a barrister. But his worst fears were soon confirmed. 'What put me off studying law,' he later told his friend the marquis d'Argenson in 1739, 'was the vast amount of useless rubbish they wanted to load into my brain. "Get to the point", that's my motto.'[1] Which, of course, is what a motto does.

By way of compensation for this arid study, the student frequented his friends at Le Temple. This particular temple was in fact a sanctuary of freethinking. Originally a late twelfth-century fortified lodge belonging to the Knights Templar, the building had been taken over by the Knights of St John of Malta, demolished (apart from its famous keep where Louis XVI and Marie-Antoinette were later held prisoner) and then graced with a beautiful residence in 1667 by the Grand Prior of the Order. This was Philippe de Vendôme, grandson of Henri IV and a law unto himself. Or at least he was until Louis exiled him in 1706. The assembly of buildings at Le Temple (on the Right Bank, north-north-east of the Châtelet) enjoyed special legal status as a place of asylum, and the police were debarred from entering. This made it an ideal refuge for debtors, and a haven for freethinkers of especially epicurean habits – like the sundry debauchees whom the exiled Grand Prior and his unexiled elder brother, the duc de Vendôme, had gathered around them. As Versailles grew ever more pious under the influence of Louis XIV's morganatic second wife, Mme de Maintenon, Le Temple was a place where a person could count on some old-style royal and aristocratic fun.

Young Arouet had been introduced into this dangerous company by his godfather, Châteauneuf, and later recalled how impressed he had been to see these high-born subversives breaking wine glasses with their teeth.[2] One in particular, the abbé Chaulieu, now in his seventies, brought a veneer of aesthetic respectability to the proceedings by celebrating them in accomplished verse. For the habitués of Le Temple, as for European high society in general, poetic composition was a form of elegant and witty social intercourse, a means of demonstrating intelligent superiority over the prosaic and the utilitarian. Moreover Chaulieu and his drinking-companions could recognize talent when they saw it. The débutant's success was assured, and he continued to mix in this circle for several years. The duc de Vendôme died in Spain in 1712, but after Louis XIV's death in 1715 the Regent quickly recalled his friend, Philippe de Vendôme (who had by then turned sixty), and the parties at Le Temple continued as never before, fuelled by the brilliant young poet's fearless satires.

François's student life was like all student life: a candle burned at both ends without any concomitant enhancement of intellectual illumination in the middle. One story has him getting home so late that the parental door was locked in his face. Having decided to sleep in a sedan chair that was lying in the courtyard of the Palais de Justice, he was very surprised to wake up the next morning still in the same chair but now in a coffee-house down by the river and surrounded by the laughter of those who had transported him there. Another anecdote, later denied by Voltaire, has him receiving a very large sum of money (a hundred *louis d'or*, the equivalent of 2,400 *livres*) from the duchesse de Richelieu, his schoolfriend's young wife, for helping her with her verse composition – not, it seems, a euphemism – and then spending it all on a carriage and horses, plus some smart livery for the driver. When he tried that same night to stable the horses with his father's, at three o'clock in the morning, there was a terrible racket – and hell to pay. Father immediately sold the lot. No such luxury for François. At least not yet.

Arouet *père* now offered to buy the reluctant barrister a position so that he could begin to practise. When his son refused, he swallowed hard and offered to buy him an even more expensive royal office in the *parlement*, which would have brought with it the beginnings of noble entitlement. Surely any young bourgeois gentleman's dream? The proud teenager merely observed that he intended to earn eminence by his own efforts, and without costing his father a penny. Undeterred but now beginning to yield to this stubborn refusal to be a lawyer, the well-connected father began to wonder about the possibility of a diplomatic career for his undiplomatic son. Following the end of the War of the Spanish Succession and the signing of the Treaty of Utrecht (11 April 1713), a new French ambassador was about to be sent to The Hague: none other than the elder brother of the abbé Châteauneuf, François-Marie's late godfather. The marquis de Châteauneuf needed a personal secretary: or rather he was persuaded that he did, and that young Arouet was just the man for the job.

Which he might have been but for Pimpette. Among the many French Huguenots taking refuge in Holland from the Protestant persecution in France there lived a certain Mme Dunoyer, who hailed from Nîmes but had sought refuge first in England and then in The Hague, where she now earned a living publishing a gossipy periodical called *La Quintescence*. Having married off one daughter to a rich old man in the time-honoured (and effective) way, she was now seeking to capitalize on her investment in a second daughter, Olympe, known as Pimpette. Alas for Mama, Pimpette and the former Zozo fell in love at first sight. She was a pretty 21-year-old – 'fresh and toothsome' like Candide's beloved Cunégonde (before she went to the bad) – and he a charismatic figure of less obvious but not insignificant physical allure. 'Thin, tall, dried-up and bony' would be his unduly modest self-assessment three years later[3] – and by 'tall' he probably meant about 5′ 10″ in his stockinged feet, which was tall for his day.[4] Theirs was a first love of true, implausible delight: they swore eternal allegiance and determined to be (unofficially) one. Why not come back to Paris with me on the pretext that you want to convert to Catholicism? Needless to say, Mme Dunoyer was horrified when she heard: a penniless nineteen-year-old was not quite the pension fund she had in mind. When she promptly informed the new French ambassador of his young secretary's behaviour, Châteauneuf was seriously alarmed at the prospect of a diplomatic incident at this very delicate moment in relations between France and its Protestant neighbours, not least because Mme Dunoyer might reveal all in her ghastly magazine. And indeed his fears were not unfounded since seven years later she published the young Frenchman's love-letters to her daughter (he being now lucratively famous and she having edited out all unflattering references to herself).

The trainee diplomat was ordered home, but there was a delay as Châteauneuf awaited the arrival of an attaché who would escort him safely and chastely back to Paris. In the interim the two lovers were placed under a form of house arrest: François was forbidden to leave the building, while Pimpette was required to sleep in her mother's bed. But where there is a will – and an irresistible urge – there is a way. The intrepid Romeo climbed out of his window, hired a carriage and bore his beloved off for a few snatched, passionate hours in Scheveningen, a fishing-village near The Hague. Urges, of course, return, and he subsequently dispatched a parcel of men's clothes to his pretty mistress, thereby enabling her admission to his room in the embassy – where they were no doubt removed. But soon, only too soon, the time came to leave, on 18 December, and François reached Paris six days later, lovelorn and once again thwarted by the grown-ups. And how! Duly informed by Châteauneuf, Arouet senior had obtained a *lettre de cachet* against his son, the equivalent of a court order that he personally could administer and which authorized his son's imprisonment in the Bastille. He had also disinherited him. Paternal patience had run out. Châteauneuf's kindness in taking young François on had been sorely abused: just think of the public outcry that could have followed the leaking of a story about a young embassy official arriving straight from France and seducing an innocent Protestant girl while trying to convert her to the Church of Rome. The political consequences did not bear thinking about.

But, for his son, Pimpette certainly did bear thinking about. He tried for several weeks by letter and amorous entreaty to persuade her to come to Paris, but good sense prevailed over romance in the mind of his mistress. After an affair with another young French man of letters, Guyot de Merville, she eventually married a certain M. de Winterfeld in 1721 and came to live in Paris, where she promptly got into financial difficulty. With a generosity of heart and pocket that would subsequently prove entirely characteristic, her former lover bailed her out. But that was eight years later. Upon his return to Paris on Christmas Eve 1713 the disgraced young diplomat wisely avoided returning immediately to the bosom of his family, and the said bosom duly calmed down, agreeing to commute the sentence of imprisonment in the Bastille to mere exile in the West Indies. His son had no choice but to accept. Perceiving his readiness to comply, Arouet *père* then went for the jugular. How about a total pardon if the reluctant barrister would agree to go and work for Maître Alain, a public prosecutor, in the Châtelet? Agreed.

In *Candide*, the philosophical tale that Voltaire published in 1759, one of the central characters, Martin, is a Manichaean: that is, he believes, after the Persian philosopher Manes, that the world is governed by the equally powerful forces of good and evil. In other words, every cloud has a silver lining, it's an ill wind that blows nobody any good, etc. More precisely put, for every dark hour that passes there is a bright spell of equivalent duration. At Maître Alain's, the study of law continued to provide the sombre moments, but the silver lining came in the person of Nicolas Thiriot, a fellow sacrificial victim to the goddess Jurisprudence. Amiable, unreliable, but usually obliging, he would be one of Voltaire's closest friends for over sixty years. He was a soul-mate: he loved poetry, quoted Virgil and Horace at the drop of a hat (as the educated then could but not necessarily did), and spent his money going to the theatre. Once again François had found literature at the heart of the law. Temporarily defeated but still unbowed, he continued to harbour his ambition to be a poet – as his father could well see. Reluctantly he was allowed to leave Maître Alain's.

It was agreed that he should go and 'think things over' while staying with one of his father's clients, the marquis de Saint-Ange, whose country seat (now vanished) was situated at Villecerf, near Fontainebleau. The marquis had previously played a central role in government as a member of Louis XIV's ruling council, and the numerous, detailed accounts of court and political life at Versailles with which he regaled his many guests were avidly registered by a retentive twenty-year-old who would later write a history of the Sun King's reign. More than that, the marquis had stories going back to the days of Henri IV (1553–1610), Henry of Navarre, the first Bourbon king of France and grandfather of Louis XIV. The French history of which young Arouet had learnt so little at school was here – in a château built by the earlier sixteenth-century king, François I – brought alive for him in the anecdotes and personal experiences of this influential man. As such, the marquis de Saint-Ange was 'father' to the Voltaire who would become not only the writer of a famous epic about the French nation but also the greatest French historian of the eighteenth century.

Louis XIV died on 1 September 1715. On the following day Arouet had not far to walk in order to attend in the *parlement* as the King's will was read out in the presence of the new Regent. The succession had been complicated by the fact that the late king's only son and heir, the so-called Grand Dauphin, Louis de France, had recently predeceased him, as had the Grand Dauphin's son, Louis, duc de Bourgogne, the so-called Dauphin. The latter's brother, the duc d'Anjou, had become Philip V of Spain in 1700. The new king was Louis XV, the Dauphin's son and Louis XIV's great-grandson, but being only five he could not rule. Hence the need for a Regent, who was Philippe, duc d'Orléans (1674–1723), the grandson of Louis XIV's only brother. Having listened to the proclamation of his great-uncle's will, the new Regent refused to accept the restrictions placed on his power by the late king, a refusal tantamount to a *coup d'état* and endorsed by the *parlement*. In return for restoring the *parlement*'s right to make remonstrances about royal edicts before (rather than merely after) registering them, the new Regent was permitted to choose his own ruling council and to govern the nation. One week later Arouet attended the royal funeral and the passing of an era.

The Regency, which lasted effectively until Philippe's death, was a period of economic recovery, relatively sound government at home, improved relations abroad (especially with England), and a moral permissiveness bordering on the dissolute. France had grown used to being ruled from Versailles by an ageing king and to heeding the pious tone set by Mme de Maintenon, whom Louis had secretly married shortly after his first wife, Maria Theresa, had died in 1683. Now the atmosphere changed radically as the country came under the direction of a man who lived in the Palais-Royal, at the heart of Paris, and was widely known to indulge mightily in the pleasures of the table, the bottle and the flesh – including, it was no less commonly believed, the flesh of his daughter, the duchesse de Berry. Mme de Maintenon's premarital royal role had been to educate the two illegitimate sons of Louis XIV and his mistress, Mme de Montespan. The elder of these, Louis-Auguste de Bourbon, duc du Maine, had been legitimated by his father in 1714 and for a time looked likely to succeed to the throne as the King's elder surviving son. (In the event Louis XIV's will stipulated – in vain – that he share the powers of Regent with Philippe d'Orléans.) His wife and distant cousin, Louise de Bourbon, was the granddaughter of the Prince de Condé, a celebrated soldier of royal Bourbon blood and a patron and practitioner of *belles-lettres*. Louise – or Ludovise, as she preferred to be known – was a feisty blonde. Diminutive in size but commandingly regal in style, the irrepressible duchesse held court with her rather feckless and partly handicapped husband at Sceaux (near Zozo's birthplace of Chatenay, just north of Paris), where they had bought a château in 1699. After elaborate refurbishment and extension, their new mini-palace became a rival to Versailles as a focus of political ambitions and a literary salon that conferred considerable cachet. More often than not, the duke was absent, and the man of the house – who had been Ludovise's lover for some years past – was the leading scientist, Nicolas de Malézieu, her husband's former maths tutor.

Thanks to his budding reputation as a poet and wit, and thanks also to his contacts at Le Temple, the young Arouet had already begun to receive invitations to Sceaux a year or so after he left school. He remained a regular visitor until 1718, when the duchesse was temporarily imprisoned at the end of the year for conspiring with the Spanish ambassador to overthrow the Regent (the so-called Cellamare conspiracy). The château at Sceaux was the perfect setting for the innumerable balls and supper-parties which the duchesse was tireless in organizing. All-night entertainments became her speciality, the number and cost of the required candles being clearly no obstacle, and she dubbed these her 'white nights' by way of allusion to the festivities at the royal palace in St Petersburg where the summer sun literally never set. Twelve such occasions took place, the first on 31 July 1714, the last on 15 May 1715.

With aspirations to becoming queen of France, she liked to play the monarch, and she had founded her own Order of the Honey Bee (in 1703), of which she was the self-styled Queen Bee and 'Perpetual Head'. Newly inducted members would swear an oath of allegiance before being presented with a medal attached to a yellow ribbon. The medal bore, on one side, her profile and, on the other, the image of a bee flying to its nest, together with an inscription in Italian that translates as 'I may be small, but my sting is all the sharper'. Accordingly, all infringements against the rules of her elegant dictatorship were duly punished, one such forfeit being the telling of a story. The resulting improvised tale, generally involving the duchesse and others of the company, would be read out and copies of it subsequently distributed among the interested parties. Which is why a manuscript version of Voltaire's first known *conte*, or tale, survived to be published: *Le Crocheteur borgne* (*The One-Eyed Porter*). Its thinly veiled sexual innuendoes suggest that the Queen Bee was not averse to being titillated by the erotic tale of a princess who is not unpleasurably raped by a man of the people in Baghdad (but mercifully only in his dreams). Just as long as the flirtatious young narrator kept his outrageous suggestions firmly wrapped in the clichéd conventions of the newly fashionable oriental tale. 'Thin, tall, dried-up and bony' though he might have been, the new socialite on the scene commanded attention: a slim and supple frame, a well-turned calf, a moderately handsome face (albeit with a slightly prominent nose), a vivacious and incipiently impish expression, and an elegance of dress that married satin, lace and wig with the skill of a portrait-artist. What presence! What restless, unpredictable energy! Young Arouet had a way with words and a twinkle in his eye that caused the ladies to forgive him (and perhaps to grant him) almost anything. Ah, those eyes! Everyone mentioned them, men as well as women, and they always would – even in his last years when he had become quite indisputably 'dried-up and bony'.

The Queen Bee's guests were also induced to provide entertainment by means of a ballot in which they drew a letter of the alphabet that would prompt a particular genre: 'f' for 'fable', 'o' for 'opera', etc. Plays were staged, both comic and tragic, as well as musical entertainments of every sort. When Mme de Montauban, the mother of one of Ludovise's ladies-in-waiting, drew the letter 'p', she delegated the task to Arouet, who composed a story in illustration of a proverb or saying. He chose 'un petit mal pour un grand bien', which translates as 'a little evil for a great good' or, more roughly, 'no pain, no gain'; and he proceeded to demonstrate the truth of the dictum in a story called *Cosi-Sancta* (*A Saint of Sorts*) wherein a married woman saves the lives of her husband, brother and son by sleeping in turn with a proconsul, a brigand chief and a doctor who has plainly forgotten his Hippocratic oath. This compliant lady thus emerges as an implausible martyr to the demands of family life and is duly canonized for what is deemed (in a deft Voltairean parody of casuistical piety) to be mortification of the flesh. The story is set in Hippo in North Africa, birthplace of the St Augustine whose writings were at the source of Jansenism and their austere, killjoy morality. Since the boring duc du Maine was given to copying out extracts of St Augustine in a little book, his unfaithful wife was no doubt delighted by this story of a young girl predestined to sainthood for selfless promiscuity.

During the early years of the Regency, therefore, young Arouet was known as someone who had been keeping bad company – at Le Temple and at Sceaux – ever since the day he had left school, if not before. Was he a threat? The Regent began to think so. Arouet's satires and epigrams were circulating freely among the 300 or so coffee-houses of Paris. Some were harmless fun, others not quite so harmless. And of course, like Rousseau, he began to be cited as the author of poems that he had not written. One such, entitled 'J'ai vu' ('I have seen'), was a skilful and entertaining critique of French life in the last days of Louis XIV. Though clearly pro-Jansenist, its anonymous author identified himself in the final line of the poem as being 'not yet twenty'. Since Arouet was only just over twenty, and since his father and brother were known to have Jansenist sympathies, the hand of Arouet was suspected – and widely praised by Philippe d'Orléans's opponents. One day in the gardens of the Palais-Royal the Regent is said to have stopped him and said: 'I'll wager, Monsieur Arouet, that there is one thing I can show you that you have *not* observed.' When the poet asked what this was, the reply came: 'The inside of the Bastille.' 'Ah, sir,' Arouet rejoined, 'I think I'd rather take that as seen.'[5]

On 4 May 1716 Arouet was ordered into exile: for 'J'ai vu' (and no doubt other satirical verses) that he had not written, and for a verse epigram about the Regent's incestuous relations with his daughter that he certainly had written – but just as had several other verse-satirists of the day. Arouet did not leave before his father had managed to change the appointed place of exile from an inconvenient Tulle, away down between the Dordogne and the Massif Central, to the more agreeable château of his clients, the Sully family, at Sully-sur-Loire (and a mere eighty-five miles from Paris). Where better to spend the summer? Obviously the Regent cannot have been too cross, especially as the duc de Sully, a bachelor in his late forties, was a known habitué of Le Temple. During the following months Arouet met the many interesting and delightful guests whom the duke had invited to visit him at his country seat. They had 'white nights' here too, and so he was able to compare them (not unfavourably) with those he had enjoyed at Sceaux during the past two years. The food was delicious, the setting beautiful, and the female guests pleasingly ready to engage in a dalliance that the warm evenings seemed positively to invite, if not demand. Hence, no doubt, the charming house-custom of taking a walk in the woods and carving entwined initials on the bark of the trees.

Arouet's companion on such walks was Suzanne de Livry, daughter of a local lawyer and tax official who was also hereditary mayor. Fortunately for her companion she had no interest whatsover in the law but wanted rather to be an actress in Paris, an ambition to which she believed herself entitled by her considerable beauty. François promised to see what he could do, and she was his. For the moment he encouraged her to practise by participating in the amateur theatricals that were a regular feature of country-house life. Later she would encourage him to have his portrait painted, which resulted in the famous Largillière painting of Voltaire (see page 8).[6]

The happy exile had nevertheless to set about winning the Regent's pardon, and Chaulieu's advice – sensible but to young eyes contemptible – was to send him a flattering poem. The resulting verse epistle had no immediate, if any, effect, so that it was not until 20 October that the Regent finally relented and agreed to end his banishment. Winter would soon be setting in, and perhaps the rascal had learnt his lesson. Alas, he had not. Seven months later, on 16 May 1717, he was arrested by order of the Regent and imprisoned without trial in the Bastille, where he remained until 15 April 1718. No more 'white nights' but a potentially endless succession of early nights and some very disagreeable living conditions. What had happened?

On being delivered from the banks of the Loire, Arouet had returned to Paris and pleaded his innocence with the Regent, who nevertheless continued – rightly – to believe him the author of the poem about his incestuous relations with his daughter. Was Arouet piqued and now determined to cast in his lot with the opposition? At any rate he renewed his visits to Sceaux, where there were very serious plans afoot to overthrow the Regent and instate Philip of Spain as king. In late 1716 or early 1717 Arouet wrote a brief poem in Latin ('Regnante puero . . .' ('Under the reign of a child . . .')), attacking the Regent in the plainest, least humorous terms and airing the suspicions and grievances of his many opponents. Not only did Philippe d'Orléans sleep with his daughter, he had poisoned members of his family in order to gain power. Two Dauphins deceased from natural causes in the space of ten months? A likely story. (It was: the father died of smallpox, the son of scarlet fever.) And now he wanted the young Louis XV dead so that he could ascend the throne himself. He had destabilized the government and undermined the authority of the Church, ruined the public finances and flouted the law. In short, France was on the brink of civil war and complete disaster: 'Gaul soon will perish.' This was strong stuff.

No one was in any doubt that this was Arouet's work, and he decided to make himself scarce by returning to visit the marquis de Saint-Ange near Fontainebleau. From here he sent to Paris a six-line poem (in French rather than Latin) transforming the story of Oedipus (son kills father and sleeps with mother before putting his own eyes out) into that of Philippe d'Orléans: the father not the son is guilty, sleeping with the daughter not the mother, and he deserves to lose his sight (the Regent had been suffering from a serious eye disease for over a year). Again there could be no doubt as to the identity of the poem's anonymous author. But why was Arouet taking such obvious risks? The Regent had in fact treated him leniently in exiling him to Sully-sur-Loire, and his whole approach to life and government – greater tolerance, less insistence on religion and ceremony, a preference for fun over duty – were exactly what Arouet and Le Temple might have approved of. It is just possible that the young poet may have had genuine moral objections to incest and debauch, but it is more likely that he became intoxicated by his own importance and the role he was playing. And he thought he was backing the winning side. If the duchesse du Maine succeeded in overthrowing the Regent, her honeycomb court of make-believe would be transformed into a hive of real power and influence.

But the Regent knew when to apply a firm hand. On being arrested and taken to the Bastille, Arouet did not at first realize the seriousness of the situation nor have any idea how long he would be held. He joked with his captors that he would enjoy a week's rest because it would allow him to keep to the milk diet that his troublesome digestive system required. Indeed if they tried to let him out after a week he would demand to be allowed to stay for a fortnight. It was Whitsun, and he apologized to the police for making them work on a holiday. As long as he could have his scissors, his iron toothpick and his essence of cloves (as toothpaste), he would manage just fine. His gaolers took an inventory of the other possessions on his person: a lorgnette (for theatre-going), a notepad bound in silk-covered leather (for being a poet), money (6 *louis d'or* – the equivalent of 180 francs – and some loose change), and a crumpled love-letter that Pimpette had sent him three years earlier. And people say he was not sentimental.

As to the Bastille itself, the place held no fears. He had already had occasion to visit his friend the duc de Richelieu there, and found him living in reasonable if rather restricted comfort. At once born to the purple and extremely red-blooded, the priapic young duke had been spectacularly grounded at the age of fifteen after forming an attachment with the wife of the King's grandson: and fourteen months under close supervision in the Bastille (April 1711 – July 1712) were his equivalent of regular cold showers. Further amorous forays had led to a repeat prescription, under the new Regent, in 1716 – which no doubt explains why Richelieu would make his third visit in 1719 after being involved in the Cellamare conspiracy to oust him. But soon the reality of his own situation dawned on Arouet. The walls of his cell were ten feet thick, the entrance was secured by a sequence of three locked and barred doors, and there was no window. After a week he was interrogated, and he realized that the police had solid evidence against him. He knew, too, that his case might never – need never – come to trial (which it didn't); that the Regent could, in the King's name, keep him here just as long as he wished (which he did). Thanks to his poems he was now learning at first hand how the law of the land actually worked: arbitrarily, despoti-cally, by royal decree. But he had only himself to blame.

The experience changed him. Voltaire claimed later that his health, as uncertain as his birth, never truly recovered (over the remaining sixty years . . .). The cockiness of the adolescent and the swagger of the successful young adult were checked; he learnt resilience and the art of self-protection; and, as he later noted (in verse) to a close friend,[7] he discovered in himself a level of courage which, amidst the foolishness and errors of youth, he had

The Bastille.

never known he possessed. As it happened, it was in the arms of the man to whom he confided these thoughts, Nicolas de Génonville, that Suzanne de Livry now sought consolation for François's prolonged and unexpected absence. But she still wanted to be an actress, and her imprisoned lover had just written a play. After the white nights and the early nights, it was time for a first night.

CHAPTER FOUR

Back to the Bastille (1718–1726)

Wherein Arouet becomes Voltaire and is beaten up all the same

A ROUET WAS RELEASED from prison just in time for Easter. Eleven months in the Bastille had proved rather more tiresome than those week-long retreats at Louis-le-Grand, and they certainly proved more of an education. The date of release – 14 April 1718, Holy Thursday – was no doubt a public demonstration of the Regent's sense of Christian forgiveness, but it may also have implied a need for repentance. On leaving prison, Arouet was required (in the customary way) to live outside Paris and under a form of house arrest, which he did at his father's home at Chatenay. There he spent the summer trying to secure his freedom. At first he was granted permission to visit Paris for twenty-four hours, then later a week, then a month. Eventually, in October, he was allowed to come and go as he pleased. Just in time for the first night of the play that would make him famous: *Œdipe*.

Like many an ex-con he wanted to start afresh. So he changed his name, to Arouet de Voltaire, which is first recorded on 12 June 1718 as the signature in his letter to an English earl requesting the loan of a horse. Later, in November, after the success of *Œdipe*, he became simply 'Voltaire' or, less simply, 'Monsieur de Voltaire'. Whatever the source of 'Voltaire' – Arouet l.j., 'le petit volontaire', Airvault – he was keen to shed the name 'Arouet' because (a) it sounded like that of a contemporary poet, Roi (sounding somewhat like Roué in the pronunciation of the day), whom he despised, and (b) because 'Arouet' continually gave rise to puns suggesting that he was 'à rouer', i.e. fit to be beaten up. Given the trouble he had got himself into, he probably was; but, as we shall see, a change of name does not necessarily alter the course of destiny.

Arouet had begun *Œdipe* in his very late teens. In his determination to become a writer and not to study law, the ambitious school-leaver had heeded Jean-Baptiste Rousseau's advice and decided to aim for the top. And the top was having a verse tragedy performed at the Comédie-Française, like Corneille or Racine. The world was waiting for their successor, and the plays of Crébillon, although they received star billing at the Comédie-Française in the early 1700s, suggested nevertheless that it would have to wait a little longer. There was a niche to be filled, and young François was minded to fill it. The subject of Oedipus was the most ambitious of all, for how could one rival Sophocles? Corneille had tried but, by common consent, had not done very well. Even the great Racine had been daunted and, though he did seriously contemplate the prospect, never attempted his own version. But that was all a fearless nineteen-year-old needed to know. He was familiar with Ancient Greek tragedy from school, he had seen Euripides performed at Sceaux, and he thought nothing of writing directly for advice to André Dacier, the leading Greek scholar and author of the most recent translations of Sophocles. At the same time, thanks to his father's allowance, he could go to the theatre whenever he wished and pick up the tricks of the trade. And perhaps more. Not that young Arouet had any designs on the leading actress of the day, Mlle Duclos: the poem he addressed to her in ostensible adoration is in fact a witty evocation of the male homosexuals for whom she was the queen of drama.[1] Had he truly adored her, nevertheless, the twenty-year disparity in their ages would have proved no obstacle: ten years later, in her mid-fifties, Mlle Duclos married a boy of seventeen – not long after appearing as Salomé in Voltaire's *Hérode et Mariamne* (1724).

Gradually *Œdipe* took shape. Arouet read the play to his friends at Le Temple and later at Sceaux, adjusting and correcting certain scenes in response to constructive comment, and on 19 January 1717 the Comédie-Française agreed to perform the finished work of this talented 22-year-old. *Œdipe* is very much in the mould of the neo-classical tragedy that flowered in France in the middle of the seventeenth century and still continued to pack in the Parisians (Racine's *Andromaque*, *Iphigénie* and *Phèdre* were performed at the

Comédie-Française over 300 times between 1700 and 1715). Written in rhyming couplets of alexandrines (twelve-syllable lines), in five acts, with few characters, it skilfully exploits the neo-classical convention of the 'three unities' (of time, place and action) to produce a claustrophobic ambience of unalleviated horror as the truth about Oedipus is gradually revealed. The verse is effective, with several memorably epigrammatic lines, and the set speeches would have been relished by the actors of the day as they sought to move their audience with the pathos of human suffering.

But what marks the play out is its depiction of destiny. Whereas Racine, with his Jansenist leanings, had used classical mythology to present a view of the human condition in which sinfulness is nobly but vainly resisted and it is our common lot to fail, Voltaire's characters rail against the injustice of the gods. From the moment the curtain rises, the emphasis is on the 'unjust anger of the gods', 'the wrath of the gods', how the 'gods have led us from torment unto torment'. Unlike Racine's Phèdre, who accepts responsibility for her monstrous, incestuous love for Hippolyte even though she has done every-thing she humanly could to resist it, Voltaire's Oedipus is tragic because he has committed monstrous deeds through no fault of his own: 'Incestuous, a parricide, and yet virtuous' (Act V, l.156). 'Merciless gods, my crimes are your crimes,' he exclaims (l.166), and the play ends with Jocasta's defiant cry: 'I have caused the gods to blush for forcing me into crime.' The Jesuit vision of a just God is thus implicitly championed in contrast to the Jansenist God of wrath and obligatory sinfulness, and the Jesuit morality of conscience and intention is opposed to the Jansenist (and Ancient Greek) morality of deed and action. But even more important is what this divine injustice has prevented: 'To be of use to my fellow mortals and to save this empire,' cries Oedipus, 'That [. . .] is the only honour to which I aspire' (Act II, ll.217–18). He could have set the world to rights but for all this daft divine intervention, having sons kill their fathers and sleep with their mothers. Yes, Freud later thought that we boys want for nothing better, but Voltaire would have had none of it. Though human free will and human action we can make the world a better place. If only the gods and their priests will cease from meddling.

The play and its message clearly struck a chord. Œdipe was first performed on 18 November 1718 and was an immediate success. Its opening run lasted for twenty-nine performances, and by the end of January 1719 some 25,000 people had been to see it. The theatre itself was located a little way south of the Pont Saint-Michel, in the direction of the Palais du Luxembourg and in what is now (therefore) the rue de l'Ancienne Comédie. The Café Procope was almost next door. At the beginning and end of the evening the tiny street would be jammed with carriages. The auditorium was rectangular in shape, with boxes on either side for the well-born or well-heeled Parisians who rented them by the year. Entry to the parterre, or pit, usually cost one *livre*, approximately the daily wage of the best-paid worker. Here there were no seats, and only men were admitted to its uncomfortable and often noisy throng. Though it was forbidden, they cheered and booed, whistled and jeered. Sometimes they heckled, obliging the players to interrupt their performance to supply a put-down. The fate of a new play lay in their hands. When it was good, they wept and groaned in deepest empathy.

The ladies and gentlemen in their boxes faced each other across this tumult, and spent much of the time surveying and contributing to a human comedy quite separate from that depicted on the stage. Indeed it was considered bad form to be more interested in the play than one's companions. A box at the theatre was a temporary drawing-room in which one received or was received. As such it constituted an extension of salon life that provided women in particular with a treasured opportunity for conversation or gossip – and a glimpse of possible recruits to the more intimate society of their boudoir. Refreshments were available throughout the proceedings, which usually lasted about four hours. But the most expensive seats in the house were on the stage itself, and this valuable source of revenue ensured that the actors were willing to give up some of the space required for their dramatic gestures. In any case the French classical stage required few sets and almost no physical action: a play was more like a verse recitation. The only extra lighting was a row of small lamps that could be raised or lowered at will to illuminate a particular actor. When the play was particularly popular, further spectators would stand at the back and sides of the stage, in front of the sets, making the dramatic entrance or exit as problematic as the traffic conditions outside. Indeed during one performance of *Œdipe* somebody stood on the hem of the High Priest's flowing robe just as he was moving forward, and so Monsieur de Voltaire (happening to be there) released it and promptly turned himself into a *de facto* page, bearing the train with exaggerated ceremony and clowning to the audience. Any opportunity to make fun of the Church would do, even if it briefly turned his tragedy into a comedy. Only in 1758 were spectators removed from the stage, and only in 1782 – when the Comédie-Française moved to new premises (the present-day Théâtre de l'Odéon, from which it has since moved) – were seats provided for those in the parterre.

Œdipe was a considerable financial success, netting its young author some 3,000 *livres*. It was also performed for the Regent and his family at the Palais-Royal, not once but four times. Since being released from the Bastille Voltaire had endeavoured to mend his fences with the Regent, sending him an affidavit, signed and witnessed (but of dubious authenticity), in which an abbé Régnier (later amended to an abbé Lebrun) confessed to authorship of 'J'ai vu'. One story has it also that on securing an audience with the Regent and having thrown himself on his mercy and that of the young king, Arouet could not nevertheless resist a joke: 'Sir, I would be most pleased if His Majesty were henceforth to provide for my board, but I beg your Royal Highness no longer to see to my lodging.'[2] Be that as it may, the Regent – in his role as enlightened patron of the arts – now awarded the recent resident of the Bastille a gold medal as the author of *Œdipe* and granted him (as was the custom) an annuity (of 1,200 *livres*). The British ambassador, John Dalrymple, Earl of Stair, reported to his superiors: 'He's ye best poet maybe ever was in France',[3] whereupon George I of England, not to be outdone, gave the young playwright a medal and a very splendid gold watch. The censor of the play, the leading poet Houdar de la Motte (whom not so long ago Arouet had ridiculed in his satirical poem 'Le Bourbier' ('The Mire')), magnanimously approved it for publication the following year in glowing terms, and the Regent's mother agreed to have the play dedicated to her (the Regent himself having declined). But perhaps the most significant plaudit came from Arouet *père*. Austere in his habits and averse to theatre-going, he had none the less been dragged along to watch. He was moved to tears by the performance and heartened by his son's success, especially when he heard about the 3,000 *livres*. Perhaps the fellow would not be a wastrel after all.

High society flocked to see the play, among them the maréchale de Villars, whose attentions momentarily turned the young dramatist's head. She was considerably older than he, and in turn married to a much older man (albeit a war hero). She invited Voltaire to stay at their house near Melun, not far from Paris (a château then called Vaux-Villars, now Vaux-le-Vicomte), an invitation which he misunderstood: she was not, it turned out, ready to play Jocasta to his Oedipus. But there was one who was. When *Œdipe* began its second run in the spring, Voltaire managed to secure the part of Jocasta for his former mistress, Suzanne de Livry. Voltaire had forgiven her lapse while he was unavoidably detained in the Bastille and fulfilled his pledge to make her an actress. But she did not do well. Her lover's coaching proved insufficient, and her thick regional accent was not quite right for a queen of Thebes. She was mocked by the rest of the cast, notably Paul Poisson, who was provoked by Voltaire's anger into challenging him to a duel outside the stage-door. Poets did not deign to duel with actors, and Voltaire, having reported him to the police, duly accompanied them round to his lodgings with the firm intention of cracking his skull open with the butt of his pistol. And if *it* could not be fired, Poisson should be. Agreement was reached by all parties that Poisson would be imprisoned on condition that Voltaire immediately petition for his release. Which he did.

Vaux-Villars was but one of several châteaux to which Voltaire was now invited. Sceaux was off limits, but he returned to the Loire valley and revisited Sully-sur-Loire in the early summer of 1719 before going to stay at the nearby Château du Bruel with the duc de La Feuillade, a known — and evidently forgiving — homosexual in his mid-forties whom he had lampooned in some recent verse. He returned to Sully in the autumn. Later, to visit his schoolfriend (during one of the latter's spells out of the Bastille) he would visit nearby Richelieu (in Voltaire's view the finest château in France, but now sadly vanished). The Château d'Ussé became a regular destination, thanks to his close friendship with the marquis d'Ussé, and a visit to La Source near Orléans, home of the exiled Tory leader Henry St John, Viscount Bolingbroke, would prove something of an intellectual watershed. Near Paris he would be invited to Maisons (now Maisons-Lafitte), the home of another old schoolfriend, Jean de Longueil, marquis de Maisons, while near Rouen he would stay at La Rivière-Bourdet, home of the marquis and marquise de Bernières. As a witty conversationalist and now a professional entertainer, he was a popular house-guest, and it spared him having to live at home under constant threat of paternal rebuke. But such visits were not necessarily a means of making economies. At Vaux-Villars, for example, it was traditional for guests to play *biribi*, a cross between lotto and roulette, where the odds were fixed in such a way as to turn a healthy profit for the 'house'. And of course there was always one's wardrobe to worry about: velvet frock-coats, richly embroidered satin waistcoats, crisp cotton shirts and lace jabots, smooth breeches, stockings of wool and silk, leather shoes with buckles of silver and gold, or even diamonds. Not to mention gifts for the ladies.

Now in his mid-twenties, Voltaire was in any case not a man for making economies. The proceeds from *Œdipe* did not last long, and over the next few years the high-living playwright would run up debts to the tune of 4,000 *livres* (eventually expunged by his father). Desirous of fame but not averse to a fortune, he was eager to follow up the success of *Œdipe*, and during the course of 1719 he wrote *Artémire*, a play about the eponymous queen of Macedonia (after the death of Alexander the Great). It was designed to be a showcase for the latest acting sensation at the Comédie-Française, Adrienne Lecouvreur, whose more natural style of understated diction marked a major break from the quasi-operatic delivery of Mlle Duclos and her even more famous predecessor, La Champmeslé (aunt of the Mlle Desmares who had first played Voltaire's Jocasta in just such a fashion). *Artémire* premiered on 15 February 1720 and flopped. The Regent's mother was keen to see it, so Voltaire mended what he could, but after eight more performances it closed. It was never published, and the text survives only in fragments. A parody of the play was performed at the rival Comédie-Italienne, and proved much more popular. For Voltaire the one compensation was that he had become Adrienne's lover.

But there were other routes to literary fame. On leaving school the young Arouet had set out to rival Sophocles. But why not Homer and Virgil too? In the autumn of 1716 it had occurred to him that he might write an epic about Henri IV, the sixteenth-century French king who had started out as the Protestant Henri de Navarre and united France by turning Catholic (because, as he famously put it: 'Paris vaut bien une messe' – 'Paris is well worth a Mass'). When he mentioned the possibility in conversation at Sceaux, Nicolas de Malézieu, Ludovise's lover, commented in a remark that has

since become proverbial in France: 'Les Français n'ont pas la tête épique' –
(roughly) 'The French don't do epic'. At that time it was a source of shame
to a nation bent on literary glory (of the kind which had been so notably
achieved in the theatre) that it had no equivalent to the *Iliad* and the *Aeneid*.
Italy had Tasso's *Jerusalemma liberata*; Portugal, Camoens' *Lusiad*. Even little
England had its *Paradise Lost*. Virgil's *Aeneid* was a particularly important
model, tracing as it does the founding of Rome. From the vantage-point of
the Regency – when the ambiguous Bourbon lineage represented a serious
cause for dispute – the subject of Henri IV, the first Bourbon king, could be
the focus for a no less 'foundational' narrative. When Arouet returned to stay
with the marquis de Saint-Ange in 1717, he was once more regaled with the
stories he had heard in 1714, eye-witness accounts of life under Louis XIV (at
the highest level) but also countless anecdotes that the marquis himself had
heard about life in the days of 'le bon Henri', the jovial Gascon soldier with
the common touch who had sought (before he was assassinated by François
Ravaillac in 1610) to put France together again after forty years of religious
civil war.

  Voltaire's great epic poem – the one single work for which he was most
celebrated throughout his lifetime but which is now scarcely read – was
begun at the Château de Saint-Ange in February or March 1717. When the
author of 'Regnante puero . . .' was then thrown into the Bastille three
months later, the task of composition became more challenging. Forbidden
the provision of paper to write on (no more seditious verses, please), he
successfully requested two books of Homer to read (one in Greek, one in
Latin), which at least gave him something to aim for. Moreover (when he got
hold of a pencil) he could write in these books between the lines. When later
recounting the episode to the philosopher George Berkeley, he claimed to
have made paper by chewing his clothes; but, as is evident in his comment to
Mrs Pope about the effect of Jesuit sodomists on his health, he seems to have
considered his British interlocutors rather credulous about strange foreign
ways. What is clear from other accounts, however, is that he composed some
sections of the poem in his head, where he carried them until he could set
them down on paper many months later. Almost as if he were Homer himself
and the repository of a venerable, orally transmitted masterpiece.

  By the autumn of 1721 it was finished, all six cantos. The next stage was to obtain the Regent's approval for its publication and perhaps even his agreement to be its dedicatee. But Arouet *père* was now seriously ill. Though his son continued to live at home when not being entertained – or entertaining – in sundry châteaux, and despite the visit to see *Œdipe*, there had been no reconciliation between the two men following the Pimpette affair. On 19 August 1721, his seventy-second birthday, François Arouet dictated his will to two notaries. His estate was to be divided equally between his three children, save that in the case of François-Marie the beneficiary should receive only the interest on the resulting capital sum. This sum, to be invested and administered by a trustee, was then to pass eventually to the beneficiary's (legitimate) children, or, in the absence of any such, to his brother and sister in equal shares. Young poets, it seemed, were not to be trusted with money. However, his father further stipulated that, if on reaching the age of thirty-five he could produce clear evidence of 'regular conduct', he would be entitled to apply to the senior magistrate in the Chambre des Comptes to have this testamentary provision set aside and to take charge of the capital himself. The terms of this will speak volumes about the father's attitude towards his talented but profligate son. On 26 December, now gravely ill, he must have felt a pang of paternal guilt, for he dictated a codicil annulling the special provision – dictated but did not sign. He died on 1 January 1722, and François-Marie was left to live on the interest from approximately 153,000 *livres*. Plenty enough one might think, except that it was to take five years for the will to be declared probate and the monies transferred. In the meantime, and now with neither allowance nor free lodging in the Palais de Justice, he would have to fend for himself – which for a poet who did not want to be a jobbing hack was not an easy matter. But fend he did, and so successfully that by the time he was thirty-five a court would duly rule (on 1 March 1730) that the special provision in his father's will be lifted. His conduct had become so 'regular' that he had in fact by then made a great deal of money all on his own.

First, he entered into business relations with the marquis de Bernières, a senior judge in the Rouen *parlement*. Before his father's death Voltaire had invested some money in the Compagnie des Indes, which traded in the Indies (East and West). He used some or all of this to buy a share, with de Bernières, in a salt-tax 'franchise', thereby securing an income through the resultant 'commission' (just as Arouet *père* had made money out of the spice tax). The Bernières lived at the Château de la Rivière-Bourdet, near Rouen, but also owned a house in Paris, on the corner of the quai des Théatins and the rue de Beaune (just along the Seine westwards from the Palais de Justice), the house where Voltaire would eventually die on 30 May 1778. For the present, however, the de Bernières were proving to be the least deadly of connections, since, while he was making money with the husband, the newly orphaned spendthrift was making love with the wife (a beautiful, buxom, 35-year-old blonde) – and would soon be renting part of their house in Paris. Clearly Voltaire was ready to contemplate almost anything at this difficult juncture in his life, because it seems that he now offered his services to the Prime Minister, the Cardinal Dubois, as a secret agent in Vienna. More sensibly, towards the end of the year, he invested with the Pâris brothers, the leading French financiers of the day, and on the basis of this and subsequent investments his future wealth was assured. As we shall see.

As to his becoming the new French Virgil, the Regent was proving as reluctant to confer official approval as Arouet *père* had been to let his son inherit. And so, for the first time since his diplomatic sojourn in The Hague, Voltaire began to look beyond the frontiers of France for his future support and recognition. At the end of August 1722 he set off for Holland with a view to finding a Dutch publisher for his new epic. The Hague and Amsterdam had long been places of refuge for French writers, notably Descartes, who found themselves unwanted prophets in their own land, and the subject of the proposed work – the Wars of Religion – was likely to be of interest in this Protestant land. The marquise de Bernières being unavailable (not only was she a married woman, she was also busy renovating her Rouen château), Voltaire travelled – and slept – with Marie-Marguerite de Rupelmonde, a very pretty young widow in her early thirties with hair like golden flame. Not that this prevented him from visiting the 'finest brothel' in Brussels when they broke their journey there (the young widow having business matters to attend to in respect of her late husband, a Flemish aristocrat who had died ten years earlier in the service of the King of Spain). The couple had earlier stopped off at Cambrai, where a major congress of European powers was taking place at ambassadorial level, a kind of EU summit minus the heads of state. Little serious business was conducted, which left time for dinners, balls

and theatrical entertainments in which the French travellers gladly participated. It was agreed by the organizers that *Œdipe* be performed, though only if
Voltaire would allow a celebrated parody of it (*Œdipe travesti*) to be staged
also.

Mme de Rupelmonde was a woman of conscience who strove earnestly to
reconcile her Christian faith with a widow's conventional licence to take
lovers as she pleased. Indeed that was the great advantage of being a widow,
which is one of the reasons why old men found it easy to secure young
brides. Her companion, who believed in God but not in Christianity, teased
her by accompanying her to Mass in Brussels and then ridiculing the
proceedings aloud, much to her embarrassment and to the outrage of the
attendant faithful. Apprehensive as she quite genuinely was that her conduct
might lead her to the fires of Hell, Voltaire then wrote her a short poem –
the 'Epître à Uranie' ('Epistle to Urania') – in which he set out his views.
The man who had sought to emulate Sophocles and Virgil now presented
himself as a latter-day Lucretius, ready to elaborate a 'natural religion' in
place of the 'sacred lies' – about hell-fire and such like – put about by the
priests. Guided by the flaming torch of reason, he rejects the Christian God
of wrath, the God who made us sinful so that He could punish us, who made
us in His image only then to wish He hadn't, who sent a Great Flood to
destroy us only then to send His son to die for us instead, and who now
continues to punish us for things we've never even done. No, says Voltaire,
'I cannot recognize in this unworthy image / The God whom I must
worship' (ll.96–7); and, now addressing the kind of God he does recognize,
the poet adds: 'People say you are a tyrant; but in you *I* seek a Father; / If I
am not Christian, it is the better to love you' (ll.104–5). The true 'natural'
God offers comfort and solace. He loves his creatures, especially if – like
Mme de Rupelmonde – they are as beautiful of face as in conscience fair and
kind.

All of which must have allowed Marie-Marguerite to find her moral
bearings, since Urania is the muse of astronomy and geometry. By the
standards of the day, the poem was not only blasphemous but highly
dangerous – for the author as well as the Church. Already in *Œdipe* Voltaire
had written the famous lines:

Nos prêtres ne sont point ce qu'un vain peuple pense,
Notre crédulité fait toute leur science.

(Act IV, ll.57–8)

(Our priests are not as foolish folk surmise,
Our credulity alone renders them knowing and wise.)

but he had got away with it because in the play the priest in question turned out to be right. But here, in the safety of this private poem, he could express his view more plainly: the Christian Church was a form of 'imposture', a con-trick by which the masses were terrified into craven subjection by lies and contradictions and denied the warming vision that the natural is beautiful and human beings potentially noble and decent. Voltaire renamed it 'Le Pour et le contre' ('For and Against') when he sent it to his friend Cideville in Rouen in 1735, by which time it had been circulating clandestinely in Paris for three or four years – a minor explosive before the great bombshell that was the *Lettres philosophiques* (*Philosophical Letters*) (1734).

Jean-Baptiste Rousseau had travelled up from Vienna to meet Voltaire in Brussels (then the capital of the Austrian Netherlands), and so perhaps it was the renewed contact with this acerbic iconoclast that had put Urania's lover in the mood for an unambiguous burst of amorous freethinking. But the happy couple bid Rousseau farewell after eleven days of his not entirely congenial company and travelled on to The Hague and then to Amsterdam, remaining in the country for three weeks. At The Hague Voltaire signed a contract with Charles Le Viers for a luxury, illustrated edition of his new epic, which now ran to nine cantos and was accompanied by historical notes and commentary. The title had been amended to *Henri IV ou la Ligue* (*Henri IV or the League*) – the *Ligue* being the Catholic forces who had combined in 1576 under Henri, duc de Guise (known as 'le Balafré' or 'Scarface') to fight the Huguenots. When the childless Henri III was assassinated by a Dominican friar after nominating the Protestant Henri de Navarre as his heir (and after having 'le Balafré' assassinated), the *Ligue* refused to recognize the new king. It was on emerging victorious from the ensuing civil war that Henri IV decided that Paris was well worth a Mass and converted to Catholicism in order to unite the country. A splendid Protestant had secured the future of a wonderful Catholic country under wise Bourbon leadership . . . in other

words a story that could be read (and spun) in a number of political ways. In
many respects it was a glorious account of the founding of the dynasty that
now ruled France, but the Regent remained suspicious of the author of
'Regnante puero . . .' and wondered about the sincerity of this new-found
sycophancy. Cardinal Fleury (1653–1743), young Louis XV's confessor and
guardian, considered that Voltaire had painted much too favourable a
portrait of the Protestants, notably Elizabeth I of England, to whom Henri
IV had turned, successfully, for military aid. It was possible also to infer an
overriding message that the King of France should be above religious dispute
and – unlike Louis XIV or XV – side neither with Catholic nor Protestant,
Jesuit nor Jansenist. Hence the reluctance in high places to grant the work a
privilège.

Having achieved the principal aim of his journey, Voltaire decided to
enjoy himself – riding, playing real tennis (jeu de paume) and relaxing with
Marie-Marguerite over a glass of Tokay. At the same time he observed the
habits and customs of the Dutch with a degree of attention which his former
infatuation with Pimpette had prevented. And his eyes were opened. Here
was a country so different from his own. Nowhere could be more pleasant
than The Hague – at least 'when the sun deigns to shine'; and, as he travelled
from there to Amsterdam, the landscape with its canals and broad acres of
fertile greenery seemed like 'paradise on earth'.[4] At Amsterdam he was
staggered by the spectacle of so much prosperity: everyone seemed to have a
job, the port was filled with hundreds of ships. At this period the fourth-
largest city in Europe, with a population of some 200,000, Amsterdam was a
thriving and heterogenous community of whom about 10 per cent were
foreign-born and some 2.5 per cent were former black slaves. The Amsterdam
Bourse was the leading financial centre in Europe (being replaced by London
only in the 1780s), and almost any book in any language could be bought in
one of its hundred or more bookshops. But what impressed Voltaire most –
as he reported in a letter to Mme de Bernières – was the simplicity,
unpretentiousness and plain neighbourliness of the Dutch. He was astonished to see the head of state walking through the streets without a single
attendant. Calvinists, Jews, Arminians (Protestant opponents of Calvinism
who advocated a more liberal, tolerant kind of Reformed religion) and
Anabaptists (who believed that only adults should be baptized, and therefore

urged the 'rebaptism' of the already christened), all mixed and spoke amicably together. Everyone, it seemed, could think or say or publish what they wanted, and for Voltaire there appeared to be a necessary link between this liberalism and the commercial vitality that was all around him. This was the future, a bourgeois world of freedom and tolerance to replace the empty coffers and vacuous rituals of his own dear bankrupt, sclerotic, hidebound France.

After staying with aristocratic friends in the Loire, Voltaire returned to Paris in the first weeks of 1723 still determined to obtain official approval for his epic. Louis XV, being now twelve, had reached the age of majority (for a king), so perhaps he could be persuaded to be the work's dedicatee. But Cardinal Fleury had begun to worry about what the Pope might say, and after he had alerted the Regent's prime minister, Dubois, to its possible dangers the poem was submitted for evaluation to the abbé Du Bos, a writer of known conservative opinions. Opposition was growing, and the chances of getting away with even an unofficial, Dutch-produced edition were slim. So Voltaire turned to a Rouen publisher, Abraham Viret, whom he had met when staying with the de Bernières at La Rivière-Bourdet, and together they plotted to produce a clandestine edition. A contract was signed at the end of March (the one previously agreed with Viers having not granted exclusive rights), and production began. His old friend Cideville, now a lawyer in the Rouen *parlement*, together with Cideville's close colleague Formont, were enlisted to supervise the operation from the Rouen end while Voltaire took care of Paris – and began writing another play, *Mariamne*, with which he hoped to expunge the failure of *Artémire*. Which it eventually would. But the demands of literary composition – not to mention the stress of city life – played havoc with the author's now notoriously unreliable digestive system. Ass's milk, he found, was the only remedy.

But soon he needed lemonade, 200 pints of the stuff. On a visit to Maisons (on the Seine, north-west of Paris) in the late autumn, Voltaire contracted smallpox. Lots of people did, and some died from it – including, in this particular outbreak, his friend Génonville (who had replaced him in Suzanne de Livry's affections during his stay in the Bastille). The marquis de Maisons appeared to have caught it also, but his bout was so benign that he caught it again in 1731 and died (as did his only son). Voltaire himself was soon at death's door. A priest was called to administer the last rites, and the author of the 'Epître à Uranie' duly confessed his sins: it was only good manners to do so. Fortunately the marquis had acquired the services of the leading smallpox specialist, Gervasi, who made it his mission to save the ailing guest. After the customary blood-letting and purges, which the patient survived, Gervasi recommended the untried remedy of drinking lots of liquid and willed the guinea-pig to live. He did: and, having fallen ill on 4 November, was well enough to leave on 1 December. Confessing his sins must have put him in the Almighty's good books, for, on casting an eye back towards the château where he had nearly breathed his last, he saw flames leaping from the window of the very room where he had lain. A fire had been kept blazing in the hearth for the three weeks of his illness and had finally set the supporting beam alight. Firemen were summoned from Paris, and the house, like Voltaire, was saved.

Specialist doctors are expensive, as are publishing costs. Voltaire's finances were stretched, and he needed to recoup some of his investment. Four thousand copies of the epic poem, now entitled *La Ligue ou Henri le Grand* (*The League or Henry the Great*), had been printed, and half of these were now 'brochés' (with pages stitched but not bound). But how to get them into Paris past the guards and customs officials that policed all entries to the capital? On 20 December 1723 Mme de Bernières dispatched from Rouen a very large waggon drawn by six horses and loaded with furniture, followed by two horses laden with saddle-packs and baskets. At a short distance from the barrier, copies of *La Ligue* were removed from in between the furniture in the waggon and transferred into the saddle-packs and baskets. After several trips Henri IV had once more entered Paris: if the city was worth a Mass, it was also worth a spot of smuggling. Were the authorities simply turning a blind eye? The Prime Minister, Dubois, had died in August, and the marquise de Villars (young Arouet's former but unyielding heart-throb) had been using her influence since then to see that they did. On 2 December the erstwhile Regent (who had become prime minister on Louis's coming-of-age) had died also. The moment was propitious. At any rate, by the middle of January 1724, the latest Voltaire *œuvre* was being discussed in the Parisian press. The author, of course, duly played the game and disclaimed responsibility, alleging that the manuscript had been stolen and reproduced without his permission. Hence its tatty appearance, the poor print quality, and the significant number of judicious blanks left in the text. But nobody was fooled, especially since the title-page announced that the publisher was one 'Jean Mokpap' from (Protestant) Geneva. Everyone knew who the nearest local 'mock-Pope' was likely to be.

The work was a huge success. The most discerning French critics praised the skill with which the conventions and set pieces of Virgilian epic had been followed and imitated and the narrative verve with which such a complex historical subject had been articulated. Plainly the French *did* do epic. Abroad, even Alexander Pope was impressed. As a Catholic in a Protestant country he could see the value of Voltaire's appeal for religious toleration based on reason and due respect for what came to be known as human rights. The clandestine edition soon sold out, and – as was inevitable in the days before copyright law – half a dozen pirated editions soon appeared to meet the demand left unassuaged by Viret's 4,000 copies. The abbé Desfontaines (of whom more later) produced a version filling in the blanks, while Guyot de Merville (who had previously replaced the undiplomatic Arouet in Pimpette's affections) produced an antagonistically annotated edition of the manuscript Voltaire had deposited with a publisher during his Dutch trip back in 1722. In short, a typical book launch in eighteenth-century France. But its author still dreamed of an official, luxury edition – as befitting a classic. In August he moved into the apartment he had rented in the de Bernières' house at the corner of the rue de Beaune, but it was impossible to write. The view across the Seine was lovely, but the noise of the traffic was unbearable, day and night, not to mention the pungent smell of the horse dung left behind on this busy riverside thoroughfare. So after a week he moved out and rented furnished rooms nearby. Not exactly salubrious since he promptly caught mange, but, despite the itching, he could at least get back to his epic. In September he wrote an additional thousand lines, bringing the total number of cantos to ten, and the great work would now be called by the title that its Parisian readers had invented: *La Henriade*. All epics worthy of the name had to end in '-iade'.

Philippe d'Orléans was succeeded as prime minister, with Fleury's consent, by the duc de Bourbon, a prince of the blood, who – since the

King was only thirteen – now effectively ruled France (with the assistance of his mistress, Mme de Prie). Already on good terms with the duke, Voltaire sought to ingratiate himself with the incoming regime. The first version of his new play *Mariamne* had flopped on 6 March 1724, which was a particular shame since the seat prices had been doubled in expectation of another 'hit' to match *Œdipe*. But the sight of the eponymous queen, wife of Herod the Great, actually poisoning herself on stage (against all the rules of decorous neo-classical theatre) seemed merely comic, so that the resultant giggles quite drowned out the pathos of her eloquent farewell and demise. Voltaire reworked the play, removing all offensive innovation and making sure that the new version, *Hérode et Mariamne*, would receive a warm reception at court with its elevated portrayal of the corridors of power. Premiered on 10 April 1725 at the Comédie-Française, with Adrienne Lecouvreur in the title-role, it brought further fame (and some fortune) to its already remarkably productive creator. A one-act, not very comic comedy in verse, *L'Indiscret* (*He Who Is Indiscreet*), soon followed, on 18 August, and was dedicated to Mme de Prie.

This important lady, meanwhile, was busy arranging with her lover, the duc de Bourbon, to find young Louis XV a bride and thus to provide France with a legitimate heir to the throne as soon as physiologically possible. The Regent and Dubois had arranged for him to marry the Infanta, daughter of Philip V of Spain, but she was still only seven – which was no good at all. So they reneged on the deal and plumped instead for Marie Leszczynska, daughter of the exiled Polish king, Stanislas. He lived and held court, at the expense of the King of France, at Wissembourg, near the border with Alsace. The young Polish princess proved – on careful inspection by Mme de Prie – at once sweet-natured, biddable, and a very useful eight years older than her husband-to-be. Voltaire was determined to be part of the show and so rented rooms in Mme de Prie's mansion in Fontainebleau, where the royal wedding duly took place on 5 September at the nearby palace. Unfortunately the entertainment he had prepared for the nuptial celebrations was rejected in favour of two plays by Molière. Undeterred, he sought out and cultivated the connections of the royal bride, went to pay court to Stanislas, now installed at Montargis (seventy miles due south of Paris), and finally met the new queen herself. *Hérode et Mariamne* and *L'Indiscret* were performed at court, and she was duly moved to tears and laughter respectively. In November the Queen even awarded him an annual pension of 1,500 *livres* (ostensibly to cover his expenses as a courtier) but the money never actually materialized. Had someone – Fleury? her husband? – whispered in her ear that this charismatic playwright was also the author of *La Henriade* and perhaps not wholly to be trusted? Still, Voltaire had the lovely vellum document with her signature on it, so he promptly borrowed money against it from the financier Pâris-Duverney – which he still owed him ten years later.

By the end of 1725, therefore, the aspirant courtier had not quite arrived. And now disaster struck, thanks to the chevalier de Rohan-Chabot, feckless and degenerate scion of one of the oldest aristocratic families in France. So important in Voltaire's life did this episode become that multiple conflicting versions of it abound. But the basic facts are more or less these. Voltaire had known Rohan-Chabot for a while, indeed had regaled him with stories of his trip to Holland in 1722. But the chevalier was jealous of this social upstart's success at court and one evening at the Opéra, towards the end of January 1726, taunted him about his change of name: 'Monsieur de Voltaire, Monsieur Arouet, just what *are* you called?' Taken aback, Voltaire muttered something about people with no less confusing (and somewhat uneupho-nious) double-barrelled names. Two days later, at the Comédie-Française and in front of Adrienne Lecouvreur, the chevalier repeated his question. No doubt armed with the weapons of his earlier *esprit d'escalier*, Monsieur de Voltaire replied to the effect that he for his part would immortalize this name while Rohan-Chabot would surely dishonour his. As the outraged aristocrat raised his cane, Adrienne called on her thespian gifts and most conveniently swooned.

When it came to matters of personal honour, gentlemen fought duels: they did not raise their cane, unless of course the offender was a scoundrel of the lowest social order. On the other hand, aristocratic gentlemen did not fight duels with mere bourgeois, however famous they might be. A few days later Rohan-Chabot sent his adversary an invitation to dinner as though from the duc de Sully (Voltaire's friend and fellow-frequenter of Le Temple), who received his 'guest' as though he had indeed been invited: 'noblesse', after all, 'oblige'. During dinner a footman tells the unexpected guest that a person wishes to speak to him at the entrance. There Voltaire is set upon by three or four men with cudgels, while Rohan-Chabot looks on from a safe distance before eventually calling them off. Furious, and injured in both person and pride, our bourgeois gentleman brandishes his sword at the departing coward before storming upstairs to protest to the duc de Sully that such an attack constitutes a slur on *his* honour as well as that of his guest. He demands that they complain at once to the police. Sully refuses, acknowledging that the attack has been 'violent and uncivil' but implicitly closing ranks with his fellow-aristocrat against an uninvited guest who, however engaging, seems to cause trouble wherever he goes. A similar response is forthcoming from Mme de Prie when the would-be courtier rushes off to the Opéra to tell her the story. No luck either with the young queen at Versailles. Everywhere he goes, people express sympathy but decline to take his side: no matter what he says, the fact remains that Rohan-Chabot is an aristocrat and he is not. Eventually on 5 February the comte de Maurepas, the King's minister in charge of law and order, gives orders for the assailants to be arrested, but no action is to be taken against their employer. The upstart poet may indeed have been insulted but he should simply not have dared to answer back.

Disillusioned by his aristocratic friends and still determined to secure justice, Voltaire now gave notice that he was going to seek Rohan-Chabot out and challenge him to a duel. The chevalier was lying low at Versailles in the residence of his influential cousin, Cardinal Fleury, but ventured back to Paris on 23 March. His adversary had now taken temporary lodgings under the assumed name of the Baron de Saint-Flor. The police placed both parties under surveillance as the 'Baron' moved from address to address to avoid them. On 28 March Maurepas gave orders to his Lieutenant of Police for Voltaire to be arrested and taken to the Bastille, but the criminal had gone to ground somewhere in the country. A few days later he was back in Paris taking lessons in fencing and pistol-shooting and busy securing the services of his least unaristocratic relative – a Daumard – to be his second. He also hired a few well-muscled pugilists, just to be on the safe side.

According to one version,[5] he finally caught up with his prey in Adrienne Lecouvreur's box at the theatre, where he challenged him to a duel next morning at 9 a.m. at the Porte Saint-Antoine (just outside the city walls, for legal reasons). Rohan-Chabot accepted but alerted his influential relatives. Other versions suggest that Voltaire and his men went to the Cardinal's residence in Versailles to settle the matter in a more direct fashion. Whichever the case, Voltaire was arrested on the night of 17 April 1726, at his hotel La Grosse Teste in the rue Maubué, and thence taken to the Bastille. In his pockets were a pair of pistols and sixty-five *louis d'or* (about 1,500 *livres*), a very large sum that was no doubt intended to fund his getaway. Voltaire responded to his arrest by protesting his innocence to Maurepas, claiming provocatively that he had sought not to defend his own honour but to restore that of Rohan-Chabot, 'which has proved too difficult'.[6] He demanded to be allowed to dine with the prison governor (as he had towards the end of his previous incarceration in the Bastille) and to be permitted to proceed with a visit to England that he had been planning for some time. The authorities were in a difficult position: they could see that, bourgeois or no, Voltaire was the injured party, and they did not want to be seen victimizing someone – and particularly not someone so much in the public eye – just because his opponent was a cousin of the King's confessor. So Maurepas instructed the prison governor to treat him liberally. Confident of an early release, Voltaire asked Thiriot to bring him some useful reading: an English grammar-book and dictionary, and a copy of *The Present State of Great-Britain and Ireland.*

Officially released on 1 May, the traveller needed further time to make the necessary financial arrangements for his trip, and so he voluntarily availed himself of the Bastille's facilities for a further night. On 2 May he set off for Calais under official escort (in case he should think of heading straight for Versailles). There, three days later, he made it plain to all who would listen that he had not been exiled: he was merely forbidden to come within fifty leagues (approximately 140 miles) of the capital. As to his forthcoming journey, he had been 'permitted' rather than 'required' to leave the country. Which he did, probably on the *Betty,* on 10 May 1726. He had been hailed as the new Sophocles and the new Virgil, but he was in the end just a poet, an entertainer. To be accepted as an equal by the aristocracy one had either to have the requisite blue blood to start with or to work one's way slowly but surely up the social ladder, heraldic quarter by heraldic quarter, generation by generation. Like a lawyer acceding to the *noblesse de robe.* Which is what his father had always told him. And which was why the marquise de Bernières, his landlady and former mistress, now chose to accompany the chevalier de Rohan-Chabot to the theatre while her former lover set off for the 'Land of Liberty'.[7]

CHAPTER FIVE

England, 'Land of Liberty' (1726–1728)

How an epic poet arrived in sunshine and left under a cloud

THE MAN WHO set foot on the banks of the Thames on a fine spring morning did not know what day it was. In France it was 11 May 1726, but here in the port of Gravesend it was actually eleven days earlier: the English — ever reluctant to enter Europe — had not yet adopted the Gregorian calendar. (First conceived in 1582, this Catholic innovation was finally adopted in Protestant England after a due period of deliberation in 1752.) Voltaire, now thirty-two according to his own personal calendar, had principally made the journey to find a publisher for *La Henriade*, but he had also come to learn. For he was not only a celebrated poet and frustrated courtier, he was a budding *philosophe* as well. And within a few months he was able to confirm in a letter to his friend Thiriot that England was indeed a country where he could 'learn to think'.[1]

In eighteenth-century France the word *philosophe* — etymologically, a 'lover of knowledge' — came to mean 'freethinker' and to be in some respects the equivalent of our 'intellectual'. By the second half of the century, after Diderot and d'Alembert began publication of their *Encyclopédie* in 1751, it was at once a badge of pride and a term of abuse affixed to those writers and thinkers who opposed Christianity and sought 'enlightenment' through the independent use of human reason. Such *philosophes* could be deists, like Voltaire and Jean-Jacques Rousseau, believing in a God whose divine hand is everywhere apparent in our well-ordered universe, or they could be atheist materialists, like Diderot, Helvétius and d'Holbach, who believed that matter is eternal and constantly evolving, so that 'nature' is simply what we call its current configuration. Being part of that 'nature', we humans are bound to see it as well ordered: all talk of a Divine Creator is mere superstition and infantile illusion. Rousseau, it is true, complicated matters by questioning the superiority of reason over feeling. For him, our heart – wherein the still, small voice of God speaks as our conscience – is the one sure guide to virtue, prompting us to do good even if we need reason to tell us quite what is the good. But reason is not necessarily to be trusted: it can be the source of duplicity and vanity, of political oppression, inequality and a singular lack of fraternity. Hence he became something of an *anti-philosophe philosophe*, which was the principal reason Voltaire condemned the man and thought *him* distinctly unfraternal.

More conventional opponents of the *philosophes* saw them as the devil plurally incarnate, as men (and some women) who had eaten rather more of the Tree of Knowledge than was entirely good for them (or anyone else). For their supporters, the French *philosophes* – like their equivalents across the English Channel (John Locke and Samuel Clarke, for example, or David Hume and other representatives of the Scottish Enlightenment) – were torch-bearers, not God's messengers bringing us news of the Light but intrepid human minds shining the light of reason into the dark corners of our ignorance. A 'natural philosopher', like Newton, was simply what we would now call a scientist or applied mathematician, and in those days before specialization it was possible for an intelligent educated person to be abreast of the latest discoveries in the natural sciences and the latest developments in philosophy 'proper' (Descartes, Locke, Leibniz, etc.). Indeed it is one of the paradoxes of intellectual and scientific progress since the eighteenth century that the more light that has been shone into the whys and wherefores of Creation, the more the average mortal has been left entirely in the dark. But bliss was it in that 'philosophical' dawn to be alive.

And bliss was it for a young Frenchman to come to England. Voltaire had already caught a glimpse of what a Protestant society could achieve when he visited Holland in 1722. The spectacle of religious toleration and humane egalitarianism had impressed him no less than the evidence of agricultural and commercial prosperity. During his visits to Henry St John, Viscount Bolingbroke at La Source near Orléans, which began at the end of that same

Henry St John (1678–1751), 1st Viscount Bolingbroke (eighteenth-century engraving).

year, he had then come into contact with the latest in English intellectual life. A highly intelligent and cultured individual, this charismatic aristocrat – then in his early forties – had played an important part as Queen Anne's Secretary for War in bringing England to the peace table with France, a policy which culminated in the Treaty of Utrecht (1713). But with the death of Anne and the accession of the Hanoverians in the person of George I, Bolingbroke's Stuart loyalties had necessitated his departure to the Loire, where he married a marquise. Impressed by the young Frenchman's verse, and especially by *La Henriade*, he set himself to remedy the defects of his Jesuit education and introduced Voltaire to the work of Newton and Locke. Isaac Newton's *Principia Mathematica*, published in 1689, had replaced Cartesian physics with the breathtaking vista of a mechanistic universe governed by the laws of attraction, or gravity. John Locke's *Essay Concerning Human Understanding* (1690; translated into French by Coste in 1700) had countered Descartes's theory of innate ideas (we are born with God-given knowledge implanted in our brains, which we then 'lead out' or 'educate') with a new form of epistemology, or theory of knowledge. *How* do we know things? Through our five senses. We are born as pieces of white paper upon which experience will write itself. Like Candide (from Latin *candidus* = white).

Bolingbroke's pupil was bowled over, and his intellectual take on the world was radically and permanently transformed. The benign Father whom he had worshipped in the 'Epître à Uranie' was revealed as God the watchmaker, a creator and guarantor of order underwriting the validity of independent rational enquiry; and his own clever-dick refusal to accept the word of authority, be it paternal, ecclesiastical or royal, could now be called 'empiricism' (from the Greek *empiros* = reality). For, like Locke, young Arouet had always wanted to argue from the particular to the general, from the facts to a sensible conclusion. As witness his response to the celebrated case of Mme Lafosse. This lady, the 45-year-old wife of a cabinet-maker (*ébéniste*) in a poor district of Paris, had been bedridden for seven years, subject to constant bleeding and barely able to move. On 31 May 1725, the feast of Corpus Christi, she had herself carried outside to witness the traditional procession of the Holy Sacrament through the streets. Having begged Our Lord for a cure, so the story went, she duly got to her feet and followed the procession before returning home a new and less menopausal woman. For the credulous this was a miracle; for the less credulous and those who were there, the story had been inflated. She collapsed when she tried to rise, she had to be virtually carried along behind the procession . . . and the 'miracle' had done nothing to correct her very poor eyesight. (Voltaire later remarked that the Holy Sacrament had cured her by rendering her blind.) In empirical terms her condition was probably psychosomatic, and her religious faith such that she could indeed be 'cured' by prayer and the placebo effect. But many people did believe that a miracle had taken place, and her case became a *cause célèbre*. Some said that she had staged the whole thing to confound the sceptical Huguenots living in her street; others suspected a Jansenist ruse. However, Mme Lafosse had plainly never heard of Jansensists for, when interrogated by the Archbishop's envoy, she replied that no, her husband was not a Jansenist, he was an *ébéniste*. (At least the 'cure' had not rendered her deaf.) The Archbishop of Paris duly declared, on the basis of the testimony of a hundred witnesses who had seen the event and four eminent doctors who proclaimed her current well-being, that a miracle had indeed occurred; and Mme Lafosse thereupon walked in procession to the cathedral of Notre-Dame, carrying a candle.

Voltaire wanted to find out for himself. The similarity between the event and Christ's healing of 'a woman having an issue of blood' (Luke 8: 43–8) made him suspicious. Mme Lafosse's husband may have done work for him at the de Bernières' house in the rue de Beaune, but at any rate he visited the couple several times and helped them out with some money. He could see that Mme Lafosse was better but he found no evidence to confirm the alleged reason for the improvement in her health. These charitable visits prompted his enemies to spread the malicious and entertaining rumour that he, a known sceptic, had been converted by the 'miracle'; and the Archbishop even invited him to a service of thanksgiving at Notre-Dame. Voltaire replied by sending him a copy of his tragedy *Hérode et Mariamne* and observing that the Archbishop was no less given to putting on good shows than he. This deist reader of Locke and Newton would now become increasingly militant in his campaign against the Catholic Church, and when in this same year he encountered the work of the mathematician and metaphysical thinker, Blaise Pascal, he discovered an intellectual enemy to savour. For Pascal was a Jansenist, like Voltaire's late father and his still-living and now detested elder brother, Armand; and, as we shall soon see in the *Lettres philosophiques*, he came to epitomize the very opposite of everything the forty-year-old Voltaire stood for.

But Bolingbroke's 31-year-old protégé still had an epic poem to publish: *La Henriade*. His English mentor has since become famously associated with the dictum, more properly attributed to Dionysius of Halicarnassus, that 'history is philosophy from examples', and he certainly warmed to the historical lesson to be derived from *La Henriade* concerning the need for religious toleration. Where the French authorities had baulked at Voltaire's vivid description of the St Bartholomew's Day Massacre – when on 23–4 August 1572 Charles IX ordered the slaughter of Huguenots in Paris and other major French cities – an English Protestant of 1726 was likely to sympathize, whether sharing Bolingbroke's own enlightened views about toleration or simply finding further grist to the mill of a prejudiced dislike of Catholics. He therefore encouraged Voltaire in the view that England would be a good place to publish such a book, better even than Amsterdam or the Calvinist city-state of Geneva. And so it proved. But not after some initial difficulties.

Voltaire had written to George I on 6 October 1725 to ask permission to visit his country and to publish a poem inspired by the values of freedom and truth of which his Sovereign Majesty was the one sure guardian. Envisaging a stay of some duration, he then transferred some eight or nine thousand *livres* via an intermediary to a banker in London, Anthony Mendes da Costa. Anthony belonged to a family of Portuguese Jews who had fled persecution at home and become immensely rich abroad. His father, John da Costa, was a pillar of the City of London, a shareholder in the Bank of England, and a perfect gentleman. Unfortunately the son was rather less of a pillar than his father, and certainly no gentleman. Soon after receiving the money he went bankrupt (in December), but omitted to tell his French client: it would help to have one creditor less. When Voltaire went to his office on arriving in London, he discovered the awful truth – and that the debtor had fled to Paris! He promptly stormed off to Highgate to visit John, only to discover that the man, aged seventy-one, was at death's door (he died six weeks later). His expostulations fell on deaf English ears, not least because they were in French, but eventually the poor man could stand no more of this tempestuous creditor making such a thoroughly unBritish fuss and placated him with the gift of a few guineas to tide him over, perhaps a hundred pounds or so in modern terms.

What to do? Here he was in a huge foreign city with barely a word of English and hardly a penny to his name. Bolingbroke had now returned from exile (though stripped of his title and his seat in the House of Lords), so his protégé called on him at his residence in Pall Mall, only to be told that the master was not at home but had gone to his country house at Dawley, near Uxbridge. Like many others he would return to the capital only with the beginning of the summer 'season', the annual round of public festivity and private ball that facilitated, among other things, the mating rituals of younger British aristocrats. For Voltaire the situation was becoming absurd. He had an official letter of recommendation from the French Foreign Minister; a letter of introduction to the French ambassador, the comte de Broglie; a letter from Horatio Walpole, the British ambassador in Paris, recommending him to the British Foreign Secretary, the Duke of Newcastle, and another to George Dodington, an influential and extremely rich patron of men of letters. Not bad for someone who had just left the Bastille. But where was everyone? Perhaps it was all for the best, however, for he was in any case not quite ready to launch himself into the world of British high society. Despite some further financial assistance, perhaps from Bolingbroke's private secretary, John Brinsden, money was still short, and the stress of his arrival in London had made him ill.

Salvation came in the figure of Everard Fawkener, a man of his own age who was a director in the family firm, Snelling and Fawkener. They traded wool for silk in the Levant. Fawkener had spent nine years at Aleppo (now Halab) in Syria, from 1716 to 1725, as the company's man on the spot, living 'native' and berobed in the local bazaar and gradually accumulating a fortune with which to return to England and marriage. Voltaire had met him in Paris the previous spring on his way back from Syria, no doubt thanks to his own family's long-standing connections with the wool and silk trade, and had presumably promised to look him up in London. For Fawkener was a man after François's heart: he loved Horace and Virgil and had taken an interest in the antiquity of the region round Aleppo (examining archaeological remains, recording inscriptions, collecting ancient coins, etc.). He also introduced the Frenchman to Islamic culture and may even have sown the seed of *Zaïre*, the successful tragedy that Voltaire would write six years later on the subject of a Christian captive loved by a sultan in thirteenth-century Jerusalem. And which he would scandalously dedicate to his English friend: not to the Queen of France, therefore, but to a mere merchant.

Fawkener had bought himself a nice house in the village of Wandsworth, just south of the Thames and not far from the City. Here Voltaire stayed throughout most of June and July. After a brief and necessarily secret trip back to Paris to fetch some money (meanwhile resisting the temptation to seek out Rohan-Chabot), he returned to spend a further three months in Wandsworth. While Fawkener had the great merit of being able to speak French (as well as Italian, then the lingua franca of Levantine commerce), his guest set about learning English, adopting the techniques he had been taught at school to learn Latin. He would copy out lines of verse or compose his own; he kept a diary in English and wrote little compositions on his impressions of England: as at Louis-le-Grand, no learning by rote but language in action. His spelling could be erratic (as it was for even the most educated in the eighteenth century): the esteemed poet Alexander Pope became Popp, while 'thoughts' were always 'taughts' – as though Voltaire had listened to too many Irishmen. His principal model was the *Spectator* magazine, founded by Richard Steele and Joseph Addison (now, respectively, retired and deceased) and first published in 1711. One early shot at an English sentence (in fact a paraphrase of Addison)[2] is particularly notable because it both recalls Voltaire's earlier comments about Holland and foreshadows a central theme of the *Lettres philosophiques*: 'England is meeting of all religions, as the Royal Exchange is the rendez-vous of all foreigners.'[3] The Royal Exchange (not to be confused with the London Stock Exchange, founded later in the century) was – and is – situated in the heart of the City, between Cornhill and Threadneedle Street. It was where merchants of every nationality met and did business, and no doubt it was the first site to which Fawkener escorted his friend. A splendid new building, erected in 1669 after the previous one had burned down in 1666 during the Great Fire of London, it testified to the importance that England attached to international commerce and bore tangible witness to the prosperity thereby created. A multicultural Britain, open to all races and all faiths, represented the way of the future. Unlike an impoverished Catholic France. What's more these lucky Londoners had running water and a postal service.

Voltaire learnt English in a phenomenally quick time. Within three months he could express himself in writing with sophistication and reasonable accuracy, while his spoken use of the language – doubtless honed in many a conversation with the patient Fawkener – was boosted by his regular attendance at the theatre. Not surprisingly, the star of the Comédie-Française was keen to see how they did things in Drury Lane – and even keener when he set eyes on Mrs Oldfield, 'an incomparable sweet girl',[4] who was London's answer to Adrienne Lecouvreur. Perfecting his English was now an even higher priority, so he cultivated the prompter at the Theatre Royal in Drury Lane and borrowed the written text for each performance. Thus, seated in the stalls in the so-called 'music-room' set aside for important visitors, he read and listened – and adoringly gazed. This man brought up on Sophocles and Racine had never even heard of Shakespeare, but he soon made up for lost time. At Drury Lane, between September and December 1726, he certainly saw *Hamlet* and *Othello*; at Lincoln's Inn Fields he certainly saw *Julius Caesar*. Beyond these he probably saw *Macbeth*, *King Lear*, some of the history plays, including *Richard III*, but none of the comedies (then out of fashion). And – as well as Shakespeare – Dryden, Otway, Congreve, Farquhar. Voltaire's own plays would never be quite the same again. And nor would he. When one day he was set upon by a mob in the street and jeered as a 'French dog', he promptly stood on a boundary stone and addressed them in English as if he were Mark Antony: 'My fine Englishmen, am I not already wretched enough that I was not born one of ye?'[5] It saved him from a baptism of mud.

At the end of October 1726 he learnt from Paris that his sister, Marguerite-Catherine Mignot, had died at the age of thirty-nine, leaving two daughters – later Mme de Fontaine and Mme Denis – and a son, the future abbé Mignot. Very little is known about Voltaire's siblings, but it would seem that his sister, though only seven years older, had been something of a mother to him. Given his antipathy to his brother Armand, she was essentially all the family he had – which is why he would subsequently watch over her children with particular care. In November he moved into rented accommodation in central London, and became a

regular visitor to the Bolingbrokes in Pall Mall. Now competently anglophone he began to move in English society, beginning with Alexander Pope
at Twickenham since he had already corresponded with him from France and
because he regarded him as the English Boileau. Pope, a Catholic, admired
the French visitor for his verse and some of his views (on toleration but not
on the Pope who lived in Rome), while the visitor felt not only envious
admiration for the translator of Homer's *Iliad* (1715–20) and *Odyssey* (1725–6)
but also compassion: openly for the minor injuries Pope had recently
sustained in a carriage accident, silently for his manifestly poor health
and physical handicaps. But contact between them lapsed the following
summer.

Meanwhile Voltaire was getting on famously with John Gay, author of *The
Beggar's Opera* (1728), who had been instrumental in getting him the seat in the
'music-room' at Drury Lane and introduced him to the prompter. And even
more famously with Jonathan Swift, whose *Gulliver's Travels* had appeared in
November 1726 and whom Voltaire met when Swift, the Dean of St Patrick's
Cathedral in Dublin, was over in London in May 1727. Hearing that the
Irishman wanted to visit France, he obliged with a letter of introduction to
the French Foreign Minister and to his old friend Maisons. But celebrated
writers were not his only company. He now began to cash in on the grand
letters of introduction with which he had arrived, not to mention his
association with the Bolingbrokes. Early in 1727 he met Sarah, Duchess of
Marlborough, who commented on the excellence of his English. Now in her
late sixties and a widow since the death of her famous warrior-husband in
1722, the former bosom-friend of Queen Anne invited Voltaire to visit her
that summer at her home, the Old Lodge in Windsor Park, where she regaled
him with stories of the past (she was writing her memoirs). One such story
concerned her husband's meeting with Charles XII of Sweden, another
extraordinary soldier, who had set out to conquer Russia and died at the age
of thirty-six. He was about to be the subject of Voltaire's first prose history.

But for the moment the author of *La Henriade* was busy doing what he had
come to do: securing publication of *La Henriade* in a definitive, luxury edition
complete with engraved illustrations. Having been presented to George I at
the beginning of 1727 (and thus in the last months of his reign), Voltaire had
supplemented the text with a eulogy of Britain's constitutional monarchy,

and he now proceeded to raise 'subscriptions' for the work from the greatest in the land. This system of publication, which was then hardly known in France, involved a subscriber securing one or more copies of an important and collectable work by paying half the cost on deposit in advance and the remainder on publication. It had recently been used by Pope himself to great financial advantage: hence the grand house at Twickenham. By the time *La Henriade* was published in March 1728, Voltaire had obtained 343 such subscribers. His success was not exceptional: Jean-Baptiste Rousseau had spent six months in England four years earlier and with similar if less spectacular results. Voltaire eventually dedicated *La Henriade* to Queen Caroline, wife of George II,[6] but it was the same Caroline who, as Princess of Wales, had also subscribed for Rousseau. This was one of the ways in which the British royal family and aristocracy managed their patronage of the arts, adorning their libraries while acquiring a reputation for civilized largesse. It was the same Queen Caroline, for example, who donated £3,000 to the Queen's College in Oxford towards the building of its front quadrangle, and whose statue now presides over the entrance under a handsome cupola. Moreover such patronage transcended party loyalties. Voltaire was known for his links to the Tory Bolingbroke, who signed up for twenty copies at three guineas each (i.e. three pounds and three shillings), but his adversary, Robert Walpole, the Whig prime minister, also subscribed and even instigated a generous gift of £200 from the royal purse as a kind of 'publication grant' to the young French author (the equivalent of about 5,000 *livres* or francs at the time). Not that the patronage was necessarily altruistic. Both men, and no doubt also the King, could see the value in associating themselves with a Frenchman who seemed to favour a Protestant rather than a Catholic reading of recent French history. For a Voltaire who had spent two periods in the Bastille and been badly let down by his French aristocratic friends over the Rohan-Chabot affair, here was paradise on earth, a land of enlightened ways. As he noted also when Newton died on 20 May 1727 and was buried alongside the kings and queens of England in Westminster Abbey. That was how one should honour the life of the mind – and how the French would never have dreamed of honouring Descartes.

By way of 'marketing' *La Henriade* and preparing his readership, Voltaire decided to publish two essays – in English (after one year in the country) –

one 'upon the epick poetry', the other 'upon the civil wars [in France]'. Accordingly he took lodgings with a dyer in Wandsworth, near Fawkener, and enlisted the services of a Quaker tutor, Edward Higginson, who provided him with further English lessons (and the pretext for some frank religious debate). On 29 June he received permission from the French authorities to return to Paris for a period of three months, but he declined the offer. Two weeks earlier, news had reached England that George I had died in Hanover: there would be a new queen, and she looked as if she might be more useful to an author than her Franco-Polish counterpart at Versailles. In any case he still had essays to write and people to see. After staying to watch the new king and queen sail down the Thames in royal state on 28 July, he set off on a tour of English country houses, subscription documents in hand. First on the list was Charles Mordaunt, third Earl of Peterborough, a colourful veteran of Marlborough's military campaigns, who lived at Parson's Green. Now in his late sixties, and having married a singer called Mrs Robinson, he was not a man to mince his words (or take advice on marrying beneath his station): he liked the poet's style and signed up for twenty copies. After the promised visit to the Old Lodge in Windsor Park, where Sarah, Duchess of Marlborough also added her name to the list, the travelling salesman proceeded to Ickworth in Suffolk, where he stayed with Lord and Lady Hervey, friends of the Earl of Peterborough as they were of the new queen. His Lordship, two years younger than Voltaire and son of the Earl of Bristol, was a fellow-poet and immediate soul-mate, and Her Ladyship a woman of great beauty. 'Hervey would you know the passion / You have kindled in my breast?' wrote the sighing guest: 'Trifling is the inclination/ That by words can be express'd. / In my silence see the lover; / True love is by silence known; / In my eyes you'll best discover / All the power of your own.' Though this unpublished manuscript poem was for a long time thought to have been addressed to Her Ladyship, the curious opening address to 'Hervey' suggests that the sighs may have been caused by the bisexual lord – or indeed by both Herveys.[7]

The subscription list grew longer, as did the list of Voltaire's British acquaintances: the future Admiral Byng, then twenty-three, who would later be court-martialled and shot at Minorca 'to encourage the others' (as we learn in *Candide*); sundry aristocrats, both English and Scottish, including

Philip Dormer Stanhope, Earl of Chesterfield, who signed up for ten copies, and the Duke of Richmond who tried to enlist *him* as a freemason; and finally one of Lord Hervey's close friends, the celebrated Lady Mary Wortley Montagu, an accomplished poet, a woman of independent views and behaviour, and the star of Queen Caroline's court as she had been of Queen Anne's before her marriage to the Member of Parliament, Edward Wortley Montagu. When the latter became ambassador to Turkey, she accompanied him to Constantinople and there learnt of the Turkish practice of smallpox inoculation – of particular interest since she had lost her looks and nearly her life to the disease in 1715. On her return to Britain in 1718 she sought to popularize the remedy, which she had administered to her only son the previous year, and – as we also learn in the *Lettres philosophiques* – persuaded Caroline, as Princess of Wales, to have her own children inoculated too. By so courageously setting this example the future queen saved many lives and earned from Voltaire the highest praise: he deemed her a *philosophe*.[8] As to Lady Mary, she had her own list – of lovers – but though she subscribed to *La Henriade* (which she hated), she did not simultaneously sign up to its rather ectomorphic author. She for one could resist his Gallic charm and the mischievous sparkle in those piercing eyes. Not that she disliked foreigners. She eventually left her husband in 1739 and ran off with – or rather, after – an Italian, subsequently spending the remainder of her life in a variety of residences in Venice, Avignon, Brescia and Padua before returning home to die.

By the autumn of 1727 Voltaire had met the cream of British society and conversed with the cutting edge of its intellectual and cultural life. He had debated in person with the leading philosopher Samuel Clarke, whose *A Demonstration of the Existence and Attributes of God* (1704) would now underpin his own deism; he had taken issue rather firmly with George Berkeley, the Irish cleric and thinker, who was in London on his way to spread the Word of God in Bermuda and who continued to maintain the view that the external world does not exist independently of the perceiving mind. He had visited George Dodington at Eastbury in Dorset, a man of dubious political reputation but a generous and broad-minded patron of the arts; and through him he had met fellow-poets James Thomson, author of *The Seasons* (1726–30), and Edward Young, who would later be celebrated at home and abroad for his *Night Thoughts* (1742–5). He had even called to see Newton's niece, Mrs Conduitt, who told him about the day, in the summer of 1666, when her uncle had first had his major insight about the law of gravity. Apparently he had got it from seeing the fruit fall from the trees, an apple perhaps – though not on his head. It was a good story, and Voltaire – who had an eye for such – made sure he published it before anyone else by incorporating it in his essay 'upon the epick poetry', where it had absolutely no relevance at all. But it did have when he repeated it in the fifteenth 'Philosophical Letter' and again in his *Eléments de la philosophie de Newton* (1738).

For his two essays – *An Essay upon the civil wars of France, extracted from curious manuscripts, and also upon the epick poetry of the European nations from Homer down to Milton, by Mr de Voltaire* – now appeared on 6 December 1727, published in the Strand by Nicolas Prévost, a French Huguenot by extraction, and printed by another Huguenot, Samuel Jallasson. Since the autumn 'Mr de Voltaire' had been living as a paying guest at the house of John Brinsden, Bolingbroke's private secretary, in Durham Yard, just off the Strand – and as rather an onerous paying guest, since he had been ill and required significant nursing. But by December he was well enough to spare them his presence and he moved into 'The White Peruke', a barber's shop run by a Frenchman called Pierre (Peter) Pellon in Maiden Lane on the other side of the Strand. Here he lived for the next six months, just behind what is now the Vaudeville Theatre: a plaque marks the spot. And from this barber's shop he could supervise the publishing process at first hand. The essays were selling at one shilling and sixpence, and now at last the long-awaited quarto edition of *La Henriade* appeared: on expensive paper, with wide margins and copious engravings, and without tedious note or commentary. In sum, a fine addition to any gentleman's library. And fit to be dedicated to a Protestant queen where once its author had hoped it might pass muster with a French and Catholic king. As a thank-you to two of the booksellers who had helped him to produce it, he temporarily waived his rights and allowed Woodman and Coderc each to publish an octavo edition (at four shillings each, i.e. at approximately one-sixteenth of the cost of the luxury edition). When Coderc passed the favour on to Prévost, Voltaire was horrified when the latter included some unfavourable lines about Louis XV that had been carefully replaced with emollient praise of his most important minister, Cardinal

Fleury. For the new darling of the English court was now trying to smooth his path back to Paris, just in case. The ensuing row in the pages of the *Daily Post* lasted some three months, which, if no publicity is bad publicity, may not have been entirely unwelcome to the disputants: for Prévost, who was making money out of this edition, and for Voltaire who had another book in mind . . . an 'account of my journey into England', of which he gave notice in an 'Advertisement' preceding the essays.

As this episode suggests, the author of *La Henriade* was now at a crossroads. He had achieved what he had come to England to do. The previous year he had already been given permission to return to Paris, albeit for only three months, and so he could presumably do so now. Hence the concern about offending Louis XV and the desire to flatter Cardinal Fleury, not to mention the dispatch on 25 April of a copy of *La Henriade* to the Queen of France (though, since he sent her only the cheap, octavo edition, she cannot have been very happy to play second fiddle to the Queen of England). But at the same time he had 'arrived' in England. The court and the City had signed up to him, literally and metaphorically; he was about to write a book about them, in English; and he now began to write a new play – also in English – entitled *Brutus* (not the one who assassinated Julius Caesar but the earlier Roman consul who put his two beloved sons to death for treason). Which way would he turn?

At the crossroads the trail goes cold. In June and July 1728 he is staying with Fawkener at Wandsworth, having written a short early draft of his book on England and having completed the first act of *Brutus*. On 15 August he writes to Thiriot, giving no indication that he is about to return to France. But four months later he has left – under a cloud. The biographical evidence is slight, but everything points to financial chicanery and disgrace. Had Voltaire made any money on the quarto edition? For a long time it was believed that he had, perhaps some £1,250 in the money of the day, which would have been approximately fifteen times the annual pension of 2,000 *livres* formerly granted to him by the Regent at the end of 1721. But more recent research has suggested that most of the income from the 343 subscriptions was absorbed by the printing and publishing costs.[9] In the summer of 1728 he seems, as usual, to have been in dire financial straits, which may be why he had to end his stay in England as he began it: as the recipient of Fawkener's hospitality. And which is why also, perhaps, he now resorted to embezzlement. For in 1733, when Voltaire's *Letters concerning the English Nation* appeared, a Quaker named Ezra responded to the Frenchman's portrayal of them as a quaint sect by accusing him, in the *Grub-Street Journal*, of an unrivalled ability to make money 'by way of erasement': that is, by doctoring cheques. Thomas Gray, author of the famous 'Elegy Written in a Country Church Yard', seems to have been reporting a commonly held view when he later commented that had Voltaire remained any longer in England, 'he would have been *hanged* for forging banknotes'.[10] Another source reported that his erstwhile admirer the Earl of Peterborough, husband of Mrs Robinson, had brandished his sword at him and threatened to 'kill the villain', following a row about some financial transaction with a bookseller. But the same Peterborough also noted, in a letter written on 25 November 1728 to Richard Towne, the intended translator of *La Henriade*, that Voltaire had left in high dudgeon, disillusioned with the inhabitants of this free-thinkers' paradise and apparently bound for Constantinople 'in order he might believe in the gospels, which he says it is impossible to do living among the teachers of Christianity'.[11]

Actually he departed for Dieppe, where he spent a very lonely winter lodging with an apothecary.

CHAPTER SIX

From Bonanza to Bombshell
(1728–1733)

In which our hero wins the lottery and lights a fuse

H AVING BEEN AT a crossroads, Voltaire now found himself in no-man's-land, marooned on the coast of the English Channel, apparently unwelcome in England and not quite sure if he was wanted in France. He was also ill, which may explain why he ended up lodging with an apothecary, Jacques Féret. But Féret was not just any old apothecary: he corresponded with some of the leading scientists of the day, and his conversation, not to mention his remedies, must have interested a man who considered himself a martyr to his physiological condition. Dieppe was a good place to lie low, being as unexciting a town as it was then possible to imagine; and the newly accomplished anglophone passed himself off as an English visitor, just to make sure that his hideaway was not discovered. After three or four months he ventured south to Saint-Germain-en-Laye, not far from Maisons, where he had once lain in bed with smallpox, and lodged with a wigmaker. Having alerted his friend Richelieu, he risked two day-trips to Paris in early April, partly to find out how the land lay and partly to see Germain Dubreuil, the man he had left in charge of his financial affairs on leaving for England three years earlier. Richelieu advised him to declare himself to the authorities, and in due course the comte de Maurepas, Louis XV's minister, granted him permission to enter Paris. But Versailles was expressly forbidden: the Rohan-Chabot affair had not been forgotten.

And so Voltaire returned to Paris in the spring of 1729. His next priority was money. So why not play the lottery? One of Cardinal Fleury's first moves on becoming Louis's prime minister in 1726 had been to sort out the public finances, and particularly to regularize a number of government bond issues that had gone to the bad. For this purpose his Controller-General (or Deputy Finance Minister), Le Pelletier-Desforts, set up a lottery for which the holders of one particular bond were eligible to buy tickets and for which the draw was made on the 8th of every month as from 1 January 1729. The purpose was to allow the state to extinguish its debt while avoiding having to repay the nominal value of every bond. Each holder who wished to participate had to purchase a ticket at a price proportionate to his holding: one ticket at 1 *livre* for a capital sum of 1,000 *livres*, one ticket at 10 *livres* for a capital sum of 10,000 *livres*, etc. If he won, he received the capital sum that governed the price of his ticket, minus 15 per cent that was carried forward to the next draw and added to the 500,000 *livres* (about £20,000 in British values of the day) with which the government sweetened the pot each month. If he lost, he said goodbye to some fairly worthless pieces of paper. (The real value of the bonds had fallen sharply since they had for some time seemed unlikely to be honoured.)

Voltaire, a bond-holder himself, attended a dinner-party at which the young mathematician Charles-Marie de La Condamine and other shrewd minds discussed the obvious flaw in the new lottery: a ticket costing 1 *livre* had as much chance of winning as a ticket costing 10 *livres* (or more). So the trick would be to form a syndicate and buy as many tickets for 1 *livre* as possible. The tickets themselves were purchased from a small number of officially designated notaries at the Châtelet, and the purchaser had to register their ownership of the ticket by inscribing it with their name and – by tradition – a good-luck motto or favourite saying. Voltaire quickly came to an 'understanding' with one particular notary and, splitting his and others' holdings into parcels of 1,000 *livres*, departed with lots of blank tickets and inscribed them with a colourful array of invented names (Magdaleine du Château) and pertinent 'sayings' ('Here's to the happy idea of M[onsieur] L[a] C[ondamine]', 'Long live M. Pelletier-Desforts', 'I brought it in a barrow and I'll fetch it in a cab').

From May onwards the names of the winners began to have a familiar and implausible air, and according to Voltaire's later testimony the syndicate won

approximately one million *livres* a month for the better part of a year. His
own winnings are thought to have amounted to some half a million in total.
Eventually the authorities got wind of the scam and closed down the lottery.
The Controller-General was sacked: he had tried to argue that the syndicate
had acted illegally, but the royal council found against him. And he was
condemned for his foolish ignorance of statistics.

Monsieur de Voltaire was now a wealthy man, and about to become even
wealthier. Nervous of the authorities' reaction, he decided that a trip to
Lorraine might be advisable at this juncture: he had had quite enough of the
Bastille, not to mention England. Having headed for the spa-town of
Plombières, he learnt that the Duke of Lorraine was just then seeking to
raise money on terms that were highly advantageous to the lender; and at
once he travelled by carriage for forty-eight hours non-stop in order to reach
Nancy in time to buy the bonds (before they rose yet further in value). On
being told that the Duke would sell only to natives of Lorraine (then a semi-
independent state), Voltaire argued that Arouet was a version of Haroué,
near Lunéville (south-east of Nancy), and managed to secure fifty bonds –
which he sold soon afterwards for three times their worth. This was in
September 1729: on 1 March 1730 the senior magistrate at the Cours des
Comptes had no difficulty in deciding that the son of François Arouet had
now so regulated his conduct as to be fit to inherit his third of the paternal
estate. Security at last; for, as Voltaire commented later in his memoirs, he
had 'seen so many men of letters who were poor and held in contempt that
[he had] long ago decided he ought not to increase their number'.[1]

Voltaire could now live and write as he pleased, no longer dependent on
royal pensions or watches, theatre takings or the elusive proceeds of book
publication. He engaged a cook and a valet and went to live in rented
accommodation in the rue Vaugirard. Unfortunately his landlady, a tripe-
seller in the local market, had found the constant 3 a.m. starts necessitated by
her trade something of a trial, to be alleviated only by regular intakes of
alcohol and much therapeutic cursing. She found similar relief in removing
her clothes and parading naked in the street, threatening to burn the place
down – and she nearly did, after which she was temporarily incarcerated. One
day she started a fight with another woman in the building where Voltaire
lived, and soon many of its inhabitants, including his cook and valet, were all

engaged in fisticuffs. When the police were summoned, the tripe-seller claimed that she had been assaulted and duly disrobed to display her bruises. Eventually, after many such incidents between August and November 1730, she was carted off to an asylum. Rich as Voltaire now was, the accommodation into which he had moved was clearly not particularly exclusive, nor indeed conducive to the concerted bout of writing that he felt to be in prospect.

During this period he had also been deflected by the death of his former mistress, the actress Adrienne Lecouvreur, at the age of thirty-seven. She had been ill for some time, and her last performance — after a severe attack of dysentery — was as Jocasta in his *Œdipe* on 15 March. She died five days later, with the playwright at her bedside. It was rumoured that she had been poisoned, but the post-mortem examination arranged by Voltaire was inconclusive. The cause of death was more probably peritonitis, brought on by typhoid. When her former lover tried to arrange for her funeral at the local parish church, to which she had left 1,000 *livres* in her will, the priest refused: she was an actress, and as such excommunicate. France was the only Catholic country in which actors were automatically barred from a Christian funeral — a case of the Gallican Church flexing its ecclesiastical muscle — and even the visiting Italian troupes had made sure to be exempt from this ruling. Some priests turned a blind eye, but not this one (in the parish of Saint-Sulpice); so that the body of the great actress was placed in a cab and taken under police escort to a patch of wasteland at the city limits, where it was cast without ceremony into a pauper's grave and sprinkled with quicklime. Seven months later her English equivalent, Anne Oldfield, was buried in Westminster Abbey. The lesson was not lost on the bereaved author, and his grief and outrage found expression in his favourite medium: a poem, among his finest. But this poem, in which he inveighs against fanaticism, philistinism and inhumanity, had to be circulated privately. Extraordinary as it may seem to us now, his outrage was shared by very few of his contemporaries: most French men and women found it quite normal to regard actors as irredeemably profane (and would do so for another century). Voltaire even tried to get his fellow-thespians to strike: they said they would but then they didn't. Always pretending.

The French authorities had sought to prevent all copies of the luxury quarto edition of *La Henriade* entering the country, and especially Paris. So Voltaire had a cheap octavo edition printed, which claimed on its title-page to have been published in London by 'Hierome Bold Truth'. Nobody was fooled, but nobody was now particularly bothered either: the censor's office and the police turned a blind eye. *La Henriade* was yesterday's news and yesterday's battle . . . But this would never do. It must be time for another play. Fresh from his experiences in Drury Lane, Voltaire took out his English draft of *Brutus* and began to rework it in French, hoping to delight his audiences with an innovative, full-blooded portrayal of republican virtue in early Rome. The first version was about to be premiered in December 1729, but – as Voltaire could see – its weaknesses would not survive the hostile publicity campaign being mounted against it by Crébillon, his old rival for billboard attention at the Comédie-Française, and the implacable chevalier de Rohan-Chabot. After revision it was eventually staged on 11 December 1730, and fifteen hundred people paid to attend the first performance. But the tragedy was still uneven: a gripping beginning and ending, but a laborious middle. And the sixteen-year-old playing the female lead quite lost her nerve on opening night. After fifteen performances the play closed. It would later do very much better after the Revolution, for obvious reasons.

The epic poet who had written *La Henriade* was also a historian in the making, and one who understood how – as in tragedies – to make the past tell a story that is relevant to the present. This time his chosen subject was Charles XII (1682–1718) of Sweden, the fabled warrior-monarch he had learnt about on his visit to Sarah, Duchess of Marlborough and from others like Fawkener and Lady Mary Wortley Montagu who had been close to the action during the Swedish king's period of captivity in Constantinople (1709–14). Above all he had gathered much authentic material from the King's close friend and right-hand man, the German-born Baron de Fabrice, whom he had met at the Earl of Chesterfield's country house in June 1727. Charles had succeeded to his father's throne at the age of fifteen and found himself ruler of (in modern terms) Sweden, Finland, Estonia, Lithuania, and parts of Denmark, Germany, Poland and Russia. Much of this territory had been won during the Thirty Years' War (1618–48). On his accession his enemies – Frederick IV of Denmark, Augustus II of Poland, and Peter the Great of Russia – decided that the teenager-king would be a pushover and that now was the time to reclaim their lost domains. They had underrated him. An exceptional, driven soldier, with ambitions to conquer Poland (which he did) and Russia (which he didn't), he was eventually killed rather randomly at the siege of Fredrikshald in Norway at the age of thirty-six. His remarkable youth and swashbuckling exploits, including his colourful dealings with the Turks, made him the dream subject for a saleable narrative (Voltaire's book would appear in more than sixty editions within his lifetime); while his bloodthirsty cruelty and the doomed nature of his warmongering would provide salutary lessons for any contemporary bellicose king. (Louis XIV had nearly bankrupted France with his campaigns, and it was feared that a young Louis XV might do the same.)

Unfortunately the verve of the adventure and an innovatively realistic – indeed quasi-journalistic – use of historical detail rather drowned out the wisdom of the pacific message. Aware of this, Voltaire added a corrective preface in which he extolled the civilizing mission of Peter the Great ('a much greater man') over and against the simple heroics of the itinerant Swede. And the final sentence left its readers in no doubt: 'If any princes or ministers should find unpleasant truths contained within this work, let them remember that as public figures they are accountable to the public for their actions: that their prominence is bought at such a price: that history is a witness, not a flatterer: and that the only way to make others say good things of us, is to do good things.' A quarter of a century later he would make the point even more firmly by writing a history of Peter the Great himself.

For the first time since *Œdipe* Voltaire managed to secure official permission (the *privilège*) for his new history before volume one was published at the end of 1730. Alas, censorship can be a two-edged sword. While the French government had no reason to fear this narrative, it realized belatedly that its ally, Augustus II, Elector of Saxony and now once again King of Poland, did not appear in a very favourable light (when temporarily dethroned by Charles in 1701) and might think that France was officially condoning such disparagement of his royal personage. All 2,600 copies of the first edition were immediately seized (and not one has been found to this day). But on being quietly told that a clandestine edition would not be so treated, the weary author contacted a rather dubious specialist in this kind of publication, Jore of Rouen, and arranged for a repeat of the cloak-and-dagger

– or rather, waggon-and-pack-horse – strategy previously employed to smuggle *La Ligue* into Paris. Here, after some tantalizing second thoughts on the part of Versailles, it finally appeared in November 1731. Unbeknownst to Jore, further editions were already being prepared in London, in French and in English: *La Henriade* had taught its author the advantages of international publishing as a means of combating the vagaries of French censorship.

In order to keep an eye on Jore, and to be on hand for the proofs, Voltaire again went to ground, this time in the vicinity of Rouen. Here he spent the early summer of 1731 attempting to live a healthy country life before taking to his bed for a month with nervous exhaustion. Valiantly he tried to soothe his troublesome digestive system with a diet of eggs, milk and salad, all the while managing as best he could to get on with his work. The locals knew him under the assumed identity of an Englishman called Mr Chevalier. A knight at last! After *Brutus* he was now determined to rival Shakespeare and write about the other Brutus, in a tragedy to be called *La Mort de César* (*The Death of Caesar*). The first results, produced in bed, were not promising, and the Comédie-Française would not touch the play for another twelve years – not least because Voltaire had dispensed with all female roles and any hint of a love interest. Despite the different Brutus, the political message of the new play resembled that of its predecessor: the glory of republican freedom as against monarchical despotism. At a deeper level, however, it suggested an ongoing and revelatory obsession with father–son relationships, for Voltaire introduces into the plot the fictitious 'fact' that Brutus is actually Caesar's son. The earlier Brutus had killed his sons; this time the son kills the father. As similarly demonstrated by *Ériphyle*, the play Voltaire was also working on at this time and which was partly inspired by *Hamlet*, it may well be that his own constant battles with royal and religious authority were indeed fundamentally Oedipal.

And an Oedipus needs a mother to love. But what fate decreed that he should find her in the rue des Bons-Enfants, the street of good children? For in September the rich but homeless playwright went to live there with the baronne de Fontaine-Martel, renting the top (unfurnished) floor of her house overlooking the Palais-Royal just north of the Louvre. In her seventies and recently widowed (but certainly not bereaved), she was another Ninon de Lenclos, as free in her views as she had previously been in her choice of lovers (by one of whom she had had a daughter). She used her box at the nearby Opéra every bit as often as she did not go to church. A lady of means, she took lodgers for the company – like former law student Thiriot, who then proposed his good friend Voltaire. Indeed it was she who paid Thiriot, to sit with her and entertain her; but when he broke the house rules and started dating (a dancer at the Opéra), she threw him out and cancelled his allowance. Young Romeos were forbidden, in case they murdered her and took her money to spend on some flibbertigibbet; but the slight frame of a 37-year-old playwright in poor health and without amorous attachments gave her just the reassurance she sought. And when he proved so witty, she put him in charge of her Sunday dinner-parties and delighted at the class of his guests. A caricature of cantankerous whimsy, she would oscillate between prodigality and penny-pinching, abusing her servants (whom she seldom paid) and dropping suggestive hints about her will that proved unfounded when she died a year later. But, avaricious or not, she was no match for the wiles of her latest lodger, who got her to pay for all manner of home entertainments, including the performance of several of his own plays. Such was the relaxed atmosphere of these productions that Voltaire himself, for the first time, ventured to take a role: and, as if he didn't know it, Mr Chevalier the showman proved to be a born actor. *Ériphyle* was duly tested in this laboratory and, after an unsatisfactory public premiere on 7 March 1732, brought back for further testing in the presence of an evidently forbearing – or somnolent – baroness. Or perhaps the play intrigued and even amused her with its (slight) variation on the Oedipal situation of a widowed mother, the Queen of Argos, who unwittingly chooses her son (whom she believed dead) as her new husband and king, only to be slain by him accidentally during a scuffle in the temple. Her nightmare scenario of being robbed and murdered in her bed by young men had been transformed into tragedy by the nation's leading playwright. Fifteen years later Voltaire revised the play and produced the much more successful *Sémiramis*.

But still he had not achieved a successful follow-up to *Œdipe*. Was he, as people now began to think after twelve long years, a one-play wonder? *Zaïre* proved them wrong. Written in a mere twenty-two days, it was vetted by the Comédie-Française on 27 June 1732 and premiered on 13 August, to universal acclaim. For many it remains Voltaire's best play, the moving portrayal of a rare love blighted by political imperative and religious divide. Given the speed of composition, one or two imperfections needed to be removed after the first night, but unfortunately the leading man, Dufresne, devoid of that humble modesty we all associate with actors, habitually made a point of refusing all corrections to a part once he had taken the trouble to learn it. However, he was obliged to relent when, at a celebratory dinner-party, the pastry was removed from a partridge pie to reveal – inserted in the beak of each culinary victim – a piece of paper bearing a corrected line of verse from *Zaïre*. He learnt them. And the play went from strength to strength. After ten performances Voltaire withdrew it, stoking the fires of audience demand and waiting on royal pleasure. In October *Zaïre* was performed before the court at the royal palace in Fontainebleau; Mr Chevalier was in attendance. Thereafter, on 10 November, the play began an exceptionally long run of thirty-one performances. No play had caused such tears – male as well as female, ecclesiastical as well as lay – to flow.

Set in thirteenth-century Jerusalem, the action concerns Sultan Orosmane, who has fallen in love with Zaïre, a Christian girl held captive since Orosmane's father, Saladin, reconquered the city twenty years earlier. Such is Orosmane's love that he, a Muslim with a harem, has decided to marry Zaïre as his one and only wife. Enter Nérestan, a young Christian knight, bringing (rather belatedly) the ransom money needed to secure the release of the Christian prisoners. Orosmane frees them all, except for Zaïre and for Lusignan, the elderly former Christian king of Jerusalem. But Zaïre obtains Lusignan's release by pleading with her kind-hearted husband-to-be, and when the venerable Lusignan emerges from his dark cell, it transpires that he is the father of Nérestan and Zaïre. For he recognizes the crucifix she is wearing. Is she still Christian? he asks. No, she replies, as a member of Orosmane's court she has had to live as a Muslim. Lusignan embarks on a long speech in which he reminds her of the crusaders and the Christian martyrs and Christ himself, who, in this city, have all laid down their lives. His daughter concedes: 'I am a Christian.' But nobody has told Orosmane about this recognition scene, so that the stereotypically jealous oriental potentate is suspicious of the new-found affection on display between his betrothed and Nérestan and only too ready to resume his robust,

authoritarian ways. Poor Zaïre! Her brother has arranged for her to be
secretly baptized that evening, but Orosmane is keen to be married. After a
number of agonizing scenes in which the misunderstanding could be resolved
but 'tragically' never is, Orosmane watches from a hiding-place as Zaïre
arrives for her baptism. 'Is that you, Nérestan,' she asks when the latter
subsequently appears, 'for whom I have waited so long?' Needing no further
proof, Orosmane stabs her, only to hear Nérestan reply: 'Ah, my sister, what
scene is this?' Realizing his error, the Sultan kills himself. Curtain.

Despite its contrived and implausible plot, the play is well written and the
pathos compelling. And of course the lesson was – is – powerful. Religious
and racial divisions are murderous: they can be overcome by love, respect,
inter-cultural compromise, and a youthful regard for the future, but they can
so easily be reinstated by an appeal to past wrongs that is all the more
frightening for being so thoroughly justified (Lusignan's wife and two other
sons were killed by Saladin's men). More subversively perhaps – in its day –
religious affiliation is presented as an accident of birth and place, a set of
rules and conventions demonstrably inferior in importance to the imperatives
of human relationships. The 'infidel' is too ready to suspect a Christian and
find infidelity in the most faithful of hearts; the Christian should have trusted
the 'infidel' to tolerate his beloved's newly rediscovered faith. Which is why
here, as in so many of Voltaire's tragedies, one cannot help feeling that the
situation is not 'tragic' in the traditional sense of being inevitable or
overwhelming, some inextricable knot that can only be resolved by death.
On the contrary, the whole thrust of his plays – as of his other writings – is
that things can be improved: if only people will listen and talk and
understand. In short, if only they will enlighten themselves. Voltaire's
Oedipus and Jocasta blame the gods for creating the present mess in which
they find themselves; in *Zaïre* an audience might blame the past for ruining
the future. That is why Voltaire, so eloquent in defence of toleration, was
and remained so intolerant of the Christian Church. And also fascinated.
When the opportunity arose to perform *Zaïre* for the baroness back in the rue
des Bons-Enfants, the apostle of deist relativism chose to perform the role of
Lusignan – the 'beau rôle' in fact, for he had given this elderly Christian the
best lines. (It would remain his favourite role for years to come, sometimes
reducing him to tears in mid-performance.) As later when he came to

denounce atheism, for example in the *Histoire de Jenni* (*Story of Jenni*) in 1774–5, he knew his enemy's arguments so well that he could speak for that viewpoint almost better than he could for his own.

But this may have been the last performance the baroness witnessed, for she died in the last week of January 1733. Her lodger failed to convince her that she should honour her testamentary promises to the servants: clearly, he observed, she was determined that no one in the household should regret her passing. But he did persuade her to one last performance of her own: the last rites, at which an understanding priest pretended to hear her confession and she for her part affirmed her belief in the Christian resurrection with a hearty 'oh, yes!' that had her grieving friend almost laughing out loud. And thus did he prevent a repeat of Adrienne Lecouvreur's appalling burial-scene, for though the baronne de Fontaine-Martel was no actress, it was a very long time since she had been to Mass.

Her passing left a large gap in Voltaire's life, and while he was able to stay on in her house for a time, he found solace only in a whirlwind of work: a new tragedy, *Adélaïde Du Guesclin*, a revised edition of the *Histoire de Charles XII*, another go at *Ériphyle*, the first draft of an opera, *Tanis et Zélide* (perhaps in memory of Mme de Fontaine-Martel's enthusiasm for musical drama), and a long allegory, *Le Temple du Goût* (*The Temple of Taste*). Here, in a format then fashionable, part verse and part prose, he narrates a 'progress' through the land of the Beautiful, past writers, painters, sculptors, actors . . . all positioned in greater or lesser proximity to the God of Taste presiding in his Temple. A wonderful opportunity for Voltaire to announce his preferences and to score some hits – and to get into trouble. The authorities were losing patience again. First it was the clandestine edition of the *Histoire de Charles XII*. Then there was the unauthorized first edition of *Zaïre* – unauthorized because Voltaire had prefaced the play with a dedicatory letter (to Everard Fawkener) in which he praises merchants and English liberty, Fawkener and Louis XIV (as a patron of the arts) and thus denounces by omission the philistinism of Fleury and Louis XV. And now here he was again, publishing without permission and upsetting people. The Bastille loomed once more, and there was talk of a *lettre de cachet* being issued for his arrest. The Garde des Sceaux (literally Keeper of the Seals but in effect Minister of Justice) was not pleased, even though Voltaire made some diplomatic revisions to his text and these were approved by the censor appointed to vet them (none other than Crébillon). But still no *privilège* was forthcoming, and the revised poem was eventually published in Holland.

It was the summer of 1733, and Voltaire's relations with the authorities were now strained to breaking point. As he put it (in English) to Thiriot: '[the Garde des Sceaux] will undo me if the letters [the *Lettres philosophiques*] come out into the world.'[2] He believed on principle that he should have the right to publish what he wanted, and the experience of doing so freely in Holland and England had made him fond of the practice. And he said so, in a 'Lettre à un premier commis' ('Letter to a Head Clerk'), fictitiously addressed to a high official in the censorship office and so outspoken that he did not dare publish it for another thirteen years. Citing the example of England, where Milton, Dryden, Locke and Pope do their nation credit because they publish unconstrained, he rejects the procedures of censorship: the state has no right to decide what the French reader should or should not read (libel excepted).

But Voltaire had to be careful: he wanted to continue living in Paris, especially as he was now involved in a new business venture. Some of his recently acquired wealth had been invested in a traditional and prudent manner: for example, by lending capital sums to reliable borrowers (therefore not the government) who undertook to pay him annual interest at 10 per cent (like M. Angot de Lezeau, a magistrate in the Rouen *parlement*). Sometimes he extended loans against property, such as 35,000 *livres* to the duc de Richelieu (through an intermediary, for form's sake). No doubt he also sought out 'opportunities' like the lottery or the Duke of Lorraine's loan issue. And now he decided to invest in the business of importing and exporting grain, with the possibility of a lucrative sideline in the sale of paper made from straw. Using his agent Germain Dubreuil's brother-in-law, Demoulin (or Dumoulin) as his own intermediary, he invested a considerable sum – and went to live over the 'shop' in what was then the east end of Paris and is now the site of the Hôtel de Ville. Here on the corner of the rue de Longpont (leading down to the river and the grain-bearing barges) and near the Portail de Saint Gervais (the gate whose architect, Jacques de Brosse, has since given his name to the present-day remains of the rue de Longpont) he came to live. And here the domestic needs of a bachelor businessman could be taken care of by Mme

Demoulin while he himself stayed close to the commercial action. *Zaïre* had been dedicated to a merchant, and a merchant its author would be. Free speech and bourgeois prosperity need not be the sole preserve of London.

And this was the message that he now proceeded to proclaim in one of his most famous books, the *Lettres philosophiques*. As we have seen, the idea of 'an account of my journey into England' had been in Voltaire's mind since 1727, when he 'advertises' it in the preface to his two essays. There he announces his intention of writing a different kind of travel-book: not a conventional guide with descriptions of St Paul's Cathedral, the palace of Westminster, and Stonehenge, but an assessment – indeed an advertisement – of the country's achievements. He wants to let the world know how men like Newton, Locke and Boyle have contributed to the sum of human knowledge, and he intends to spread the news of the latest scientific and medical advances. Accordingly he invites his readers to send him any information they can that might demonstrate the excellence of English enterprise and invention. It is not known if they did, so providing this shrewd author with free research material, but the spirit of the undertaking was plain: a loud proclamation of the benefits of freethinking. A first draft, completed in May 1728, proved something of a false start, concentrating as it does on 'the character of this strange people':[3] their love of royalty and horse-racing, the fun of their fairs and the dull animosities of their politics, the tea-parties and the upper-class snobbery, the coffee-houses with their evening jollity and morning gloom, the suicidal depression when the wind is in the east. But then he began again, and over the next three months wrote a major part of what would be first published in London in 1733 as the *Letters concerning the English Nation*. Such was this book's success that it would appear in a further fourteen editions before 1800, an eighteenth-century British bestseller.

'I think and write like a free englishman,'[4] Voltaire proclaimed in April, and it has been a recent orthodoxy that he wrote this first group of letters in English. But new research shows that, good as his English was, he nevertheless wrote the whole work in French (from which it was subsequently translated by the accomplished translator, John Lockman).[5] Of the twenty-four eventual 'letters' or chapters published in 1733, Voltaire had written part or all of more than half by the time he left England late in 1728, and with particular emphasis on those aspects of English life and culture that especially interested him: its religious — albeit predominantly Protestant — pluralism (the Quakers, Anglicans, Presbyterians and Unitarians), its parliamentary government and its trade, its theatre, and its men of letters (Pope, Rochester, Waller, etc.). But the apparently ignominious manner of his leaving seems to have put a temporary stop to his anglophilia, such that it was not until towards the end of 1731 that he could bring himself to think about the place again and duly consulted his friend Formont in Rouen as to how he might 'finish his letters about the English'.[6] When Thiriot visited London the following May (still in pursuit of his dancer, Mlle Sallé), Voltaire recommended him to Lord Hervey and George Dodington among others, and from his correspondence it is clear that the old enthusiasm for this 'free and generous nation' had been reignited.[7] Now returning to his former project, he reread Locke and Newton and supplemented the earlier letters with an account not only of the substance of these men's work but also of the great esteem in which they were held by their countrymen (unlike Descartes). He also added further letters on Lady Mary Wortley Montagu and the practice of inoculation (as an example of moral courage and innovative science), on English parliamentary government, and on the Royal Society (of which he himself would subsequently be elected a Fellow in 1743).

The tone of these later letters is much more sober and the content more weighty, at once less witty and altogether more daring. In the first version of his new letter on Locke he writes provocatively about the immateriality (and thus the immortality) of the soul: 'I speak by the lights of philosophy, and not according to the revelations of faith. All I can do is to think humanly; the theologian decides about things divinely, which is quite another matter. [. . .] Humanly speaking, it is a question of knowing what the soul is.' Rejecting the ideas of Plato and Aristotle, of Descartes and Malebranche, Voltaire sides with Locke's so-called 'sensationalism' and sees the 'soul' as just a fancy word for the human mental processes dependent on our five senses. This was fighting talk, and since the letter verged on an expression of atheist materialism, he toned it down. But only so far: 'I am no more disposed than [Locke],' he continued to write in the final version, 'to imagine that a few weeks after my conception I was a very clever soul who knew a thousand things that I then forgot when I was born.'[8] So much for Descartes's theory of innate ideas. And so much for the theologians: 'human reason is so little capable on its own of demonstrating the immortality of the soul that religion has been obliged to reveal it to us instead.' For 'reveal', read 'invent'.

In early 1733 Voltaire sent Thiriot a package containing the earlier letters, written in England if not in English, together with the new letters he had just completed. Thiriot was to have them all translated into English and the whole work published as soon as may be. Which turned out to be August, in a print run of 2,000 copies, produced on the presses of William Bowyer and published by C. Davis and A. Lyon. At the same time Bowyer printed a French version (of 1,500 copies) with the title *Lettres écrites de Londres sur les Anglois et autres sujets*. Ready by the end of July, it would not be circulated (in London and Amsterdam) until the following March (and a year later in Frankfurt, in 1735), with a title-page that said it had been published in Basle. One cannot be too careful. Meanwhile Voltaire had instructed Jore of Rouen to produce a French edition (2,500 copies), aiming to publish it in the same clandestine manner that had earlier brought *La Henriade* and the *Histoire de Charles XII* to a Parisian readership by pack-horse and waggon. Voltaire would pay all the production costs: Jore could have the profits in return for the risk of ending up in the Bastille. (Which he duly did, for a fortnight, temporarily ruined.)

The result was the first major work of the French Enlightenment, at once an attack on religious and political intolerance and a defence of empiricism and the experimental method in science. In short, the blueprint for a bourgeois liberal society of progressive views and prosperous ways. Janus-like, Voltaire now found himself facing in two directions. On the one hand, in the *Letters concerning the English Nation* (which bore no evidence that it was a translation), he was addressing an English readership who knew his *Henriade* and his essays, and indeed his *Histoire de Charles XII*. They would be gratified by this flattering portrait of their country: they would read his knowing comments on government and the abuse of ministerial power within the context of their own party-political debates between Whig and Tory, and they would see irony in his deadpan admiration of English religious toleration at a time when both Catholics and Nonconformists alike were far from enjoying its benefits. On the other hand, in the *Lettres sur les Anglois*, he would now also be addressing a francophone public which, since French constituted the lingua franca of educated eighteenth-century Europe, was potentially very large and — who knows? — perhaps ready to embrace these bourgeois liberal values. But what of his specifically French readership? Accustomed as they were to pseudo-travelogues about their own country — for instance, Montesquieu's *Lettres persanes* (1721) in which two Persian visitors provide an amusingly subversive new take on Regency France — perhaps they would appreciate a variation on the formula. Perhaps he could tell a silent story about the crippling conservatism and religious bigotry of the French by loudly singing the praises of their irritating neighbour. It was a tempting prospect.

But the French authorities were poised to pounce. The history of Charles XII, the preface to *Zaïre*, the *Temple du Goût* . . . What next? they wondered. Voltaire knew it. He had tested the water by showing the letters on the Quakers to Cardinal Fleury and the comte de Maurepas at the end of 1732, and they had even been mildly amused. When he asked the abbé de Rothelin what he would say if he were appointed censor, the influential theologian thought that most of the work would be acceptable except for the letter on Locke. Which, as we have seen, Voltaire duly revised. With the result that, when he instructed Jore at the end of January 1733, he foresaw no insuperable problems. Indeed he began to plan another French edition, to be produced in Paris itself. Not that he informed Jore, of course. Nevertheless the authorities were gradually becoming more hostile, both to him and — as they began to gain a clearer idea of its scope and thrust — to his new book. As we have also seen, the Garde des Sceaux was beginning to threaten him with the Bastille. Hence the frustrated outpourings in the 'Lettre à un premier commis'. And so he was faced with a major decision: to trim or to proceed. He decided to go for broke.

The legal profession in general and the law courts of the Paris *parlement* in particular were dominated by men with Jansenist sympathies, like his late father and his now increasingly fanatical brother. In 1730 the King had declared the papal bull *Unigenitus* (rejecting Quesnel's Jansenist views as heretical) a law of the state, which gave the magistrates a headache when Jansenist ecclesiastics lodged official complaints alleging abuse on religious grounds. Would the magistrates support the King or their fellow-Jansenists? Since *Unigenitus* could be interpreted as being imposed on France from without (even though Louis XIV himself had wanted the Vatican to issue it), they were able to side with Jansenist plaintiffs in the name of Gallican independence. But this had brought both litigants and magistrates into serious dispute with the crown, and the situation was tense. At that moment François de Pâris, a leading Jansenist deacon of exemplary asceticism, died and was buried in the Saint-Médard cemetery in Paris. Having given most of his possessions to the poor, he had become something of a cult figure, and his grave was now a place of pilgrimage. 'Miracles' were reported, and alleged cures proliferated, with many 'pilgrims' suffering violent convulsions in the process. Armand Arouet was one of these so-called 'convulsionaries'. In 1732 the authorities closed the cemetery, and someone posted a mischievous notice: 'By order of His Majesty the King, God is forbidden to do miracles in this place.'

Voltaire chose this moment to attack the brightest intellectual star in the Jansenist firmament, Blaise Pascal: not only a mathematical prodigy and an innovative metaphysician, but also the brilliant polemicist of the *Lettres provinciales* (1656–7), his defence of Jansenist doctrine and devastating onslaught on Jesuit casuistry and moral laxity. His famous *Pensées* (*Thoughts*), fragments of a projected apologia for the Christian religion, were published after his death and remain a powerful and moving testimony not only to his profound religious faith but also to the pain and turmoil of metaphysical anguish. His primary lesson was that faith cannot be based on reason, indeed is superior to reason and must come from the heart. It is the one sure source of human happiness. For the heart to be receptive to faith, the body must be disciplined; to be granted faith is to be the beneficiary of divine grace. In its absence, human reason can decide between two options (the famous Pascalian wager). Assume that God does not exist and enjoy unbridled earthly pleasure, at the risk – if God does exist – of eternal hell-fire in return for a few brief moments of delight. Or believe in God and adopt a self-denying Christian way of life, secure in the knowledge that, if God exists, such a choice will ensure eternal bliss and that, if He does not exist, the pleasures forgone are as nothing compared with the risk of hell-fire. For Pascal this choice was what some modern investment analysts call a 'no-brainer'.

Jore's French edition had already been typeset when in July 1733 Voltaire sent him the additional 'Lettre sur les *Pensées* de M. Pascal': the *Lettres sur les*

Anglois was now well and truly the *Lettres philosophiques*. Given that an attack on Jansenism was tantamount to an oath of allegiance to the crown in these tense months, perhaps Voltaire was hoping to mitigate the furore that would be caused by other aspects of his letter on Pascal. For this letter not only constituted a withering attack on the pessimism of the Jansenists, it was also a bold profession of deist belief. He was throwing down the gauntlet to the Roman Catholic Church. 'It seems to me,' he writes:

> that the general spirit in which M. Pascal wrote these *Pensées* was to show man in an odious light. He is at pains to depict us as wicked and unhappy. He attacks human nature rather as he once attacked the Jesuits, imputing to us as an essential part of our nature that which is to be found only in certain human beings, and hurling elegant insults against the human race. I hereby dare to take humanity's part against this sublime misanthropist; and I dare to assert that we are neither as wicked nor as unhappy as he says we are.

Voltaire then highlights fifty-seven quotations from the *Pensées*, refuting Pascal as he goes with logic, scorn and ridicule, and calling on his reader to 'judge if I am right or wrong'. The wager argument is 'puerile' and 'rather indecent'. Why should I bother to be good if only a chosen few will be granted divine grace? To liken human existence (as Pascal does) to being imprisoned in a dungeon like criminals on death row is 'a fanatic's way of thinking'. Where Pascal says that 'we should recognize the truth of religion by its very obscurity', I Voltaire say that 'it would be much more sensible to show us the light of faith rather than the darkness of your erudition'.

For Voltaire, Pascal was a kind of touchstone of everything he abhorred: metaphysics, asceticism, anguished self-absorption, portentous assertion. For him human nature was not inherently base and sinful but a wonderfully complex blend of animality, emotion and reason: 'The passions are what make us act, and reason is there to govern our actions.' To believe in God you have only to look around you; and Pascal's arguments about faith 'would serve only to create atheists if the voice of nature did not everywhere proclaim that there is a God'. And what is the most precious of all human gifts? The capacity to hope, 'which alleviates our sorrows and offers us the prospect of future joys even as we enjoy the pleasures of the present'.

In their earlier manifestation as the *Lettres sur les Anglois*, the *Lettres philosophiques* had already represented, by implication, an explosive critique of French absolutism. Now primed by the defiant letter on Pascal, it became what the venerable critic (and first modern editor of the French text), Gustave Lanson, famously called 'the first bomb thrown against the *ancien régime*'. Compared with Protestant liberalism, the Catholic Church was here openly challenged as an agent of monarchical oppression, and the whole fabric of French social, political, economic and intellectual life was condemned as inimical to freedom, tolerance and prosperity. 'Humanly speaking', France was just not human.

For a right-thinking French reader of the early 1730s (even a man like Cardinal Fleury therefore) the opening sentence of the *Lettres philosophiques* offers beguiling reassurance as the author prepares to devote his first four letters to the Quakers: 'It seemed to me that the doctrine and history of such an extraordinary people were worthy of the curiosity of a reasonable man.' Well, that's all right, then. At least he thinks these Quakers – and no doubt the English in general – are 'extraordinary', and perhaps I too, as a reasonable person, should read what he has to say. How quaint these Quakers are, with their strange garb and informal, 'friendly' ways, calling everyone 'thou' and not hesitating to ask their French visitor if he is circumcised – to which unceremonious question 'I replied that I did not have that honour'. And fancy them not believing in baptism or the Eucharist or needing priests ('We do very well without them'). Quite a decent lot actually, especially that William Penn who founded a colony in America. Still, it wouldn't do here in France, would it? We're civilized already. But all these Presbyterians and Unitarians and so on do seem to produce a beneficial muddle: 'If there were only one religion in England, there might be a risk of despotism; if there were two, they would cut each other's throats; but there are thirty, and they live together in peace and happiness.'[9] But look here, have these English lost all respect for the divine right of kings? And what's this about giving yourself smallpox on purpose? 'Don't the French love life?' you ask: 'don't French women care about their looks? In truth, we are a strange people.' Well! Speak for yourself, Voltaire! I'm not at all sure I should read any more of this rubbish. I think I'll skip these wearisome pages about optics and Newton and things falling out of trees and see what you have to say about tragedy. Ah, that's better. All that glisters is not English gold. No wonder we've never heard of this Shakespeare: sounds perfectly dreadful. Good for Addison, I say. At least he knows how to write a proper tragedy. Mmm . . . not sure I like the sound of these English comedies, though. That's not how *I* see high society. But hold on, what's this about Pascal? But, but . . . this is blasphemy! Burn it, burn it!

Voltaire knew what he was in for, and signals the fact in the second sentence of the letter on Pascal:

> Do not compare me, I beg you, to Ezechias, who wanted to burn all of Solomon's books. I respect the genius and eloquence of Pascal; but the more I respect them, the more I am persuaded that he would himself have corrected many of these *Pensées* that he simply jotted down on paper with a view to going back to them later: and it is while in the very process of admiring his genius that I take issue with some of his ideas.

Voltaire believes in free speech, not book-burning. And he signals his fears again when commenting on the persecution of the wise men who told the pagans that there was only one God: 'just as today a man would be persecuted if he were to preach the need to worship one God independently of the officially recognized religion'. Socrates, says Voltaire, 'was condemned to death not for saying "there is only one God" but for opposing his country's religion and because he had most ill-advisedly made powerful enemies'.

Voltaire-Socrates had primed his bomb and lit the fuse in full knowledge of the consequences. And why? Because he had found a bolt-hole and the dearest creature with whom to bolt. Enter Émilie, marquise du Châtelet, the great love of Voltaire's life and the best of all possible women.

*Voltaire in his forties. Early nineteenth-century lithograph
by François Seraphin Delpech, after a contemporary portrait.*

MIDDLES
(1733–1749)

'My Wife' Émilie

CHAPTER SEVEN

Sex in Blue Stockings (1733–1735)

How the lawyers had themselves a lovely holocaust,
and how two cuckolds turned a blind eye

L IFE BEGINS AT FORTY, especially if you have just met Émilie du Châtelet. Similarly, the love of knowledge becomes infinitely more exciting if you can pursue it in bed. For Émilie – the delectable, passionate, fun-loving, tempestuous, unpredictable, unreasonable, extremely intelligent Émilie – was the leading female scientist and mathematician of her day, an intellectual power-house bedecked in ribbons and all manner of functionless haberdashery. My 'Pompon-Newton', Voltaire called her. She was the first woman to be published by the Académie des Sciences. Her translation – from the Latin – of Newton's *Principia mathematica* remains the standard French edition to this day. In her company over the next sixteen years Voltaire became fully a *philosophe*, a natural scientist as well as a freethinking deist. In her company he would know great joy and great pain. And they, too, would make him philosophical.

The story begins back in 1714 when the twenty-year-old Arouet left Maître Alain's law firm and was sent away by his father to think things over during a visit to his client, the marquis de Saint-Ange, at his château near Fontainebleau. Here, in the marquis's anecdotes about life under earlier French kings, the seeds of *La Henriade* and all Voltaire's great prose histories were sown. And here young Arouet met one of the marquis's cousins, Louis-Nicolas Le Tonnelier de Breteuil, a man with a colourful and chequered past who had squandered a fortune but given excellent service to his king. The latter promised to reward him the day he settled down and got properly married. Having previously made his unmarried cousin pregnant, Breteuil had married the lady on her death-bed after she retired to a convent and fell ill. Now a widower but ever fertile, he begat another illegitimate child, Michelle, who spent her life in religious seclusion. In 1697, at the age of forty-nine, he finally got remarried – to a model of virtue named Anne de Froulay – and the King duly appointed him to a well-remunerated post at court. Louis-Nicolas now fathered six legitimate children, of whom only two boys survived, and a daughter, Gabrielle-Émilie, born on 17 December 1706. And it was this young girl whom Arouet met in 1714 when he went to call on her father in Paris after returning from Fontainebleau.

The Le Tonnelier de Breteuils lived in a grand house overlooking the Tuileries gardens – that is, when they were not staying at their château in the Loire valley at Preuilly-sur-Claise, near Loches (and where Arouet may well have visited them in subsequent summers). Both properties had been recently acquired, along with a baronetcy. The new baron, a cultured man with a ready pen and a huge library, kept freethinking company and patronized the arts. And he had progressive views on the education of women. His little daughter was not going to be packed off to a convent school to learn deportment and the finer points of the Mass. She would stay at home and be taught something useful. A clever and attentive child, there was no reason why she should not grow up to be a leading classical scholar like Mme Dacier. Thus Émilie learnt Latin and soon began to translate the *Aeneid*. She might have been at Louis-le-Grand with the boys. But unlike its former pupil she quickly developed a taste for mathematics and metaphysics, having a natural talent for mental arithmetic. Her admiring lover later noted that she could divide a nine-figure number by a nine-figure number in her head.

But nine plus nine equals eighteen, and it was time for her to get married. Having the means to provide his prodigy with a dowry of a mere 150,000 *livres*, a modest sum in top aristocratic circles, M. de Breteuil nevertheless decided to marry his daughter penuriously up rather than affluently down, and so plumped for one Florent-Claude, marquis du Châtelet, a descendant of Charlemagne with barely a *livre* to his illustrious name. His ancestors had fought in the Crusades and one or two had even been dukes of Lorraine, but the family had fallen on hard times. He personally could just about rub together a nearly ruined château at Cirey-sur-Blaise in Champagne (just west of his native Lorraine) and the governorship of a small town in Burgundy, Semur-en-Auxois. But, if his future wife were so minded, he did have one trump card: his marquisate was of sufficient vintage that it carried with it the right, usually associated only with certain dukedoms, for his wife to sit down in the presence of the Queen. Though not really the sedentary type, Émilie would later have some fun with this so-called privilege of the *tabouret* (the foot-stool on which such ladies were thus permitted to perch) – even if, as we shall see, she could have done with rather more trump cards in her hand at the time.

Born in 1695, Émilie's husband-to-be was an army officer, and had been since the age of seventeen. Now almost thirty and a colonel in the infantry, he was a decent and intelligent man – her father would not have settled for less – and his decency, not to mention his frequent absences on military campaigns, would make him an ideal husband for a young woman with a mind of her own. The marriage took place on 20 June 1725, a few months before the royal wedding at Fontainebleau. Soon after Louis was joined in holy matrimony with his Polish princess, the nineteen-year-old marquise du Châtelet was being welcomed with energetic local festivities to the governor's residence in the little town of Semur. Motherhood followed with respectable immediacy, and she returned to Paris. For her confinement she went not to her father's house (which says something about the unsatisfactory nature of her relations with her mother) but to another governor's residence, that of a cousin on her husband's side, the marquis du Châtelet-Clémont, at the Château de Vincennes. The governor's wife was the duc de Richelieu's eldest sister. Here she gave birth to her first child, Françoise, on 30 June 1726, whom she would eventually marry off to an Italian prince. On returning to Semur she soon became pregnant again and gave birth to a son, Florent, on 20 November 1727: he would become ambassador to Great Britain (1768–70) and die – as a duke – on the scaffold during the Terror (1793–4). Her part in the conjugal bargain complete, she entrusted her two children to wet-nurses – as women of her class and time quite conventionally did – and, when M. du Châtelet departed on military exercise, returned to Paris ready for some fun. Whereupon, to her great sorrow, her father died on 24 March 1728. Her mother withdrew to the country, at Créteil, where Émilie would rarely visit her, and she herself went to live in the house her husband had rented in the rue Traversière-Saint-Honoré.

After a due period of genuine grieving, the good life could begin; and at the age of twenty-three, now a married marquise with two conveniently absent children, she sought out the high life of Paris. Operas, balls, private parties . . . and gambling, which she loved beyond reason (and she a mathematician). But her capacity for mental arithmetic had soon to be devoted less to calculating the odds than to counting her debts. And to cap it all she fell in love, for the first time, with a Don Juan who merely wanted to add her to his list, the comte de Guébriant. Much to her husband's credit she had yet to experience the full egotism of the priapic male, and it took her time to realize the truth of the situation – and not before she had alienated her lover further by the frenzy of her tantrums and the possessiveness of her love. Eventually, according to the memoirs of the comte de Maurepas, Louis XV's minister and Voltaire's policeman, she determined to give Guébriant a fright. When he visited her to announce the end of their relationship, she answered him civilly from her couch and begged him to be so kind, before leaving, as to pass her a bowl of broth warming by the hearth. She drank and then handed him a letter, which he was not to open until he was outside in the street. When he duly read the words 'I am dying of the poison you handed me', he rushed back and – whether through his agency is not clear – she vomited up the 'poison' in question, an overdose of opium. Like Voltaire she adored the theatre: that is, she loved making a scene, and she enjoyed teaching people a lesson.

Not that she learnt such lessons herself. For she promptly fell into the arms of the duc de Richelieu, a Don Juan *pur sang*. ('For ever deceiving women', as Voltaire put it to the young writer Marmontel twenty years later, 'but a man that other men can count on.')[1] Richelieu had just returned to Paris in the summer of 1728 from his posting as French ambassador in Vienna. Now thirty-three and as handsome as Adonis, he soon met her through his sister: and Émilie was powerless to resist. For he had wit and tenderness to match his good looks, and when their relationship ended she continued to maintain a cordial bond of affection with this man who was also one of Voltaire's closest friends.

Eventually it was time to return to Semur, where her husband was missing her, and at the beginning of 1732 she made the journey. It was a lonelier place now that her father-in-law had died and her two sisters-in-law had married and moved away. But at least she had her books and her equations. At the end of the year, pregnant once more, she returned to Paris with her husband – only for him to be called away to war (now of the Polish Succession, for these thrones were troublesome). Ever in search of entertainment, Émilie became companion to the duchesse de Saint-Pierre. This lady, recently widowed from a much older Spanish nobleman, was a young-looking fifty-three and most determined to make up for time lost in the stifling atmosphere of the Spanish court where she had lived under the jealous surveillance of her husband since 1704. The merry widow began by taking the 23-year-old comte de Forcalquier as her lover, and the three of them painted the town red with all the decorum of their station and condition. By way of minor interruption, Émilie gave birth to another son, on 11 April: he died sixteen months later, in August 1734. She recovered quickly from her labour and plunged back into Parisian life with a flatter tummy and a space in her heart. Enter François-Marie Arouet, once known as Zozo.

Voltaire had remained in touch with the baron de Breteuil over the intervening years, seeking his help or influence on a number of occasions. The baron for his part was a great admirer of the young man's work – though quite evidently not of his eligibility as a husband. Indeed that thought would never have occurred to him. As to his daughter, she was not unlike Monsieur de Voltaire: she shared his deism, she too led a life divided between serious intellectual study (in her case, mathematics and physics) and serious partying (when she was very careful to conceal her blue stockings). And she too loved the theatre. Though not a beauty – some said her hands were coarse, her feet too big, her nose too long, and there was even the suggestion of a squint when she lost her temper – she was an attractive woman with long, dark hair and a fiery personality that beguiled and bewitched. Not only could she count, she could act like a pro and sing like a diva. She was fun. And Voltaire fell for her at once.

They must have met at the Opéra – where else? – in late April or early May 1733. Voltaire was helping a friend, Moncrif, with the libretto of his latest work *L'Empire de l'amour* – what else? – and the couple were introduced by a mutual acquaintance, Jean Dumas d'Aigueberre. Voltaire, it must be said, was not a notable – or noted – lover. He had a weakness for actresses, it is true, both bad (Suzanne de Livry) and good (Adrienne Lecouvreur), and he had been very fond of Mme de Bernières. He had had various casual affairs (as with Mme de Rupelmonde and doubtless others whose anonymity has been preserved by history). But he had adapted easily to the chaste regime imposed by the baronne de Fontaine-Martel. His digestive system continued to plague him, and his general state of health was sometimes such – whether real or imagined – as to banish all thoughts of romance. But with Émilie he felt like a new man, and they became lovers quite soon afterwards. He would call on her in the rue Traversière, and she would visit him at his granary in the rue de Longpont. Sometimes she would arrive with the duchesse de Saint-Pierre and her young count, and together they would seek out entertainment. On one occasion they set off to have supper in a country village (Charonne), but more frequently they would go to the Opéra, where it had all begun.

Voltaire was just finishing a new play, *Adélaïde Du Guesclin*, a historical drama set in the early years of the Hundred Years War, and he had given it a happy ending. (The play was premiered at the Comédie-Française on 18 January 1734, the first of his dramas to be based entirely on a French historical subject.) He was simply not in the mood for tragedy, which is probably why he was also working on a mock-heroic verse epic, similarly set in this period. The result of an after-dinner conversation with the duc de Richelieu, who dared him to try, it was entitled *La Pucelle* (*The Maid*) and offered an irreverent account of the life of Joan of Arc. The two men had been discussing the serious verse epic on this subject by Jean Chapelain (1595–1674), half of which was published in 1656 (the remaining cantos were not published until 1882). Chapelain had been much admired by Cardinal Richelieu, the illustrious ancestor of Voltaire's friend, but the duc himself took a dim view of Chapelain's clunking verse and his pious attempt to portray Joan as a saint. (Beatified only in 1909, she was not finally canonized until 1920.) For eighteenth-century aristocratic soldiers like the duc de Richelieu, the prospect of an innkeeper's servant-girl hearing voices and donning a military uniform to lead her people to victory over the English was indeed potentially comic, whether or not she ended up being burned at the stake. And for Voltaire there was much fun to be had from the centrality of the girl's virginity to this rousing tale.

But despite these various projects (and he was still putting the final touches to the *Lettres philosophiques*) François entered into the swing of Émilie's operatic enthusiasms and began – having helped Moncrif and Dumas d'Aigueberre with their own libretti – to turn his hand to some of his own. *Tanis et Zélide*, set in Egypt, is a kind of anti-clerical pastoral idyll (young princess Zélide loves handsome, intelligent shepherd Tanis and marries him, despite all manner of priestly interference and after Isis and Osiris have sorted the villains out with a few natural disasters); while *Samson*, commissioned by the composer Rameau, allowed for the depiction of further anti-clerical drama as the shorn hero recovers his strength to bring the temple crashing down on the idol-worshippers. Except that Rameau lost interest and the libretto was never staged.

Voltaire was bowled over by Émilie: by her body and the sexual pleasure they shared, by her mind and all the things they could discuss, from Newton to the latest developments in geophysics. They felt the earth move, and then they debated how best to measure its meridians. But people were beginning to talk, especially when Émilie threw caution to the wind and gave François a smacking kiss on the mouth in full public view. No matter what one did in private, keeping up appearances was crucial, and neither of them was much given to playing such a dull role. In July they seem to have made a secret visit to Cirey-sur-Blaise to inspect M. du Châtelet's derelict château. With Voltaire's money they could transform it into a very comfortable residence, far from the prying eyes of Parisian gossips. She was sure her husband wouldn't mind. And François would be there to help her with her Newton . . . But if they were keen to protect Émilie's reputation, they were no less keen to save François's bacon. For this visit came just after he had sent the incendiary letter on Pascal off to Cideville in Rouen: he had primed his bomb and needed somewhere to take cover. Perhaps the intoxication of love had made him, like his beloved Émilie, throw caution to the wind.

There are two ways to look at what happened next: a Voltaire overtaken by circumstance, or a Voltaire who contrived to appear overtaken by circumstance. At any rate, the bomb went off. The letter on Pascal had been typeset and printed by Jore by the middle of July. Chauvelin, the Garde des Sceaux, gets wind of Jore's edition and threatens Voltaire with the

Bastille if it ever appears. Voltaire duly warns Jore to keep all 2,500 printed copies carefully under wraps – in fact in a stable in Passy, just outside the city walls. Since Jore is well known to the police, Voltaire asks him for two unbound copies, on the pretext of undertaking further proof corrections but actually in order to pass one to a Parisian publisher, François Josse. He knows that Josse, without being told, will print off a pirated edition of his own, and so if anything happens to Jore . . . Now, in August, the English edition appears (but without the Pascal letter therefore) under the title of *Letters concerning the English Nation*; and by October the French and Dutch press begin to review what Voltaire refers to (in a letter to Formont in Rouen) as these 'philosophical, political, critical, poetical, heretical and diabolical letters'.[2] He instructs Thiriot in London to hold back publication of the French translation, not least as a means of restraining Jore, who is eager to publish and make his profit on the French edition containing the 'anti-Pascal' bombshell. Impatient, especially as he has not yet been fully reimbursed by Voltaire for the production costs, Jore circulates a small number of copies, sufficient to have him hauled before Hérault, the Lieutenant of Police, and given a formal warning. Hérault's officers find nothing when they search Jore's premises in Rouen.

Winter passes, and the French version of the *Letters concerning the English Nation* – the so-called 'Basle' edition – appears in London in March 1734. Jore can wait no longer, particularly as this has also triggered the appearance of Josse's pirated edition (ostensibly without Voltaire's approval), and he decides to publish (without reference to Voltaire). He is immediately arrested, stripped of his licence as a printer and bookseller, and sent to the Bastille for a fortnight. Voltaire just happens to be out of town – or has planned the moment carefully. For he and Émilie have gone to attend the wedding of their mutual friend, the duc de Richelieu, at Montjeu near Autun in Burgundy.

Like an unmanageable young colt, Richelieu had been obliged by royal order at the age of fifteen to marry Anne-Catherine de Noailles in order to divert his youthful ardour from the duchesse de Bourgogne, wife and soon-to-be-widow of the Dauphin. Anne-Catherine came from a family of gratifyingly ancient nobility, but in her appearance she was quite ungratify-ingly plain. (Which was perhaps why she had to pay the young Voltaire handsomely for his help with her versification.) So in protest the bridegroom refused to consummate the marriage – a refusal in part facilitated by his fourteen-month stay in the Bastille. His wife then conveniently died some five years later. Now thirty-eight, it was time for the widower duke with the roving eye to secure his lineage – and, as an increasingly influential confidant of Louis XV, to enhance his connections. With Émilie's assistance, Voltaire arranged a marriage with Elisabeth, the beautiful and intelligent daughter of the prince and princesse de Guise, with whom he had stayed from time to time in the Loire. Elisabeth was a woman of good sense and few illusions, both necessary qualities if she was to marry Don Juan. Voltaire and Mme du Châtelet left Paris on 2 or 3 April, and the wedding took place on 7 April. Remaining at Montjeu after the celebrations, they soon learnt that the 'bomb' had duly exploded and that Paris was in uproar. At once Voltaire wrote letters to Cardinal Fleury and Maurepas, claiming that he had made every conceivable effort to prevent publication of this incendiary work (he could, of course, have chosen not to write it in the first place) and that he had even paid booksellers not to publish it. He wrote to Hérault denouncing Jore, fully aware that Hérault needed no such tip-off. He wrote to Jore himself, obliquely implicating him while knowing full well that the letter would be intercepted and read by the police. All to no avail. At the beginning of May an order is issued for Voltaire's arrest, and the chief of police at nearby Dijon is instructed to apprehend the culprit and imprison him in the château at Aussone. The said culprit promptly leaves for Cirey-sur-Blaise, carefully avoiding Dijon, while Émilie and the duc de Richelieu inform the police that they believe him to have gone to the spa at Plombières, for his health. They will surely find him there.

On 10 June the Jansenist lawyers of the Paris *parlement* officially condemned the book, and – according to custom – it was ceremonially shredded and burned outside the Palais de Justice (at the foot of the grand stairway leading up to its entrance) at 11 o'clock that morning, just close by where its author had once lived. Except that the *Lettres philosophiques* itself was not actually burned. The officiating clerk, Ysabeau, wanted to read it himself, and had quietly substituted a book about Spanish revolutions. Ysabeau was also something of a bibliophile and thought he knew a collector's item when he saw one. This symbolic holocaust nevertheless heralded a very real police operation. Jore's storage facilities were raided: first, a flat on the corner of the rue de Bièvre and the rue de la Tournelle, where the authorities found twenty-three copies of the *Lettres*, both looseleaf and stitched, together with some other unsuitable publications such as *The Fifteen Joys of Marriage* and *The Reluctant Nun*, not to mention an array of anti-Jansenist tracts; and then a few weeks later the stable at Passy, where another thirty-one copies were found, this time in the company of *Amorous Intrigues at the Court of France* and a rather sceptical treatise on the doctrine of papal infallibility. The police could thus claim some success, but in reality the bird had flown; and thanks to further pirated editions in France, England and Holland, some 20,000 copies of the *Lettres philosophiques* were soon in circulation throughout educated Europe (thus rendering Ysabeau's copy less rare than he would have wished). This fell far short of the circulation levels of the penny-dreadfuls of the day, but nevertheless constituted a major diffusion for a book of such consequence.

The bird had flown, and so had Voltaire, who now found himself at Cirey but without Émilie. Presumably she would soon join him at her husband's tumbledown residence. Or would she? Their relationship, no less incendiary than the *Lettres philosophiques*, had started with a bang: an immediate rapport, blissful sex, the rapid and enchanting discovery of common interests, and all the excitement of Parisian night-life. But could it survive? For François, unquestionably. But for Émilie? The first months of madness and passion quickly took their toll on Voltaire's health and he ended up in bed, alone: in September 1733 and then again in December. He couldn't stand the pace. While he was profiting from the enforced rest to catch up on his writing, so Émilie decided to take her mind off this enforced chastity by learning English – which she acquired even faster than Voltaire – and by going back to her mathematics. Accordingly, her fallow lover suggested that she take tuition from the man who had helped him with his chapter on Newton for the *Lettres philosophiques*, the brilliant Pierre-Louis Moreau de Maupertuis. It was a generous suggestion. Although very short and a terrible fidget, Maupertuis was handsome as well as brilliant, a man of the world with a taste for salon life and a passion for figures, female as well as numerical. From January 1734 he began to teach his new pupil some very advanced mathematics, initiating her into the wonders of Newtonian physics. The pupil was soon smitten and became mistress to her master: the laws of attraction were followed by lessons in applied physiology of the kind administered by Dr Pangloss. Voltaire, the cuckolder, was now the cuckold.

Was he surprised? He knew Maupertuis's reputation and Émilie's susceptibilities, especially as her latest bout of child-bearing had left her more determined than ever to enjoy all that Paris had to offer a woman in her late twenties. Perhaps not, therefore. And he may also have predicted what would happen. For Maupertuis soon tired of his pupil's demanding nature and, like the comte de Guébriant before him, began to fear for his independence. He would eventually leave Paris for Basle, towards the beginning of September, to work with the great Swiss mathematician Jean Bernoulli on integral calculus. But meanwhile Voltaire enjoyed a rest, and his beloved Émilie made considerable progress in the field of learning that would one day make her reputation. And she had not broken off her relationship with Voltaire. So he knew she cared, as indeed she continued to demonstrate throughout the events surrounding publication of the *Lettres philosophiques*. No doubt it appealed to her own impatience with convention and intellectual conservatism to be associated with public enemy number one, and it was demonstrably true that – sex or no sex – life with Voltaire was incomparably exciting. But if it came to it and her lover had to go into hiding at Cirey, could she possibly give up Paris? And could she stand the draughts?

For the place was a ruin. Its foundations dated back to the tenth century, but the house had twice been razed to the ground: once during the sixteenth-century Wars of Religion, and then again in the first half of the seventeenth century following Gaston d'Orléans's conspiracies against Cardinal Richelieu and the King. The current marquis's great-grandfather had partly rebuilt it, but the works has been abandoned for want of funds. Not only was it not fully restored, it was also in the middle of nowhere. The village of Cirey-sur-Blaise consisted of no more than a dozen houses, all buried away in a tiny river valley surrounded by forest. Idyllic but remote. It was ten or fifteen miles to the nearest small towns, Bar-sur-Aube and Wassy. Nevertheless two sections of M. du Châtelet's two-storey château had been more or less restored, and they did have roofs. Admittedly the windows were few in number, narrow and badly made, letting in little light and far too much air. But, for Voltaire at least, it was better than the château at Aussone, let alone the Bastille. He was free, it was spring, and the country life meant fresh eggs, milk and poultry to soothe his tortured innards. And he had money: he could improve the place. He would build a new wing and make it *their* château, as wonderful – if not as big – as all those grand country residences he had frequented in the Loire. Here in Champagne, some forty miles east of Troyes, life could be made to sparkle. Just as soon as Émilie would join him.

But for the moment, to preserve both her own reputation and the secret of Voltaire's hideaway, Émilie remained at Montjeu until 20 June (her husband was away on military service). And Voltaire was glad that she did. As he wrote to the comte d'Argental, a close friend since their schooldays, he owed her his freedom, and he urged d'Argental to defend her good name in Paris. She had so often endangered it by her own reckless behaviour in the past, and he was particularly anxious now that she should not lose it, least of all on his account. As for Émilie, she heeded François's warnings but missed him dearly. Had he been simply a lover, she wrote to one of her own friends, she would have got over him; but he had become a friend, and she was astonished at the pain she felt. He for his part got on with the business of living, settling in as comfortably as he could and calling on two neighbours who were friends of the du Châtelets: the young and pretty comtesse de La Neuville, and the slightly older, plumper and less pretty Mme de Champbonin. Their husbands, too, were away with the army, and the ladies were delighted to have such a diversion here in deepest Champagne.

Voltaire now found himself in a situation that would with two exceptions – the periods spent at the courts of Louis XV and Frederick the Great – become the norm for the remainder of his life: living at a distance from the main centres of civilized Europe and communicating with the outside world by letter. In this particular situation such correspondence had to be discreet, so that he had his own letters posted from distant towns while requiring that his correspondents wrote to him c/o the abbé Bonaventure Moussinot in Paris. By these means he learnt that he had been denounced by Jore, who had been freed, and that his apartments at the rue de Longpont had been searched and ransacked. He learnt, too, that the *parlement* had banned and burned his book. And he heard also that his friend the duc de Richelieu had been wounded in a duel and now lay gravely ill in his camp near Philippsburg (on the east bank of the Rhine, north of Karlsruhe). He must go at once. When he got there, he discovered the truth. Richelieu had been insulted by a member of his new wife's family, François de Lorraine, prince de Lixin, who regarded Richelieu's family as unworthy (being not of royal blood like the de Guises and the de Lorraines). The alleged parvenu had then dispatched the princely snob with his sword and was himself perfectly well: just a slight cut, nothing to worry about. Much relieved, Voltaire stayed for a month as the French continued to besiege Philippsburg. Life at this army camp was considerably more comfortable than his billet at Cirey, and Richelieu's fellow-officers and aristocrats welcomed the famous poet to supper each day with flattering courtesy and entertaining conversation. One of them was the marquis du Châtelet, who was fighting under Richelieu's command, and so this was an opportune moment to ask if it was all right if he lived in his draughty château. Permission granted. Especially if he was planning to spend money on it.

The marquis's wife was now in Paris, finding out what she could about official sentiment and trying to intercede on the fugitive's behalf in so far as propriety allowed. But the news was not good. Fleury refused to withdraw the *lettre de cachet* – the order for Voltaire's arrest – and there was talk of permanent exile in the manner of Jean-Baptiste Rousseau, who had not been allowed to return to France for the past twenty years. Émilie was particularly eager that Voltaire should not have to spend the winter at Cirey: his health was uncertain enough as it was, and she for her own part had no desire to share such rigours with him. She continued to prefer Paris, and she still hankered after some more lessons – of whatever kind – from Maupertuis. While her 'friend' was wandering round the French lines at Philippsburg and confirming his view that war is 'human folly in all its glory and in all its horror' (as he wrote to Mme de La Neuville),[3] Émilie was once again pursuing her 'lover', the diminutive but handsome mathematician. Relations were still stormy, particularly when she dragged him off on a picnic, but following the death of her infant son she quickly sought solace in his capable arms. Voltaire soon heard the news: and once again, like Émilie's husband, he too chose to turn a blind eye. Writing to Mme de La Neuville, he hopes that she may continue to extend her customary good-will towards him: 'as to that of my wife [ma femme], I trust in providence and a cuckold's patience.'[4] Clearly Mme de La Neuville was every bit as discreet as she was pretty and faithful to her husband.

On returning to Cirey, and having secured the owner's permission, Voltaire set about designing a new wing for the property, which would be altogether better lit and better insulated than the existing parts. Financially there was no problem. His grain business was flourishing, especially since he had begun to import North African corn not only into France (via Marseilles) but, at much greater profit, into Spain and Italy. At the same time he had invested in the import–export market at Cadiz, then an important hub for trading the commodities and produce of European colonies in South America, the West and East Indies, and North Africa. Through a reliable agent, Gilly, he was getting a return of 30 per cent on his capital. But better still – especially now that he had had a chance to inspect military operations at first hand – were the investments he began to make through the brokerage of the Pâris brothers, who were financing the supply of the French army. Horse fodder, clothing, food supplies . . . Gradually Voltaire invested more and more, and his annual income from this source grew steadily over the ensuing decades. At the same time he continued to make loans to high-placed individuals whose creditworthiness could be relied upon, and it was the abbé Moussinot's job back in Paris to collect the interest payments. The subversive poet was becoming very wealthy indeed, and certainly wealthy enough to employ his own little army of masons and carpenters to build a love-nest. And as they banged and chipped, he wrote: the *Traité de métaphysique* (*Treatise on Metaphysics*), more of *La Pucelle*, and the rest of a new play, *Alzire ou les Américains*, begun early in the previous year and set in sixteenth-century Peru, at the time of the Spanish conquest.

But the tranquil author was as keen as his 'wife' to avoid spending the winter at Cirey. The duchesse de Richelieu had now returned to Paris and was trying, like Émilie, to intercede on his behalf. Chauvelin, the Garde des Sceaux, seemed disposed to resolve the matter, but the public prosecutor (Guillaume-François Joly de Fleury) was sceptical about the sincerity of both Voltaire's denial of responsibility for publishing the *Lettres philosophiques* and his strenuous promise to mend his ways. Accordingly, and Maupertuis having now departed for Basle, Émilie decided to make the trip to Cirey, where she arrived on 20 October at the same time as some 200 boxes and parcels containing the furnishings and household equipment that Voltaire had recently ordered. It was chaos, as Voltaire wrote soon afterwards to

Mme de Champbonin: 'We have beds but no curtains to go round them, rooms but no windows, lacquered cabinets but no armchairs, lovely phaetons but not a horse to draw them. Amidst all this mess Mme du Châtelet simply laughs and is her charming self.'[5] And continues to have a mind of her own: 'She wants windows where I intended doors. She turns staircases into chimneys and chimneys into staircases. And she plants limes where I had wanted elms.'[6] Still, the main thing is that she has come, and Voltaire cannot wait to take her off to visit Mmes de La Neuville and Champbonin in their elegant phaeton, even if it does have to be drawn by a carthorse.

But as winter set in, the inevitable happened: Voltaire fell ill, and Émilie was eager to be off back to Paris, especially as Maupertuis had now returned from Basle. Pleading the need to look after her friend the duchesse de Richelieu, who was having a difficult pregnancy, and pointing out how useful it would be if she delivered *Alzire* to the comte d'Argental in person so that he could offer it to the Comédie-Française (as the work of an anonymous author), Mme du Châtelet duly fled back to a city where the rooms had windows and the beds had curtains. And a city where the authorities were beginning to relent towards her friend. The draft letter that Voltaire had submitted to Chauvelin, officially denying all responsibility for the pub- lication of the *Lettres philosophiques*, had been amended by Joly de Fleury to his own satisfaction, and to that of Cardinal Fleury also, so that Hérault, the Lieutenant of Police, wrote to Voltaire on 2 March granting him permission to return to Paris — much against the wishes of the Jansenist *parlement*, who had not forgiven his treatment of Pascal. Not that Voltaire was totally in the clear: the *lettre de cachet* issued in May had not been annulled, and if he did not behave he risked being arrested and imprisoned in the Bastille at any moment.

The master of Cirey delegated supervision of his building works and returned to Paris on 20 March 1735. It was time for a showdown with the mistress of Cirey: did she intend to continue her relationship with Mau- pertuis and fritter her life away on the ephemeral pleasures of Parisian society, or did she wish to return with him to Cirey to a life of serious study and quasi-monogamous tranquillity? Six weeks later, having delivered the question, he left Paris on 12 May with the duchesse de Richelieu and headed for Lunéville in Lorraine, where his travelling-companion — as a member of the Guise family – was a leading member of the ducal court. For Émilie this was indeed decision time, and she discussed the matter with her friends, taking long walks in the Tuileries gardens and confiding her thoughts by letter to her friend and former lover the duc de Richelieu. She admired and cared deeply for Voltaire and wanted to be of help to him. But how best to do this? Her position at court was growing: she had dined with Cardinal Fleury and been invited to some of the best houses, and she did after all have that privilege of the *tabouret*. Could she not be of more assistance to her vulnerable hero by remaining in Paris and using her influence in high places to temper the inevitable consequences of his incautious subversions? And yet what hurt her most was his accusation that she did not love him. He cared less that she might have slept with Maupertuis than that he now counted for nothing in her heart. The decision was soon made: she did love him, and she wanted to demonstrate the fact unambiguously. She would give up the high life and join him at Cirey. He deserved this sacrifice – for sacrifice was how she saw it.

She had concluded that only her total commitment would resolve the situation:

> In my mind I am devastated, but in my heart I am bursting with joy. The hope that this decision will convince him that I do love him blots out all other considerations, and all I can see is the sublime happiness of quelling all his fears and of spending my life with him [. . .] But I must admit that I find his anxieties and suspicions thoroughly upsetting. I know that they are the torment of his life. And necessarily, of course, they are what poison my life too. But perhaps we are both in the right. There is all the difference in the world between jealousy and the fear of not being sufficiently loved [. . .] The one is a tiresome emotion, and the other an insidious uncertainty against which there are few weapons and remedies other than that of simply going to Cirey and being happy.[7]

She had decided, too, that she had a better chance of keeping him safe if they lived at Cirey: 'I love him sufficiently, I confess, to be able to sacrifice everything for the happiness of living with him without cause for alarm, and for the pleasure of saving him from himself, from his own recklessness, from his own fate.' And she asked Richelieu to present matters in a favourable light to her husband, knowing that the latter had great respect for his commanding officer's judgement. Voltaire and she would be engaged on important scientific work: there was no need for jealousy, and Voltaire was an honourable man. Not only did her husband heed Richelieu's words, he proceeded to obtain permission from the Garde des Sceaux to be allowed to house this dangerous man under his roof (and any new one he cared to construct).

At Lunéville the author of the *Lettres philosophiques* heard the news of Émilie's decision with understandable delight, though he was not missing her as much as he might. The court of Lorraine was presided over by Elisabeth, widow of the duc de Lorraine (who had died in 1729) and now regent – a role that no doubt came readily to her since she was the sister of Philippe d'Orléans. The court was noted for its unstuffy charm and devotion to the arts, notably the theatre. Voltaire was in his element. Moreover his new-found passion for physics was shared by Elisabeth de Richelieu – as it was by many others at that time – and together they made good use of a laboratory that had been set up with all manner of apparatus. They conducted experiments together, and Mme de Richelieu gave a lecture on Newton to a select audience. When a Jesuit tried to contest the theories she was so ably expounding, he was booed,

5. - Environs de Doulevant. - CIREY-sur-BLAISE. - Le Château. - Cour Intérieure
(Ancienne demeure de Mme du Châtelet. - Séjour de Voltaire (1733-1740)

The château at Cirey-sur-Blaise. The wing added by Voltaire
and Mme du Châtelet is facing, with the older, taller building to the right.

especially by a number of Englishmen who were present. Here in miniature was the controversy that would rage in French intellectual circles for several decades: a reactionary and xenophobic defence of Cartesian physics against the progressive adoption of Newtonian science and British empiricism. According to Voltaire, who tells the story,[8] the Englishmen were left with a dim view of French clerics and a very favourable impression of French ladies. And Émilie wasn't even present.

It was almost as if Voltaire was rehearsing for his life at Cirey. For there, together, he and Mme du Châtelet would hold similar court. They too would have laboratories; they too would perform plays; and they too would have visitors from abroad.

CHAPTER EIGHT

A Marriage of True Minds (1735–1738)

How Adam and Eve feasted on the Tree of Knowledge

A FTER A JOURNEY of some fifty miles from Lunéville, Voltaire reached Cirey on 25 June 1735. Mme du Châtelet arrived a few weeks later with her two children and accompanied by the abbé Linant. The abbé had originally been wished on Voltaire by Cideville, who had known the young cleric in Rouen and wanted to find him a position. His kind-hearted friend had taken him on in a quasi-secretarial role, but Linant had done a poor job defending his patron's interests in the rue de Longpont. Fat and lazy, he was a sort of feckless Friar Tuck with pretensions; and he stammered. But at least he was unlikely to distract the lady of the house, to whose children he was now to be tutor – except that, as Voltaire remarked, the mother would first have to teach the tutor his Latin before the tutor could pass it on to her son. And only her son: for, untrue to her father's principles, Émilie had sent her daughter to a nearby convent.

The idyll began. It was summer; the house was being daily improved, albeit noisily; M. du Châtelet was happy with the arrangement; the local priest was turning a blind eye to the adultery in his parish (as local priests did throughout France if the adulterers were high-born or rich); and for Voltaire all reason for doubting his 'wife' had gone. He proclaimed himself 'at peace, happy, and busy'[1] and had started work on a new history, *Le Siècle de Louis XIV* (*The Age of Louis XIV*). And, as a letter to Thiriot shows, he knew how lucky he was:

What she has done for me throughout the vile persecution I have undergone, and the ways in which she has helped me, would make me her slave for ever if the singular lights of her mind and her superiority over all other women in this domain had not already bound me in chains. You know how my heart is capable of friendship; consider therefore what infinite attachment I must feel towards a person in whom I find the reasons to forget everyone else, in whose company I learn new things every day, and to whom I owe everything.[2]

Émilie was pleased that her 'sacrifice' had had the desired effect, and together they abandoned themselves gaily to life in the country: walking, riding, shooting. Many happy hours were spent on interior design, debating colour schemes and arguing about where to put the furniture. But neither was a recluse. They called regularly on their neighbours, where they played chess and backgammon. Linant, alas, rather exceeded his role as paid eunuch by developing a passion for Mme de La Neuville, who was rather surprised, not least because her husband was home on leave. And despite all the works being carried out on their home, the happy couple began to receive visits from their friends, not least from Richelieu, who came to see the results of his diplomatic intervention with M. du Châtelet. 'So you will come and observe the phenomenon,' a delighted Émilie wrote to him on hearing his intention, 'two people who have spent three months alone together and who love each other all the more as a result [. . .] I swear to you that if anyone had told me two years ago that I would voluntarily be leading the life I now lead, I would have been well and truly astonished.'[3] In short, it was paradise.

But the whole object of the enterprise was work, and so the two students devised a daily timetable for themselves, setting certain hours aside for quiet study, others for discussion, and the rest for recreation. Their principal shared interest remained Newton, and because his physics had consequences for metaphysics and for the bases and validity of religious belief, they conducted a joint programme of what we now call 'research'. They would meet for coffee about eleven to discuss their early-morning reading but then take a light lunch alone and separately, surrounded by their books. A proper midday meal was served for other members of the household: for Linant and his pupil; for Mme de Champbonin, who was often there, and her son, who performed a secretarial role making fair copies of the researchers' latest scribbles; and of course Émilie's husband, who had every right to be there, quite frequently was, and seemed thoroughly pleased to be so. Though he preferred to be off fighting, he did like to inspect his estate, walking round the farm and taking a close interest in the metalwork being produced in his own forges. But the highlight of the day was supper and the evening entertainments that sometimes followed. Most of contemporary Europe would have paid to be present, so that they could be privy to Voltaire's witty conversation and marvel in his showman's skills. He would tell stories and do brilliant impersonations; sometimes there was a puppet show, or else the assembled company would perform a play, with hilariously variable results. One evening was never quite like the next, and there was rarely a dull moment. After which François and Émilie would sit up half the night, working.

Their common purpose was to understand the universe and the world we live in. Nothing less. But they had arrived at this ambitious undertaking from different directions: Voltaire – the arts student – after visiting England and studying Locke, Newton and Pascal for the purposes of the *Lettres philosophiques*; Mme du Châtelet – the science student – after a more concerted and advanced study of mathematics and physics. Each complemented the other. Now that they were settled, they took forward their earlier debates about religion by studying the book that was supposed to have explained the universe already: the Bible, and more especially the Book of Genesis and the New Testament. Few modern lovers spend early married life reading the scriptures but this couple did just that, and it fell to Émilie to write up the results: in her *Examen de la Bible*, which was much too dangerous to be published. Their practice was to examine key passages in the light of published commentaries by a range of authorities, their favourite being Augustin Calmet's *Commentaire littéral sur les livres de l'Ancien et du Nouveau Testament* (*Literal Commentary on the books of the Old and New Testaments*), published in several volumes between 1707 and 1716. Mme du Châtelet knew this Benedictine monk well – indeed he would later write a history of her family – and Voltaire soon came to share her enthusiasm for his work. In his valiant attempts to explain away apparently absurd or implausible aspects of scriptural narrative, Calmet thereby revealed the places where deists could attack it – and demonstrated a certain literal-mindedness that caused considerable hilarity during their coffee-breaks. Together they confirmed what they already both thought: that a book so full of improbability, immorality and inhumanity could scarcely be thought sacred. How could such a work be at all conducive to respect for the deity? As Voltaire later observed: 'If God made us in His image, we have certainly returned the compliment.'[4]

These months of biblical study provided Voltaire with an arsenal of anti-clerical ammunition, which he would deploy over the coming decades. At the same time he and Mme du Châtelet sought to formulate their own brand of deism, a project which the author of the *Lettres philosophiques* had already begun in the letter on Locke, and which he had then continued in his *Traité de métaphysique*. Intended for private consumption only,[5] this work was never published during his lifetime. As its author noted in the dedicatory verse written on Mme du Châtelet's fair copy: 'The author of the metaphysics/ Here placed upon your knee/ Deserved to be burned in the public square/ Whereas he only burned for thee.' In the autumn of 1733 Voltaire had been rereading the work of Samuel Clarke, the rationalist theologian and adherent of Newton whom he had met in England some six years earlier. *A Demonstration of the Existence and Attributes of God* (1704) had provided an important direction for his thinking and a basis for the second chapter of his treatise ('If there is a God'). Then, after arriving at Cirey in the summer of 1734, Voltaire had drafted much of the remainder, in which (under the influence of Locke) he is principally concerned with the existence of the soul and the nature of consciousness. By November he is able to announce to Cideville and Formont in Rouen that he has 'a little treatise on metaphysics all ready'.[6] His conclusions are now fairly firm: it is more plausible to human reason that God exists than that He does not exist; God has endowed matter (in the shape of human beings) with the power of thought (rather than giving each of us an immaterial and immortal soul); we learn about the world through our senses rather than being born with this knowledge. But perhaps Voltaire's firmest conclusion is that he hates metaphysics: the abstractness, the logic-chopping, the seeming lack of practical relevance to the realities of living.

His research partner no doubt shared his impatience with metaphysical speculation (though to a much lesser degree), for their conversations soon turned to questions of ethics. It is no accident that the *Traité* begins not with God but with a discussion of what we understand by the term 'human being'. Each of us means something different, according to our assumptions or desires or social situation. For a king, a human being is an obedient subject; for a pretty Parisienne, a potential admirer; for a young Turk in his seraglio, the human male is a superior being who is obliged by law to take an enslaved human female to bed every Friday; for Pascal, the human being is a wretched sinner, damned to Hell unless he or she happens to be the lucky one in five or six million arbitrarily preselected for salvation and eternal bliss. In an attempt to rise above this ignorance and prejudice and fanatical ideology, Voltaire imagines himself instead as an extra-terrestrial arriving from Mars or Jupiter. How then would this phenomenon called 'man' really look? Suppose that E.T. landed in East Africa . . . Well, elephants seem pretty sensible creatures, but once this little black creature on two legs gets bigger, it seems to be superior. It is not as strong as some animals nor as agile as the monkey, but it appears to be cleverer and its language is more complex. But suppose E.T. then went to China and the Dutch East Indies . . . and found yellow creatures and blond creatures, the hairy and the hairless . . . and suppose E.T. went to Goa and found another creature dressed in a long black cape, who said that it was his job to teach every other human being the truth and that all these human beings were born of the same father . . . Well, E.T. might think that this Jesuit was off his head, and that in fact human beings are not all the same. Human beings are like trees: they come in all shapes and sizes. In other words, it takes all sorts, and we need to begin by respecting difference.

And how do human beings behave? Indeed how *should* human beings behave? Their instinct for self-preservation makes them inherently selfish, but they do show some natural benevolence towards other human beings. They are free: not as free as they sometimes think, but free none the less to think and do certain things. As health is the body's state of being, so freedom is our mental and spiritual state of being. And free to do what? Free to deny ourselves, yes, but what an abuse of freedom that is. No: free to enjoy.

To improve her knowledge of English (partly so that she and Voltaire could speak freely in front of the servants) Mme du Châtelet had been reading and translating *The Fable of the Bees*, the verse allegory of the English moralist Bernard Mandeville, and she and her lover had been amused and half-persuaded by his argument: asceticism is bad for business and thus for the human race. Rather than content themselves with the bare essentials, human beings can foster economic growth by the desire for and purchase of 'luxuries' – Émilie's pompons, for example, or the splendid bathroom facilities they were having installed in their new wing. Mandeville's defence of so-called 'vice' – let us luxuriate in sloth, greed, envy, pride, etc., and boost the gross national product – was music to Voltaire's anti-Jansenist ears, and he wrote his own verse account of the argument, *Le Mondain* (*The Man of the World*), which ends with the famous line: 'Paradise on earth is here to hand' ('Le paradis terrestre est où je suis'):[7] i.e. wait not upon heavenly bliss but enjoy the good things in life. All of which is very persuasive, of course, if you find yourself at Cirey with your Eve instead of being imprisoned in the Bastille.

If Mandeville's *Fable of the Bees* had been music to Voltaire's anti-Jansenist ears, these ears had already been attuned by reading Alexander Pope's *Essay on Man* (1733–4). At the end of this work Pope claims to have

> Shew'd erring Pride, WHATEVER IS, IS RIGHT;
> That REASON, PASSION, answer one great aim;
> That true SELF-LOVE and SOCIAL are the same;
> That VIRTUE only makes our Bliss below;
> And all our Knowledge is, OURSELVES TO KNOW.

Where Pascal and other Jansenist ascetics condemn our passions as inherently suspect, to be suppressed or punished as the occasion demands, here is a harmonious vision of social order based on the pursuit of individual desires tempered by the realization that it is in our interests to love our neighbours as ourselves. In other words, deist ethics begin to resemble Christ's original teaching, but this teaching has long been obscured and traduced over the centuries by the accretions of sophistical theological doctrine and the power-crazed, money-driven abuses of the institution known as the Roman Catholic Church.

And this is the message which, in the middle of their research programme, Voltaire conveyed in his latest play, *Alzire ou les Américains* (*Alzire or the*

Americans), first performed by the Comédie-Française on 27 January 1736. Set in Lima at the time of the Spanish conquest, the play opens with the governor of Peru, the ageing Alvarès, handing over the reins of power to his son, Guzman. Alvarès has ruled in the name of a merciful Christian God, a God of love and forgiveness. With this gospel and by the example of his own benign governance he has converted Montèze, an Inca ruler, and his beautiful daughter Alzire, to his faith. But Guzman aims to overcome continuing Inca resistance by fear and violence. Moreover he is determined to marry Alzire, even though she still loves Zamore, the leader of this resistance, to whom (as it happens) Alvarès owes his life and who is himself believed dead. Reluctantly commanded by her father to wed, Alzire duly does so, only to find that Zamore is alive. After some recriminations and much pathos Zamore mortally wounds Guzman, whereupon he and Alzire are to be executed. Alvarès offers them their freedom if Zamore will convert. They refuse. Enter a dying Guzman who has now seen the light: he pardons Zamore in the name of Christianity and instructs him to marry Alzire after his death. Zamore, won over by this spectacle of mercy and magnanimity, is converted: Guzman dies content, and Alvarès is proved right. The lovers, we may presume, live happily ever after.

When published (and by royal permission), the play bore as an epigraph Pope's famous phrase 'To err is human, to forgive divine' and was dedicated openly to Mme du Châtelet: 'I composed it in your house and before your eyes.' In the dedicatory epistle Voltaire sings his beloved's praises (as well as those of Queen Caroline of Great Britain) and asserts the right of women to pursue scholarly interests. In the preface that follows, he makes a profession of faith on behalf of himself, indeed as if he were the true defender of *the* faith:

A barbarian's religion consists in offering up the blood of his enemies to his gods. A poorly educated Christian is often scarcely more righteous. Observing a few pointless customs while failing to carry out his real duties as a human being; saying prayers but not renouncing his vices; fasting while simultaneously hating, plotting, and persecuting: that is his religion. Whereas the religion of a true Christian is to regard all men as his brothers, to do well by them and to forgive them their evil [. . .] People

will find humanity of this kind in nearly all my writings, a humanity that
must be the first and foremost attribute of a thinking being: and they will
recognize [. . .] a desire for the happiness of mankind, a horror of injustice
and oppression. That alone is what has hitherto saved my works from the
obscurity to which their defects had otherwise consigned them.[8]

Voltaire had been stung by the abuse heaped on the *Lettres philosophiques*, not
least that it was the work of a godless heathen (or 'American'), and he had
been angered by the dangers and the indignities to which its publication had
exposed him. We may smile at his guileful, politic attempt to present himself
as the truest of Christians: perhaps the French 'governor' would pardon him?
And yet his statement is heartfelt, sincere, and uncharacteristically personal
('For once in my life I have felt obliged to speak thus about myself in
public').[9] Why was he the object of so much vilification and misrepresentation when his aims were indeed so pure? Freedom, humanity and justice, are
they not what everyone wants? Aren't we all Quakers really? It seemed not.

But delight rather than outrage was the order of the day at Cirey, at least to
begin with, and the Champagne life of love and laughter was more conducive
to comedy than tragedy. Between sessions on metaphysics and ethics the
workaholic playwright was tidying up a play originally called *Monsieur du Cap-
Vert* (perhaps *Captain Evergreen*), later amended to *Boursoufle* (literally *Blister*, or
Mr Bloater) and then *Grand Boursoufle*, and later still *Les Originaux* (*The
Originals*).[10] The eponymous character is a seventy-year-old mariner who
has a wife in every port but who is prevented from acquiring the latest one
when a wife he married twenty years ago escapes from the convent where he
had put her and arrives to repossess her conjugal catch . . . Voltaire had
probably written it – and may even have privately staged it – while living
with Mme de Fontaine-Martel; and shortly before fleeing Paris in 1734 he
had shown it to Mlle Quinault at the Comédie-Française. Mlle Quinault, the
fifth child of the great actor Jean Quinault and the sister of Dufresne (the
leading man who had played Orosmane (*Zaïre*) and Zamore (*Alzire*)), was the
star soubrette of the company and also now its artistic director. At once free
in her thinking and enterprising in her pursuit of theatrical innovation, she
was nevertheless not entirely persuaded of the play's merits and gave its
famous author an idea for a new comedy instead: the story of the prodigal

son in modern dress and with a love interest. Written in three months, *L'Enfant prodigue* is a mix of situational farce and tear-jerking moments of amorous separation and reunion – and was thus in tune with the contemporary taste for sentimental comedy.

Where once there had been a sharp divide between tragedy (Corneille, Racine) and comedy (Molière), now the boundaries were beginning to blur. Tragedy – as is evident in Voltaire's previous plays – had come to mean a succession of poignant scenes of serious purport but not necessarily excluding a happy ending, while in comedy the laughter provoked by the absurdities of character, situation, behaviour and language had sometimes become a way of softening the audience up for a jolly good – and happy – cry. For Voltaire, despite all his Jesuit training in the classics, was no last-ditch defender of the old ways. As he put it in the preface to *L'Enfant prodigue* when eventually it was published: 'any genre will do, except the one that bores'. Nevertheless he was nervous about how the play might be received: normal theatre-goers might like it, but the critics and the academics would be sure to object. So he insisted on remaining anonymous. Then Mlle de Quinault played a shrewd trick. On 10 October 1736 Racine's tragedy *Britannicus* was on the bill, but at the last moment she pretended that a member of the cast was ill and offered the audience *L'Enfant prodigue* instead. They loved it. They had come to cry in any case, and to be able to laugh as well was a bonus. The theatre-going public flocked to see it; the old guard duly objected; and Voltaire revealed his authorship of yet another success. France's *enfant terrible* had no need to repent the prodigality of his talent.

If Pope's *Essay on Man* had helped to clarify the views of Voltaire and Mme du Châtelet concerning ethics, it had also offered them a way through the major metaphysical problem that threatens any belief in God: the problem of evil. If God is omnipotent and benevolent, why is there evil in the world? In relation to physical evil – floods, earthquakes, volcanic eruptions, etc. – Christians answer that God moves in mysterious ways His wonders to perform, while in respect of moral evil they argue that we have abused the great gift of freedom granted to us by God. In other words, it's not His fault. In Catholic terms, the ever-present evidence of man's inhumanity to man is the inevitable result of Adam's 'original sin' in the Garden of Eden, when at Eve's suggestion he ate of the Tree of Knowledge of Good and Evil. (Some say it was an apple, but that's just a pun on the Latin *malum* meaning both apple and evil.) Eve, of course, was tempted by the devil, so it was all *his* fault really. Deists like Voltaire shared the Christian view of physical evil while taking the view that moral evil was (a) not inevitable, and (b) not evidence against the existence of God. For Pope, as well as for other English thinkers of the day such as Shaftesbury and Voltaire's friend, Viscount Bolingbroke, the watchword was indeed 'Whatever is, is right'. For they were Optimists, believing that God created an optimal world and that if it does not quite look that way to us, then ours not to reason why. 'Submit,' says Pope in the first Epistle of his *Essay on Man*:

> [. . .] In this, or any other sphere,
> Secure to be as blest as thou canst bear:
> Safe in the hand of one disposing Pow'r,
> Or in the natal, or the mortal hour.
> All Nature is but Art, unknown to thee;
> All Chance, Direction, which thou canst not see;
> All Discord, Harmony not understood;
> All partial Evil, universal Good.
> And, spite of Pride, in erring Reason's spite,
> One truth is clear, 'Whatever is, is RIGHT.'[11]

For Voltaire and for Mme du Châtelet at this period, as for the Optimists, there is a limit to our metaphysical knowledge of the universe, but we can make the best of what we have got. There are necessary evils, but the evils of intolerance, bigotry and fanaticism, of religious, political, intellectual and cultural oppression, are far from necessary, even if occasionally they may seem ineradicable. And of course if 'All Nature is but Art, unknown to thee', it might still be possible to know it a little bit better – and to help other people to know it better – through the study of the physical world. Especially since that new knowledge – in the shape of Newtonian physics – seemed spectacularly to bear out the contention that the universe is a beautifully designed and wonderfully complex piece of 'art' or knowing craftsmanship.

So after *Alzire* came their joint project to make Newton's work more widely known in France. Following Mme du Châtelet's arrival in the summer of 1735 the couple's first visitor had been a brilliant and handsome young Italian, Count Francesco Algarotti, whom Émilie had met through Maupertuis. Only twenty-three, he was an accomplished mathematician and natural philosopher, and he was writing a book about Newton for an Italian readership (which was eventually published in 1737 as *Il Newtonianismo per le dame* (*Newtonianism for the Ladies*)). His presence was a delight, for he spoke several languages, was very widely read, and had as much enthusiasm for the arts as he did for the laws of gravity and the philosophy of Locke. And his visit was instructive – for him and for his hosts. After he left, Voltaire's principal project became the preparation of his own *Éléments de la philosophie de Newton*. For her part, Mme du Châtelet determined to assist the cause of disseminating Newtonian science by translating his *Principia mathematica* from Latin into French and thus for the benefit of readers all across Europe, who read and spoke the latter very much more readily than they could now understand the former.

Almost every member of the French Academy of Sciences was firmly opposed to Newton's theories: Jean-Dominique Cassini, his son Jacques Cassini, Réaumur, Fontenelle, Bignon, Saurin, de Mairan . . . all the big names of the day. For them Descartes had already given a satisfactory account of interplanetary space as consisting of an ethereal fluid (*materia subtilis*) in which the celestial bodies were supported and conveyed by a system of 'tourbillons' or vortices. (Imagine ping-pong balls bobbing about in an intelligent way around the plug-hole of an emptying bath.) Instead of the Cartesian *plenum* the academicians were being required to countenance a Newtonian vacuum in which invisible forces of gravitational attraction held the planets and their satellites in harmonious equilibrium while the whole lot whirled around the sun. Put more precisely, the gravitational pull of any two objects is proportional to the mass of each and varies inversely as the square of the distance between them. Halve the distance between the two objects and the tug becomes four times stronger. Moreover this mad Englishman was suggesting that the centrifugal force of the earth's spin would make the earth slightly flat at its two poles and just as slightly fat at its equator, a squished-earth policy that would upset all manner of calculations. No, they said, the earth was like a lemon not a mandarin, an onion not a date.[12] Which was why Maupertuis was now, in 1736, setting off for Lapland to measure one degree of the earth's meridian to see if it was the same as or longer than one degree measured in France. He would return in the following year – followed ten months later by two Lapp sisters, Christine and Ingebord Plaiscom, who had fallen in love with him and absolutely refused to leave his side – and announce that it was longer. Newton was right. As was further confirmed by La Condamine (of lottery fame), funded and dispatched by the Academy in 1735, when he (and his colleague Bouguer) returned years later from measuring one degree of the meridian near the equator. His trip had taken him to the Andes, but he had not returned with Alzire – nor indeed with very much of his (frostbitten) ears.

Voltaire and Mme du Châtelet were thus at the cutting edge of contemporary science, and the former pupil at Louis-le-Grand was as keen as ever to compete. Accordingly he asked his agent in Paris, the abbé Moussinot, to find out what the subject for the Academy's annual competition was going to be for 1737. 'Fire,' he was told: what it is and how it spreads. In other words, contestants were required to explain the secret that Prometheus had once stolen from the gods. Voltaire's study of physics had hitherto been more theoretical than experimental. Nevertheless, a small room had been set aside as a laboratory in the older part of the château, and arrangements were also in hand to install a camera obscura for experiments relating to Newtonian optics. Larger pieces of apparatus – globes, mirrors and other instruments – were accommodated at Cirey in a long gallery that also served as the dining-room. Further instruments were now ordered from Paris, with Moussinot's help, many of them specifically related to the new project on fire: four concave mirrors of equal size; a large, double-sided convex mirror; a barometer; two thermometers; two earthenware receptacles designed to withstand high temperatures; crucibles; glass shards; iron rods. Moussinot was sent off to ask Fontenelle, as a member of the Academy, quite what they meant by 'how it spreads', while another expert was asked for his opinion on whether or not fire can be said to have weight. The marquis du Châtelet's forges now proved most convenient as his house-guest undertook a number of experiments intended to answer this very question. After three months engaged in the calcination of metals, Voltaire reckoned it did: the resultant calx, or mineral substance, weighed more than the original metal.

Mme du Châtelet meanwhile was delighted at her companion's new-found enthusiasm for experimental science, and from her letter to Maupertuis at the beginning of December 1736 it seems that the mathematician (also a member of the Academy) may have had equal reason to be pleased: 'You have long wanted to make a [natural] philosopher of our leading poet and you have succeeded, for your advice has played no little part in making him yield to his thirst for knowledge in this way.'[13] Did Maupertuis think that Voltaire was wasting his talents in merely furthering the 'public understanding of science' when he could actually have been making his own original contribution? Quite likely. At any rate, it is clear that Voltaire was having tremendous fun trying to make this original contribution to knowledge, and the couple discussed his work daily. Gradually, however, Émilie began to draw conclusions from the evidence that differed significantly from those of François, and so she decided that she, too, would enter the competition. But secretly. She did not want to upset her lover, and of course women were not supposed to meddle in science or enter public competitions like that. Secrecy meant that she could not do her own experiments, but this did not matter unduly since she could learn from Voltaire's. In any case she wished to write a largely theoretical treatise, arguing that fire is a manifestation of what Descartes had called *materia subtilis* and is therefore weightless and in itself imperceptible.

In the event the prize was shared between the eminent geometer Leonard Euler and a couple of unadventurous Cartesians: the former had done little to advance our knowledge of fire, describing it as an elastic fluid, but at least he had come up with the formula for the speed of sound. The other joint-winners had merely 'explained' fire in terms of Descartes's vortices. The two papers from Cirey (entries numbers 6 and 7) were remarkable – if not a little suspect to xenophobic eyes – in making so much use of the work of foreign scientists like Newton, Boyle and Boerhaave (whose book on chemistry Voltaire had relied on heavily). Nevertheless, given the fame of their authors, the Academy agreed to publish them along with the winning entries in the summer of 1738 – while explicitly distancing themselves from their findings in a short preface. Mme du Châtelet's authorship of entry number 6 was revealed (she had told Voltaire herself once the result was known, and he was even prouder of her than ever), and thus she claimed the honour of being the first woman to have a paper published in the proceedings of the Académie des Sciences. Eve had made good use of that apple.

Voltaire's paper was an object of curiosity, and the Academy presented it as the work of 'one of our best poets'.[14] Few in Paris yet appreciated just how far advanced in his understanding of Newton he was, but one who did was the royal censor appointed to assess his *Éléments de la philosophie de Newton*. Which is why he sat on it. Mme du Châtelet was keen that this work should be published by royal permission, thus securing official recognition and some breathing space for her controversial companion. And so in June 1737 Voltaire had submitted a revised version, this time to an expert, Pitot, known for his Newtonian sympathies. His old schoolfriend, the marquis d'Argenson, was enlisted to use his influence. But the Academy, supported by the court, continued to contest Newton's theories, even when Maupertuis returned from Lapland in the middle of August 1737 with the irrefutable evidence that the earth is not a perfect sphere. (As Voltaire put it, he was 'the man who flattened the earth and the Cassinis'.)

The research team at Cirey was beginning to acknowledge that Voltaire's new book would have to appear outside France when, on 10 April 1738, Ledet published the unfinished and uncorrected manuscript that its author had left behind two years earlier. Not only was the newly published version full of errors and misprints but Ledet had also commissioned an incompetent jobber to 'finish' it. The result was a travesty, and Voltaire was furious – especially about the subtitle that Ledet had thought fit to append: 'à la portée de tout le monde', or 'as may be understood by everyone'. Voltaire and Mme du Châtelet both considered Algarotti to have simplified Newton unduly, and Voltaire in particular was not at all pleased at the suggestion that he himself had not done full justice to the difficulty of Newton's mathematics.

Over the next two months, and making himself ill in the process, he worked on a 'second' edition, obtaining 'tacit' permission to publish it – officially in London, actually in Paris. His enemies used the Ledet edition to mock him, but more illustrious readers of the authentic 'second' edition recognized his merits. Father Tournemine, his teacher at Louis-le-Grand and a leading Jesuit thinker, praised the clarity with which his former pupil had expounded the complexities of Newton's optics and the laws of gravity. Many expressed open regret at the lack of consideration shown to Descartes, but most were forced to recognize the value of the book as being the first to make Newtonian physics intelligible to those who read French. Mme du Châtelet reviewed it most favourably (and anonymously) in the *Journal des savants!* It was a major, ground-breaking contribution to the 'public understanding of science'. This particular Adam had also made good use of that apple. Like Newton himself.

CHAPTER NINE

Worms in the Apple (1736–1739)

In which a great man rides high and stoops low

THUS WAS THE backwater of Cirey transformed into a lovely château and a leading centre for scientific research. Needless to say, Europe was intrigued. And no one in Europe was more intrigued than Crown Prince Frederick of Prussia. Born on 24 January 1712, he was twenty-four when he wrote his first letter to Voltaire. Unlike his father Frederick William, a military man with firm ideas about discipline and the benefits of regular exercise, the young Frederick had spent his adolescence with his nose in a book and listening to music. French books and French music were his especial favourites. His father suffered from porphyria, the hereditary disease that eventually drove George III of England mad, and was given to wild tantrums and unpredictable cruelty. At the age of eighteen young Frederick planned to run away to France with his close friend and lover, Lieutenant von Katte. The two men were caught and imprisoned. On 6 November 1730 von Katte was beheaded in the presence of his devastated prince, who had the good fortune to faint at the crucial moment.

In 1733 Frederick William forced his son to marry Princess Elisabeth of Brunswick-Wolfenbüttel, niece of the Holy Roman Emperor. The Princess fell in love with her arranged husband, who was five foot seven and had large blue eyes. But the young prince remained indifferent to his bride. At his father's instigation he took command of a regiment and lived the military life: the future warrior-king emerged later from that experience. But the future philosopher-king could be seen more immediately in Frederick's rejection of the hidebound pieties of the Prussian court and in his enthusiastic embrace of freethinking, particularly French freethinking. Voltaire was the young man's hero.

In 1736 Frederick and his new wife set up home at Rheinsberg, 175 miles north-west of Berlin, surrounded by a small circle of Frederick's close friends and courtiers. The household consisted of about twenty people: Princess Elisabeth had six ladies-in-waiting and a chaplain. There was no mountain – or 'Berg' – to be seen, and the Rhine in question was a trickle of a thing, not the great river on the other side of present-day Germany. But when a university professor at Rostock suggested that 'Rhein' was actually a corruption of Remus, Remusberg sounded altogether more Roman and grand (mountain or no mountain) and that became Frederick's new address. Like Ludovise, the duchesse du Maine, he set up his own little 'Order' – a group of twelve who would play Round Table to his Arthur. Literature, music and theatre were the pastimes of choice, to be written, composed and performed as well as merely read, heard and watched.

Frederick was a keen dancer and flautist, and he enjoyed acting in Voltaire's *Œdipe*. Its depiction of the father–son relationship was no doubt as suggestive for him as it was for its celebrated author. And he studied, compulsively, rising at four in the morning and going to bed at two, also in the morning. Sleep was a waste of time, but when he tried to do without it altogether he fell seriously ill. He also corresponded widely, asking advice on intellectual matters from experts in the relevant field, and he was eager to be abreast of the very latest developments in the arts. He had heard rumours about Voltaire's apparently hilarious mock-epic about Joan of Arc and simply decided that he would write – on 8 August 1736 – and ask the poet for a copy. Accordingly he surrounded his (in the end implicit) request with an elaborate eulogy of his addressee, together with an account of his own intellectual and artistic interests. Metaphysics was a particular hobby, he said, and he mentioned the work of a certain freethinker, Christian Wolff, which seemed to him absolutely splendid. Perhaps he might send Voltaire an account of it. And if only he were already king. Because then he could provide the great Frenchman with the peace and security that a man of his genius needs and deserves for the accomplishment of his life's work.

Some letter, and some correspondent. Voltaire was hugely flattered to be thus lionized by the future ruler of one of Europe's leading nations. How different from the usual response in Paris. He replied in kind, praising the young philosopher-prince for his enlightened views. And thus began a relationship and a correspondence that would continue for the rest of Voltaire's life: two men acting out the respective roles of mentor and pupil, of sage and ideal ruler, while in the event performing a number of scenarios more suggestive of a mistress hounded by a jealous lover, or a star attraction used and manipulated by a ruthless impresario.[1] For the moment, however, the future looked promising, and even Mme du Châtelet was moved to comment (to Thiriot) that 'since it seems that we have to have princes, although no one knows quite why, then at least it would help if they were all like him'.[2]

But she was wary, and right to be wary. For Frederick was already paying Thiriot to inform on his friend. Here was the further purpose of Émilie's 'sacrifice' in abandoning Paris for Cirey: not only to show Voltaire that she loved him, to disarm his jealousy and to provide a refuge where he could work; but also to protect him – from himself, from all the many enemies that he had managed to accumulate, and (most dangerous of all) from would-be friends. Voltaire, of course, could fight his own battles, but the trouble was that he all too frequently did. For him, discretion was very rarely the better part of valour. As soon as their first winter together at Cirey was over, he was off to Paris in the spring of 1736 to sort things – and people – out. First, he sacked Demoulin, his manager and agent at the granary in the rue de Longpont. Profiting from his absence, Demoulin had embezzled him to the tune of 20,000 *livres*. The abbé Moussinot, his brother-in-law (just as Demoulin had been the brother-in-law of his predecessor Dubreuil), was to replace him. As a canon of the church, with special responsibility for the finances of his chapter, Moussinot had credentials as a competent and trustworthy agent. He was also very good at shopping, which would be vital as Cirey was gradually upgraded, and he was soon dispatching all manner of goods in the direction of Champagne, from wig-powder to commodes (*chaises percées*). Candles, coffee, citrus fruit, quill pens, gilt-edged writing-paper, confectionery, diamond shoe-buckles, slippers, feather-dusters, parquet brushes, canaries, a little parrot with a black collar . . . Everything that was essential to life in paradise. As to Mme du Châtelet's make-up and gloves, he delegated their selection and purchase to his sister and nieces respectively.

With his supply lines thus secured, the doughty combatant then entered the lists of legal dispute and confronted three opponents of disparate valour and resources: a tailor and a printer — doubtless both demanding payment, but eventually routed — and then Jore of Rouen, his old accomplice in clandestine publishing. This was a more serious joust. For Jore was now in league with Demoulin, who had taken advantage of Voltaire's absence to comb his personal papers and effects at the rue de Longpont in search of incriminating or blackmailable evidence (like the extracts from *La Pucelle* he had recently obtained from Dubreuil and then leaked). As his former agent, of course, Demoulin already knew the ins and outs of Voltaire's financial affairs. Jore had written to Voltaire in March 1736 saying that the Garde des Sceaux was minded to restore his bookseller's licence if he, Jore, would make a clean breast of his role in the dissemination of the *Lettres philosophiques*. Would Voltaire be so kind as to provide a letter that would serve to exonerate him? In an act of generosity that speaks volumes about both the kind-heartedness and the recklessness of Voltaire, he duly did so — thus falling into a trap.

The Garde des Sceaux's offer was a fiction: but now Jore had a letter identifying Voltaire explicitly and in writing as the author of the *Lettres philosophiques* and furthermore admitting that he, Jore, had yet to be reimbursed for the costs of the book's production. In so far as anyone was to blame in the affair it was François and René Josse with their pirated edition. Duly armed with this letter, Jore threatened to show it to the authorities unless Voltaire paid him 22,000 *livres* at once. On 5 May Voltaire offered him a thousand. Whereupon Jore published a so-called *factum* or official statement of complaint against him, detailing at length his alleged meanness in money matters and a fine array of unsavoury business practices. (Given the cloud under which Voltaire had left England, he may not have been making these up . . .) Unbeknownst to Voltaire a court order was served at the rue de Longpont on 16 May, which Demoulin of course concealed from him, and this was followed on 21 May by an order distraining his goods. Whereupon Jore published the text of his official statement of complaint and sold it outside the theatres of Paris. He made some money, and the ensuing scandal promised more.

The statement had been drawn up by one of Voltaire's inveterate and most determined enemies, the abbé Pierre-François Guyot Desfontaines. This individual had first entered the picture in the spring of 1724 when he published a pirated edition of *La Ligue* in which he had filled in Voltaire's diplomatic gaps with unsuitable text of his own. A Rouennais and distantly related to the de Bernières family, he was nine years older than Voltaire. Educated by the Jesuits, he had then taught for them in Rennes and Bourges. After fifteen years he changed careers – having perhaps been dismissed for his homosexuality – and soon afterwards he became a journalist, as the editor of the prestigious *Journal des savants*. On 18 December 1724 he was arrested and imprisoned after being denounced by a sixteen-year-old boy he had taken to bed, and then, having been tried and found guilty, was transferred on 25 April 1725 to the prison at Bicêtre, where all 'sodomites' were sent. They could expect to be burned at the stake in the Place de Grève.

Voltaire soon learnt of the case, no doubt through Thiriot, and quickly intervened on behalf of someone whose literary and journalistic talents he considered worthy of respect. More especially he did not regard homosexuality as a capital offence – or even an offence (at least between consenting adults). The marquis de Bernières used his considerable influence

Abbé Pierre-François Guyot Desfontaines.

on behalf of his distant relative and spoke to the Prime Minister, the duc de Bourbon, requesting that the abbé be placed under his supervision at his Rouen home, La Rivière-Bourdet. Voltaire, meanwhile, pleaded with Mme de Prie, the duc de Bourbon's mistress, and with Hérault, the Lieutenant of Police, arguing that Desfontaines was a man of superior worth and character and had merely been guilty of a regrettable 'indiscretion'. One month later Desfontaines was duly released, placed under the supervision of the marquis de Bernières (the presiding judge in the Rouen *parlement*), and 'exiled' – that is, forbidden to approach within thirty leagues (eighty miles) of Paris. Desfontaines then sent Voltaire a long letter of thanks, attributing his recent misfortunes to the malice of his enemies and asking if Voltaire would now be so kind as to get the sentence of exile lifted. To this end he even drafted the text which the Prime Minister had only to sign (in the King's name). Undaunted by this rather discourteous demand, Voltaire did as he was told, and Desfontaines was freed completely on 4 June. Whereupon, in the comfort of La Rivière-Bourdet, Desfontaines sat down to write a pamphlet attacking Voltaire and all that he stood for . . . Thiriot, shocked, persuaded him to destroy it (or so he later claimed). Desfontaines's ingratitude and treachery remain a mystery. Conceivably Thiriot was his lover and perhaps had so frequently and petulantly complained of Voltaire's behaviour towards him that he had taken up a journalist's eloquent pen on Thiriot's behalf. Or perhaps Desfontaines simply hated Voltaire – the person and the views – and hated him even more now that he was beholden to him. At any rate, come the spring of 1736, he had found useful allies for his hatred in Jore and Demoulin, and the wide circulation afforded to his latest attack on Voltaire (in Jore's public statement) constituted a signal victory.

But not his first. The previous year Voltaire had received a request from the abbé Asselin, headmaster of a boys' school (the Collège d'Harcourt) and a man of some standing in the world of letters. Was there a play Voltaire could recommend for performance at his school's annual prize-giving? Since Asselin had done him a favour by admitting Mme de Champbonin's son as a boarder on very charitable terms, the famous playwright offered him his own *La Mort de César*, still unstaged and just right for a boys' school since there were no female roles. Performed on 11 August 1735 before an influential audience, it was a considerable success, being reviewed in the Parisian press, but what Voltaire had most feared – and warned the headmaster against – now came to pass. A copy of the play was published, without his permission, and containing not only many misprints but also all the revisions and bowdlerizations that Asselin had thought necessary for a schoolboy production. He would be pilloried – and by Desfontaines most of all, for, as he well knew, this man lived for such opportunities. So he wrote to Desfontaines, disclaiming responsibility for the unsatisfactory edition. Foolish man! Desfontaines published his article, already written, ridiculing the play and its many shortcomings, and then appended Voltaire's letter – which was addressed from Cirey. This was in September 1735 when only a few people knew where Voltaire was. His cover was blown, and his hosts, the marquis and marquise du Châtelet, were severely embarrassed. On top of which the authorities now began to complain about the seditious, republican message of the play. And just when his intention had been to lie low and let the storm caused by the *Lettres philosophiques* abate. He was furious with the well-meaning Asselin and even more furious with the decidedly not well-meaning Desfontaines. Why should anyone have to read the bugger's tedious articles: 'It would after all have been better that a priest should burn than that the public be bored.'[3]

But Desfontaines was not alone in his hatred of Voltaire. Jean-Baptiste Rousseau had also fallen out with him some time ago. In 1722, when he met Rousseau in Brussels, Voltaire had begun to find the exiled poet something of a ponderous and self-important bore. When he met him again a few weeks later, on his way back from Holland, relations worsened. During a carriage-ride Rousseau read out some of his latest satirical verses, and Voltaire commented – with only too characteristic directness – that his 52-year-old fellow-poet seemed to have kept his bite but lost his wit. As to his new 'Ode to Posterity', it was unlikely to reach its destination. Whereupon Rousseau listened as his former protégé recited some of his 'Epître à Uranie' and asked to be set down before he had to listen to any more of this terrible blasphemy. Voltaire, scornful of such piety in a man who had once been so politically subversive, then proceeded to malign Rousseau wherever he went. As Rousseau knew. When Voltaire published his own, corrected edition of *La Mort de César* in 1736, he included in his preface a number of insulting remarks about Rousseau – who responded, quite reasonably, by sending an anonymous article to a Parisian booksellers' journal (*La Bibliothèque française*), detailing his previous dealings with Voltaire (the anonymity was for form's sake only) and offering a sample of the man's 'turpitude' that would be more fully illustrated in a forthcoming book (in two volumes).

Apparently oblivious to this new threat, Voltaire now responded to Jore and Desfontaines by publishing his own signed statement, witnessed by a lawyer, in which he answered Jore's various accusations. Then he wrote a stream of letters to Chauvelin, the Garde des Sceaux, and Maurepas, the minister in charge of security, and Hérault, the chief of police . . . He has been the victim of theft and blackmail; his former agent Demoulin has robbed him and even now is in possession of his personal papers; his enemies have taken everything; he has hardly a penny to his name (all this on the best note-paper) . . . Are the authorities going to let the law be trampled on in this ghastly fashion by men – Jore and Desfontaines – who have previously been detained at His Majesty's pleasure? (asks this former inmate of the Bastille . . .) Jore counter-attacked by republishing Voltaire's original, self-incriminating letter, together with new 'information'. But the authorities were becoming thoroughly weary of this affair, and especially of Voltaire's implausible and hyperbolic role as the innocent victim. So Hérault hastened to end it. Jore was obliged to return the letter, and Voltaire was required to 'settle' by donating 500 *livres* to the poor. 'Condemned to give alms, and thus I am dishonoured', as he put it.[4] But at least he could choose the recipients of his charity, so he began by giving 100 *livres* to 'a young man of letters' – probably Baculard d'Arnaud, one of many young protégés in Voltaire's life.

After this sortie, Voltaire returned to Cirey exhausted and temporarily chastened, not to say feeling a little guilty at having owed the relatively satisfactory outcome with Jore to the intervention of the powers that be. This visit to Paris is illustrative of the bearpit that Voltaire and Mme du Châtelet considered the French capital to represent. His enemies sought every opportunity to do him down, while his celebrity meant that much money was to be made out of pirating his work and libelling his name, even by those who bore him no particular grudge or malice. But Voltaire himself thoroughly enjoyed jousting and duelling with his pen, and above all, of course, he liked nothing better than being read. After Algarotti's visit in 1735, for example, he wrote a charming verse epistle in which he professed no envy for Algarotti's forthcoming participation in Maupertuis's expedition to Lapland. When it comes to astronomical observations, 'Émilie' is the only star he wants to gaze at: 'And I attest in the name of the heavens you are measuring / That for her charms divine I would soon forsake / The equator and the arctic pole.' It was so good that he just had to send it to his 'friend' Thiriot, who showed it to Desfontaines, who disingenuously asked Voltaire for permission to publish it and then, on being predictably refused, published it anyway on 10 November 1735. The damage to Mme du Châtelet's reputation was not negligible, and her husband felt badly let down.

For such reasons the 'divine' Émilie despaired of Voltaire's incaution (thus born of vanity and a natural belligerence), and she had reason to do so again one year later. Copies of *Le Mondain* began to circulate in Paris, and its irreverent humour, not to mention its apologia for the life of luxury, was upsetting pious souls. 'My dear Adam, my good father, lover of fine food / Just what were you up to in those gardens at Eden? [. . .] / Were you busy caressing my mother, Madame Eve? / Admit it now, isn't it true? / Your nails were long and dirty, / Your hair not looking just as tidy as it ought. / Quite a tan you had, and what leathery skin! / Love unwashed, even the fondest love, / Is love no longer, but a basic, shameful urge.' In other words, thank God for bathrooms. Not exactly an atheistic or revolutionary sentiment, and Voltaire did not think so as he parodied the potential po-faced clerical commentary to which his poem might be subject. Tut, tut: such verses

> might lead anyone straight to the conclusion that there were no scissors or razors or soap in the earthly paradise, which of course would be the worst possible heresy. Moreover it is supposed in this pernicious pamphlet that Adam was caressing his wife in paradise, whereas in all the stories about Adam's life found in the archives of the Ark on Mount Ararat by St Cyprien, it is expressly stated that the good fellow never had an erection in paradise, and that he only did so once he was driven out. According to the rabbis, that's why we say the poor are 'hard up'.[5]

How could anyone still regard the Book of Genesis as literally true?

But this was Voltaire's problem. If he had written less wittily and less often, it wouldn't have mattered so much. Maurepas laughed at *Le Mondain*, but once Cardinal Fleury saw it, the issue assumed more serious dimensions. With each new witticism and each new book published without permission – whether Voltaire had tried to prevent it or not – he was becoming an acknowledged adversary of religion and an ever more troublesome irritant in the body politic.

Mme du Châtelet was once again genuinely anxious about his security, and he for his part thoroughly frustrated and angered both by the undue sensitivity of the authorities and by his own vulnerability to its consequences. A sword seemed to be hanging over his head, and so he decided to visit Holland for a while, for a breath of good Protestant air. In Amsterdam he could oversee publication of some of his works by Ledet, while in Leyden he could attend lectures and classes given by 'sGravesande, the distinguished expert on Newtonian physics, which would help him with the finer points of his forthcoming book. Partly to put pursuers off the track and partly to avoid any suggestion that he was running away or had been banished, he spread the rumour that he was going to see Frederick at Rheinsberg/Remusberg. On the night of 9–10 December 1736 Mme du Châtelet accompanied him by carriage to Wassy, where he was to catch the stagecoach at 4 a.m. She was at once relieved and heartbroken to see him go. For herself she dreaded remaining at Cirey without him, especially during the dull months of winter, and for him she feared the effects on his health and the publishing temptations into which Dutch freedoms might lead him. She worried too about what might happen if he did go to visit Crown Prince Frederick. Might not his father, the King of Prussia, be just as hostile as the King of France? She may even have wondered if Voltaire would return, for the letter which he wrote that day to d'Argental – when still unsure whether the situation was really so grave as to require his departure – expresses a similar pain at parting but puts a rather different slant on the possible results: 'When I see the moment approaching when I shall have to part for ever from someone who has done everything for me, who left Paris for me, as well as all her friends and all the delights of her previous life, someone whom I adore and should adore, you can well imagine how I feel. It is a horrible state to be in.' It hurts him deeply to see his dearest Émilie in tears, to have to consign her to the loneliness of a house she built for him (*sic*) and all because he has enemies in Paris. He would rather not leave. But if he has to . . . 'I would leave with inexpressible joy, I would go and see the Prince of Prussia . . . I would live abroad . . . I would be free.'[6] Mme du Châtelet had provided him with freedom, and yet her shelter could be stifling.

It would have been much better if they could have gone together. And later they would. But for the moment Voltaire visited Holland alone, and there gloried once more in that other 'paradise on earth'. Especially as he was fêted wherever he went. *Zaïre* and *La Mort de César* were both staged during his visit, the latter in a Dutch translation by Jacob Vordaagh. At Amsterdam he dined with the finest freethinking minds, young and old, some Dutch-born, some Huguenot refugees, and some – like the young marquis d'Argens – just plain French. At Leyden he followed 'sGravesande's lectures on Newton and consulted the eminent chemist and medical scientist, Hermann Boerhaave (whose book he found so useful for his work on fire), both of whom attracted large numbers of overseas students to the city and made it notably cosmopolitan in atmosphere. In his letters to d'Argental Voltaire expressed muted enthusiasm for his new life, in order not to upset Mme du Châtelet (to whom d'Argental would certainly have communicated their content), but in others he was more explicit. To Mlle Quinault at the Comédie-Française he was unambiguous: 'They don't treat me like this in my own country . . . I wish you the new-found happiness that is currently mine to enjoy',[7] while to Frederick of Prussia he summarized just why he wasn't treated like this in France: 'I've been persecuted ever since I wrote *La Henriade*. Would you believe how often people have reproached me for depicting the Saint Bartholomew Massacre in such an odious light? I have been called an atheist because I said that men weren't born to destroy each other.'[8]

But even in Holland he was pursued. Impoverished French refugees would eke a living by acting as conduits for the latest Parisian libels that came from men like Desfontaines, spreading false rumours and feeding misinformation to the press. That Voltaire had abandoned France in the name of liberty . . . That he had fled under threat of imprisonment on account of *La Pucelle* and its attack on religion . . . That he had so outraged 'sGravesande with his atheist comments that the eminent scientist had been obliged to flee the lecture-room . . . Both Voltaire and 'sGravesande had to issue separate formal denials of these allegations. And Mme du Châtelet fretted the while. Surely Voltaire would not be mad enough to let Frederick have a copy of the

Traité de métaphysique? It was much more dangerous than *La Pucelle*. What further ill-advised verses might he send to Thiriot and others? She felt that she needed more political wiles to protect him 'than the entire Vatican deploys to keep Christendom in irons'.[9] In the end, she despaired of the power of her epistolary eloquence and resorted to the rather obvious tactic of getting d'Argental to tell him she was seriously ill. Her endless warnings – her 'sermons', as he called them – had made Voltaire cross, but he could not call her bluff. So he cut short his visit and left Amsterdam – and an unfinished version of his *Éléments de la philosophie de Newton* – behind. He was back in Cirey by the end of February 1737. She had given up Paris – and her freedom – for him; and he had given up Holland – and liberty – for her.

Now that she had him under close supervision again, Mme du Châtelet began to act as custodian of his works, locking his manuscripts away where he could not get at them and on occasion even refusing him access to them. As long as he was working on the *Éléments* or his study of fire for the Académie des Sciences, all well and good. The experiments he was doing following 'sGravesande's lectures were harmless, as for the moment was a new play, *Mérope*. He had gone back to tragedy . . . He was also writing his own version of Pope's *Essay on Man*, his *Épîtres sur le bonheur* (*Epistles on Happiness*), later to be entitled *Discours en vers sur l'homme* (*Discourses in Verse on Man*). These would have to be watched, not least because they were particularly intended for Frederick's eyes (and education). That relationship was developing fast, and she was anxious. On the other hand, Frederick had – as promised – just sent Voltaire a French translation of Christian Wolff's writings on metaphysics, which, to her at least, seemed of considerable interest. Heavily based on the work of Leibniz, they met with Voltaire's scorn – since he was on Newton's side in that particular battle – but she herself warmed to Leibniz's attempts to found faith on reason and to offer a convincing metaphysical explanation of the universe and its workings. However, when Frederick then sent his personal envoy, Baron Keyserlingk, to Cirey with strict instructions to return with every written Voltairean word he could lay his hands on, she excelled herself in her new police role, and the baron returned home with the least inflammatory of portfolios. No *Traité*, no *Pucelle*. Admittedly Keyserlingk had managed to persuade Linant to swap Cirey for Prussia (the tutor continued to have pretensions to intellectual stardom), but Mme du Châtelet got to hear of it and told her son's tutor what she thought of him. However, when she then discovered that Linant's sister, her own treasured maid, had been writing all manner of scurrilous things about her to the abbé Desfontaines, she sacked the pair of them. And all was consternation in the most beautiful and most agreeable of all possible châteaux.

Life at Cirey could indeed be no less turbulent and no less riven by gossip and enmity than life in Paris or Prussia or even Holland – as we know from the letters of Mme de Graffigny. Increasingly celebrated today as the author of the *Lettres d'une péruvienne* (1747), an epistolary novel about a captured Inca princess who adapts to French customs without sacrificing her proto-feminist independence, she was a distant relative of the marquis du Châtelet. As her full name suggests, Françoise d'Issembourg d'Happoncourt de Graffigny was descended from many generations of Lothringian nobility, but she had recently suffered singularly ignoble treatment from her husband, Huguet de Graffigny, whom she had married while still very young. Something of a psychopath, he had not only kept her in penury but regularly beat her, until she managed to have him sent to prison, where he died. Destitute but for the small pension granted her by the regent, Elisabeth d'Orléans, she nevertheless moved in the best circles at the court of Lunéville, where her wit and intelligence constituted a ready passport and a reliable bread-ticket. Among her close friends she counted a rather insipid poet and hanger-on, François Etienne Devaux, whose immaturity was reflected in the childhood nickname, Panpan, by which he was known. While she cared for him as for a poodle, the man she loved was an army officer, Léopold Desmarest, who would presently come to fetch her from Cirey and take her to Paris (where she would become companion to the duchesse de Richelieu). For her, life was beginning at the age of forty-three.

When she arrived on 4 December 1738 at two o'clock in the morning, exhausted and covered in mud, Françoise de Graffigny was warmly wel-comed. Her hosts were keen to hear news of the court at Lunéville where in the preceding year Stanislas Leszczynski, father of the Queen of France, had been installed by his son-in-law as the ruler of Lorraine and permitted to retain the courtesy title of King of Poland. Louis XV had put his own man, M. de la Galaizière, in charge of the things that mattered – taxes, the courts, the civil administration of the duchy – which left the 'King' free to command his guard and preside over his court (and to enjoy the company of his mistress, the beautiful marquise de Boufflers). The two men understood each other perfectly, and with the annual allowance of 1,500,000 *livres* granted him out of the French purse Stanislas was able to live life on a regal scale. A palace and fine châteaux, servants galore, the best food and wine that money could buy, and the most accomplished of musical and theatrical entertainments. In short, a mini-Versailles and something to make the inhabitants of Cirey almost regret their rustic isolation.

Mme de Graffigny for her part was most intrigued to see life at Cirey from the inside. So many rumours, so many stories . . . what was the reality? To begin with she was rather shocked to discover that the alleged luxury of this earthly paradise did not extend to the guest rooms, nor even that of Émilie's tolerant husband. Perhaps the soldier in him would have considered undue home comforts detrimental to a ramrod military bearing, or perhaps his wife was keen not to dissuade him from returning to the delights of his army encampment. At any rate the rooms in the old part of the house were large, draughty and shabbily decorated, with huge fireplaces that let in more air than they generated heat. But life was much more agreeable in the new wing, reached by a door at the foot of the main staircase. A tiny hallway gave on to Voltaire's own room. Evidently designed for warmth in winter, it was quite small, with a low ceiling, and hung with crimson velvet that kept out the draughts and retained the heat from the fire. An alcove, surrounded by a gold fringe, contained his bed. The wood-panelled walls were decorated not with tapestries (as in the older part of the house) but with paintings neatly framed by the panels. Lacquer corner-cabinets held displays of porcelain, while a clock supported by marabou storks told the time. Mme de Graffigny's eyes widened at the spectacle of expense and good taste: a canteen containing a silver service (presumably the safest place for it) and a jewellery box containing an assortment of rings mounted with cut stones. Oh, the diamonds! And everything was so spotlessly clean, she said, she could have kissed the parquet floor.

Beyond Voltaire's room one passed into a gallery some thirty or forty feet long with lacquered yellow panelling. Here, too, warmth was paramount, and a stove set into the wall pumped out the heat. Work was currently in hand to conceal this essential technology behind a statue of Cupid loosing an arrow. At whom? Between the windows that punctuated the other side of the gallery stood two pedestals, the one bearing a statue of Venus, the other of Hercules. At the centre a door opened on to the garden, and the outside of the door bore the depiction of an ornamental grotto wherein gods might disport. Thus did these playful lover-scientists see themselves. On either side of the soon-to-be-camouflaged stove stood two large cupboards: one for books, the other for scientific instruments. For the latter this was a temporary home until the camera obscura (for testing Newtonian optics) and the laboratory (for other physics experiments) were ready to accommodate them. The furnishing in the gallery was at once functional and decorative: looseleaf tables, writing-desks, one sofa, a few rather unforgiving chairs, more porcelain, sundry clocks. Portable screens adorned with exquisitely patterned paper matched those panels that had been similarly covered.

But Mme de Graffigny had seen nothing yet. Émilie's personal suite was an object of wonder. First, there was the bathroom with tiled walls and ceiling and a marble floor. Then came her dressing-room (*cabinet de toilette*). Beneath a painted ceiling the lacquered wood-panelled walls were a pale and subtle green, each panel framed by gilded mouldings. In the corners stood perfectly proportioned cabinets. A small sofa and a selection of delicate armchairs occupied the centre, while around the walls were displayed a fine array of porcelain and engravings. In her bedroom the panelling was a pale yellow and similarly lacquered, while the recessed bed was upholstered in pale blue moiré silk. Everything was in yellow and blue, even the dog-baskets. And the furniture gleamed: armchairs, corner-cabinets, a bureau, a writing-desk, silver-framed mirrors. A large door with mirror-panels led into the unfinished library, where the Veroneses were to hang.

To one side of the recessed bed lay a private cloakroom (*garderobe*) with its essential commode (*chaise percée*). The floor was of marble, and the walls were covered in grey linen panelling hung with prints: embroidered muslin curtains prettily framed the windows. To the other side of the bed a plain wooden door opened into a delightful little blue-panelled boudoir. Its ceiling had been painted in the style of Martin, a leading contemporary artist: one of his students had been working at Cirey for the past three years. Beneath this beautiful ceiling each tiny wall-panel was decorated with a Watteau miniature. Some of the miniatures depicted the five senses, others evoked two of La Fontaine's fables: each was surrounded by gold filigree. One corner of the room was taken up by a fireplace, the others by cabinets or shelves designed by Martin. One displayed an amber writing-box (*écritoire*) given to Mme du Châtelet by Frederick of Prussia. The only seating was a large armchair covered in white taffeta, with two stools to match. Daylight came from a French window that led out on to a terrace at the back of the château, and from it Émilie could gaze across the gardens towards the river valley and the woods beyond. It must all have helped her not to miss Paris too much. And Mme de Graffigny – who had seen some impressive châteaux in her time – was speechless: 'if I had an apartment like that, I would have myself woken in the night just to look at it.'[10]

But her first experience of supper at Cirey was a disappointment. The food was not copious, though it was served on solid silver, and the setting in the gallery – surrounded by globes and scientific instruments – was surprising to say the least. On her left Voltaire was an assiduous and attentive host, but on her right the marquis du Châtelet seemed rather quiet – and indeed left the table as soon as the meal was over. An ailing cousin of the marquis was also present, the marquis du Châtelet de Trichâteau, who was the object of much deferential concern since his hosts were rather hoping he might leave them his extensive estates. After supper Mme de Graffigny received visits in her draughty and ill-heated room: from Mme de Champbonin, whom she judged a kindly woman utterly devoted to Voltaire and likely to be a useful source of gossip; and from M. du Châtelet, who shared with her his seemingly inexhaustible knowledge of the Lothringian aristocracy, not to mention some elaborate accounts of his military exploits. Afterwards she was left alone to peruse the reading matter that Voltaire had kindly lent her: his book on Newton, and his latest attack on Desfontaines, *Le Préservatif* (because it would preserve the reader from the abbé's errors), a work intended by Voltaire as revenge for Desfontaines's role in the Jore affair.

In the days and weeks that followed Mme de Graffigny had much time for reading, since guests were expected to fit in with their hosts' timetable. But the suppers turned out to be more entertaining than on the first day. She enjoyed one particular magic-lantern show when Voltaire used the projected images as prompts for a witty impersonation of the duc de Richelieu and his art of seduction. The sex life of the abbé Desfontaines was another favourite pretext for caricature. If there was a sufficient number of guests – and guests of the

right calibre – then a play was performed: *Boursoufle*, for example, for which
Mme du Châtelet's twelve-year-old daughter was fetched from her convent.
Though he had usually written the play in question, Voltaire sometimes knew
his lines rather less well than the other members of the cast, but it was his
privilege – and talent – to improvise, often bringing the show to a halt as
everyone else collapsed in helpless laughter. And of course he was not the only
talented performer present: Mme du Châtelet was a gifted actress, and she was
often requested to sing. Eventually Mme de Graffigny was prevailed upon to
tell the story of her unhappy life: it reduced Voltaire to tears.

The longer she stayed, the more critically Mme de Graffigny assessed the
happy couple. She found Voltaire's preoccupation with his health irritating
and considered his fastidiousness about diet probably counter-productive.
Even worse, his obsessive hatred of Desfontaines and Rousseau became
tedious in the extreme. As to Mme du Châtelet, she admired her intellect
greatly but was wary of her rather volatile and temperamental character.
Émilie seemed to fuss a lot, and she could see how her fussing made Voltaire
cross. Not only did she keep his manuscripts under lock and key, she also
kept a sharp eye on what he drank (Rhine wine was bad for his digestion)
and what he wore (he looked silly in too much lace). Rows were relatively
commonplace, if brief, though the fact that they were often conducted in
English meant that it was quite difficult to tell who was winning. After some
three weeks it began to look as if there were some serious rift between them,
and François in particular seemed especially taciturn and cast down. The
reason, as it transpired, was once more Desfontaines. In *Le Préservatif* Voltaire
had attacked the abbé's latest periodical, *Observations sur les écrits modernes*
(*Observations concerning Contemporary Writings*), by listing all the erroneous and
foolish comments made by the 'observer' and then finishing with a letter
detailing the abbé's imprisonment at Bicêtre and the ingratitude shown by
him towards his subsequent benefactors. Desfontaines had now replied in *La
Voltairomanie* (*Voltairomania*), a devastating attack fuelled by a very genuine and
very considerable anger. Each of Voltaire's works is slammed on specific and
not necessarily unreasonable grounds, but most of all it is the egotistical
vanity of the man – Voltaire's mania for Voltaire – that so deeply infuriates
Desfontaines. Not a single criticism of his works can be voiced, it seems,
without attracting the most violent and personal counter-attack. *Le Temple du*

Goût – in which, it is perfectly true, Voltaire had mocked many writers and artists, living or dead – is the work of 'a small mind drunk on arrogant pride', while the man himself is 'a foolish and reckless writer, for whom neither morals, nor the conventions of polite society, nor humanity, nor truth, nor religion have ever been in the remotest degree sacred'. And so it goes on. Voltaire is accused of mendacity and acting under false pretences, of chicanery and sundry frauds, of a high-handed disregard for others and a readiness to ride roughshod over the demands of decency and justice.

La Voltairomanie was probably the most sustained and detailed piece of vilification to which Voltaire was ever subjected throughout his life, and there were many similar. It found its mark, especially when Desfontaines recalled the Rohan-Chabot affair, which had been – with the possible exception of his mysterious departure from England at the end of 1728 – Voltaire's darkest hour. And it found its mark doubtless because the missile was well directed. Its target was not the most scrupulous of businessmen, and the damage caused as he lay about him with his sharp-edged pen was sometimes needless and often disproportionate. Desfontaines, of course, neglects the honourable values and objectives for which Voltaire was fighting, but in focusing on the obsessive, almost paranoid energies of this driven, mercurial temperament he was simply magnifying what several people thought. Voltaire was a vain exhibitionist who cared about nobody but himself, a wheeler-dealer opportunist, an arrogant shyster riding for a fall. Desfontaines's pamphlet sold 2,000 copies in a fortnight.

Voltaire and Mme du Châtelet both received a copy of *La Voltairomanie* on 26 December, and each then thought they were concealing its existence from the other. Hence the tense and taciturn atmosphere noted by Mme de Graffigny. The marquise was now controlling the arrival and dispatch of the post even more assiduously than before, trying to keep from Voltaire the news of the furore raging in Paris while also endeavouring to ensure that he did not fan its flames with any ill-advised letters or verses to friends. Or that anyone else did. Unfortunately Mme de Graffigny had been indiscreet in her correspondence with Panpan, sending him passages from *Le Siècle de Louis XIV* and reporting the gist of those sections of *La Pucelle* that Voltaire had recently read to her aloud (having obtained Émilie's permission to have access to his own manuscripts). On the evening of 29 December Voltaire visited Mme de Graffigny in her room and told her that he would have to flee to Holland because, so it appeared, *La Pucelle* was now circulating in manuscript in Lunéville. When she showed no signs of penitence or guilt, he lost his temper and accused her of leaking the material. She assured him that she had taken no copy of the poem. Enter Émilie in highest dudgeon, brandishing Panpan's latest letter to Mme de Graffigny (in which he referred to *La Pucelle*) and accusing her guest of stealing the original from her (locked) bureau. Voltaire had physically to restrain Mme du Châtelet, who was beside herself with rage at the thought of Mme de Graffigny's supposed treachery and with alarm at the possible consequences for Voltaire. But the latter soon realized what had happened: Panpan had been overheard referring to his correspondent's account of *La Pucelle*, and that person had then alerted Mme du Châtelet, who had immediately imagined a full-scale pirated edition. Still Émilie continued to rant, until five in the morning, leaving Mme de Graffigny in a state verging on seizure. The kindly Mme de Champbonin found her vomiting and trembling uncontrollably.

Mme de Graffigny would have left at once had she had the means and the escort. Voltaire sought to repair the damage done by his companion's histrionics, but Mme du Châtelet continued to open her guest's letters and barely spoke to her. At last Desmarest arrived, but good manners dictated that he stay for a while before accompanying Mme de Graffigny to her intended destination in Paris. Almost as though to forestall any awkward silences, Mme du Châtelet now initiated a frenzy of theatrical activity – Desmarest had been instructed by his mistress to prepare for certain roles in advance – and together they performed play after play. And one or two operas, which occasionally required the two ladies to share a duet. Ever the perfect hosts, Voltaire and Mme du Châtelet tried to persuade Desmarest and Mme de Graffigny to stay on until the spring – though Mme de Graffigny thought that this was because Émilie had taken a fancy to her escort – but, no doubt to the relief of all parties, the couple left on 12 February 1739.

Meanwhile, on 3 January, Voltaire had told Mme du Châtelet that he knew all about *La Voltairomanie*. At first he seemed to be reacting calmly, so much so that he had begun a new play, *Zulime*. But he was plotting – and trying to deal with the fact that Thiriot had betrayed him with Desfontaines. Originally Thiriot had said that Desfontaines had written a pamphlet against Voltaire on being released from Bicêtre and that he, Thiriot, had made him destroy it. In *La*

Voltairomanie Desfontaines claimed that he had never written such a pamphlet, that this was just another of Voltaire's terrible lies; and Thiriot now said he couldn't quite remember . . . The entire Cirey household, it seems, began to write to him: Mme du Châtelet, who hated him; her husband, who urged Thiriot to uphold Voltaire's good name; Mme de Champbonin, begging him to see reason; and Voltaire, who appealed to their friendship of twenty-five years' standing. And throughout January Mme du Châtelet, Thiriot and Voltaire all corresponded with Crown Prince Frederick, who seemed remarkably well informed about the whole business . . . and eventually pressed Thiriot to make a public statement in support of Voltaire. But, for the moment, Thiriot refused. Not so the wonderful Mme de Bernières (separated, widowed and remarried since those days in Rouen), who wrote a letter to her former lover carefully and indignantly refuting Desfontaines's allegations about his behaviour twelve years earlier. Voltaire was deeply touched and deeply grateful, returning the letter to her as she requested but taking numerous copies which he then dispatched to his allies in Paris (d'Argental, the marquis d'Argenson) and to the authorities (Maurepas, Hérault). Why? In part to try to restore his reputation, and in part to prepare the ground for his next move: court proceedings against Desfontaines. Much to Émilie's despair. But it was less her despair than the characteristic good sense of d'Argental and the inside knowledge of the well-connected d'Argenson that gradually dissuaded Voltaire from this doomed course. Two days after the departure of Mme de Graffigny he finally renounced his plan to institute formal legal proceedings against Desfontaines in the *parlement* of Paris.

On this occasion discretion was indeed the better part of valour, but it pained Voltaire exceedingly. Some three weeks later d'Argental managed to get Thiriot to sign a satisfactory statement, partly thanks to further pressure from the interfering Frederick (because a Thiriot reconciled with Voltaire would be much more use to him than a stubborn ally of Desfontaines). Next it was proposed that both Desfontaines and Voltaire – who had in any case never admitted authorship of *La Voltairomanie* and *Le Préservatif* – should each sign official statements disavowing the allegations made in each pamphlet. Desfontaines did so on 4 April, and Voltaire finally followed suit – in craftily ambiguous wording – on 2 May. Peace. For now. In any case it was time to help Émilie, who had some court proceedings of her own to attend to.

CHAPTER TEN

Court Proceedings: Berlin or Paris? (1739–1745)

In which a bourgeois gentleman becomes a Gentleman in Ordinary

WHEN VOLTAIRE AND Mme du Châtelet left Cirey for Brussels on 11 May 1739, it was the end of a chapter in their relationship. Apart from a six-month stay in 1744, never again would they spend so much time together far from the madding crowd; and while Cirey remained Voltaire's base for the next ten years, he henceforth resumed the more nomadic existence to which he had been accustomed before publication of the *Lettres philosophiques*. The safe-house had been useful – and very comfortable – but it had also become something of a prison. The locals themselves seemed to recognize that the couple's departure marked the passing of an era. M. de Champbonin, writing to his son a few days later, remembered Voltaire with great fondness and gratitude: 'Never has there been a friend with a kinder heart or more worthy of respect.' And he observed wistfully: 'The happy times we spent with him must remind you, my son, as it reminds us, of all the marks of friendship that he bestowed upon us. [. . .] He leaves adored by the whole district, and we all lament his absence.'[1]

The immediate reason for the journey to Brussels was a court case that Mme du Châtelet had recently reopened concerning the rightful ownership of some estates at Beringhen and Ham, not to mention a little principality near Cleves. While the prospect of becoming a princess no doubt had its charms, the promise of substantial extra income was even more exciting, and she hoped that the long evenings with her relative Trichâteau would now pay dividends as she renewed the sixty-year-old dispute with a rival branch of her family. Conscious that the proceedings might no doubt last another sixty years, she had taken not only Voltaire along with her but also a new mathematics tutor, the Swiss Samuel König, whom Maupertuis had recommended to her during a rapid visit to Cirey in March. For not only was Mme du Châtelet continuing with her translation of the *Principia*, she was also writing – ostensibly for the educational benefit of her son – her own account of Newtonian physics, the *Institutions de physique*, begun the previous year and eventually published to considerable acclaim in 1740.

In Brussels the couple rented a fine house on the rue de la Grosse Tour, on the edge of the medieval city, taking separate floors for the sake of appearances. Voltaire promptly announced their arrival by throwing an extravagant party complete with fireworks. Styling himself the Ambassador of Utopia on the invitations, Voltaire felt that he had caught the intellectual measure of the place when he discovered that no one understood what 'Utopia' meant, or indeed where it was! (Jean-Baptiste Rousseau, living close by, would have got the joke, but then he was certainly not invited. He was busy having Desfontaines's *La Voltairomanie* republished in Holland.) Alas, the firework display was somewhat marred when two helpers fell from a third-floor window, and Émilie was scathing about the vulgarity of François's decision to display a gaming term in flaming letters as the centrepiece of the show. She did not like being teased about her weakness for gambling. Things scarcely improved when they went to stay with the duc d'Arembourg at his nearby château. He had not a book nor an idea to his name, and they spent much of the time playing cards, admiring his beautiful garden, and drinking some Hungarian wine that Frederick had kindly sent them as a present. They did perform Molière's *L'École des Femmes* together, having persuaded the duke's companion, the princesse de Chimay, to join them in taking a role. But boredom soon returned. Three weeks was quite long enough: it was time for work.

For Mme du Châtelet this meant closeting herself away with König, while for Voltaire the immediate tasks in hand were two new plays, *Zulime* and *Mahomet*, both set in the world of 'the Orient' – about which he was also reading extensively in preparation for what would eventually become his history of the world, the *Essai sur les mœurs* (*Essay on the Manners and Spirit of the*

Nations). But in the middle of August — and after a distinct lack of progress with her court case — Mme 'Pompon-Newton' proposed a visit to Paris, where their friend, the duchesse de Richelieu, was in the throes of a difficult pregnancy . . . and spitting blood. She had less than a year to live. Once more for the sake of appearances the couple took separate accommodation, Mme du Châtelet at the house of her friend, Voltaire in a hotel in the Marais (while M. du Châtelet and König were packed off to Émilie's mother's at Créteil). But together they participated in the celebrations then taking place to mark the marriage of the King's sister to the Crown Prince of Spain. More fireworks. And there were innumerable supper parties: with old friends (Cideville, the d'Argentals, Mme de Champbonin), dubious friends (an increasingly antagonistic Mme de Graffigny, a forgiven Thiriot), and influential friends (de Mairan, Réaumur, Buffon, Fontenelle, all members of the Académie des Sciences). Nevertheless even Voltaire began to weary of Parisian gaiety and hanker after the backwater of Brussels. Moreover the stress of keeping up with the indefatigable queen of his heart had made him ill.

The duchesse de Richelieu wished to leave Paris for her family home at Chaumont, south of Cirey, and so Mme du Châtelet agreed to accompany her towards the end of October — without König, who had had enough of Cirey, Brussels, and especially his pupil. Voltaire, alone and ailing, now learnt on 24 November that the police had seized copies of an unauthorized miscellany of some of his unpublished works that included the opening pages of *Le Siècle de Louis XIV* and a poem dating from 1732, the 'Ode sur le fanatisme' ('Ode on Fanaticism'). In this poem he had extolled the good sense of Émilie's deism in contrast to the murderous and implicitly unChristian fanaticism of religious zealots. That safe-house in Champagne began to look attractive again, and he reached it within forty-eight hours. Just in time, no doubt, since one week later the Paris *parlement* gave orders for *Le Siècle de Louis XIV* to be ceremonially burned (for its implicit critique of Louis XV). But was Cirey safe enough? After all, it was still in France. Voltaire proceeded on at once to Brussels, while Mme du Châtelet returned to Paris from Chaumont and tried, once again, to mend fences and build bridges on her companion's behalf. And to see if she could make König change his mind. She could not, no more than she could persuade a no less distinguished and no less Swiss alternative, Jean Bernoulli, who had accompanied Maupertuis on his recent visit to Cirey. She was not the most docile of pupils nor the most restful of companions. Voltaire, for his own part, was delighted by the breakdown in relations with König, for he held him responsible for persuading his friend of the merits of Leibnizian metaphysics. This nonsense about monads and the best of all possible worlds and God having had a 'sufficient reason' to do everything . . . 'It is highly deplorable,' he later wrote to Maupertuis, 'that a French woman like Mme du Châtelet should have given her mind over to the spinning of such spiders' webs.'[2] And to make the point he published his own *Métaphysique de Newton* in Amsterdam almost on the same day that his companion's *Institutions de physique* appeared from Prault in Paris (with an opening chapter that offers an accomplished résumé of Leibnizian thought).

Hungarian wine had not been the only gift from Frederick. At the end of 1739 he sent the couple the first twelve chapters of his most recent work, in which he rejected the cynical *Realpolitik* set out in Machiavelli's classic work, *The Prince*. The Prussian heir-apparent, now twenty-seven, professed his adherence instead to a policy of non-violent and altruistic humanitarian rule in which the personal interests of the sovereign are set aside in the name of virtue and reason and for the better good of his people. Voltaire's lessons of tolerance and pacifism had apparently borne fruit, and even Mme du Châtelet began to warm to her rival, being now 'curious to see this phenomenon on the throne'.[3] Indeed this throne now beckoned, for Frederick's father was gravely ill, and died soon afterwards on 31 May 1740. Alas, as the moment approached, Frederick began to regret some of his expansiveness and warned Voltaire that he could not let the work appear under his own name. He had been rather too frank about a number of other princes. Nevertheless the new king appeared to remain true to his ideals when, one week into his reign, he wrote to his French friend and fellow-*philosophe*: 'By God, write to me only as man to man, and share in my disdain for all titles and names and outward glory.'[4] At this particular moment Voltaire was preoccupied by the failure of his latest tragedy, *Zulime*, which – as he had rather feared – was poorly constructed and, despite its intriguing multiracial *dramatis personae*, proved much too sugary and sentimental for the Parisian public ('his worst tragedy,' commented one critic).[5] He asked d'Argental to have it taken off at once and instructed Mlle Quinault to ensure that no copy reached a pirate press. Moreover he had upset the duc de Richelieu, whose wife was now very seriously ill (she died six weeks later) and who thought that his friend might have had the decency to postpone his latest premiere.

But if the news from Paris was disappointing and sad, the latest letters from King Frederick were becoming a cause for deep concern. True, he had at once refounded the Berlin Academy and – like the wealthy owner of a twenty-first-century football club – had signed up the best international talent he could seduce with money and luxury-living. 'I have acquired Wolff, Maupertuis, Vaucanson, Algarotti,' he informed Voltaire (with a revealing choice of verb), 'and I am waiting for a reply from 'sGravesande and Euler.'[6] But he had also signed up sixteen new battalions for his army, plus five squadrons of hussars, and a squadron of guards. Was this the behaviour of an anti-Machiavelli? Needless to say, he would like to have 'acquired' Voltaire also, but he realized full well that the attachment to Mme du Châtelet was insuperable (and of course she couldn't come too). And he duly told the lady so: 'I bear you no ill will, Mme du Châtelet, but may I be allowed to envy you that which you possess, and which I would prefer to own in preference to many of the other possessions I have recently inherited.'[7] The language – and later his actions – give the lie to any notion that Frederick viewed human beings as anything but pawns and objects in the pursuit of his own private and public ends. So much for 'man to man'.

But if he could not possess Voltaire, he could at least order him about, and he duly bade him ensure that his *Anti-Machiavel* (*Against Machiavelli*) was withdrawn from the printers. It was on no account to be published. When Voltaire reached The Hague on 20 July 1740, he found the publisher – Van Duren – unsurprisingly reluctant to comply, not even for ready money. For there was yet more ready money to be made out of publishing a royal book. So Voltaire sabotaged it, amending the manuscript in such an intrusive and bizarre way as to render it unpublishable. Van Duren published anyway but sued. Not content, Voltaire then secured permission from a busy Frederick to amend the text as he saw fit and to publish a revised edition, which indeed proved highly successful. Except that it was now largely Voltaire's own work: Frederick disclaimed authorship. The original text, with its contradictions and inconsistencies (and approval of powerful armies), had reflected the profound ambiguity at the heart of Prussia's new ruler. Voltaire, his erstwhile 'tutor', had simply amended what he did not wish to read or believe.

And if Frederick could not possess Voltaire, he could also at least meet him – and they set eyes on each other for the first time on 11 September 1740, at the Château de Moyland, some five miles outside Cleves (and 150 miles north-east of Brussels). It was night-time, and the philosopher-king had flu: 'In a small room, lit by a single candle,' Voltaire later wrote, 'I saw a modest-sized bed some two and a half feet wide, and on it a little man wrapped in a thick blue dressing-gown. It was the King, sweating and shivering beneath a scruffy blanket and running a very high temperature.'[8] Despite his fever Frederick rose from his bed to have supper with Voltaire, in the company of Maupertuis, Algarotti and Keyserlingk (he who had once visited Cirey in search of the latest Voltaire manuscripts). The visitor was impressed by Frederick's lack of ceremony and his simple readiness to speak his mind, while the young Prussian king was filled with admiration and delight to hear the philosopher-poet recite extracts from *Mahomet*. The intimate excitement and mutual congratulations of their epistolary relationship had survived a flesh-and-blood encounter in the least auspicious of circumstances, and the temptations of life at Frederick's court now seemed particularly real to a Voltaire who had grown weary of being hounded for every word he wrote. As Mme du Châtelet well knew. Anxiously she confided to Maupertuis: 'I do hope [Frederick] will soon send me back the man with whom I intend to spend the rest of my life. I only lent him for a few days.'[9]

And how could she keep him when he did return? The implausible turn that Voltaire's existence took over the next five years suggests a clever strategy on the part of the divine Émilie. If her dear companion was minded to be a courtier, then let him try the French court first. As Voltaire returned to Holland to work on his own *Anti-Machiavel*, Mme du Châtelet headed for Paris, where her mother had recently died. But instead of returning directly to Brussels and the tedium of the ongoing legal proceedings, she travelled on to Fontainebleau where the King and Queen were in residence, and took advantage of that *tabouret* she was allowed to sit on. It was time to play her court card – of which she promptly, if obliquely, informed Frederick by letter on 10 October. Her trump card, on the other hand, was the knowledge that

Voltaire's close friendship with Frederick could be useful to France as it came to terms with the new king's accession and vainly attempted to second-guess his political and military intentions. Soon Cardinal Fleury was extending a forgiving hand of friendship to the author of the *Lettres philosophiques* and the French ambassador in Holland was lending his support to the idea of a Voltairean 'mission' to Berlin. Though he covered himself by warning Fleury about some of the irreligious opinions expressed in the *Anti-Machiavel*, the Cardinal turned a pragmatic blind eye: the opportunity was too good to miss.

Which is just what Voltaire thought, too. For he had wanted to go and see Frederick's court at first hand, and now he could pretend to be pleasing Émilie by doing just that. Never the patient diplomat and perhaps unwilling to be the lady's puppet, he immediately set off without waiting for the official word, informing Fleury on 26 November that 'I have followed the orders that your Eminence has not given me.'[10] Except that Émilie wasn't at all pleased, as she told the duc de Richelieu:

> I obtain for M. de Voltaire an honourable return to the country of his birth, I restore him to ministerial favour, I open doors to the Academies, in short I give him back within the space of three weeks everything that he has done his utmost to lose over the last six years, and how does he reward such devotion and zeal? He leaves for Berlin and informs me just like that, knowing full well that his matter-of-fact tone will pain me deeply.

But her shrewdness and her love are unabated: 'But, do you know, the thing that worries me most [. . .] is how terribly hurt M. de Voltaire is going to be when his infatuation with the Prussian court wears off.'[11] How right she was, and how sadly ironic that she never lived to see the full measure of that hurt . . .

As Mme du Châtelet shared these thoughts with her ex-lover, Voltaire was being fêted in Berlin and finding the new king's assiduities rather exhausting. There was something excessive, even disingenuous, about all these concerts and balls, all this feasting and card-playing, and he began to view with some distaste the egotistical flirtations of his promiscuously homosexual host. Though Voltaire's body was probably not the object of

Frederick's desire, his person certainly was, and the visitor felt uncomfortable
– not least when the putative pacifist absented himself to go and play with
his armies. What *was* he up to? The Emperor Charles VI had died that
October, leaving no male heir to the Habsburg throne and designating (by
the so-called 'Pragmatic Sanction') his daughter, the Archduchess Maria
Theresa, to succeed him as ruler of Austria, Hungary and Bohemia. (As a
woman she could not become Holy Roman Emperor, but her husband,
Francis, Duke of Lorraine, could – and did in 1745.) The husbands of the late
emperor's nieces – the Electors of Saxony and Bavaria – rather thought that
one of them should succeed. Spain was opposed to Maria Theresa, while
France (meaning Fleury) was beginning to regret its decision to recognize her
and contemplated seeking an alliance with Prussia in support of the Elector
of Bavaria. Frederick, for his part, simply saw a golden opportunity to seize
Silesia, to which his country had been laying claim since 1537.

Power relations within the European political theatre had thus become
particularly volatile, and Voltaire was not at all sure what part Frederick
meant to play in the forthcoming drama – except that the Prussian king
seemed to place little faith in the capacity of France or its armies to be of any
use to him whatsoever. When Mme du Châtelet was reduced to her
customary last resort of claiming to be seriously ill, it suited Voltaire to
play along, and he requested permission to leave – and to be reimbursed the
cost of his travel. Though he agreed, Frederick carped about the expense and
was unable to resist some valedictory bitchiness: '[Mme du Châtelet] must be
delighted [. . .] to see how promptly you obey her orders.'[12] He hated it
when a 'favourite' escaped his clutches. Voltaire's parting shot, to Maupertuis, was less feline: he merely called Frederick 'a most respectable,
singular, and amiable whore'.[13]

More relieved to have left Berlin than anxious to return to Brussels,
Voltaire broke his journey for two nights at the castle of Bückeburg, between
Hanover and Minden, where he was the guest of Count Albrecht-Wolfgang,
the ruler of this tiny, independent fiefdom, and his mistress the Countess
Bentinck, whom Voltaire had probably first met some years earlier in
Holland. She was a ravishing beauty, a highly intelligent reader of Newton
and Locke, and a fan. They would become great friends – and quite possibly
lovers. For the moment the traveller enjoyed the elegance and sophistication

of their civilized, Francophile court, buried in the middle of nowhere; but on 11 December he set off again, still travelling due west from Berlin and then by boat down the Rhine and along the Dutch coast. Though he wrote Frederick a flattering letter about his court and tried to refute the charge that he was at Émilie's beck and call, he was genuinely glad to be reunited with her. And she, already jealous of Frederick and now thoroughly disillusioned by the invasion of Silesia, was relieved: '[Frederick] can take all the provinces he wants as long as he does not deprive me of the charm of my life.'[14]

Exhausted and ill after his long journey, Voltaire soon recovered and began to put the finishing touches to *Mahomet*, which was first performed at Lille on 25 April 1741. His niece's husband, Nicolas Denis, had been appointed to a senior post in the military administration there, and his dear niece had herself instituted a salon that brought together some of the more enlightened and cultivated inhabitants of the city. At the Comédie-Française in Paris there had been a change of personnel: Mlle Quinault had retired, and her brother Dufresne had also left. Thus when the actor La Noue – whom Voltaire had met through Cideville in Rouen and who was now director of the Théâtre de Lille (and author of a *Mahomet II*) – suggested that they put the play on, Mme Denis's famous uncle leapt at the chance. Privately he was worried about La Noue's suitability for the role: he was small and thin and looked like a pet monkey, but in the event he performed the role of Mahomet 'better than Dufresne would have done'.[15] The premiere was a great success, and three further performances were given by public demand. During the interval of one such performance Voltaire appeared on stage and read out a letter from Frederick, announcing his victory at Mollwitz. Since a French alliance with Prussia against Austria was now very much in the wind (even though the 'whore' was secretly negotiating with the English), this was a propaganda coup for Frederick and a flattering moment for Voltaire, the would-be player on the world stage.

This aspiration – and the sense that he was indeed 'living' contemporary history from a privileged vantage-point – may have been sharpened by the historical research that he was continuing to carry out (notably in the extensive library of a Brussels resident, Johan de Witt). The author of *La Henriade* had been intending for some time to write a prose sequel in the form of an account of the Age of Louis XIV, and it was his pacifist intent to demonstrate that what had made that age great was not Louis's military campaigns but the extraordinary flowering of literary, cultural and scientific achievement over which he had presided and that he had in no small measure fostered. (Louis XV, please note.) Gradually Voltaire had extended his field of enquiry to three other 'great ages' in the history of (Western) man: Greece under Philip of Macedonia and Alexander the Great, Rome under Julius Caesar and Augustus, and the Italian Renaissance under the Medicis. On 1 June 1741 he wrote to Frederick of his intention to write a history with a broader focus than the Age of Louis XIV, and by 1743 he had produced the first draft of a history of Europe from Charlemagne (742–814) to the Emperor Charles V (1500–58). The new book would present 'the mind and spirit, the manners and usages, of the principal nations'[16] over many centuries. As was the case with the more limited study of France in the seventeenth century, the intention was to demonstrate and glorify the achievements of mankind, to show just what the human mind was capable of under conditions of peace, prosperity and enlightened rule – and just what was sacrificed by war and religious fanaticism. Through reason and tolerance human beings could become more and more civilized. Progress was possible . . . if only men and women would learn the lessons of the past and rise above violence, self-interest and petty enmities. If only.

As for Frederick, his future place in history remained unpredictable. On the one hand, he had signed a treaty with the French on 4 June under which he retained Silesia and Breslau and promised to support French efforts to have the Elector of Bavaria become emperor (which he did on 24 January 1742). But one year later Frederick ratted on his alliance with France and Spain and signed a peace treaty with Maria Theresa of Austria, in which she, too, agreed to his retention of Silesia. (Whereafter Frederick's subjects called him 'the Great'.) Interpreting this change of alliance as the act of a pacifist rather than of a Machiavellian opportunist, Voltaire wrote to praise the Prussian king: 'So you are no longer our ally, Sire? But you will be the ally of the human race instead.'[17] Unfortunately this letter found its way into the public domain, perhaps having been opened by the French secret police, and Voltaire was now accused of a lack of patriotism – just when *Mahomet* was about to be premiered at the Comédie-Française (on 9 August 1742). The play was a great success, but more trouble loomed. The Lille audience had interpreted *Mahomet* as an orthodox Christian attack on 'false' religions (its subtitle is '*ou le fanatisme*'), but the Parisians – and notably the Jansenists – saw a different message, or rather the old Voltairean message: that all official religions are an imposture in the service of political oppression.

In the play, the founder of Islam – Mahomet being derived from the Turkish for Muhammad (reflecting a prevalent eighteenth-century view of Islam as essentially the religion of the Ottoman Empire) – is presented as bent upon world domination: the East is sunk in decadence, the Arabs' hour has come. Opposed by the wise and elderly Zopire, who governs the city of Mecca, Mahomet decides with his second-in-command Omar to have Zopire assassinated – by the young and fanatical Séide (aided by his beloved Palmire). As the old man lies dying, the young couple discover that he is their father and call on the people of Mecca to revolt against Mahomet. But Omar has previously slipped Séide a slow-acting poison so that he dies in the middle of his rousing speech, as though struck down by Allah, and Palmire duly takes her own life as a young girl should. Stifling momentary feelings of remorse and compassion, Mahomet holds firm and proclaims the dominion of the new religion: 'I have deceived these mortals, but to myself I must be true' (V. iv). The parallel between Islamic fanaticism and Jansenist zealotry was plain to see, especially when a dying Palmire expresses the hope that 'some more just God may offer a future to innocent hearts'. Accordingly the Jansenists did everything they could to get the play banned.

Voltaire had taken the precaution of sending a copy to Cardinal Fleury, who took a relaxed view. (Now almost ninety, and with less than a year to live, he was perhaps losing the will to care.) So his new Lieutenant of Police, Feydeau de Marville, made no attempt to ban the play, despite the adverse opinion expressed by the official censor, Crébillon (who had no reason to help Voltaire). But when the Jansenist *parlement* objected, Fleury was keen to avoid a confrontation, and so Marville summoned Voltaire in the middle of the night (Mme du Châtelet accompanied him for moral support) and leant on him to withdraw the play by reminding him that the order for his arrest following publication of the *Lettres philosophiques* had still not been withdrawn. Furious, the playwright agreed; and *Mahomet* was not staged again until 1751.

Voltaire, of course, had not been entirely fair – to the Prophet Muhammad. The founder of Islam committed no such murder, he was a genuine visionary, the teaching of the Koran had brought dignity and moral discipline to a region given over to idolatry, and the Muslim world subsequently contributed handsomely to the glories of civilization – all of which the playwright later acknowledged as a historian in his completed *Essai sur les mœurs* (1756). But in the 1740s the subject did provide an opportunely oblique means of attacking all forms of religious fanaticism, especially that of the Jansenists; and the play has chilling contemporary resonance (now as then) in its depiction of the ease with which Mahomet and Omar transform the youthful idealism of Séide into murderous and inhuman zeal. 'Whoever dares to think for himself is not born to believe in me,' the Prophet warns the young man: 'Silent obedience shall be your only path to glory.' The effect is compelling – as it seems to be in Voltaire's dramatic productions each time he has a son kill his father – and *Mahomet* ranks among his finest plays. Once again the message is clear: tragedy is what comes of not allowing – and encouraging – people to think for themselves. The unfettered – but assumed-to-be-intelligent – use of human reason is the secular means to our no less secular salvation. Roll on the Enlightenment.

Near-nonagenarian or not, Fleury was still a key figure. After Voltaire had paid another brief visit (from Brussels) to Frederick at Aix-la-Chapelle (where the weary warrior was taking the waters in the late summer of 1742), he wrote to Fleury intimating that he could be of use to his country by reporting on the Prussian king's intentions towards it. Mme du Châtelet's strategy was now beginning to bear fruit. Frederick had offered him a fine house and gardens in Berlin, but Voltaire told Cideville proudly that he preferred 'my second floor in the house of Mme du Châtelet'.[18] He was wary of Frederick, he still cared deeply for Émilie, and of course he had always loved prestige and success. So, just as he had in his twenties, he resolved to become *persona grata* at the French court – by signalling his allegiance to Louis in his offer to inform on Frederick, and by seeking election to the Académie Française. But if he was to achieve the latter he would have to improve his reputation. Thus, when he returned to Paris in late November – with Mme du Châtelet, who wished to present her future son-in-law, the Duke of Montenero-Caraffa, at court – Voltaire did what he could to suppress the inevitable pirated version of *Mahomet* and an even more damaging five-volume edition of his 'works', which included a number of libellous pamphlets written against him and his closest friends.

This attempt – his first – to gain election to the French Academy was ill-prepared, but it served as a trial run, a demonstration of just where he needed to rewrite his C.V. And it sent a strong signal of his wish to be accepted by the Establishment. However, he still lacked the support of key salon figures, and, needless to say, the Church was strongly opposed. The winner was the highly successful comic dramatist, novelist and journalist, Pierre de Marivaux. Elections to the Academy were political events, and in this case Marivaux's election was part of a broader strategy, supported by the duc de Richelieu, to weaken Maurepas's ministerial influence over the King. The duc, who had himself been elected to the Academy at a very young age (thanks to his connections), therefore reluctantly voted against his friend. But the political climate was gradually changing, and other schoolboy connections were now coming to prominence. The Minister of War, François-Victor de Breteuil (Émilie's cousin but most distinctly not a freethinker) died of 'apoplexy' on 9 January 1743, to be replaced by the comte d'Argenson. The comte's elder brother, the marquis, would become Foreign Minister at the end of the following year.

Fleury himself died on 29 January and, being one of the forty so-called 'Immortals' (waggish critics called them the 'Invalids'), thereby precipitated another Academy election. As luck would have it, Voltaire's credentials as the leading dramatist of his day were spectacularly readvertised by the triumph of another tragedy, *Mérope*, completed four years earlier but first staged on 20 February 1743. Summoned by audience acclaim, its author appeared in the box of the duchesse de Luxembourg and received a standing ovation lasting a full fifteen minutes. The play's ingredients are familiar: a widowed queen, a no-good aspirant to her hand and throne, a long-lost son who returns, is nearly murdered but eventually avenges the murder of his father and brothers – and becomes king, whereupon a roll of thunder seems to indicate to the assembled populace that his accession has met with divine approval. The play's success, however, derived from an unusually coherent plot, from an especially poignant scene at the end of Act IV when the royal mother risks her life for her son and declaims a speech worthy of Racine, and above all from the brilliant and moving performance of Mlle Dumesnil in the title-role. (As Voltaire modestly noted subsequently, that was why the play would be much less successful when read.) And once again, of course, the tragedy was not a tragedy. Virtue and justice triumph: the feel-good factor was secure.

But Voltaire's second attempt at securing election to the Academy failed like the first. Following Fleury's death, the King's closest religious adviser was Boyer, formerly Bishop of Mirepoix and now tutor to the King's son. He was no admirer of Voltaire, however good his plays might be. Like most churchmen he regarded the author of the 'Epître à Uranie' and the *Lettres philosophiques* as a godless and dangerous subversive – whereas, as we know, he was merely subversive. It was (and is) traditional in the Académie Française for the incoming Immortal to eulogize his predecessor, and the thought of the eminent cardinal being praised by the devil's advocate was simply too rich. Desperate to succeed, Voltaire wrote to Boyer, disowning the *Lettres* and protesting his purity: 'I can honestly say, as God is my witness, that I am a good citizen and a true Catholic, and I say this for the simple reason that I have always been so in my heart. I have not written a single page that does not radiate a love of humanity.'[19] In a sense – and no doubt to Voltaire's own keen, legal eye – this was not strictly a falsehood: as a deist he considered himself less removed from the teaching of Christ than the purveyors of incense and superstition. But of course Boyer was not fooled, and Voltaire's friends were dismayed that he could abase himself in this way, especially Frederick. (Whereupon Voltaire simply disowned the letter.)

On 22 March 1743 the Bishop of Bayeux, brother of the influential duc de Luynes, was elected to succeed Fleury at the Academy. Frederick had been waiting for his moment and now thought it had arrived: if Voltaire was to be so mistreated at home, why not come and live in Prussian luxury and under his sovereign protection? When Crébillon recommended that permission be withheld for the staging of *La Mort de César*, Frederick at once promised to have it performed in Berlin. It looked – and Voltaire allowed it to look – as though the time had indeed arrived for a parting of the ways. 'I shall abandon Minerva [Mme du Châtelet] for Apollo,' he wrote to Frederick in the middle of June. 'You, sire, are my greatest love, and in the end one must seek one's own satisfactions in this life.'[20] It was even rumoured that Voltaire had been exiled.

But one week earlier the King had decided to use Voltaire as his secret envoy. Though no war had yet been officially declared, things were going badly in the field for the French as they retreated before the Austrians and tasted defeat by the Hanoverians-cum-British at Dettingen. Richelieu, now increasingly influential, was clear that Frederick held the balance of power and that it was therefore vital to have him on the French side. Maurepas, the comte d'Argenson and other ministers concurred: Voltaire would be best placed to convince the Prussian king that France had the military and financial means to constitute a staunch and valuable ally. And Voltaire was pleased: to be able to have another taste of court life in Berlin no doubt, but above all to be important. As for Mme du Châtelet, she would be losing him for a time but at least his heart and loyalty still belonged to France and to her. Meanwhile she busied herself enlisting Maurepas's help to get the ban on *La Mort de César* lifted. She succeeded, but after the glorious triumph of *Mérope* the first night on 29 August was a lukewarm affair.

Since Frederick was away from Berlin reviewing his troops, Voltaire had begun his 'mission' in June by going to stay with the Prussian ambassador, the Count von Podewils, in The Hague (in a crumbling sixteenth-century palace that nevertheless survived until it was burned down in 1948). This youthful diplomat was having an affair with the wife of a high-ranking member of the Dutch government, and so the intrepid spy found himself with fortuitous access to an additional source of 'intelligence'. While the Dutch held a very poor opinion of French capabilities, they were not minded to support Maria Theresa, or the Hanoverian British, any more than they already were – which it was helpful to Louis and his ministers to know. And Frederick was getting cross with the Dutch for marching across his territory without permission. All of which Voltaire conveyed back to Paris in coded messages, some of them carried by his capable niece, Mme Denis, on her trips from Lille to Paris. The French ambassador in The Hague was impressed by the secret envoy's assiduity and skill and reported warmly to his superiors on the gentleman's devotion to his king. This was progress: the author of the *Lettres philosophiques* now mentioned in dispatches!

Not that Frederick did not realize full well what was going on. Deviously he sent his ambassador at Versailles an extract from Voltaire's mid-June letter, doctoring it so that both the King and Boyer appeared to be ridiculed for their stupidity. When there were no official repercussions after it was leaked, he knew that his philosopher friend had court backing for his visit. But he played along with him all the same: every minute that Voltaire spent in Berlin and Potsdam was a minute away from Émilie and a further chance to secure the great man's permanent presence at the Prussian court.

And Émilie was indeed beginning to suffer more and more. How could François be so cruel as to abandon her for such a long time (nearly four months)? The intervals between his letters were getting longer and longer. And now he had accompanied Frederick to Bayreuth, where Frederick's two charming sisters held court: Wilhelmine, who had married the Margrave of Bayreuth, and Ulrike, who would soon be Queen of Sweden. Life here was good: fine food and wine, beautiful gardens, excellent music, a constant round of operas and plays, of balls and supper-parties, of delightful female company and much sophisticated wit. As Frederick took himself off on military business, the would-be secret agent was fêted and flattered and entertained. It was easy to forget that he was on a mission.

But Voltaire still wanted to demonstrate his worth to the French king. If only he could bring home written evidence that Frederick regarded the French as serious and useful allies. The Prussian ruler, however, was playing a waiting game and refused to give his visitor what he wanted before his departure. Moreover he had formed the view that in military and political matters Voltaire was a lightweight, and that such influence as he was beginning to acquire at the French court was unlikely to endure. This lightweight had in turn formed the view that while Frederick would stop at nothing in the pursuit of his political ends, his love of the arts and his freethinking views on religion nevertheless made him a better king than most. The course of European history might yet be changed by the influence of Voltairean views. And so, even as he left Berlin, he promised to return.

By the time Voltaire reached Brussels on 6 November 1743, he and Mme du Châtelet had been apart for nearly five months. The marquise was bitterly hurt by what she regarded as her companion's indifference, while he for his part had become increasingly irritated by her possessiveness, illustrated most publicly and spectacularly when — at great expense — she had sent a dispatch rider to intercept him on his journey from The Hague to Berlin in August. As though to make his feelings clear, he had done nothing to hasten his journey home, spending six days at the court of Brunswick with another of

Frederick's sisters, and then travelling to Bückeburg in the hope of seeing Countess Bentinck (who was regrettably absent). Their eventual reunion brought forgiveness and a renewal of affection, but relations remained difficult and soon deteriorated again. Mme du Châtelet's gambling losses were further depleting her already meagre resources, and Voltaire began to set limits to his previous largesse. Gifts became loans. Then, on their return to Paris, she soon discovered that François was having an affair with the actress, Mlle de Gaussin, who had played Zaïre and Alzire in his plays and whose forte was the meltingly irresistible damsel in distress. Meanwhile M. du Châtelet, whom she had not seen for four years, was back at Cirey and asking her (and Voltaire) to join him there. A wife could but obey.

Following Voltaire's not altogether decisive contribution to Franco-Prussian diplomatic relations, the duc de Richelieu – now a First Gentleman of the King's Bedchamber and in charge of court entertainments – decided to further his friend's court career by enlisting his talents in a more obvious way: by asking him to write the libretto for a musical entertainment celebrating the forthcoming marriage of the Dauphin (aged seventeen) to the Infanta of Spain (aged twelve). Having been charged by the King with the task of negotiating the terms of this marriage, Richelieu was determined to crown his own diplomatic success with a great spectacle. The composer Rameau would provide the music. And so Voltaire, his passion for Mlle de Gaussin spent and himself once again ill, decided to accompany Mme du Châtelet back to Cirey in the spring of 1744. Perhaps the country air and the solitude would do him good, restoring his health and providing leisure in which to pursue his royal commission (with helpful advice from Émilie, that expert singer and actress). Piqued, Frederick informed Voltaire that he was 'unfurnishing' the house he had been preparing for him in Berlin.

The 'musical entertainment' that Voltaire had been asked to write was a 'comédie-ballet', a lavish spectacle of variously amusing or poignant scenes interspersed with dance and song. His brief was to celebrate the Bourbon lineage that united the French and Spanish royal families and to combine an idealized portrayal of love with amusing and decorous references to the circumstances of these glorious nuptials. It was to be called *La Princesse de Navarre*. Irony was out of the question. Which meant that it took Voltaire the best part of ten months and an awful lot of advice – from Mme du Châtelet, the d'Argentals, the marquis d'Argenson and others – to complete it. He hated every moment. But the fact that he stuck to the task in hand shows just how much he wanted to succeed at the French court. After four months at Cirey an outbreak of foot-and-mouth disease drove the couple back to Paris (M. du Châtelet having returned to the front): the local meat and dairy produce was no longer safe to eat. There they learnt that the King lay seriously ill at Metz (in Lorraine) following a visit to Flanders to rally his troops. The idea had been Richelieu's, and his opponents were making much of the physical risk to which he had exposed the monarch and of the moral risk to his soul represented by the fact that the King's latest mistress, the duchesse de Châteauroux (an ally of Richelieu's), had accompanied him on his military journey. But as the King recovered his health, so Richelieu's position was likewise restored. Voltaire could continue the pursuit of his courtly aspirations.

For the sake of the play he and his companion went to stay for several months with the duc de La Vallière – a key member of the King's retinue and possessor of one of the finest libraries in Europe – in his château at Champs (now Champs-sur-Marne). Where Richelieu's role was to organize public functions, La Vallière was charged with the King's private entertainments (a role that would later include pimping): his advice would be invaluable, especially as he was himself a talented actor. The duc and duchesse enjoyed high living, and their guests were among the wittiest and cleverest that nearby Paris had to offer. Some consolation, then, for the tedium of *La Princesse de Navarre*. As for the courtly aspirations, Voltaire and Mme du Châtelet attended the public festivities in Paris on 13 September to celebrate the King's recovery, which largely meant getting caught up in an enormous traffic jam, at some considerable risk to Émilie's diamonds, and then having to send out for some chicken from the local rotisserie.

They were present again on 14 and 15 November for the ceremonies to mark the King's return. *La Princesse de Navarre* was now ready for rehearsal, so the couple moved into temporary accommodation at Versailles, where the riding school was being converted into an enormous theatre for the forth-coming extravaganza. With Richelieu and the d'Argenson brothers all now key figures in Louis's administration, Voltaire and Mme du Châtelet felt that their royal hour had come. And with the marquis d'Argenson in particular newly appointed as Foreign Minister, a fellow *philosophe* had the ear of the King for the first time – and was urging an alliance with Frederick. But Voltaire still hated his play (and the uncooperative Rameau), and in his gloomier moments he despised himself for his craven role. 'Will you not sympathise,' he wrote to Cideville, 'with a poor devil who has become court jester at the age of fifty.'[21] And it was very hard work. Actors, actresses, dancers, singers, set designers, stagehands . . . all had to be marshalled and directed and told. Every nuance of the play's text was inspected for possible unseen slur or innuendo, while the flattery had to be carefully aimed and regulated according to the hierarchical sensitivities of its royal targets. To cap it all, his brother Armand – always the killjoy – died in Paris five days before the performance, which meant a funeral to attend and a will to administer. And what a will. Like father, like son. Armand (who never married, though he was alleged to have caused many a convulsion among lady Jansenists) had bequeathed half his estate to his brother and the other half to his two nieces and their husbands. But while they could have the capital, his wicked brother was to receive only the interest on his portion.

La Princesse de Navarre was performed on 25 February 1745. It was scheduled to begin at 6 p.m., but too many people had been allowed into the makeshift auditorium and some had to be removed before the King and his party eventually arrived at 7. The show ended at 10. The creaking plot for this royal celebration turns on the plight of the eponymous Princess of Navarre, Constance, who has ended up in the home of a Spanish country gentleman called Morillo as she flees from a variety of pursuers, including her guardian, Don Pedro, who is the tyrannical King of Burgos, and a handsome French soldier, the duc de Foix, who is keen to press his unwelcome suit. (Unwelcome because their two families are feuding.) The duc appears in disguise, purporting to be Alamir, a nondescript relative of Morillo – who for no apparent reason asks him to arrange a party. Not an undue burden perhaps, except that Morillo's daughter, the comically dim Sanchette, falls in love with 'Alamir' and thinks the party is for her. At which point Don Pedro's troops arrive to take Constance home to Burgos. Cue the beginning of 'Alamir's' party, with people dancing and singing to Rameau's music. 'Alamir' then declares his love for Constance, who accepts his offer of help without accepting his love (thinking him socially unsuitable). For a moment it looks as if the daft troops may abduct Sanchette by mistake, but when they come for Constance, 'Alamir' routs them — and disappears. Whereupon Constance realizes she loves him. Which is when he briefly returns — before dashing off again to fight for the French against Don Pedro. What a hero! Now Sanchette asks Constance to renounce 'Alamir' for her sake, which Constance broken-heartedly does (still thinking him socially unsuitable) — a scene played to tear-jerking perfection by the lovely Mlle de Clairon. Enter 'Alamir', who at last reveals his true identity, whereupon a delighted Constance consoles Sanchette by offering to find her another husband. But Morillo is inconsolable: he had loved Constance all along. Cue more singing and dancing, and a final flourish: at the back of the stage the Pyrenees gradually sink from view! France and Spain are one.

Everybody loved the music, but for many it was hard to hear what the actors were saying. Those who *could* hear were not sure they had the advantage. Wasn't it all just a little too flattering to the French? Would the Spanish visitors not take exception? But Louis, it seemed, was content, and the royal reward was great: an audience with the King, in which the humble courtier was promised an honorary position in the royal household (Gentleman in Ordinary to the Royal Bedchamber) as soon as one became vacant, appointed to the post of Historiographer Royal (for which Voltaire had asked), and accorded permission to attend in the royal apartments. Richelieu had done his friend a considerable favour. Zozo had arrived. And the historian had a key to the royal archives.

CHAPTER ELEVEN

The Way of the World (1745–1748)

The courtier courts disaster and his niece

FOR VOLTAIRE THE pleasures and advantages of courtly success were various but seldom unalloyed. Outwardly he was delighted. 'Behold, I am happy in this world,' he wrote to the librettist Moncrif in March 1745: 'and the prayers of Mme de Villars will secure me bliss in the next.'[1] All well and good, then. Except that he saw the irony: fame at last, but for what he himself regarded as no better than a fairground display ('une farce de la Foire').[2] And now that he had arrived, the thrill of the chase was gone. Writing a few weeks later to his new friend, the ex-soldier and like-minded *moraliste* the marquis de Vauvenargues, he noted that court life did not suit him at all and that he stayed 'more out of gratitude than self-interest'.[3] A fortnight later he and Mme du Châtelet were off to Châlons, where her son was ill with smallpox (he survived). Quarantine rules meant that they were forbidden to return to Versailles for a further forty days. Another cloud with a silver lining.

But life at court offered the prospect not only of writing history but also of making it, through his high-placed connections. As Foreign Minister the marquis d'Argenson was particularly important, since he was pursuing an alliance with Frederick as a means of securing peace throughout Europe. But the marquis had adversaries: Maurepas, Maurice de Saxe (a brilliant military leader who had recently come to prominence), and above all his own brother, whose job as Minister of War was to wage it not stop it – a policy the comte d'Argenson was much encouraged to pursue since he was making a personal fortune in the business of army supplies. So, too, as it happened, was Voltaire, also in association with the Pâris brothers, but these financial affairs did not prevent him from supporting the marquis d'Argenson vigorously in his pacific but doomed intent.

Meanwhile Voltaire noted the unexpected rise of a new ally, Jeanne-Antoinette Poisson, god-daughter of the financier Pâris-Monmartel (through whom he had met her). Born in 1721 and brought up at the château d'Etioles by a very wealthy tax-collector (her real father had been exiled for financial malpractice), this beautiful, intelligent and extremely well-educated young woman had first been obliged to marry her guardian's unappetizing son, for which the young couple were rewarded with the château itself − a fine place to institute a salon to rival those of Mmes de Tencin and de Geoffrin (where she herself was nevertheless warmly received). Guided by her mother, the Pâris brothers and the highly influential Mme de Tencin (who was seeking to secure that influence by providing the King with a compliant successor to the recently deceased duchesse de Châteauroux), Jeanne-Antoinette had succeeded in being noticed by the King − by turning up in the forest where he was hunting. Invited to the performance of *La Princesse de Navarre*, she found herself two days later being led away from a masked ball by the King himself . . . who then gallantly escorted her home the following morning. Now his officially recognized mistress, Mme d'Etioles (née Poisson) was about to be ennobled as the marquise de Pompadour. She admired Voltaire greatly and had much enjoyed acting in *Zaïre*: she would prove a staunch friend, as would her newly appointed mentor, the abbé de Bernis.

The King himself had departed once more for Flanders, in the Austrian Netherlands, where − in the company of his son the Dauphin, the marquis d'Argenson and other high-ranking members of the court − he presided over the famous French victory of Fontenoy on 11 May 1745. Having been present, he was deemed to have secured the victory personally over the British adversary (itself supported by Dutch and Austrian elements) and to have avenged the shaming defeat at Dettingen. In fact the victory was owed to the military prowess of the maréchal de Saxe and the brains of the duc de Richelieu. But sycophancy soon followed, not least from the pen of M. de Voltaire, whose poem celebrating the victory was permitted the honour of being dedicated to His Majesty. He would later, as Historiographer Royal, give a more nuanced account of the event in his history of the War of the Austrian Succession (the *Histoire de la guerre de 1741*), but for the moment it was imperative to be fulsome in one's praise and first into print. Once in print, he could revise the poem at leisure, and soon it grew from 100 to 350 lines. The rapid and apparently endless sequence of new editions, each one dropping yet more names than the last, was soon a cause for merciless parody. Desfontaines and his ilk enjoyed a glorious day on the field of polemical battle. After the fortieth edition of the poem people stopped counting. But Voltaire was more or less sincere in his praise. Since his illness and recovery at Metz the King had become a more human – and much more popular – figure in France, even being dubbed 'le bien-aimé' ('the well-beloved'), and it was conceivable that this new-found popularity, combined with his military success, might make him a strong ruler. Where an insecure and inexperienced despot in thrall to the Church will connive in the politics of faction and shelter behind the ramparts of injustice and arbitrary decree, so an absolute monarch, confident of his power and correctly steered (perhaps by an enlightened new mistress), might be able to improve the lot of his subjects and usher in a new age of tolerance and humanitarian concern. Just the opportunity a certain Prussian warmonger seemed unready to grasp . . .

The King was delighted with the poem, as was the new marquise de Pompadour. Aware of the hostility harboured towards her by the Church (for obvious reasons) and from the nobility (because she was a commoner), she was glad to be associated with this particular Gentleman in Ordinary and to draw on his reflected prestige. Especially as he was now going to write an opera, *Le Temple de la Gloire* – again with music by Rameau – in which France's new royal hero would be fêted. The ducs de Richelieu and de La Vallière wanted to repeat the success of *La Princesse de Navarre*, and so another court entertainment was demanded of the author of the *Lettres philosophiques*. Which meant another summer visit to stay with the duc and duchesse de La Vallière at Champs, and more illness-inducing stress. At the same time the historian-journalist in Voltaire was frustrated not to be able to spend more time following the course of contemporary events as the French army continued on its victorious way through the Austrian Netherlands (taking Ghent, Ostend, Tournai in successive months). He wanted to write a faithful history of this war, to which end he now wrote to the man who had led the English forces in Flanders, the Duke of Cumberland, son of George II. Or rather he wrote to his secretary, none other than Everard Fawkener, former merchant and enlightened resident of Wandsworth. It would be good, Voltaire observed, if he might one day introduce him to the marquis d'Argenson. They would have so much to talk about – and to agree on. The court jester was a serious research historian, and he still believed in the international republic of letters.

And he still wanted to be elected to the Académie Française. Conscious that the main obstacle to this election remained the Church, he embarked on a charm offensive – by writing to the Pope (in fluent Italian) and sending him his poem about Fontenoy and a copy of *Mahomet* (to be read, of course, as an attack on false religions). The Pope in question, Benedict XIV, was of a kindly and broad-minded disposition, which helped; but when he replied on 15 September he was careful to praise the poem and to omit all mention of the play. Undeterred, Voltaire had only to amend his letter slightly – and have it retranscribed – for it to appear that the Holy Father had praised 'la sua bellissima tragedia di Mahomet'. Moreover, the authentic letter had ended with an apostolic blessing addressed to his 'dear son'. The pious of Paris were appalled: how could His Holiness have let himself be manipulated in this way? But the pious were also circumspect, and said nothing. All Voltaire needed now was for an Immortal to prove himself mortal.

Meanwhile that other Temple of Glory beckoned. The court jester's latest entertainment was performed at Versailles (once more in the riding school) on 27 November 1745. No expense had been spared in providing lavish sets and costumes, and no compliment had been left unturned in the playwright's apparent attempt to celebrate his master's recent heroic deeds. The meagre plot turns on a competition between three victorious heroes to enter the Temple of Glory: Bélus, King of Babylon, the epitome of the bloodthirsty tyrant; Bacchus, the conqueror of India, who ushers in a reign of sensuality and debauch; and Trajan, the very model of an enlightened monarch who forgives his enemies and acknowledges the equal right to happiness of each and every citizen. Despite the intended flattering parallel with the Roman Emperor, it seemed to those present that the French king looked rather put out. Did he perhaps think that this new and notoriously unreliable courtier was implying certain royal shortcomings, perhaps even telling him what to do? At the subsequent supper-party Louis appeared to snub Voltaire, paying pointed compliments to Rameau's music. Or perhaps the whole thing just left him perplexed. For he ordered the opera to be staged again in one week's time, which was followed by a performance at the Opéra on 4 December. Now the critics could get their knives out: anyone would think Rameau had written the words, they said, and Voltaire the music.

When Richelieu then asked him to produce a shortened version of *La Princesse de Navarre*, the court jester had had enough. Let someone else shorten it. So the duc gave the job to a young musician and opera-composer who was just beginning to make his way in the world: Jean-Jacques Rousseau. At this early stage he was still very much an admirer of Voltaire. He had wept at a performance of *Alzire* (in Grenoble in 1737), and the *Lettres philosophiques* had left a profound impression. His first letter to Voltaire is purest hero-worship: 'Sir, for fifteen years now I have been working and studying to make myself worthy of your notice and to merit the support with which you favour the young Muses in whom you discover some talent.'[4] But after six weeks' hard slog trying to do what he was asked, he became notably less starry-eyed. He could never get hold of either Voltaire or Rameau to discuss his proposed revisions. And, in the former case, no wonder. For he was busy seducing his niece.

Marie-Louise Denis, née Mignot, was the elder daughter of Voltaire's beloved sister, Catherine, who had died in 1726 soon after he arrived in England. Following her marriage to Pierre-François Mignot in 1709 (when her father had given her that handsome dowry), she had given birth to three children: Marie-Louise (1712), Marie-Elisabeth (1715) and Vincent (?1718). When her widowed husband died subsequently in 1737, the two girls were still unmarried, and the miserly and miserable Armand Arouet decided that they would have to go into a convent. But their younger, wealthier and kindlier uncle gave them dowries instead. Marie-Elisabeth married Joseph de Dompierre de Fontaine in 1738 and bore him two sons – through whom Voltaire's modern heirs, the Dompierre d'Hornoy family, are now exclusively descended. In the same year Marie-Louise married Nicolas-Charles Denis, an army supply officer, for whom she had developed a passionate regard.

Voltaire had always had a soft spot for Marie-Louise, and at first he had proposed to marry her off to Mme de Champbonin's son, his rather dim secretary at Cirey. It would be nice to have his niece living nearby . . . But much as she was grateful to her uncle – and fond of him, too – Marie-Louise had no desire to bury herself away in the depths of the countryside. She was an attractive, lively and intelligent young woman in her mid-twenties, and Paris, not to mention Nicolas-Charles, was worth some disobedience. Piqued, and jealous, her uncle reduced his offer of a dowry from an annual income of 8,000 *livres* to a one-off lump sum of 25,000. Needless to say, he did not attend the wedding. For what are weddings? 'Assembled relatives, facetious jokes about marriage, dirty stories to make the bride blush and the prudes purse their lips, a lot of noise, interrupted conversations, excessive and indifferent food, forced laughter, slobbering kisses slobberingly bestowed, and little girls taking it all in out of the corner of their eye.'[5]

But his absence mattered rather less to his niece than the fact that her husband was promptly posted to Landau, on the eastern front. The happy couple stopped off at Cirey on their way, where Marie-Louise noted her uncle's uncertain health (with concern) and commented (with disbelief) on the state of apparent subjugation in which he was held by a rather rotund Mme du Châtelet. On reaching the garrison at Landau the new bride was reassured. She had lost Paris, but she had gained 'a very fine house' and 'four hundred officers at my service', amongst whom she resolved to choose a dozen of the nicest – 'who will come often to have supper with me'.[6] She was the adaptable sort: she knew how to make the best of things.

When, as the novels she read might have put it, she finally gave herself to Voltaire in the last weeks of 1745, she had been a widow (without children) since the spring of the previous year. On that occasion Voltaire – from whose mind her new situation banished all thoughts of his latest actress, Mlle de Gaussin – had then immediately invited her to spend a month at Cirey (where he was working on *La Princesse de Navarre*): 'I talk of spending a month with you, my dear niece, when actually I would like to spend my whole life with you [. . .] I imagine that we might get on rather well.'[7] She had declined the invitation – for the present, and to good effect. Announcing his return to Paris in August 1744, Voltaire seemed even keener: 'I feel somewhat ashamed at my age to be forsaking philosophy and solitude to play the royal minstrel

[. . .] but leave I must, since I shall see you, and together we shall console each other, you for your recent loss, and me for the ridiculous life I'm leading, which is quite contrary to my temperament and my way of thinking.'[8] He rarely unbuttoned in this manner, and his openness is a sign both of his fondness for Marie-Louise and his yearning for a companion less strident and possessive than the wonderful, incomparable, but exhaustingly demanding Émilie. His niece enjoyed the theatre and the opera, and while she was no intellectual she was shrewd and witty in an unselfconscious, if occasionally vulgar, way.

Uncle François knew well that he was not the answer to a young widow's sensual prayers, and he could see that Marie-Louise — for all her easy-going affability — had a very sharp eye to the main chance. But he wanted and needed her; and she, in her way, wanted and needed him. Despite the legacy from Uncle Armand, her husband's death had left her only modestly well-off, and in the spring of 1745 she had gone to live with her sister and brother-in-law in the rue Pavée in Paris. As a consolable and potentially merry young widow she had the independence but not quite the means. And now here she was receiving love-letters from a man of considerable wealth, fame and position. No matter that he was her uncle: such relationships were not uncommon, and if marriage was intended (which in the present case it was not) one could even apply to the Pope for special permission. As La Condamine, Pâris-Monmartel and the journalist Fréron, among others, could all attest on the basis of personal experience. And of course the illegitimate Voltaire believed that she was only his 'half-niece'.

And so, as young Jean-Jacques Rousseau got on with revising the great man's work, Voltaire and Mme Denis embarked on a relationship that would last until Voltaire's death. The ageing Romeo now began to write notes to his newly beloved in Italian, just in case the servants found out just how explicit the sender was being about the anatomical pleasures afforded by the recipient. Mme Denis's bottom seems to have been a particular joy. And the champion of free speech was unabashed when it came to conveying the nature of any physical malfunction that might stand — or not — between them. Though eager in his benevolence, Voltaire Almighty was not, after all, omnipotent. Again, no matter: the resourceful Marie-Louise found consolation where she could. Once she had moved into her own accommodation near the Palais-Royal in 1747, she began to throw dinner-parties, and the young writers whom her uncle regarded as his protégés – François de Baculard d'Arnaud and Jean-François Marmontel, for example – were often invited. And sometimes stayed, discreetly.

For the moment, however, the King's minstrel was still 'married' to Mme du Châtelet, with whom he continued to bask in royal favour at Versailles but also to share an increasingly painful relationship. Not the type of courtier to dance eager attendance on the person of the King as he rose from his bed or retired for the night, the minstrel was now finding time to be Historiographer Royal, scouring the archives as he researched Louis's two recent military campaigns. He was also writing a new play, *Sémiramis*, based on the earlier *Éryphile* that he had set aside in 1732. Then came news that an Immortal had died: Jean Bouhier, a senior judge in the Dijon *parlement* from the age of thirty and an immensely learned scholar, who had himself been elected to the Academy at the age of thirty-four. Might a playwright who had entertained the King and been blessed by the Pope now at last have a chance of succeeding him? Voltaire began as one should, pretending to have no interest in being elected. Then he lobbied the Jesuits. Writing to the current Recteur of the Collège Louis-le-Grand, Father Simon de la Tour, he professed a wish to 'live and die quietly in the bosom of the Roman, Catholic and Apostolic Church without doing harm to anyone'.[9] Some chance. His correspondent replied with suitable, Jesuitical charm, implying everything and promising nothing. Unfazed, the would-be academician calculated that since the Jansenists were bound to oppose him, so the Jesuits would have no option in the end but to support him. And they did. Even the implacable Boyer bowed to the inevitable, and the King himself raised no objection (whereas he had before). Voltaire was duly elected to the Académie Française on 25 April 1746 by a majority of the twenty-nine Immortals who had turned up to vote.

Needless to say, the election had precipitated an especially poisonous campaign of vilification on the part of his enemies. Desfontaines had died on 16 December 1745, Jean-Baptiste Rousseau four years before that. But a new generation of satirists and libel-mongers had come to the fore, led by the man whom Desfontaines had been grooming as his chosen successor, Élie-Catherine Fréron. Now twenty-six, he joined others in a concerted and sustained onslaught on Voltaire's reputation, attacking the poem about

Fontenoy, the opera *Le Temple de la Gloire*, indeed every word that the sycophantic courtier now produced. And the alleged sycophant undoubtedly deserved some of it: 'his brilliant successes and his laurels without number,' wrote Fréron, 'have procured him the right to produce bad work.'[10] As usual Voltaire fought back, with a mixture of intelligent resolution, foolish obstinacy and impolitic fury, accompanying the police in person as they sought out offending documents and authors, ill-advisedly pressing official charges when this simply gave his enemies the oxygen of publicity and fanned the flames of their ardent hatred.

As happens in all wars, the combatant soon found himself a hostage to events. On 29 May he followed the police into the house of one particular suspect called Mairault, only to find him lying in bed terminally ill. He died six weeks later. On 3 June Voltaire obtained a warrant to search the premises of one Louis Travenol, a violinist at the Opéra. Louis had fled, but the police commissioner took it into his head to arrest his eighty-year-old father in the presence of Louis's terrified wife and invalid daughter. When the man was flung into prison, Voltaire's opponents had another field day depicting him as a cruel grandee lording it over the defenceless poor. Travenol *père* was soon released and went straight round to beg his tormentor for mercy: Voltaire, in a characteristically spontaneous and generous moment, invited him to lunch and promised protection and support to him and his family. But the whole affair nevertheless ended in a court case that lasted for over a year. An initial judgement, in December, found against Louis for libel and awarded Voltaire 300 *livres* in damages, but found also against Voltaire for the treatment of Travenol *père* and awarded the latter 500 *livres* in damages. Neither party was content, and Voltaire appealed – apparently forgetting that the court of appeal was the *parlement*, where he had many (Jansenist) enemies. In August 1747 it confirmed the judgement of the lower court. Meanwhile, Voltaire's good name had been dragged through the mud. Travenol, ruined by the cost of litigation, had merely been the instrument of Voltaire's shrewd opponents, while Voltaire emerged with no credit from his stubborn and counter-productive pursuit of a defenceless violinist with an elderly parent and a handicapped daughter. Let alone poor Mairault on his death-bed. Voltaire's friends and influential advisers had looked on with regret and distaste. If only, for once, he could have responded to the slurs with silent disdain. But that was not our hero's way.

During this period Voltaire and Mme du Châtelet had been dividing their time between the court (at Versailles or Fontainebleau) and Paris (in the rue de la Traversière). Émilie was painfully conscious of the deterioration in their relationship. She had been hurt by her companion's passing affair with Mlle de Gaussin – and may even have had a retaliatory fling of her own with Charliers, her agent in Brussels (when she went there alone in October 1744) – though she probably did not know that Voltaire and Mme Denis had become more to each other than merely uncle and niece. But the cohabitation in Brussels had ceased (just as the city fell into French hands): her adversary, the marquis de Hoensbroeck, had agreed to settle out of court. And increasingly Voltaire made trips into Paris on his own. To fight his fights, and to see his niece. His principal project during the spring and summer had been *Sémiramis*, since the King had requested a play from him to celebrate the end of his daughter-in-law the Dauphine's confinement. But unfortunately she died in childbirth in mid-July, just a few days after the death of her father, Philip V of Spain. The exhausted courtier, who had himself been ill, commented wryly (in a letter to Richelieu) on his own confinement: 'I was busy with the fourth act when Madame La Dauphine died, and when poor little me was on the point of dying also in the service of her pleasure. See how destiny toys with crowned heads, first gentlemen of the bedchamber, and those who write verse to entertain the court.'[11] Having achieved every official success he had set his sights on, Voltaire seemed to be overtaken by a new sense of world-weary fatalism. Now in his early fifties he had seen and done it all. Honour and glory are mere baubles once attained, just as kings and queens seem only too human when viewed up close. The war continued despite all talk of peace, and the successes of Maurice de Saxe, now eager to invade Holland, encouraged the King to dismiss the peace-seeking marquis d'Argenson (while retaining his more bellicose brother as his Minister of War). Illness threatened constantly (as he had recently been reminded). So perhaps did death. Which indeed it did – albeit from an unexpected quarter.

Less gloomy moments were to be enjoyed during visits to the duchesse du Maine, a widow since 1736. Now seventy, she was as imperious as ever in the pursuit of her pleasures – whether at Sceaux or at her summer residence, the château d'Anet, some forty miles east of Paris and just north of Dreux. Here her guests could relish the idyllic river-valley setting and marvel at the fine Renaissance building constructed for Diane de Poitiers by Henri II. Voltaire and Mme du Châtelet were invited for a short stay at the end of August 1746, a signal favour which the duchesse's two companions, the baronne de Staal and Mme du Deffand, did not wish to see extended to the bossy marquise. But the duchesse knew that if she were to secure the company of one of her favourite – and most entertaining – men, Voltaire's companion had to come too. The bossiness became more apparent on the second visit, the following August, when at Émilie's instigation the couple arrived twelve hours early and in the middle of the night. One guest had to be evicted from his room, and it was several days and a change of rooms before Mme du Châtelet was quite sure that she had all the creature comforts she required. In the evenings they would earn their keep by contributing to the entertainments – for example, performing Voltaire's comedy *Boursoufle* – but during the day (and sometimes night) both of them wanted to work. Mme du Châtelet was drafting the commentary to her translation of Newton's *Principia*, and – as the baronne de Staal cattily reported – appeared to require at least six writing-tables and various other pieces of furniture for the purpose. It was such hard luck on the marquise, was it not, when she knocked over a bottle of ink and it went all over her algebra? Mmes de Staal and du Deffand were relieved when the famous couple departed as abruptly as they had arrived, in a hurry to bid farewell to the duc de Richelieu who was off to govern Genoa. He was to be accompanied by Émilie's son.

This departure had its compensations for Voltaire also, who wrote to Mme Denis (in Italian):

> I have been ill at Anet, my dearest, but I hope to recover my health in your company. [. . .] Today is the day I shall see you once more, today is the day when I shall be reunited with the one consolation that can sweeten the bitterness of my life. Nature has graced me with the tenderest of hearts but forgot to give me a stomach. I cannot digest, but I am able to love. And I love you, I shall always love you, until the day I die.[12]

Doubtless Marie-Louise was able to console her ailing uncle, but Émilie was never far away, and she now dragged Voltaire off to Passy, then a most fashionable spa village just outside Paris. Perhaps the waters would be good for his non-existent stomach. But no: 'I am a hundred times worse than I was before,' he informed his niece. 'You are my one consolation, for my life is otherwise wretched.'[13] He certainly knew how to play on her maternal instinct. As the two courtiers now left Passy for Fontainebleau, Mme Denis bided her time – and enjoyed it in the company of young poets. The lovers kept in touch by letter, and Marie-Louise even invited her uncle to attend an important sermon to be given by her brother (his nephew), the abbé Mignot. But, malleable in her hands as he may have wished to be, Voltaire was not about to abandon his sure sense of priorities: 'I imagine that on my return you will wish to show me something more profane and rather more to my taste than a sermon.'[14] He was obviously feeling better.

At Fontainebleau disaster loomed. Much card-playing went on in royal circles, and for very large sums. The less scrupulous took lessons in cheating and fleeced their fellow-courtiers. For knowledge of what happened next all students of Voltaire are indebted to Sébastien Longchamp, his secretary, whose biography of his master now becomes an important source of information. Longchamp's sister had been Mme du Châtelet's maid, and when her brother left the employ of Mme de Lannoy, wife of the governor of Brussels, in mid-January 1746, she got her mistress to take him on. But after a row with Mme du Châtelet about their pay – Émilie, always broke, was being stingy – they left. In any case Longchamp had not much liked the way she had treated him. As a servant, apparently, he no longer counted as a human being in her aristocratic eyes. She removed her clothes in front of him, and on one occasion required him to pour hot water into her bath while she was in it. As she parted her legs he blushed and averted his eyes, which rather complicated his task. 'Take care,' said his mistress, 'or you will scald me.' 'And so, despite my sense of modesty,' Longchamp continues, 'I was forced to see what I should not have seen [. . .] I was regarded as one regards an inanimate piece of furniture, and the lady appeared to make no distinction between myself and the kettle.' It is true that Émilie, like many aristocrats, regarded servants as sub-human. Even the abbé Linant, her son's tutor and thus above the rank of servant, had been told that he should never presume to sit down in the presence of a marquise from the House of Lorraine. And Mme de Graffigny had been shocked at Cirey to see the way in which the bourgeois Voltaire had adopted his lover's ways and insisted on being attended hand and foot by his valet. But Émilie also had a sense of fun, and Longchamp may have been just the sort of po-faced prude she loved to shock.

Be that as it may, Longchamp was aggrieved. But he knew a good employer when he saw one, and when Voltaire – who knew a good secretary when he saw one – soon afterwards offered him a job, he accepted. In time to record the evening at Fontainebleau when Émilie lost her head – and a vast amount of money. She had always loved gambling, but in this company she was out of her depth and she fell into the trap of trying to recoup her debts by risking yet more. Voltaire, ever loyal and ever generous, stood close by, funding her losses as requested. But as they mounted alarmingly he intervened, whispering to her furiously in English that she was surrounded by cheats. Since they were in the Queen's apartments, and since they were not alone in understanding English, the couple realized the sudden danger they were in. For Voltaire to say such a thing in the vicinity of the Queen herself . . . Longchamp was ordered to pack their trunks, and they left in the middle of the night. A wheel on their carriage breaks, they have it repaired but lack the means to pay the wheelwright, a passing marquis of their acquaintance saves the day, and then – like fugitive cowboys – they split up: Mme du Châtelet heads for Paris, while Voltaire sends ahead to ask the duchesse du Maine for refuge at Sceaux. Which she grants. The official court always constituted the opposition for her, and she was delighted to house the runaway subversive, especially if he was on his own. He would help her while away the winter evenings.

Mme du Châtelet, meanwhile, set about finding the money to pay her huge debt of 80,000 *livres*. She already owed Voltaire a considerable sum, and he could help her no more. Through connections and some dubious practices she raised 24,000 and, perhaps working on the uneasy conscience of her debtor, persuaded him to accept this as honouring the debt in full. Then she returned to Fontainebleau to smooth ruffled feathers and prepare the way for Voltaire's return. She arrived at Sceaux at the beginning of December to remove him from the clutches of the duchesse du Maine. Worthy of a novel by Alexandre Dumas, the whole episode had lasted less than a fortnight, but it had been a close call. And it did nothing to endear Émilie to her former lover. Was the wild gambling perhaps an expression of her pain at losing him, a desperation born of an increasing sense of powerlessness? The duchesse du Maine was grateful to Mme du Châtelet for restoring Voltaire's reputation, and so invited her to stay. A celebration was called for, and Voltaire saw a golden opportunity to try out his new comedy, *La Prude*, written in 1739 and tinkered with since. It was to be performed on 15 December, and its author sent out at least 500 invitations. There was a tremendous crush, and the duchesse had a firm word with her guest about it afterwards. At her age she was not partial to such upheavals in her palace. Based on Wycherley's *Plain Dealer* (itself based on Molière's *Le Misanthrope*), the play had its moments, but the playwright did not subsequently offer it to the Comédie-Française. Nor did he stay long at Sceaux.

Clearly his remark about cheats had been forgotten, for by the end of the month the King was attending a private performance of Voltaire's more accomplished comedy *L'Enfant prodigue* in the royal apartments at Versailles. These private performances – at which sometimes the King was the only person in the audience – were given by his closest companions and advisers for his pleasure, and indeed for their own. In this case Mme de Pompadour and the duc de La Vallière played two of the roles. But it was not customary to invite the author to be present. When Mme de Pompadour persuaded the King to change this rule, and in future to invite Voltaire (and others), the poet-playwright – though now weary of honours – thanked his patroness in some elegant verses that were nevertheless rather too frank about her new relationship with the King. Everybody knew, of course, but one was not supposed to say – especially if you were famous and your verses would soon be circulating in the streets of Paris. At the very least one should be mindful of the feelings of the Queen. It is not clear how serious this new *faux pas* really was. The King appeared unconcerned, and Mme de Pompadour was sufficiently flattered and delighted to allow the poem to circulate. But rumours flew that the Queen was displeased, and when Voltaire and Mme du Châtelet then departed in the middle of January 1748 the rumours seemed to be confirmed.

Which all suited Émilie rather well . . .

CHAPTER TWELVE

Death of a Lover (1748–1749)

What became of Émilie and her soul (if she had one)

W AS THE QUEEN in fact displeased with Voltaire's thank-you poem to Mme de Pompadour? It was difficult to say. But when the marquise de Boufflers, daughter of the Prince de Beauvau-Craon, expressed a desire to return from Paris to Lunéville in their company, Voltaire and Mme du Châtelet each saw an opportunity. The marquise de Boufflers was a great admirer of France's leading playwright, and she had been present in the duchesse de Luxembourg's box on the triumphant first night of *Mérope*. What better way for Voltaire to demonstrate his loyalty to the French queen than to revisit her father's court, albeit in the company of her father's acknowledged mistress? (The 66-year-old Stanislas was at least now a widower, so his daughter had less reason to disapprove.) Indeed what better way to imply to the world at large that the Gentleman in Ordinary was still *persona grata* in the royal bedchamber?

What was convenient to Voltaire was also convenient to Mme du Châtelet, who saw in her companion's predicament just the opportunity she needed to whisk him off to Lunéville. For she had a particular aim in view. In alliance with her friend and former lover, the duc de Richelieu, Émilie had succeeded in her objective of getting her dearest François accepted at the court of Louis XV and keeping him from the unreliable clutches of Frederick the Great. But she could see that it did not make him happy, and his inevitable indiscretions meant that he continued to be vulnerable. Moreover their relationship had suffered. Had she by now also realized the true nature of Voltaire's interest in his elder niece? Quite possibly. At any rate she now decided that they would both be far better off at the court of Lorraine. Her husband would soon be retiring from active military service, and if she could secure him a post there – after all, his ancestors had once ruled the province – then she would have a pretext to live at Lunéville in the proximity of the man she continued to love. Which was a much more agreeable prospect than a return to the prison-paradise of Cirey.

Mme du Châtelet's particular ambition was to obtain for her husband the post of commander-in-chief of the Lothringian army, and her charm offensive began at once. The King must be entertained: by a performance of *Mérope*, about which his mistress had told him so much, and by Émilie reprising an operatic role (in a version of Houdar de la Motte's *Issé*) that had brought her rapturous acclaim when she sang it for the duchesse du Maine. In this way the court at Lunéville was made the equal of Versailles and Sceaux, and the 'King' could delight in the reflected glory. But kings with favours to bestow are not always in a hurry to bestow them: on the contrary, while the issue hung in the balance the entertainments would continue and his famous guests would remain. Which was a nuisance for Voltaire, since he was keen to return to Paris to rehearse *Sémiramis* and to seek 'consolation' with Mme Denis.

Had Mme du Châtelet planned just this? Did she foresee that Stanislas's procrastination would extend a visit which she had promised Voltaire would be brief, and that this prolonged absence from Paris might serve to moderate the avuncular passion she had begun to note in her companion? Perhaps. But what she cannot have foreseen is that she herself would fall head over heels in love. With a soldier, Jean-François de Saint-Lambert. A close associate of Mme de Graffigny's Panpan, he came from an old but impoverished aristocratic family and had grown up with the children of the Prince de Beauvau-Craon. Through the Prince's patronage and that of his daughter, Mme de Boufflers, he had been given command of the garrison at Nancy, but he spent little time with his soldiers and preferred life at court – where women heavily outnumbered men precisely because of the demands of military life. A handsome man of elegant and even foppish ways, he was also a poet: his success with the ladies was assured. Indeed in 1735, at the age of nineteen, he had sent some verses to Voltaire, who commended his efforts in some courteously generous but unwittingly prophetic lines: 'Venus smiles no more on me; / the Graces turn their steps away; / My Muse, with tearful eye, / To Saint-Lambert doth run. / On you she lavishes her charms: / I read your verses, and I wish that they were mine.'

One of Saint-Lambert's 'conquests' was Mme de Boufflers herself, who had a room set aside for him near the royal apartments. At Commercy, where the court resided during the summer, he lodged with the local priest – in a room from where he could see the royal mistress's window. When she blew out the candle, he knew that it was safe to visit her. But during the summer of 1747 this marquise tired of her poet and took another lover – as she frequently and capriciously did – so that Saint-Lambert resolved to make her jealous. And the return of Voltaire's marquise seemed opportune. Now forty-two, Émilie lacked the beauty of Mme de Boufflers but more than made up for it in energy and personality. With the result that after the merest hint of flirtation from Saint-Lambert – with which he intended to goad his former mistress into a reconciliation – she allowed him no escape. And what Émilie wanted, Émilie got. After dinner one evening, when the two of them were unexpectedly and briefly alone, our operatic heroine swooned artfully into his arms. For Mme du Châtelet there followed a passion such as she had not felt for many years; for Saint-Lambert, there followed long months of exhaustion as he experienced the uncompromising and possessive infatuation that Maupertuis and Voltaire had known before him. And for Voltaire himself, more long months at Lunéville. For, as though he were a cuckolded husband, his companion's new relationship did not imply his own release. Come the end of April 1748 he was still at Lunéville. Émilie would not let him return to Paris alone, and he remained devoted: to her, to the past they had shared, and to the thought that after all that they had been through, and all that she had done for him, he could not possibly throw her over. Indeed, in his way, he still loved her.

Eventually Mme du Châtelet agreed that they might return to Paris, but she was deeply reluctant to leave her new lover behind with Mme de Boufflers. Stopping off at Cirey, she summoned Saint-Lambert to visit her there, despite Voltaire's presence. Then, during the subsequent journey to Paris, she made a detour alone to see him at Nancy before rejoining Voltaire at Bar-le-Duc on the main road to the capital (which they reached on 13

May). In short, she was besotted. And Voltaire weary. 'You are my
consolation,' he wrote once more to Mme Denis, after they had been
reunited in the capital: 'and I have no other desire than but to make you
happy during my lifetime and after my death. I shall love you always,
tenderly, until such day as nature's law separates that which nature and love
have joined together. Let us love one another until that day comes.'[1]
Meanwhile he got on with rehearsing *Sémiramis* at the Comédie-Française,
though he missed the indispensable advice of the d'Argentals: they were
taking the waters at Plombières.

But Voltaire's moment of Parisian freedom was short-lived. Émilie was
yearning for Saint-Lambert and once more pleaded the pretext of securing
her husband's future at the court of Lorraine. At the end of June they set off
for Commercy, where they were accommodated in a wing of the château –
Mme du Châtelet on the ground floor, easy of access, and Voltaire on the
second, with a view. He was ill again, and deeply depressed. In a letter to the
marquis d'Argenson, with whom he had had little contact since the former
Foreign Minister's fall from grace, he reflects on the vagaries of fortune and
the ironies of fate. His historical research has shown him how often the best
intentions and the most sensible decisions go unrewarded, and his own
situation shows how difficult it is to be happy in this world. Here he is,
lodged in a beautiful palace, free to do as he pleases (even under a king's
roof), surrounded by his books and papers, in the company of Mme du
Châtelet: 'and yet despite all this I am one of the most wretched thinking
creatures alive'.[2] To his niece, on the same day, he is even more frank: 'My
situation is most cruel. Pleasure and work are alike denied me, and I am
deprived of your presence. In truth I feel that I do not have long to live.'[3] He
omitted to mention the rows he was having with Mme du Châtelet about
Saint-Lambert.

Mme Denis suspected him of disingenuous self-pity and in any case
despaired at the hold Émilie continued to exert over her uncle. She now
informed him that she intended to marry the commanding officer of the
garrison at Lille. Voltaire's reaction was robust: he wished the said officer
dead and poured out his affection for Marie-Louise's body in the frankest
Italian. Evidently restored to good health, he now resumed work on *Sémiramis*,
and at the end of August he was delighted to be offered a lift to Paris by King

Stanislas, who was off to visit his daughter. The itinerant playwright arrived on 30 August, one day after the premiere of his new play – but untroubled by the delay (for reasons we shall presently discover). Mme du Châtelet, meanwhile, had been sent off to Plombières by the King to accompany Mme de Boufflers, with whom she was now at daggers drawn. Perhaps the waters – and the boredom of spa life – might cool their animosities.

Sémiramis, Voltaire's latest tragedy, was innovative in French terms in having a plot that spans fifteen years and figures a ghost. The latter, unfortunately, appears in broad daylight and in a very public place, which (as several critics pointed out) was rather unghostly of it. Once again Voltaire sought to move his audience without resort to a love plot (as he had so successfully managed in *Mérope*), and on this occasion he hoped to impress them with extravagant Babylonian sets, sponsored by King Louis to the tune of 15,000 *livres*. The fact that some of the audience habitually stood on the stage at the Comédie-Française rather detracted from the scenic splendour, and tragedy turned to farce on the first night when a policeman had to order some of them to 'make way for the ghost'. Despite the presence of a paid claque numbering 400, the play nearly failed, and so on the days following his arrival Voltaire disguised himself as a scruffy abbé and sat in the Café Procope nearby, listening to people's comments after the show. Basing himself on this consumer research, he rewrote some 200 lines and saved his play. Its first run lasted twenty-one performances, and ushered in a new taste for spectacular melodrama.

His job done, Voltaire left Paris on 10 September but fell seriously ill at Châlons with a very high fever. As usual the stress of work had taken its toll. He later told Frederick that this illness had made his teeth fall out and left him deaf in one ear.[4] After five days he moved on to Nancy, and reached Lunéville the following evening. In Paris his friends in high places, including Mme de Pompadour, were trying to suppress a parody of *Sémiramis*, while his new enemy, Fréron, was asking his readers very sensibly how the freethinker who had hitherto caused the authorities such a headache could write such a play, in which crime is punished and virtue rewarded, and religion emerges triumphant. Voltaire, it seemed, had become a toady.

But what Fréron did not yet know was that on the very day he left Paris Voltaire published – without permission, at his own expense, and in a brilliantly subversive manner – his first major *conte philosophique*, or philoso-phical tale: *Zadig, ou la Destinée* (*Zadig, or Destiny*). A first version had been published in Amsterdam the previous year, anonymously and under the title *Memnon*; but it had gone unnoticed. This would never do. As to the new version, he had got Prault in Paris to print a thousand copies of the first 144 pages and Lefèvre in Nancy the remaining 51. Having then brought copies of the second half back to Paris (in the unimpeachable company of the King of Poland), he bought up Prault's stock of the first half, got Longchamp to employ two women to sew the gatherings together – and published the assembled volume privately. Hey presto! Neither printer could immediately market a pirated edition, and the author would be very difficult to trace.

Under the guise of an Oriental fable *Zadig* is an entertaining but uncompromising attack on kings and ministers, and on the ruses and hypocrisies of court life. It lambasts religion as surely as it condemns the judiciary, the medical profession, the world of high finance – and the fickleness of women. And it does so within the framework of one question: can a virtuous man of enlightened views be happy? The answer is not encouraging. Fine morals get you nowhere: indeed they can get you into trouble. And when the hero has everything 'explained' to him by a hermit spouting a mixture of Leibnizian and Popean Optimism, he begins to object. 'But . . .' he stammers, before the hermit rather unhelpfully turns into an angel and flies away. Zadig – from the Hebrew for the 'just' or the Arabic for the 'truthful' – is none the wiser in his truthful goodness, and the story's happy ending has all the irreality of a fairy story. (And subsequent additions, in the light of experiences in Prussia, were to make the ending less happy.)

In thus giving expression to his disenchantments the world-weary courtier had intuitively created a type of prose narrative that would serve him well in the years to come, and by which indeed he is now best known to posterity. Instead of the 'high' genres of epic and tragedy or the grand narratives of history, here was a playfully subversive medium that lent itself brilliantly to Voltairean irony. In *Zadig*, as in subsequent tales like *Candide* and *L'Ingénu*, the foolish fables of complacent assumption and unthinking prejudice, of religious superstition and grand philosophical system, are briskly juxtaposed with the brute facts of human existence, leaving the reader at once hugely entertained by the irreverent puncturing of illusion and provoked into some serious but inconclusive thoughts about the true nature of reality. Voltaire's *contes philosophiques* were intended for those who had a mind to be enlightened.

A mind like that of Babouc, the hero of *Le Monde comme il va* (*The Way of the World, or Let the World Be*), a much shorter and much less effective tale published earlier in 1748. This story had probably been written in 1746 or 1747 when Voltaire was entertaining the duchesse du Maine, who had fond memories of the tales (*Le Crocheteur borgne* and *Cosi-Sancta*) that he had produced for her some thirty years earlier. Babouc is a clear-thinking messenger of the gods, dispatched by the angel Ituriel to investigate the present state of Persia and report back what he finds. For Persia and its capital Persepolis, read France and Paris – and read Voltaire reporting to the duchesse du Maine. Being a commendable empiricist, Babouc embarks on his voyage of discovery with an open mind and encounters a mixture of the good and the bad. The good is limited (architecture, music, politeness), whereas the bad is reflected in a familiar checklist of Voltairean bugbears: war; religious practices; ecclesiastical, legal and conjugal hypocrisy; the sale of military commissions and public offices; tax-farmers and money-lenders; dull preachers; the low condition of actresses; monastic luxury; Jansenism; the 'glitterati'; bitchy lampoons and vapid novels; bureaucracy.

Wondering how best to make his report, Babouc hits on the idea of presenting Ituriel with a statue consisting of every conceivable metal or mineral – the most precious and the most base – and then facing him with a question: 'Will you smash the statue just because it is not made entirely of diamonds and gold?' Ituriel gets the point: there is nothing to be gained from destroying Persepolis, or even from trying to improve it. It is better to 'let the world be'. Here again, despite the impeccable philosophical method, was the voice of a world-weary and defeated courtier, the very opposite of the reforming campaigner of the *Lettres philosophiques* – and of the reforming champion of human rights who was still to come. For this was his nadir.

Once reinstalled at Lunéville on his return from Paris, Voltaire became increasingly agitated at the flagrancy of Mme du Châtelet's relationship with Saint-Lambert, and his jealousy and sense of injury seemed to increase in proportion to her perceived duplicity. There were furious rows, and he threatened to pack his bags – or rather to get Longchamp to pack them. She argued that she still loved him and was not being unfaithful, merely protecting his health by seeking her pleasure elsewhere! How much better that she should do so with a man he regarded as a friend. Voltaire saw the force of her improbable argument and asked merely that she spare him the spectacle. Letters of assignation secreted in Mme de Boufflers's harp were one thing: letting him walk in on her amours (as he just had) was quite another. But they remained bound by the closest ties of friendship: he still supported her, as indeed she had always supported him. And now she needed his support more than ever. Saint-Lambert was wearying of his role and her demands, while King Stanislas had appointed as his commander-in-chief Count Ladislas de Bercsényi, a Hungarian, who had served him exceptionally in earlier days. The Count had always been his first choice. By way of compensation, however, Stanislas named the marquis du Châtelet Grand Marshal of the Royal Household, an office more honorific than real. Which meant that the marquise had ostensible reason to take up more permanent residence at Lunéville, much to the chagrin – for quite different reasons – of both her friend and her new lover.

Her principal objective secured, Mme du Châtelet acceded to Voltaire's request for another visit to Paris, and they departed at the end of the year, spending Christmas at Cirey. And there, against all expectations, they remained a while longer. For it was evident that Émilie was pregnant; that, as Longchamp recorded in his memoirs: 'the assiduous attentions of M. de Saint-Lambert had placed her in the position of becoming a mother'.[5] The consequences were potentially catastrophic: for her body, for her reputation both personal and scientific, for her husband's prospects at Lunéville, and for Voltaire, who could just see what Fréron and others might make of this situation. Desperate straits required desperate remedies. It would be essential to convince M. du Châtelet that he was the child's father. But how? His wife had not been in receipt of *his* 'assiduous attentions' for many years. On the pretext of requiring his advice about a legal matter, and with the enticement that Émilie had money to pass to him, they secured his arrival at Cirey and entertained him royally. Plying him with drink and listening to every one of his anecdotes, they managed – as though they were staging one of Voltaire's comedies – to put the new Grand Marshal in such excellent spirits that amorous thoughts sprang unprompted to his mind. Having feigned surprise and blushed with becoming modesty, the lady consented; and when the very minimum of time had elapsed to make the story half plausible, Mme du Châtelet stunned her husband with the news of his fertility. He was as pleased as Punch and hoped for a boy. And off he went.

Mme Denis was put out. What was Voltaire up to at Cirey? Why was he always at his companion's beck and call? She had decided against her garrison commander at Lille but was threatening her uncle with a new match, M. de Caseique, a lieutenant-general who happened to be very rich. In mid-January Voltaire told her to grasp the opportunity at once, and he explained his continuing loyalty to Mme du Châtelet in the clearest terms:

> Have I not told you quite openly what I feel? Surely you know that I see it as my duty to the public not to cause a scandal which they can then use to make fun of me? That I see it as my duty to steer a straight course, to respect a relationship of twenty years' standing, and to seek shelter – even at the court of Lorraine or in my present isolation – against the persecution by which I am continually threatened?[6]

But he promised her some extra-special gossip on his return, which came a fortnight later and despite the heavy snowfalls that were making travelling conditions atrocious throughout northern France that year.

Voltaire and Mme du Châtelet spent the next few months together in Paris, in the rue Traversière. Saint-Lambert was proving shiftless and unfaithful at this moment of crisis, responding to his mistress's stream of passionate letters with vacuous banalities while being content once more to be taken to bed by the marquise de Boufflers – as Émilie's innocent husband unwittingly revealed to her in a letter. Feeling very much alone and increasingly anxious about her pregnancy, Mme du Châtelet sought solace in work and pressed on with her translation of Newton, determined to finish it before her confinement. At least in Paris she could shut herself away in her study rather than have to spend her time entertaining the ex-King of Poland. Her faithful companion, now plagued by back trouble, was miserable too, feeling at once excluded and powerless to help. The result was a series of rows, one broken door, and the smashing of an extremely expensive porcelain coffee-cup. (Subsequently replaced, but it wasn't the same.) Soon the time was coming when they would need to return to Lunéville, where the marquise wished the Grand Marshal's latest heir to be born. Having prepared the ground with Mme de Boufflers, she had asked King Stanislas's permission while he was on a visit to his daughter in mid-April. His response was munificent: he would furnish a little house for her and make sure he was present on the occasion of the birth. Conscious that he would now be spending more time at Lunéville, Voltaire requested permission to resign from his office as Gentleman in Ordinary. This king's response was also munificent: M. de Voltaire could, if he so wished, sell the post. It was worth some 60,000 *livres*. And he could retain the title and privileges that went with it.

Voltaire and Mme du Châtelet travelled to Lorraine towards the end of June, stopping off for a few days at Cirey. The weather was still unseasonably cold, with frosts round midsummer's day. Frederick had been pressing his friend to make another visit to Berlin, and he promised to do so – but not before October: 'I shall not, even for Your Majesty's sake, abandon a woman who may die in September.'[7] They then proceeded to Commercy, where the court was again spending the summer. But after a fortnight, in search of privacy, they returned with Saint-Lambert to Lunéville, to join M. du Châtelet and Panpan. Mme du Châtelet wanted to be with her lover as much as possible, but he sought desperate refuge in the pretexts of military duty. Voltaire, for his part, stood by to help out with the gambling debts and to discuss his companion's commentary on Newton. During the hours that remained at his own disposal he worked on a new play, *Le Duc de Foix* (derived from *La Princesse de Navarre*), and reworked a comedy, *Nanine*, which had been performed at the Comédie-Française in May and offered a wry take on Samuel Richardson's sentimental novel *Pamela* (first translated into French in 1742). It occurred to Voltaire also that he could settle some scores with Crébillon if he rewrote the latter's *Catalina*, a recently successful tragedy by his ageing rival, and so he drafted what became *Rome sauvée* (*Rome Saved*). On 15 August the court returned from Commercy. Saint-Lambert was becoming increasingly elusive as Mme du Châtelet's pregnancy reached its term, while she became increasingly anxious about the forthcoming birth. As a precaution and fearing the worst, she deposited all her manuscripts at the royal library in Paris.

Need she have feared? She gave birth on the night of 3–4 September. The following morning a relieved and proud Voltaire wrote joyfully to all their friends, including the marquis d'Argenson:

> Madame du Châtelet begs to inform you, sir, that last night while she was sitting at her desk and scribbling out some Newtonian diagram, she felt a call of nature. The call in question was a little girl, who arrived at once. She was laid out upon a book of geometry, of in-quarto format. The mother went to bed, for one does after all have to go to bed, and if she were not now asleep, she would be writing to you herself.[8]

Where once the weather had been unusually cold, it was now unseasonably hot: the mother's puerperal fever was not immediately identified. On 10 September a large glass of iced barley water brought on a severe headache and choking. Stanislas's doctor summoned experts from Nancy, who gave Mme du Châtelet some pills that appeared to calm her. Everyone went down to supper, except for Saint-Lambert, Longchamp and the marquise's maid. A quarter of an hour later Émilie died. Uncertain if she had, Saint-Lambert and Longchamp tried to rouse her: pulling her hair, rubbing her feet and hands. To no avail. The maid was sent to inform the company. Voltaire came at once. Eventually, with Saint-Lambert, he was the last to leave Émilie's room. According to Longchamp he fell at the bottom of the stairs, near the sentry box where guards stood regular watch, and cracked his head on the stone floor. As his footman and Saint-Lambert helped him to his feet, Voltaire turned, the tears streaming down his face, and looked at Saint-Lambert: 'In God's name, what possessed you to give her a child?'[9] The baby girl in question died some days later.

There were traces to be covered over. The resourceful Mme de Boufflers ordered Longchamp to go and remove the diamond locket-ring from the dead woman's finger. When he brought it to her the next day, she carefully removed the portrait of Saint-Lambert and told him to give the ring to M. du Châtelet. Voltaire, slower in his reactions, asked Longchamp about the ring some days later, anxious that it might contain his own portrait. When he learnt what had happened, the crudeness of his response bespoke the depth of his grief. 'That's women for you,' he said, throwing his eyes up. 'I removed Richelieu from that ring, and Saint-Lambert expelled me. One nail to drive out another. Such is the way of the world.'[10] He wrote more appropriately to Mme Denis: 'My dear child, I have lost a friend of twenty years. It is a long time, as you know, since I regarded Madame du Châtelet as a woman, and I trust you will share in my grief. To have seen her die, and in such circumstances! And from such a cause! It is all quite dreadful.' Informing his niece that he would be accompanying M. du Châtelet to Cirey to collect important papers, he assured her of his continuing devotion: 'From Cirey I shall return to Paris to embrace you and be reunited with my one consolation, my one and only hope in this life.'[11]

Mme du Châtelet was buried on 11 September at 10 a.m. in what is now the Église Saint-Jacques in Lunéville, from where her remains were removed during the Revolution and later, in part, returned. As she had instructed, Longchamp delivered into the hands of her husband a parcel and a small casket, each containing her personal papers. The key to the casket was contained in a sealed envelope on which she had written: 'I request M. du Châtelet to be so kind as to burn these papers without perusal, they being of no use to him and quite unconnected with his own affairs.'[12] According to Longchamp, her husband began to inspect what appeared to be letters and grimaced with displeasure. His brother, the comte de Lomont, objected to this act of disrespect towards the dead, tipped the contents of the casket into the fireplace, and set fire to them. To this day people have wondered if these were Voltaire's letters to his divine Émilie. For those letters – like almost all of hers to him – have disappeared without trace, and their relationship remains for the biographer a phenomenon to be observed at one remove: in what other people said about them, or in what they said about each other to other people. Our prying eyes cannot truly know the closeness that they enjoyed for some sixteen and a half years, a closeness born of great intelligence, shared interests, and a fundamentally similar world view. For – had things turned out differently – theirs was a deep affinity and companionship that would surely have persisted through such years as might otherwise have remained to them.

It was obligatory upon the death of a propertied person to proceed at once to the preparation of a detailed inventory of their possessions. Accordingly, Voltaire accompanied M. du Châtelet and his brother to Cirey to accomplish the painful task and, in his own case, to bid farewell to the place that had been the nearest thing to home that he had known since his days in the Palais de Justice. On 23 September he wrote to the d'Argentals, the couple's closest friends and advisers over the past ten years or more:

> I would even say that a house in which she once used to live is not – though it causes me pain – disagreeable to me. I do not fear my affliction, I do not flee from what speaks to me of her. I love Cirey. Though I would not be able to tolerate Lunéville, where I lost her [. . .] But the places that she made beautiful are dear to me. I have not lost a mistress, I have lost half of myself, a soul for whom my own soul was made, a friend of twenty years whom I had seen born. The most loving father could not love his only daughter more. I delight in finding the thought of her everywhere. I delight in talking to her husband, to her son. Well, they say that no two people grieve alike, and so there you have how my grief is.[13]

Voltaire the *philosophe* may have refused to believe in an immaterial soul. How could he believe in it? There was no tangible evidence of such a thing. But now in the very absence of the person he had loved more than any other – or ever would – he beheld an ineffable human essence that transcends corporeal reality and lives on in the memory of those who are left behind. Generation after generation.

And Émilie? Some three or four years earlier she had written a *Discours sur le bonheur* (*Discourse on Happiness*), entrusting the manuscript to Saint-Lambert shortly before her death. Here she reflects that a life without passion is no life at all, even if passion is what brings pain and tumult to an existence that might otherwise be serene and untroubled. Some passions, like a passion for work, are safe passions: they entail no dependence on others. Unlike gambling, ambition and love. And, of these, love reigns supreme, bringing the greatest happiness even as it also brings the greatest suffering – like the thunderstorm that is the price we pay for a beautiful summer's day. And when it comes to suffering for love, women suffer most. For they love more passionately than men: 'I have received from God [. . .] one of those tender, unchanging souls that can neither disguise nor moderate its passions, that knows neither what it is for a passion to cool nor what it is to feel disgust, a soul so tenacious that it can resist anything, even the certain knowledge of no longer being loved.' Whereas men tire of such love, and their thoughts soon turn back to work and ambition. Women, therefore, must love for two, as she has done:

> I have been happy for the past ten years in my love for the man who conquered my soul, and I have spent those ten years in intimate contact with him without a moment's disgust or indifference. When his interest in me declined on account of advancing age, illness, and perhaps also a certain difficulty in obtaining sexual satisfaction, it took me a long time to realize the fact: I loved for two. I spent every living moment with him, and my heart, empty of all suspicion, delighted in the pleasure of loving and the illusion of believing myself to be loved. It is true that I lost that happy state, and that the loss of it caused me to shed many a tear. It takes terrible blows to break such chains: the wound in my heart bled for a long time; I had good grounds for complaint, and I forgave all.[14]

Voltaire knew that in his body he had betrayed her with Mme Denis. Yet in his heart he believed himself faithful, and he had been determined not to leave her. Formerly bed-mates, they had remained soul-mates. For Émilie that was no longer love, but for François it was. Her fatal affair with Saint-Lambert left him feeling that he, too, had good grounds for complaint. But he forgave them both. And indeed he came to regard Saint-Lambert's poem *Les Saisons* (1769) as the poetic masterpiece of the century. As to his own poetic talents, he penned a few simple verses and attached to them a portrait of the person who had been – and would remain – the greatest love of his life:

> L'univers a perdu la sublime Émilie.
> Elle aima les plaisirs, les arts, la vérité.
> Les dieux, en lui donnant leur âme et le génie,
> N'avaient gardé pour eux que l'immortalité.

> (The universe has lost the sublime Émilie.
> She loved pleasure, art, and truth.
> The gods gave her genius and their soul,
> Everything they had – save immortality.)[15]

LATE MIDDLES

(1749–1768)

A Kingdom of One's Own

CHAPTER THIRTEEN

Hello and Goodbye to Berlin
(1749–1753)

Wherein a royal chamberlain is squeezed like an orange

W HERE SHOULD VOLTAIRE GO? Lunéville was too painful, and too dull – though the *baba au rhum* was delicious.[1] He loved Cirey, but it did not belong to him. Nor did the house in Paris, in the rue Traversière, and anyway it held the wrong sort of memories. There was only one answer: he would go to Mme Denis, wherever she was. 'My life is yours, and you may do with it as you please.'[2] Perhaps he would buy a grand house for them, for he was now a very rich man. He had continued over the past decade to invest in the colonial trade centred on Cadiz, making substantial sums every time his ship came in. Through the Pâris brothers he continued to make no less sizeable profits out of the French army. He was quite genuine in his aversion to war – in a civilized world rational discussion would be a much better alternative – but he would have seen it as hopelessly naïve to boycott lucrative investment in military supplies. Moreover, even in time of peace (and the War of the Austrian Succession had just ended), the army still needed food and uniforms. As each profit became the opportunity for further investment, he continued also to lend significant sums to the impecuniously grand, who paid him good interest. His annual income rose steadily. By 1749 it had reached some 75,000 *livres* (by Longchamp's calculations): that is, roughly half the capital sum he had once been left by his father. It was also about half the total debt that Émilie was found to have accrued at the time of her death. Alas for her husband the marquis.

Voltaire was mindful of Frederick's open invitation to revisit Prussia, but it was too soon for that: he had still to grieve. And so he decided after all to return to the rue Traversière, which M. du Châtelet had agreed to sublet. Here, for the time being, he would mourn his loss in private solitude. He arrived on 12 October, a month after Mme du Châtelet's death. He was ill and forlorn. Around him lay twenty-five packing-crates containing the personal effects he had removed from Cirey: sundry scientific instruments stood about, bearing silent witness to the shared enthusiasms of the past. During the nights that followed he would leave his bed and wander round his old apartment on the first floor, calling for his beloved Émilie. On one occasion he stumbled into a pile of books in the dark and collapsed on the floor, too weak to get up. When Longchamp eventually heard his cries, he found his master frozen to the core, and wrapped him in warm towels. But gradually he regained his strength and a taste for living. Mme Denis visited frequently and was solicitous. He wrote to Dumas d'Aigueberre, the man who had introduced him to Émilie, and invited him to share the house. The librettist declined the offer. Doubtless he knew that he could not displace a ghost. But then at the turn of the year Mme Denis moved in on the ground floor, where the marquise had lived. She at least was not afraid to fill the void. And did so for the next twenty-eight years.

After his prolonged absences at the court of Lorraine, the Historiographer Royal found that he had fallen out of fashion. Mme de Pompadour, long a devotee of Crébillon, had encouraged the celebrated playwright to make a comeback, and his *Catalina*, premiered at the Comédie-Française on 20 December 1748, had been a great success. The King was as enthusiastic as his mistress. Now seventy-four, Crébillon lived alone in the Marais with a housekeeper, in a house full of innumerable cats and dogs, and this had been his first play for twenty-two years. Voltaire's initial response to this renewed threat to his own pre-eminence had been *Rome sauvée*, his still-unstaged version of *Catalina*, but he now decided to compete with the old has-been by rewriting his *Électre* (*Electra*) of 1708. Crébillon was again appointed as censor, and, no doubt feeling magnanimous in his new-found glory, he passed his younger rival's latest play fit for public consumption: 'May the brother bring you as much honour as the sister did me,' he graciously wrote.[3] He may also have realized that the 'brother' – *Oreste* – was not much good: it was first performed on 12 January 1750 and flopped. Voltaire revised it for a second performance but, though he personally exhorted the audience to applaud it, the play failed again. An excellent cast could not disguise how poorly conceived and how badly constructed this new play plainly was. Mme de Pompadour, conscious of Voltaire's hurt, did what she could by having *Oreste* publicly staged at Versailles and by taking the lead role in a private performance of *Alzire*. But the comparison served only to underline the inadequacies of the more recent play, and to confirm the King in his preference for Crébillon.

As to *Rome sauvée*, the Comédie-Française refused to take it, and Voltaire was obliged to install a makeshift stage at home in the rue Traversière. He had created a theatre in the attic at Cirey, so why not here in Paris? Having auditioned a rival troupe in a performance of *Mahomet*, he invited a large and select audience to a performance of *Rome sauvée* on 8 June. Over a hundred guests squeezed into the adapted, second-floor room: they included the duc de Richelieu and the duc de La Vallière, the King's own entertainers; Father Simon de la Tour, head of the Collège Louis-le-Grand, along with a number of fellow-Jesuits; and Jean Le Rond d'Alembert, the leading mathematician who had been elected to the Académie des Sciences at the age of twenty-three and who was now celebrated for his collaboration in the forthcoming *Encyclopédie*. The play went down well. Further performances were called for, extra seating was somehow provided, and the duchesse du Maine agreed to a gala performance at Sceaux on 22 June. With sets and costumes now to hand, other Voltaire plays were performed at the rue Traversière, sometimes with Mme Denis and her sister Mme de Fontaine in the cast. Indeed Mme Denis had written a comedy of her own, *La Dame à la mode* (*The Lady of Fashion*) – later retitled *La Coquette punie* (*The Coquette Confounded*) – and would soon be at work on a verse tragedy, *Alceste*. Her uncle managed to avoid having to stage them.

Such thespian delights were good therapy for a grieving man but a paltry sop to his ambitions. Was his star on the wane? Louis XV seemed to be ignoring him, the Parisian theatre-going public was currently enthusing about Mme de Graffigny's sentimental comedy, *Cénie* (*Cenia*), and the cause of freethinking seemed to have passed into other hands. During the previous year Denis Diderot had been imprisoned in the Château de Vincennes for publishing his *Lettre sur les aveugles* (*Letter on the Blind*), a radical philosophical treatise that questions traditional arguments in favour of God's existence and foregrounds the relativity of human knowledge and morality. With d'Alembert, Diderot was now launching the *Encyclopédie*: his prospectus had just been published, and the work itself — in seventeen volumes with eleven volumes of plates — would start to appear the following year. In addition, Jean-Jacques Rousseau had sent Voltaire a copy of his recent discourse, on the arts and sciences, in which he begins to propound his radical thesis that man, originally a natural and simply virtuous creature, has been morally corrupted by the so-called 'progress' of civilization. Had those years with Mme du Châtelet been wasted? Had he spent too long playing the courtier? What had happened to the author of the *Lettres philosophiques*?

Voltaire decided to revisit Prussia. There at least he would be fêted, and there he could once more engage in 'philosophical' study and conversation in the freethinking company of Frederick and his court. His official posts as royal historian and gentleman of the bedchamber obliged him to ask the King for permission, and he duly went to Compiègne, where the French court was spending part of the summer. Perhaps Louis might again want to use him as his envoy? But the King barely acknowledged his presence, granting him leave to depart but apparently quite indifferent as to whether he did so or not. The country's greatest poet and playwright? The man who had entertained him and celebrated his royal victories? The friend of Mme de Pompadour? In retrospect it seems barely credible, but at the time nobody knew — least of all Voltaire — that this would be his last appearance at the French court. Nor did anyone realize that the great man would not set foot in Paris again for the next twenty-eight years. For the moment, as he crossed the French border on 30 June 1750, everyone thought — including Mme Denis — that he was absenting himself for a matter of months. He himself was aware that Frederick might once again try to persuade him to become a permanent member of his entourage, but he was not yet minded to accept. There was Italy to visit, perhaps even an audience with the Pope to think about, and then he would return to Paris and once more become the toast of the court and the Comédie-Française.

With no Émilie to warn him, Voltaire walked straight into Frederick's trap. For the Prussian king was no less of a strategist with his friends than he was with his soldiers. Realizing Voltaire's anxieties about being *passé*, he had recently invited the young poet Baculard d'Arnaud, Voltaire's protégé (and one of Mme Denis's nice young men), to join him at Sans Souci, his new palace at Potsdam. As befitted his invitee, he did so in verse and addressed him as the new Apollo: 'Come and shine in your turn. As he [Voltaire] sinks, so shall you rise. / Thus does a fine sunset / Promise a yet brighter dawn.'[4] And Frederick made sure that these lines were seen by the old Apollo too. Just when Voltaire was assuming that Frederick's invitation was as generous and as flatteringly open-ended as ever, the possible prospect of its withdrawal was designed to stimulate his eagerness to accept. He had already decided to go, but now he hastened to do so – in so far as the appalling state of the Westphalian roads permitted. He reached Potsdam on 21 July 1750 and was reunited with Frederick six days later in Berlin, a further twelve miles east.

At first all was well. Old Apollo was given magnificent accommodation at Charlottenburg, the royal palace. He would spend two hours each day with the King, advising him on his poetic, historical and philosophical writings, and then in the evenings he would join in the supper-parties at which the conversation seemed invariably brilliant in its wit and licence. Frederick was showing himself and his court off to very best advantage, and appeared genuinely attached to his new guest. Voltaire was bowled over. In such a setting was he born to live. On 7 August he officially requested to be admitted into the King's service. Frederick asked his ambassador in France to secure the necessary permission from Louis, which was granted with unflattering speed (through his new prime minister, the comte de Saint-Florentin). Thereupon Voltaire was appointed a chamberlain in the royal household, admitted to the Order of Merit, and paid an annual salary of 20,000 *livres*. Mme Denis was aghast, as were Voltaire's other friends in Paris. Did he realize what he was doing? When the new chamberlain told his master of their worries, the Prussian king replied by letter: 'I am firmly persuaded that you will be thoroughly happy here as long as I live.'[5] 'Firmly persuaded' perhaps, but would he ensure it? Voltaire, however, needed no convincing. Berlin seemed to offer paradise on earth: there were balls and operas and concerts, a seemingly endless round of festivities. Here was a haven of sound reason and civilized taste, with not a Jesuit or Jansenist in sight. A true home for philosophers, a new Athens! And as he accompanied Frederick and his family across the square before a particularly spectacular royal tournament, the crowd acclaimed him by name. He was still a star.

But the star had burned his bridges, both French and Prussian. The French court regarded his request to serve Frederick as an act of treachery. He was allowed to retain his royal pension and indeed his title as Gentleman in Ordinary of the Royal Bedchamber, but he was relieved of his duties as Historiographer Royal. How could he record the life of the King of France if he was never there? The fact that he planned to return to Paris in November was of no consequence. And in Prussia, too, he had taken an irrevocable step. Though he did not yet realize the implications of the change, he had become the King's servant and no longer a distinguished guest who needed to be wooed. The seducer had achieved his purpose: he had 'acquired' the one 'possession' he had always coveted, and he now had a court to rival Versailles. And a palace too – the rococo château that he had personally designed and to which he had given the French name of Sans Souci (literally, 'Carefree'). Built on top of a hill in the garrison town of Potsdam, its elegant wings stretch out on either side of a central rotunda in which the assembled international team of literary and scientific celebrities were accustomed to join their king at supper-parties, the symposia of this latter-day Athens. A room was allocated to Voltaire in the west wing.

But Voltaire spent more of his time in Berlin, at Charlottenburg. The Prussian capital numbered approximately 110,000 inhabitants at this period and was a fifth the size of Paris or London. It had been expanded significantly at the beginning of the century by Frederick's grandfather, the Great Elector, who turned himself into a king and his city into the most important German city after Vienna. As the Habsburg capital of the Holy Roman Empire Vienna continued to retain its Roman Catholic character, but the population of Berlin was predominantly Protestant and contained a significant proportion of French Huguenots, perhaps 8,000, from families who had fled from France after the Revocation of the Edict of Nantes in 1685. But Voltaire had little contact with them, confining himself to the royal circle, in which French was also the language of choice. Like Potsdam the city was dominated by the presence of the army, not least because many civilians used to wear second-hand military uniforms as a cheap form of clothing. Prussian blue was everywhere. Evidence of enlightened rule could be found in

recent urban developments, be it the elegant avenue of Unter den Linden or
the finest opera house in Europe or the Catholic church then under
construction – ostensibly as a symbol of religious toleration but also as
a means of encouraging Catholic Silesians to come and work in the capital.
Nevertheless the army's needs took priority. Thus the ground floor of the
Academy of Arts and Sciences housed the stables of the royal cavalry, while
above them Maupertuis presided over more intellectual pursuits, ably assisted
by the second-generation Huguenot and former pastor, Samuel Formey.

But Voltaire had little opportunity to mix with the younger Enlightenment
figures who were then coming to prominence in the Prussian capital, men such
as the future dramatist Gotthold Lessing or the philosopher Moses Men-
delssohn or the publisher and writer Friedrich Nicolai. Instead he was obliged
to keep company with the ladies of the court: the 67-year-old Queen Mother,
Sophia Dorothea, daughter of George I of England, or Frederick's neglected 35-
year-old wife, Elisabeth Christine, or one of his six sisters, either the unmarried
Amelia or another who happened to be visiting. Voltaire's favourite, just as she
was Frederick's, was Sophia Wilhelmine, married to the Margrave of Bayreuth.
Of the potential male company, Frederick's three brothers were often absent on
military duty. A particularly important contact was the French ambassador to
Prussia, Richard Talbot, Earl of Tyrconnel, a jovial and corpulent gourmand
of Irish extraction who died of a heart attack two years later. Of more
philosophical bent there was Maupertuis himself; Frederick's beloved Algarotti, who had once visited Cirey; the marquis d'Argens, whom Voltaire had first
met in Holland some years earlier; La Mettrie, the resident atheist and author of
L'Homme-machine (Man-Machine) (1748), who would die a materialist's death (of
indigestion) in November 1751. And finally there was the 35-year-old Countess
Bentinck, Voltaire's charming and vivacious friend, who had sought refuge at
Frederick's court from an estranged husband (the first Earl of Portland)
determined to dispossess her. Such persons provided welcome relief for the
chamberlain as he attended the endless round of ritual events that filled the
court calendar, from a variety of royal birthdays to the no less inevitable
military parade. The Countess in particular proved to be engaging company: in
all likelihood the two friends became lovers.

And there was always his own work. After the tumult of life with Émilie
he now had the time and seclusion to complete long-standing projects. Le

Siècle de Louis XIV became a central focus of his efforts, although some source material was hard to come by. In Prussia, he complained, 'there are prodigious quantities of bayonets but very few books'.[6] Fortunately he had access to the excellent library at Sans Souci, and he could always order books from his own publisher in Dresden, Conrad Walther, who had brought out his first collected edition of Voltaire's works in 1748. And it was to Walther, on 12 January 1751, that he sent the completed version of *Micromégas*, his latest 'philosophical tale' and indeed the first to bear that label as its subtitle. Over a decade earlier, at Cirey in 1739, Voltaire had sent Frederick an amusing story of interstellar travel entitled the *Voyage du baron Gangan*. Now, perhaps at Frederick's instigation but more probably in fond memory of his life with Mme du Châtelet, he revised the original text (of which no copy exists, only the evidence from Frederick's letter of thanks).

In *Micromégas* the Newtonian universe becomes an allegorical superhighway for the mental journeys of empiricist thought. 'On one of the planets that orbit the star named Sirius,' it begins, 'there once was a young man of great intelligence, whom I had the honour of meeting when last he journeyed to our little anthill. He was called Micromégas, a most suitable name for all men of stature.' Therein lies the message of the story: everything is relative, and to the tallest the tall are short. If human beings think they are the greatest, they must be out of their tiny minds: but mega they are in their arrogant ignorance. The Sirian's interplanetary journey has been unproblematic: 'Our traveller had a marvellous grasp of the laws of gravity and of all the forces of attraction and repulsion. He put this to such good use that he and his retinue managed, sometimes with the help of a sunbeam, sometimes by means of a convenient comet, to proceed from globe to globe like a bird flitting from branch to branch.' Following their arrival on Saturn the diminutive size of the inhabitants causes some initial Sirian mirth; but 'as the Sirian was no fool, he very soon realized that a thinking being may perfectly well not be ridiculous just because he is only six thousand feet tall.' Indeed he rather admires the Secretary of the Saturnian Academy, and after a most interesting conversation 'they resolved to make a little philosophical journey together'. To reach the answers you need first to find out the facts.

But the 'globe of Earth' proves very difficult to make out. So small, and so bizarre. Having fished a microscopic whale out of the water and been unable to locate its soul, 'the two travellers were therefore inclined to think that there is no intelligent life in this abode of ours'. But then they find Maupertuis and his Lapp girls on their way back from the Arctic Circle. Plus a motley bunch of philosophers, who each explains what he means by 'soul'. Micromégas is rather more impressed by the diffident disciple of Locke than by the self-assured representatives of Aristotle, Descartes and Leibniz. Whereupon 'he promised to write them a nice book of philosophy, in very small script just for them, and that in this book they would discover what was what'. Alas, when the book is opened at the Académie des Sciences in Paris, the pages are blank. Sirians, like God, move in mysterious ways their teachings to perform. Especially when the lesson is the need for intellectual humility and the benefits of E.T. We can all enjoy Enlightened Travel.

Not that all travellers are necessarily enlightened. If Voltaire had moved home, he had not nevertheless changed character. Soon he was embroiled in a series of quarrels that brought him little satisfaction and much opprobrium. Baculard d'Arnaud was piqued at having been used by Frederick to goad Voltaire into coming, and when he found himself subsequently sidelined he took his revenge by libelling his former protector, notably in some letters to arch-enemy Fréron. Voltaire secured his dismissal and declared smugly that 'the rising sun has gone off to set'. But Frederick soon resented having been bounced into the decision. Then Voltaire became embroiled in a financial dispute with two Jewish businessmen, a father and son both called Abraham Hirschel. The sums were large, the transactions opaque, and the legality in doubt. In brief, Voltaire was buying in Saxon government bonds at a reduced price in the knowledge that 'as a Prussian' he could redeem them for their face value under the terms of the Treaty of Dresden (between Prussia and Saxony in 1745) by applying to the Saxon tax authorities. He quickly changed his plan when he realized how it might embarrass Frederick, who was currently engaged in delicate diplomatic discussions with Saxony over this and related matters. But when Hirschel junior was unable immediately to repay the money he had been lent for the purpose and gave his client some diamonds to the same value as surety, Voltaire sued – for he thought the man had cheated him over the value of these diamonds. The royal chamberlain had barely been in the post a few months, and here he was already mired in litigation. Hirschel senior promptly and inopportunely died – Voltaire's more vulnerable enemies had this unfortunate propensity – while his son made counter charges: that Voltaire had ripped a diamond ring from his finger, that Voltaire had forged his signature . . . Shades of England and that cloud, perhaps. Voltaire won the case, but yet again his name was on gossipers' lips throughout Europe. Such 'business' and such court cases did his reputation no good whatsoever, and did more than embarrass Frederick. The King suppressed all local press coverage of the affair and wrote a furious letter to his chamberlain, admonishing him in the most categoric terms and issuing a stern warning as to the consequences of any such future meddling in Prussian diplomatic affairs. Semi-disgraced, Voltaire requested permission to withdraw temporarily from the court and to live just outside Potsdam in a house recently vacated by the marquis d'Argens. Permission granted. But no, he could not renounce his salary as chamberlain: he was still the King's servant. And he would do his bidding. Voltaire duly remained in this semi-exile until the marquis d'Argens's return at the end of August, after which he returned to his grace-and-favour accommodation in the royal palaces of Berlin and Potsdam.

All thoughts of travelling back to Paris or on to Italy had now evaporated, and Voltaire returned to his one sure source of solace: work. He continued to advise the King on his writings, and he would send him the occasional flattering poem. Sometimes he would be invited to supper at Sans Souci, and it was almost like old times. But the King's attitude towards him had changed, as he learnt from La Mettrie the following summer. Apparently a courtier had objected to the King that the special favour with which he was accustomed to treat Voltaire was causing jealousy and unhappiness amongst other members of his court. Frederick is said to have replied: 'I shall have need of him for another year at most, no longer. One squeezes the orange and one throws away the peel.'[7] Was La Mettrie making trouble? Voltaire convinced himself that the story was genuine, and was deeply disillusioned. After corresponding with each other for nearly twenty years, after all those protestations of admiration, friendship, and even love, after all the conversations they had enjoyed, after all the help he had given Frederick with his work . . . Frederick, of course, may have made the remark (if indeed he did make it) in a moment of impatience or to placate jealous courtiers. But the damage was done. Voltaire felt used, and vulnerable: 'I resolved thereupon to place the orange peel in safe keeping.'[8]

Paris once more looked attractive. Mme Denis was refusing to come to Prussia, and Voltaire's reputation as a playwright was about to be restored. The ban on *Mahomet* was lifted, and the play would enjoy a successful run in the autumn. *Zaïre* and *Œdipe* were once again delighting the royal court at Fontainebleau. His friends pressed him to return, leaning on him with the suggestion that *Rome sauvée* might finally be given a public performance if he himself consented to be present. Before the remark about oranges, Voltaire had been adamant: a return to France would simply mean more persecution; the terrible Boyer was poisoning the Dauphin's mind against him, so that even if something should happen to Louis XV . . . ; and life with Frederick had many advantages. But now, at the end of September 1751, he enquired of Mme Denis whether Richelieu might not seek his rehabilitation at court through the good offices of Mme de Pompadour. Surely she could be brought to see that he was a far better dramatist than Crébillon! So he was beginning to prepare his exit.

But first more work. *Le Siècle de Louis XIV* was published in Berlin at the end of 1751, in two volumes, under the name of 'M. de Francheville', a (real) member of the Berlin Academy. Profiting from this alias, Voltaire introduced some bold innovation – in spelling. Here appeared for the first time the now standard distinction in French between *oit* and *ait* endings that reflect a different pronunciation. Where once the written form 'François' denoted both François (like Monsieur de Voltaire) and 'français', now the different pronunciation was recorded. Similarly 'avoit'/'avoient' became 'avait'/'avaient', and 'étoit'/'étoient' were altered to 'était'/'étaient'. Very sensible. Less sensible, perhaps, was Voltaire's other innovation: using capital letters only at the beginning of paragraphs (thus saving copy-editors several headaches). but this capital idea never caught on. More importantly, *Le Siècle* marked a new advance in the writing of history, rejecting legend and hearsay in favour of well-attested empirical evidence. At the same time it replaced the depiction of events as the mere unfurling of divine providence with a more complex and contextual account of the evolution of human society and culture in which the epoch-making role of powerful individuals is manifest. Louis XIV was not just God's instrument, he created a 'great age' to rank with those inaugurated by Philip of Macedonia and Alexander the Great, by Caesar and Augustus, by the Medicis.

The prospect of a return to Paris loomed again in the spring of 1752, particularly since *Rome sauvée* had finally been staged – without him – at the Comédie-Française on 24 February. But the success was moderate, and there was no request for it to be performed at court. Moreover Voltaire worried that *Le Siècle de Louis XIV* was likely to meet with royal disapproval. On the other hand he missed Mme Denis, who was again threatening to remarry; this time, the marquis de Ximénès. And another theatrical success – *Amélie ou le duc de Foix*, on 17 August 1752 – continued to bode well for the prospect of a triumphal return, though the success in this case owed more to the new acting star, Lekain, than to the play itself. Nevertheless he stayed. Despite his royal duties he was not always at Frederick's beck and call, and he enjoyed a significant amount of leisure in which to pursue his own interests. Whatever he said or wrote, moreover, he did not have to worry about the Bastille. Thus his latest and particularly savage onslaught on the Judaeo-Christian religious tradition, the *Sermon des cinquante* (*The Sermon of the Fifty*), was circulating, albeit anonymously, in both manuscript and print. Many responded warmly to its rousing call to replace Christianity with 'the wise and simple worship of the one and only God'. The lesson was clear: deism was the natural culmination of the Reformation, a sensible, rational and potentially all-embracing improvement on Protestant and Nonconformist sects. And Voltaire was free to repeat the lesson in his *Défense de milord Bolingbroke* (1752). In part an apologia – in the name of a 'Doctor Goodnatur'd Wellwisher, chaplain to the Earl of Chesterfield' – for the beliefs of the enlightened aristocrat who had so influenced his thought as a young man and who had died on 21 November 1751, this text was also a response to the Protestant Samuel Formey's recent attack on deism. Must we continue with this sectarian bickering, asks Voltaire: everyone shares the same moral code, so why fall out over dogma and superstition that have needlessly and tragically divided human beings for over 1700 years?

No wonder he stayed. He was having fun. This freethinking company was interesting, not least that of the abbé de Prades, a young theologian on the run from Paris having contributed an article to Diderot's *Encyclopédie*. There was even talk of d'Alembert succeeding Maupertuis as the President of the

Voltaire aged forty-one, by Maurice Quentin de la Tour
(1704–88). Pastel.

Ninon de Lenclos, attributed
to Louis-Ferdinand Elle
(1612–89). Oil.

Jean-Baptiste Rousseau, by
Nicolas de Largillière
(1656–1746). Oil.

Louise-Bénédicte de Bourbon, duchesse du Maine, by
François de Troy (1645–1730). Oil.

Alexander Pope and his dog,
Bounce, attributed to Jonathan
Richardson(1655–1745).Oil.

Jonathan Swift, by Charles Jervas
(1675–1739). Oil.

Queen Caroline (1683–1737), wife
of George II of England, by Charles
Jervas. Oil.

Louis XV by Maurice
Quentin de la Tour. Pastel.

Marie Leszczynska, wife
of Louis XV, by Jean-
Marc Nattier
(1685–1766). Oil.

Cardinal André Hercule
de Fleury by Joseph
Siffred Duplessis
(1725–1802). Oil.

Jeanne Poisson, marquise
de Pompadour, by Jean-
Marc Nattier. Oil.

Gabrielle-Émilie Le Tonnelier de
Breteuil, marquise du Châtelet, by
Maurice Quentin de la Tour. Oil.

Françoise de Graffigny in her
later years, by an anonymous
French artist. Oil.

Jean-François de Saint-Lambert, by Louis
Carrogis (1717–1806), known as
Carmontelle. Watercolour.

Frederick II of Prussia,
by Antoine Pesne
(1683–1747). Oil.

Jean-Jacques Rousseau, by
Maurice Quentin de la Tour.
Pastel.

Jean Le Rond d'Alembert, by Maurice
Quentin de la Tour. Pastel.

Voltaire and Marie-Louise Denis, by Charles Nicolas Cochin
(1715–90). Crayon.

Marie-Louise Denis in her
late sixties, by Joseph Siffred
Duplessis. Oil. The laurel
wreath recalls Voltaire's
'coronation' at the
Comédie-Française.

Lekain, of the Comédie-
Française, in the role of
Genghis Khan, by Simon
Bernard Le Noir
(1729–91). Oil.

Voltaire's levée (at Ferney), by Jean Huber (1721–86). Oil.
The Carmontelle engraving of the Calas family can be seen
hanging on the wall.

Berlin Academy. And of course he enjoyed taking issue with La Mettrie and his materialist views. Indeed they spurred him to write a first draft of *La Loi naturelle* (*Natural Law*), originally entitled *La Religion naturelle* and eventually published in 1756. In this long poem he rejects La Mettrie's argument that moral values are an illusory and irrelevant commentary on ineluctable physiological processes. As a deist he defends his faith in a just God whose hand is everywhere visible in nature and whose presence we can feel in our hearts, a God whose orderliness can be imitated on earth by a just and enlightened ruler. It was a faith he would find himself defending stoutly as the atheist/materialist camp grew more numerous and more vociferous over the remaining twenty-five years of his life.

He now employed a new secretary, Cosimo Alessandro Collini. The previous one, Richier, had been sacked after lending a manuscript copy of *Le Siècle de Louis XIV* to the student who had helped interpret during the Hirschel court case. This student, none other than Lessing, had gone off with it, and Voltaire was eager for its return (to prevent a pirated edition). If Lessing would like to translate it into German, Voltaire would gladly let him have a corrected version . . . Lessing declined: to translate Voltaire well, he said, one would have to sell one's soul to the devil.[9] Not such a bad bargain perhaps, since in the following year Lessing agreed to translate Voltaire's *Essai sur le siècle de Louis XIV*. Collini, albeit Florentine, was more trustworthy than Richier, and Voltaire was soon confiding in him the outline of an exciting new project that had been mooted during one of Frederick's philosophical supper-parties: a philosophical dictionary to be written by divers hands. Voltaire's hand had soon produced at least half a dozen entries, on religious topics (Abraham, atheism, baptism . . .): the seeds of his own, single-handed *Dictionnaire philosophique portatif* (*Portable Philosophical Dictionary*), eventually published in 1764, had been sown. Like the philosophical tale, the dictionary entry would soon become one of his most effective polemical weapons.

In the autumn of 1752 Voltaire turned his weaponry on Maupertuis, and in two short pages published in an Amsterdam journal he burned his Prussian boats once and for all. The question at issue was the reputation and actions of Maupertuis, President of the Berlin Academy (and a member of the French Académie des Sciences). Appointed by Frederick in 1746 and granted sweeping powers, he was effectively the King's Minister of Science, and his marriage to one of Princess Amelia's ladies-in-waiting, the rather dull Mlle de Borck, indicated his ambition to be integrated into Prussian society. It also drove him to drink (not to mention a predilection for parrots). A distinguished but much smaller fish in the Parisian pond, Maupertuis had come to Berlin to be important. And of course Voltaire could not stand importance unless it was his own. He had known him since 1732, and relations had never been easy, not least because of Émilie's affair with her handsome tutor when they were supposed to be doing their sums. Voltaire had been grateful for the expert's help with his book on Newton, but that had not prevented him making the most of Maupertuis's unfortunate experience at the Battle of Mollwitz. The famous mathematician had been captured by Moravian peasants, or so the story went, and stripped of his clothes before being saved in the nick of time: 'then they robbed him of more than fifty theorems he was carrying in his pockets'.[10] In Berlin Voltaire had quickly outshone his rival, which made the President of the Berlin Academy all the keener to be important.

In 1750 Maupertuis published his *Essai de cosmologie* (*Essay on Cosmology*) in which he sought – as Voltaire described it – to demonstrate the existence of God by an equation. (In his *Essai de philosophie morale*, published a year earlier, he had defined human happiness in a mathematical formula . . .) This demonstration turned on the 'principle of least action' whereby, so Maupertuis claimed, the amount of action required for any natural change will always be the least amount needed to effect it. Samuel König, another of Émilie's old tutors, begged to differ. Now working in Holland, König had been elected to associate membership of the Berlin Academy (by Maupertuis) in 1749. When he visited Berlin in September 1750 he pointed out what was wrong with Maupertuis's calculations: furious, the President refused to listen. So König published his objections, in March 1751, also pointing out that this principle had already been established by Leibniz. By way of evidence he quoted part of a letter that Leibniz had written to a Basle professor called Hermann. When Maupertuis demanded to see the letter, König replied that he only had a copy, sent to him by a man called Henzi – who, alas, had just been beheaded in Bern. So Maupertuis accused König of forging the letter. Using his influence (and Frederick's), he then had Henzi's papers searched. No letter. Still refusing to debate the mathematics with König, as the latter proposed, Maupertuis continued to demand the evidence that his own 'discovery' was not original. Poor König could only reply that no letter had been found among the papers of the alleged recipient, Hermann. Accordingly, at Maupertuis's instigation, the Berlin Academy declared König guilty of forgery and of wrongfully impugning their President's reputation. Since no other academician understood the theoretical physics at issue, and since they all depended on the President for their livelihood, the verdict was a foregone conclusion.

Maupertuis published his academy's report in May 1752 and sent copies to the Académie des Sciences in Paris. König resigned his associate membership and sought redress, arguing in a published 'Appeal to the Public' that no individual academy had the right to be judge and jury in deciding such a matter. In the domain of science all are equal: truth is the sole criterion of justice. Meanwhile Maupertuis was foolish enough to publish a 'Letter on Scientific Progress' (and to include it in the newly published edition of his collected works) in which he sketched out some of the ways in which he thought scientific enquiry might go forward. Though his ideas were avowedly speculative, his vision of the 'cutting edge' had a daft look to it even then: let's bore a hole to the centre of the earth, let's locate those giants that are said to live in Patagonia and dissect their brains, let's try and see into the future by an opium-induced 'exaltation of the soul' . . . With enemies like these, Voltaire must have thought, who needs friends? For he had been following the affair closely since König's visit in September 1750. And now he struck – in the July–September issue of the Amsterdam critical quarterly, *La Bibliothèque raisonnée*. First, he reviewed the new edition of Maupertuis's works, rubbishing his more fanciful ideas and casting doubt on the 'principle of least action'. Then, in the same issue, he published a two-page statement: 'A Fellow of the Academy of Berlin [i.e. Voltaire] replies to a Fellow of the Academy of Paris [i.e. Maupertuis]', denouncing his handling of the König affair as a 'tyrannical abuse of his position'.

Voltaire thought he had judged his moment and his tactics to perfection. In May Maupertuis, seriously ill, had received permission from the King to seek medical help in France. Hence the rumours that d'Alembert might succeed him. Also Voltaire knew that Frederick was no more impressed with

Maupertuis's latest publications than he was, and indeed his more outlandish suggestions had become stock jokes at court. But Frederick was furious to see his academy, its President, and indeed by implication himself thus publicly attacked and ridiculed across Europe – just when his whole point had been to establish Berlin as an important centre on the world intellectual map. So he published a defence of Maupertuis: the 'Letter from a Fellow of the Academy of Berlin [Frederick] to a Fellow of the Academy of Paris [Voltaire]'. More eulogy than reasoned argument, it did not convince. Voltaire, having first flatteringly and opportunely sought permission of the ruling council in Bern to dedicate his *Rome sauvée* to them (as the epitome of quasi-Roman republican virtue), then wrote a long, detailed letter of support to König, knowing that the latter would publish it. This was his response to Frederick. Heedless of his own safety, Voltaire saw in the behaviour of Maupertuis and now Frederick an example of what he had thought they all three despised: obscurantism and the self-serving use of arbitrary power. Maupertuis, he knew, had long since been lost to the cause of enlightened thought (why, he even went to church now), but Frederick! In this argument over theoretical physics it should be the truth, not personal interest or reputation, that was at stake.

And then Voltaire published his brilliant masterpiece of intellectual assassination, the *Diatribe du docteur Akakia* (the doctor's name being the ancient Greek for 'without malice'). It consists of four sections: the 'Diatribe of Dr Akakia, physician to the Pope', the 'Decree issued by the Inquisition at Rome', the 'Judgement delivered by the professors of the College of Sapience', and the 'Letters examined'. The satire turns on a plot device whereby Maupertuis's writings are examined by various authorities as the forgeries of a young unknown writer – who is exposed as a fraud. For how could the great Maupertuis have written such nonsense! The kind Dr Akakia has to forsake his care of the Holy Father and treat the evidently deranged young writer, who thinks that the surest way to cure someone of apoplexy is to get them dancing a pirouette. And how did Voltaire manage to have this published? By sending the printer the handwritten permission Frederick had recently given him to publish the *Défense de milord Bolingbroke*. But the eagle-eyed military author of a book on fortifications spotted the *Diatribe* in the bookseller's presses and alerted the authorities. It was seized and burned.

Things were coming to a head. 'Your effrontery astounds me,' wrote Frederick: 'people erect statues to you for your works, but you deserve to be clapped in irons for your conduct.'[11] To his sister Wilhelmine he confided that 'if it were not for his wit, which still delights me, I should in all honour have been obliged to send him away'.[12] Voltaire simply demanded 'justice or death'.[13] He was in his element. A second edition of the *Diatribe*, published in Leyden, began to circulate in Berlin: Frederick ordered all copies to be seized, shredded and burned – on the public square, by the public executioner, just the way the Paris *parlement* liked to do things – and then sent the ashes to Maupertuis as an earnest of his support. Voltaire watched the proceedings from Francheville's apartments, where he was living (he had not been invited to Charlottenburg this time): he smiled to see Maupertuis's ideas going up in smoke. How thick and black that smoke was!

On New Year's Day 1753 Voltaire sent Frederick a letter of resignation, together with the gilt key denoting his office as chamberlain and the cross of the Order of Merit. He respectfully informed His Majesty that he had placed himself under the protection of the French ambassador (now the chevalier de La Touche) and begged leave to quit the country. Within half an hour Fredersdorff, the King's aide, was standing in front of Voltaire, clutching the key and the insignia and with orders that the chamberlain write a nicer letter. Voltaire wrote again, but would not withdraw his resignation. Keen to leave but with his head held high, he embarked on a policy of passive resistance – and a media campaign of European dimensions. But the King was equally resistant. 'It would be easier to leave Siberia,' Voltaire remarked to Mme Denis in the middle of January.[14]

One problem was money: how to transfer it out of the country? The answer was the Duke of Württemberg, ruler of the duchy in the south-west of Germany that is now part of Baden-Württemberg. For like many German princelings of that time the Duke needed cash. By a procedure that amounted to buying an annuity, Voltaire had already transferred the equivalent of 150,000 *livres* in German thalers to the Duke on 27 November 1752: for which he was to receive in return an annual income (payable quarterly) of 15,750 *livres* (i.e. at a rate of 10.5 per cent), with Mme Denis to receive 7,500 *livres* (5 per cent of the original capital sum) in the event of his (Voltaire's) death.

On 31 January 1753 Voltaire repeated the procedure: this time transferring the equivalent of 112,500 *livres*, for which he was to receive an annual income of 12,375 *livres* and Mme Denis a lump sum of 2,250 *livres* in the event of his death.

Voltaire was nearly sixty: even if he lived another ten years, the Duke would effectively have repaid the capital and ended up having paid virtually no interest on these 'loans'. Meanwhile Voltaire could count on a reliable income flow. Alas for the Duke, Voltaire would live till he was eighty-four; alas for Voltaire, the Duke fell constantly behind with his payments. Still, it seemed like a good deal at the time, and this type of annuity would become a major form of investment for Voltaire from now on. Especially as he was so good at telling everyone he was ill and not long for this world, which helped considerably to boost the annuity rate. From his point of view, on the other hand, such investments were a marvellous spur to longevity.

Having thus successfully arranged for the transfer of his funds out of the country, Voltaire began to think of making a run for it, disguised as a Protestant pastor. Collini would drive the waggon, and his belongings would be hidden in the hay. But finally Frederick yielded and (on 9 March) granted him leave to go. But still Voltaire wanted to depart in style: he requested an audience at Potsdam, when he could return the key and the cross.

Unfortunately a London bookseller chose this moment to publish a collection of the various articles and pamphlets relating to Maupertuis's part in the König affair, plus two pieces by Frederick (eulogizing La Mettrie and another former favourite, Charles-Etienne Jordan) in which the King champions freedom of thought. A bitter irony was evident in the contrast displayed by this so-called *Maupertuisiana*. When Voltaire received a copy from König, together with a letter from him that had plainly been opened by the police, he quickly sought to convince Frederick that he had had nothing to do with this publication. But the damage was done, and on 17 and 20 April there appeared in the Dutch press the 'précis' of a very blunt letter (dated 16 March 1753) in which Frederick had purportedly dismissed Voltaire from his service and demanded that he return 'his contract of employment, the key, the cross, and the volume of poetry'. This mysterious volume was now to play a central role in the extraordinary events that followed. But had the King actually sent such a letter? Voltaire denied it, and moreover the 'précis' was dated the day before Frederick (according to Voltaire) had granted him a very civil audience at Potsdam. Nor did Frederick subsequently refer to it as justification for what happened next.

At nine o'clock on the morning of 26 March Voltaire departed from Potsdam in orderly fashion: his salary had been paid up to date, and he had promised to return in October. All very polite. But he would never set eyes on Frederick again. Travelling in a commodious carriage with Collini, two servants and his most precious belongings, he reached Leipzig on the following evening. Having supped at The Blue Angel he was escorted to rented accommodation secured by his publisher Walther, and there he remained for the next three weeks, supervising the production of his collected works. Rather more German was spoken in these parts than he was used to, but he managed as best he could. And he met some interesting people, notably Johann Christoph Gottsched, who was Professor of Poetry at Leipzig's distinguished university. Also the octogenarian field-marshal Count Heinrich von Seckendorff, a veteran of all three Wars of Succession (Spanish, Polish and Austrian), who invited him to his home for Easter. He had a special story to tell. When Crown Prince Frederick had run away from home at the age of eighteen (with his subsequently executed lover, von Katte), it was he who had persuaded his father not to execute Frederick also. No doubt Voltaire expressed due relief and gratitude.

Voltaire left Leipzig on 18 April. He was making his way slowly towards France, waiting for a sign from Mme Denis that she had succeeded in smoothing his path back to the French court. He was to meet her in Strasbourg. Three days later he reached Gotha, where the Duke and Duchess of Saxe-Gotha invited him to their castle at Friedenstein. He stayed a month in the company of this engaging couple, who entertained him royally with grand dinners, and concerts, and – as always – the performance of his (and other people's) plays. The Duchess, aged forty-three, was particularly charming: intelligent, very well educated, an enthusiast for philosophy, but sadly quite hopeless at French versification. So lavish were the couple's tastes that Voltaire had later to lend his delightful hostess a large sum of money to allow her to make ducal ends meet. At a decent rate of interest, of course.

With some reluctance he departed on 15 May, and reached Kassel some ten days later. Though he intended to put up at The Inn of London, he was invited to stay by the local ruler, the Landgrave of Hesse-Kassel, whose subjects numbered some 350,000. Voltaire had met the Landgrave's son and heir, the enlightened Friedrich von Hesse-Kassel, in Berlin, and together with his wife (daughter of George II of England and of Voltaire's erstwhile patroness Queen Caroline) he was to become a lifelong friend. But what was Baron von Pöllnitz, one of Prussian Frederick's trusted courtiers, doing in these parts? Spying perhaps? On 30 May Voltaire set off again, travelling via Marburg, and reached Frankfurt-am-Main the following evening at about 8 p.m. As a self-governing entity within the broader jurisdiction of the Holy Roman Empire, Frankfurt lay wholly outside Frederick's control, but that had not prevented the Prussian king from writing on 11 April to Baron Franz von Freytag, his representative in the city, with the strictest instructions. He was to stop and search a Monsieur de Voltaire's luggage and repossess the chamberlain's key, the Order of Merit, all letters and papers in Frederick's hand, and the 'volume of poetry'. Should Voltaire resist, he was to be threatened with arrest, and if that failed . . . then just arrest him! Since the King had previously refused Voltaire's resignation, and since he was supposed to be returning in October, there had been no call for him to return the key and the insignia before leaving Prussia. But Frederick was not only furious about the *Maupertuisiana*, as well as all the published polemic for which Voltaire actually *was* responsible, he was also extremely anxious about the satirical use to which his witty and clever 'friend' might put his own writings, notably his poems. Though the said volume (which included non-poetic works) had been printed (on the royal presses), its circulation had been tightly restricted to a very small number of intimates. In essence Frederick was enlightened enough to have written his *Œuvres du philosophe de Sans Souci* but thoroughly despotic about who read them.

Freytag now set up a network of paid lookouts and informers and nervously bided his time. Having confirmed the identity of the two travellers who had arrived at The Golden Lion the night before, Freytag called to see Voltaire at 9 a.m. on the morning of 1 June, accompanied by a local Burgmeister (for the form) and an army officer (for the force). No doubt he relaxed somewhat when he discovered that his target 'looked like a skeleton' and claimed to be ill, and he proceeded to spend the next nine hours searching the man's belongings (two trunks, a large suitcase and two document-folders). Voltaire co-operated and proclaimed his undying devotion to the King of Prussia. The key and the cross were seized, plus sundry papers – including two bundles of Voltaire's own, as a 'caution' in case he should try to leave. But no sign of the 'volume of poetry': it was in another trunk. They would all have to wait for it to be sent on from Leipzig. By the end of the day Voltaire had obtained two signed notes from Freytag: a receipt for the two bundles of his own papers and a promise to let him go once the poetry arrived. He agreed to remain in Frankfurt for the time being but urged Freytag to send a dispatch rider to Fredersdorff, Frederick's aide, requesting 'permission' for him to leave. Freytag objected to the extra expense: the request was sent by normal post. Not so Voltaire's letter of protest to the Emperor in Vienna: that went special delivery on 5 June. But neither the Emperor nor even Frankfurt's ruling council chose to intervene in the dispute, for it was not worth upsetting the King of Prussia over some skeletal Frenchman and a book of poems. Both parties turned a blind eye to this gross infringement of their jurisdictions and an innocent traveller's freedom.

Mme Denis arrived on 9 June and immediately wrote a long letter to Frederick on her uncle's behalf, mixing remonstration with sundry professions of good faith. On 17 June, late on a Sunday evening, the all-important trunk arrived from Leipzig, only to exacerbate the situation in the most unexpected manner. For, as a token of his co-operativeness, Voltaire had given orders for it to be sent direct to Freytag's house: and Freytag refused to open it. He had received orders to do nothing until he had heard from the King – i.e. Fredersdorff – by post the following Thursday. But what about his written promise? Freytag deemed it non-binding and abjectly awaited further orders from Potsdam. So Voltaire decided to escape. On Wednesday, taking Collini and one servant, plus a chest containing his money and manuscripts, he hired a carriage and was about to make his getaway when he found himself stuck in a traffic jam – of haycarts. The delay was sufficient for word to be sent ahead to the city gate, where the fugitive was stopped. Just as well perhaps, for Freytag had given orders to shoot him if he left Frankfurt. Freytag arrived, stepped into the carriage, and accompanied his prisoners back to the centre of the city, surrounded by a detachment of soldiers. They stopped at the house of

J.F. Schmidt, Freytag's assistant as Prussian representative, where the fugitives were searched like common criminals. When they took Voltaire's snuff-box he complained that he was unable to live without his snuff, but they insisted. So he made a run for the door (or so Freytag claimed in his subsequent report to Frederick) but, when cornered, claimed merely that he had been going to relieve himself.

After negotiations with a conscientious but eventually compliant magistrate the two men were disarmed and taken to a nearby hostelry called The Goat's Horn, where they were held under guard. Meanwhile Freytag's secretary, called Dorn, went to The Golden Lion, lured Mme Denis out of her room on the pretext that he was fetching her on her uncle's behalf, and then escorted her in the company of three soldiers back to The Goat's Horn. There he locked the shocked and very frightened woman in a room with himself as guard and ordered dinner. After a certain amount to drink he became amorous, and Marie-Louise had to scream for help. The scandal was complete.

On Thursday Freytag received a letter from Fredersdorff ordering that Voltaire be released in return for a written promise to return the book in question. But Freytag began to play his own game: he was worried about the consequences of Dorn's overzealous behaviour, and he feared that he might end up having to pay all the expenses incurred during the previous three weeks of skulduggery. The Frankfurt authorities had required him to underwrite these as a condition of their acquiescence in Voltaire's arrest. Accordingly he ordered the trunk to be brought and recovered the 'volume of poetry', forwarding it reluctantly to Potsdam four days later. At the same time he and his accomplices helped themselves to the more valuable contents of the trunk: clothes, cash, gold and silver shoe-buckles, some gold scissors. Then they got Voltaire to sign for all the expenses himself. He and Mme Denis were in no state or mood to argue. And Voltaire also signed a document exonerating Freytag, Schmidt and Dorn – though he managed to subvert it with irony: 'I am thus most justly imprisoned, and although I do not know why my niece has been imprisoned, I own that this too has been most justly done.' Neither he nor his niece knew that Frederick/Fredersdorff had already given orders for Voltaire's release. They had not seen the letter of 21 June, and Freytag had also intercepted Frederick's reply to Mme Denis.

But then Dorn told them. Gradually the truth about Freytag's conduct became clear to Voltaire, as it did to Frederick — not least because he was being bombarded with letters from Voltaire's friends and supporters. He was horrified by the treatment of Mme Denis.

Freytag could only stall for so long. After dragging out his negotiations with the Frankfurt authorities and protracting his correspondence with Frederick so as always to be ostensibly awaiting further orders, he finally gave way: his prisoner could return to The Golden Lion. He was no longer under armed guard, and his sword was returned. Now it was Voltaire's turn to appeal to the Frankfurt authorities for justice, but to little avail. He did secure a court order enabling him to recover some money from Schmidt, but when it was brought to him by Dorn he was so furious that he grabbed his pistol and would have shot Mme Denis's unwanted dinner-companion on the spot had Collini not sprung forward and deflected his arm. More trouble with the courts. But the Frankfurters had had enough. Would M. de Voltaire be kind enough to leave! And he did so, on Saturday, 7 July 1753. The orange peel was safe.

CHAPTER FOURTEEN

A Niece for a Wife, or
House-Hunting in the 1750s (1753–1755)

How a man may be shipwrecked in Strasbourg
and find heaven in Switzerland

WHERE COULD VOLTAIRE go now? On the day following
her uncle's departure Mme Denis left Frankfurt and headed for
Paris to prepare the ground for his return. Meanwhile he
himself proceeded with Collini to Mainz, where he spent the next three
weeks enjoying the hospitality of the Prince-Bishop and his court. 'I have
been rather like one of those knights errant who leave an enchanted castle
and end up in a cave; but then they leave the cave and end up in another
castle.'[1] Amidst the partying he continued to seek redress from the Frankfurt
authorities, and even returned to the city for a couple of days, this time
staying at The Golden Apple. But still to no avail: the ruling council would
rather ignore the matter, especially as Frederick had written in full support of
Freytag's actions.

So Voltaire travelled to Mannheim, where the Elector Palatine became the
latest of his lavish German hosts. At the castle of Schwetzingen, between
Mannheim and Heidelberg, Prince Karl Theodor presided with intelligence
and gusto over a court that was one of the most brilliant and culturally rich
throughout the Empire. No expense was spared: indeed the Prince immediately asked his guest for a loan of 100,000 *livres*. Granted, in the form of
an annuity at 12 per cent per annum. The bruised but wealthy philosopher
felt at home once more: 'French comedies, Italian comedies, opera buffa,

ballet, fine food, conversation, good manners, nobility, simplicity . . .' Two weeks of this did much to restore his spirits, and the performance of so many of his own plays – *Zaïre*, *Alzire*, *Nanine*, *L'Indiscret* – set him thinking about writing another: an account of Genghis Khan, to be known as *L'Orphelin de Chine* (*The Orphan of China*). He had come across the subject while doing research for his history of the world, the *Essai sur les mœurs et l'esprit des nations*, begun in 1739 and finally to be published in 1756. He had also been thinking about tyrants and how to enlighten them.

On 15 August 1753 Voltaire reached Strasbourg, where he took lodgings at The White Bear, run by the father of a valet who had charmed him at Mainz. Here he remained for six weeks, awaiting the green light from his niece. Instead he received a letter informing him that she was pregnant. In this respect if in no other their sojourn in Frankfurt had proved productive. But this astonishing news was soon followed by a sadder tale: she had miscarried. Nearly sixty, Voltaire was saddened when he thought of what might have been. Marie-Louise, on the other hand, was probably relieved: would her child have called its famous progenitor 'Great Uncle' or just plain 'Papa'? We shall never know. Nor shall we ever know what would have happened if Voltaire had gone to live in Normandy. His old friend Cideville was madly in love with Mme Denis and thought Rouen might suit the couple well, especially with all those subversive booksellers to hand. But our homeless hero was thinking more in terms of a château in the country. His niece, alas, was not: she much preferred Paris.

Strasbourg was a convenient place to consult local experts and libraries for another of Voltaire's projects, a history of the Holy Roman Empire. So, too, was Colmar, where he proceeded to spend the next eight months. Lodging with Mme Goll, at 10 rue des Juifs, he completed this history and looked about for somewhere permanent to live in Alsace. The Duke of Württemberg had sold Voltaire his annuity against a château near Hobourg, just outside Colmar. The Duke was proving to be a bad payer, so why not buy the collateral and deduct the rent in arrears? But the place turned out to be a dump. To add insult to injury the Duke's agent then insisted on making payments in *Reichsthalers* (the currency of the Empire) when the exchange rate for conversion into French *livres* was much more favourable against the Brandenburg thaler that was the official currency in Berlin (where the contract had been signed). Lending money to aristocrats was not always straightforward.

As he continued to wait for some favourable news from Paris, Voltaire exorcized his anger about Frederick by composing a work of semi-fiction in epistolary form based on the actual letters that he had sent Mme Denis from Prussia. She had been reluctant to return them in case her uncle did something foolish. But he reassured her: he had posterity in mind. The result – some sixty pages comprising forty-two letters – was a po-faced spoof of the sentimental fictions of Samuel Richardson (hence Voltaire's reference to it as his *Paméla*)[2] in which the former chamberlain presents his experience at the Prussian court in terms of guileless virtue abused by cynical despotism. The squeezed and discarded orange (in his late fifties) has become, with delightful implausibility, a naïve and maidenly victim whose heart lies elsewhere (with Mme Denis in Paris) while he, the poor innocent, is seduced into the philosophical arms of a man who then betrays the truth (in his support for Maupertuis over König). The result was simply too dangerous to publish. Indeed it got buried away among Voltaire's corre-spondence, as though the letters were in fact real, and it has only recently been reconstructed and brought to light. It is the nearest to a novel that Voltaire ever wrote (he who despised novels) and was composed over a period of ten weeks, mostly in bed.

On 27 January 1754, three days after finishing *Paméla*, he received unwelcome news: the King had refused him permission to set foot in either Paris or Versailles. Having burned his bridges and his boats, Europe's most celebrated writer and thinker was again in no-man's-land. And sinking. 'Life is one vast shipwreck,' he wrote to Cideville the following day: 'and it's a case of every man for himself.'[3] His one safe haven remained Mme Denis, but she was jibbing at all the errands he kept asking her to run. Nor did she like the way he harped on about her extravagance. He, for his part, considered that she could be protecting his interests rather better. In other words, it was time to make up: and so they agreed to meet soon at Plombières in Lorraine, which the d'Argentals were once again about to visit (the comtesse was partial to taking the waters). For Voltaire it was also time to make up with the Church: the Archbishop of Paris had just denounced him publicly for a pirated and incriminatingly doctored version of the *Essai sur les mœurs* that had recently been published at The Hague. And the Jesuits of Colmar, surprisingly numerous and altogether less flexible than their sophisticated Parisian counterparts, were circling with ominous intent. So the deist went to say Easter confession. Not with the Society of Jesus – Heaven forfend! – but with a nice Capuchin monk. In the penitent's own account he told his confessor that having been in bed ill for most of the past six months he had suffered little from temptation: his one sin had been to lose his temper with a Jesuit. 'Ah,' said the monk, 'if it was only a Jesuit, there's little harm in that.' The sinner was absolved and duly went to Mass to take communion. Collini, eager to witness this unusual event, also recorded it: 'He presented his tongue [to receive the host] and looked the priest firmly in the eye. I knew that look!'[4] By way of thanks the communicant sent the monk a case of wine and a loin of veal. Paradise was cheap at the price. To save his real soul, however, he also sent a number of articles to d'Alembert for publication in the *Encyclopédie*. But they were too pithy. Wearily he agreed to make the one on literature 'as boringly useless as people wish'.[5]

On 9 June he set off for Plombières for the reunion with Mme Denis. He had intended to pay a brief visit *en route* to Dom Calmet at the Abbaye de Senones: this was the Benedictine monk whose commentaries on the Bible he and Mme du Châtelet had once found so useful and so entertaining at Cirey. But when he learnt from Mme Denis that Maupertuis was also headed for Plombières, the brief visit turned into a three weeks' stay. Which he greatly enjoyed. He should have been a monk, he told Mme Denis, for the life suited him. Perhaps she might like to become a nun? 'I'm rather an old monk, though. You'd probably rather be with a novice' – especially as a novice was a trainee monk not yet bound by the vow of chastity. But it was not just the peace and quiet that Voltaire relished. The abbey's library was a godsend, or so to speak, and the octogenarian Dom Calmet raced up and down the library ladder on the devil's behalf. For Voltaire was researching further articles for the *Encyclopédie*: 'it's always a good idea in war to go and steal the enemy's artillery and then use it against them.'[6] Responding with his usual pugnacity to the merest hint of adversity, he was gradually deciding to make a virtue of necessity: if he was beyond the pale, then he might as well let rip and truly speak his mind. He had been a fawning sycophant too long: now he would have a kingdom of his own and court disaster in the name of truth.

But first he needed a queen. He reached Plombières on 4 July and was reunited with the d'Argentals, perhaps his closest friends. His 'angels' he called them, for they watched over his interests in Paris with shrewd wisdom. They were also the indispensable arbiters of taste to whom he always submitted a new play. Mme Denis arrived with her sister, Mme de Fontaine, the following day. Voltaire had promised his elder niece with customary impropriety that they would be able to 'cleanse their blood' together as they took the waters at this fashionable spa. But since he only actually took them once – being as sceptical in this domain as in that of religion – it is to be presumed that he attended to the needs of his circulatory system in other ways. In any case, as he pointed out, 'taking the waters' appeared for most people to mean eating as much as they possibly could. But Plombières was at least an oasis of calm in which to reflect on the future, and over the course of the next three weeks Voltaire and his niece came to an understanding that would shape the rest of their lives. It was time for him to settle down, he told her (with a temporarily straight face). He wanted to set up home. He cared nothing for Louis or Frederick, wished only that she would consent to be his life's companion. He was also rewriting his will . . . This moment of decision had been looming for several years, and Marie-Louise made the same choice as Émilie had done twenty years earlier. She would give up Paris (and Cideville's Rouen) and attach herself permanently to this extraordinary man. Now in her early forties, she would become his helpmeet, his châtelaine. He was sixty and not in the best of health, so she might soon be a very wealthy widow. If not, she would still be able to enjoy the wealth – and the lovers – and her uncle too! For she was fond of him, and life in his company was most certainly never dull (even if he did spend long hours working alone). It was not a difficult decision. She presumed that they would live in France and – unlike Henri IV, who had renounced Protestantism because Paris was well worth a Mass – she was not willing to give up everything for its capital.

And so Voltaire returned to Colmar in the company of his niece, whose official role was to be that of nurse-companion to the ailing sage. Plombières had served its purpose, and he had books to write. And a house to find. Mme Denis's eyes turned westwards, but her uncle was thinking of Switzerland. There was a château at Alaman, between Rolle and Morge, on the north shore of Lake Geneva. He could offer 225,000 *livres*: over half in cash, and the remainder as shares in his Cadiz investments. But the vendors proved unduly demanding, so he decided to rent something in the same area while he and his niece continued their hunt. A Parisian banker, the baron de Guiguer, had offered him the use of his château at Prangins, north of Nyon. Perfect. On 11 November the happy couple set off, but not before a row with the increasingly unhappy Collini. As they were preparing to leave, Voltaire decided that there was too much luggage on the carriage: it would be dangerous on such a long journey. (Perhaps he remembered the time he and Mme du Châtelet ended up sitting in the snow when their axle broke on the way from Cirey to Paris.) So he ordered Collini to remove his own trunk and sell the contents. He could buy more clothes when he got there. After several exhausting years in the service of this impossible workaholic, Collini could take no more: he resigned. Then Voltaire argued over what wages he was due, refusing to pay him for the whole month of November. Impasse. Eventually Mme Denis made the peace, and off they went. No accident overcame the carriage. And Collini did not throttle his master.

A Voltairean journey now resembled a royal progress. After Dijon, where he and Mme Denis supped with a senior judge in the *parlement*, came Lyons and a number of meetings: most importantly with Jean-Robert Tronchin, his new banker, with whom he deposited 500,000 *livres* at 4 per cent; most enjoyably with his favourite Prussian, Frederick's sister, the Margrave of Bayreuth; least satisfactorily with the Archbishop, Cardinal Tencin, who refused to dine with Voltaire on the grounds that he had fallen from royal favour (Tencin was d'Argental's uncle and indeed, unofficially, d'Alembert's, for it was his sister, the leading salon hostess Mme de Tencin, who had in 1717 abandoned the future *encyclopédiste* as a baby on the steps of the church of Saint-Jean-Le-Rond in Paris); and finally, and least formally, with the duc de Richelieu, who had become a *maréchal de France* in 1748 and was now widely regarded as a great military hero. The famous playwright was given a standing ovation at the theatre after a performance of his *Brutus*, just as he was graciously received at the Academy, of which he had been a member since 1745. The couple stayed almost a month, and once again Mme Denis felt a sacrificial wrench as they departed from France's second city (and its shops) and headed for the Alps.

Next came Geneva, where they arrived on 12 December. They were greeted by the annual celebrations of the day in 1602 when the city had been saved from the men of Savoy who had tried to scale the city walls. Now the Genevan authorities kept the gates open late in order to receive its celebrated visitor: for, as his hosts graciously told him afterwards, these gates were always open to people of merit. His principal host was Jean-Robert Tronchin's brother, François, a lawyer and one of the twenty-five members of the ruling council. Now fifty and a man of enlightened views, François Tronchin was also a playwright, and his tragedy on the subject of Mary, Queen of Scots, had been performed at Fontainebleau and at the Comédie-Française exactly twenty years earlier. With a French wife and French tastes he had always longed to meet the star of the Parisian theatre.

The ostensible reason behind this visit to Geneva was for Voltaire to consult Théodore Tronchin, the internationally celebrated doctor whom he had met many years earlier in Holland and a cousin of François. This consultation – the first of many – took the form of supper on the following evening, at which Voltaire met several leading intellectual and diplomatic figures, helpfully including the French envoy to Geneva, the so-called Résident. Voltaire was keen for Louis to know that he had not abandoned France but had come to Switzerland simply for his health. In the event Théodore Tronchin saw nothing particularly wrong with the visitor's physiological state, even if it was clearly a subject of the most profound interest to the visitor himself.

Voltaire and Mme Denis departed on 14 December for Prangins, both of them moved by the warmth of their welcome and the delightful character of their hosts. Geneva itself was a beautiful city. Did they really have to leave? But leave they did, and, having crossed the Franco-Swiss border six times in barely more than ten miles, they reached Nyon and then, a few miles further and higher, their new home. The house itself was huge and rather bleak, especially in winter, but the views were spectacular, whether southwards to the lake and the Alps beyond or eastwards along the shore towards Lausanne. Still visible to the west lay Geneva itself, huddled at the mouth of the nascent river Rhône, while behind them the great range of the Jura Mountains arced north-eastwards from Geneva up beyond Lake Neuchâtel and north of Bern. Mme Denis began nesting at once, ordering furniture and warm clothing, especially a thick padded house-coat for her uncle. She approached the solitude with determination, 'for women are more courageous than people think' (*dixit* Voltaire)[7] and took on a cook and servants to help her do so. One boy, just turned fifteen, seemed a cut above the rest, and was made assistant to the hard-pressed Collini. His name was Jean-Louis Wagnière, and he would shortly become the best secretary Voltaire ever had, serving him until and beyond his death with his quite beautiful handwriting, his scrupulous efficiency, and his keen eye for detail. And unlike Longchamp he did not steal his master's manuscripts. Nor indeed was he called upon to attend Mme Denis in her bath.

Equipped with house-coat and proper office support, all Voltaire needed now was a local publisher. But that was perhaps the principal reason why he had come to Switzerland. While at Colmar he had received a letter from the Genevan booksellers Gabriel and Philibert Cramer in which they offered their services and even suggested that he might like to come and live in Geneva. When Philibert arrived in person to press the point, Voltaire was much taken with the man and his proposal, so much so that he wrote to his Parisian publisher, Lambert, and mooted a prospective programme of Franco-Swiss co-publication. Now, on his recent visit to Geneva, he had met the two brothers to take the matter further, and he continued to be impressed. Aged thirty-two and twenty-seven respectively, Gabriel and Philibert came from a long line of printer-booksellers, and the firm had established a highly effective distribution network throughout Europe. Philibert, more charming but less industrious than his elder brother, would soon leave the business and go into politics, eventually becoming a member of Geneva's ruling council. But Gabriel was no dullard: a lover of fine wine and good food, he would turn out to be a brilliant actor in Voltaire's amateur theatricals. The two men became firm friends, and 'caro' Gabriel would be Voltaire's most trusted publisher for the remainder of his life. Just now his presses were about to start printing his new client's history of the world.

Based at Prangins, uncle and niece began to house-hunt in earnest. Voltaire had learnt that no Catholic, however lapsed, could own property in the Calvinist city-state of Geneva nor in the neighbouring Swiss cantons of Bern or Vaud. But he could take a lease. Local landlords began to beat a path to Voltaire's windswept door, offering him any number of desirable residences all along the northern shore of Lake Geneva. A young banker from Lausanne, called de Giez, arrived one day to propose a property on the western outskirts of that small city, at Montriond. The man and his description both appealed to Voltaire, who accepted in principle but subject to a visit when the weather improved. The Cramers, fearful that he might prefer a rival publisher in Lausanne, prompted François Tronchin into asking permission of the Genevan ruling council for Voltaire to take up residence in the city. At the same time they called their client's attention to another property, a country residence on the hillside of Saint-Jean just outside the city gates, with gardens that stretched down to the banks of the Rhône. Its owner, the banker Jean-Jacques Mallet – also a member of the ruling council – was putting it up for sale, fully furnished, at a price of 90,000 *livres*. It was a fine house, in a glorious position, with commanding views: and Mme Denis was keen. Despite the poor weather the couple visited the property on 19 January and were immediately taken with what they found: simple, classical architecture, elegant reception rooms opening directly on to a generous terrace, and exquisite gardens. To one side a long gallery extended out from an oval vestibule: it would be perfect as a summer drawing-room, and large enough for their theatricals.[8]

But Voltaire liked to drive a hard bargain. Eighty thousand was all that he was prepared to pay: Gabriel Cramer was to negotiate a lower price. And just to unnerve Mallet, the couple visited the property next door (which had an even better view). Not wholly unnerved, Mallet agreed to a reduction of 2,000 *livres*. So Voltaire went to visit another house, at Cologny, and made an offer. In fact he was all the while ready to pay the full 88,000 for the Saint-Jean property; he was just trying to pressure Mallet into paying the purchaser's costs as well as his own. (Thus do rich men become richer.) Meanwhile our good and communicant Catholic was arranging to buy the house in the name of a Genevan while retaining all the customary rights of ownership and securing Mme Denis's inheritance. On 1 February 1755 he received official permission to become a resident of the city of Geneva, and after some inevitable Voltairean complications he agreed to buy Councillor Mallet's house in the name of François Tronchin's brother, his banker Jean-Robert. The latter would pay a third of the original asking price of 90,000 *livres* but grant full rights of occupation to Voltaire. He in turn would contribute the remaining 58,000 and give Jean-Robert 20,000 towards his costs – on condition that Jean-Robert paid 38,000 to Mme Denis in the event of his death. The Swiss thus stood in due course to acquire this splendid house for a maximum of 48,000 *livres*, while Voltaire ended up paying less than the 80,000 that had always been his upper limit. Honour satisfied. And Montriond? He would rent that and use it in the winter. All the best people liked to have two residences – as did nervous fugitives who wanted a foot in two separate jurisdictions (Geneva and the Canton de Vaud). Meanwhile it would be handy for Countess Bentinck, who had also decided to come to Switzerland: she could live there while she found somewhere permanent. Finally he entrusted Jean-Louis Labat – the local banker who had overseen the sale of the Saint-Jean property – with oversight of his financial affairs in Geneva. They, too, became firm friends.

Voltaire and Mme Denis moved into their new house on 1 March 1755 and renamed it Les Délices. After the paradise of Cirey here was a garden of delights, a happy place of friendship and freedom far from the Bastille. Having established his new base, Voltaire then found that it was not he but everyone else who had been exiled. Where he had spent sixty years of a quasi-nomadic existence in constant search of fame and fortune, not to mention safety and freedom, he now discovered that the world came to him. Lekain, for example, the new star of the Comédie-Française, announced his imminent arrival (during the Easter recess when the Comédie-Française was closed), no doubt anxious to secure a copy of *L'Orphelin de Chine*. The playwright bestirred himself to finish it. Soon there were so many visitors that they had to extend the already spacious house, converting barns and outhouses into guest rooms for fear that cramped surroundings might otherwise frighten these welcome distractions away.

And, like a fresh young couple who have just moved into their first home, they decided to cultivate their garden. Unfortunately it was already perfect, but optimists can improve on perfection. Every plant they could think of was ordered at once, every herb that ever flavoured or soothed – 'and hyssop to cleanse us of our sins'.[9] A huge greenhouse was ideal for growing artichokes and asparagus to be eaten out of season (in imitation of Louis XIV), although it could be difficult to get hold of asparagus plants. Friedrich von Hesse-Kassel was a sure source, however, and Voltaire wrote letter after letter to his princely and enlightened friend, requesting further supplies.

Scores of fruit-trees were ordered and planted: mostly apple-trees to begin with, then a series of eighty early- and late-fruiting peach-trees that would ensure a ready supply from July through to October. (Later, at Ferney, he would repeat the exercise, buying from Carthusian monks whose catalogue offered forty varieties of peach and fifty of pear.) Four gardeners, twelve servants and twenty artisans assisted the couple in the gilding of their lily. Money was no object: but happiness was. 'Here I am, finally leading the life of a patriarch – a gift bestowed by God only when our beard is grey, in the last gasp of old age.'[10] It would have seemed quite improbable to him that he had another twenty-three years to live – twenty-three years in which to enjoy a freedom that even at Cirey he had never really known.

> Here am I, by reason drawn to this retreat,
>> At peace, at liberty;
>> Freedom, that wise divinity,
> Whom all mortals desire, whose loss we all regret,
>> Is here the source of my felicity. [. . .]
> Study sustains me, and reason guides me with its light;
> I speak what I think, and I do as I will.[11]

Geneva, of course, in true Calvinist style, had no theatre: such places were immoral. But who needs a theatre when you have a large summer drawing-room? (The winter one needed to be small and warm.) So on 2 April the mountain came to Mahomet – or rather to *Zaïre*, in which Lekain played Nérestan to perfection. As usual Voltaire took the role of Lusignan, while Mme Denis played his daughter Zaïre, and quite brilliantly too. Almost every member of the ruling council was present, including Mallet; and what Voltaire called the 'Tronchin tribe' was there in force. After all, one of them did 'own' the place. The evening was a huge success. 'I never saw so many tears,' their host exulted (and indeed he had cried at his own performance). 'Little did Calvin know that one day Catholics would come and make Huguenots weep in the city of Geneva.'[12] As in Paris, so here in this rather more austere moral climate, Voltaire sought to win friends and influence people by the glamour of his theatrical celebrity. But as in Paris and indeed throughout Europe there were those who suspected him of diabolical intent, seeing in his talents no more than the meretricious and beguiling work of Satan. Hostile rumours circulated, as did unauthorized and traduced versions of his writings. There were increasingly audible mutterings about *La Pucelle*, his irreverent and satirical take on the story of Joan of Arc; and Voltaire's Genevan friends grew nervous – on his account and on their own, for they had risked position and reputation to make him welcome. To reassure them he read or circulated an authentic version of *La Pucelle* to trusted individuals, and then, in order to pacify the so-called Venerable Company of Genevan pastors, he wrote to the ruling council, urging them to condemn and burn the manuscript of eleven lines of *La Pucelle* that had somehow come into the public domain. They complied, and everyone duly inferred – or pretended to infer – that he could not possibly have written them.

But there was still the problem of his amateur theatricals at Les Délices, just outside the city gates. To right-thinking Genevans these smacked not only of immorality but also of provocation. And so Voltaire could see that here was another paradise from which he might very easily be evicted. Accordingly he secured the agreement of the 'Tronchin tribe' to an amendment of his contract of purchase whereby, should he decide to leave his new house, the sum of 38,000 *livres* originally intended for Mme Denis after his death would be payable to himself. The success of *L'Orphelin de Chine*, premiered on 20 August at the Comédie-Française, again raised the prospect – in the mind of this optimist, if in no one else's – that he might be allowed back to Paris. But it did nothing to help his relations with Geneva – nor indeed with Jean-Jacques Rousseau.

The message of this play is essentially that Chinese 'civilization' is morally superior to – and will prevail over – the 'natural' barbarism of the Mongol hordes. The art of the theatre being central to Chinese culture, it followed that Calvinist strictures against thespians belonged with the unreconstructed world view of Genghis Khan. In case the point was missed, Voltaire then included in the first published edition of the play a letter to Rousseau in which he takes issue with the latter's view of 'natural' man, as expounded in his recent *Discourse on Inequality* (1754). For Rousseau, human beings had once lived in a harmonious and unreflective state of nature. With their God-given reason they had invented language and evolved loose-knit communities in which families lived in happy independence, occasionally providing help for

each other but functioning more or less as free agents. But then they abused
that reason. With the advent of agriculture and metallurgy it became possible
to produce more food than any individual or family required, and soon the
lazy became dependent on the industrious. The notion of property emerged
– and the scourge of inequality. Worse still, increased social interaction
revealed the manifold diversity of human behaviour patterns, such that the
cleverer human beings began to realize that certain types of behaviour could
prove more profitable than others in the cause of their selfish interests. A rift
opened between reality and appearance: and the poison of insincerity and
hypocrisy began to ooze from that rift. Hence, for Rousseau, the appalling
inauthenticity of contemporary 'civilization', a society of sham in which an
artificial code of honour and an overwhelming emphasis on show had
replaced the natural 'virtue' of compassionate and peaceable humanity. All
the world had become a stage, a morally corrupt domain of pretence and
spectacle.

It was these views that prompted Voltaire in his open letter to thank the
now-famous citizen of Geneva for sending him a free copy of 'his latest
attack on the human race'.[13] At the same time he prefaced this edition with a
dedicatory letter to the duc de Richelieu (master of Louis's royal spectacles)
in which he proclaims the beneficial effects of theatre on public life. As the
history of ancient China, Greece and Rome testifies, by bringing people
together in the shared enjoyment of the 'pure pleasures of the mind' public
theatre renders human beings more sociable in their dealings, more moderate
in their behaviour, and keener in their judgement. Those nations that are
without it cannot be 'included in the ranks of civilized countries'. Well, at
least the pastors of Geneva now knew where they stood. And Rousseau too.
'Reading your book,' Voltaire told him, 'fills one with the desire to walk on
all fours.'

While delivering his own broadsides the pugilist continued to ward off
the attacks of others. To demonstrate the inauthenticity of the various
versions of La Pucelle now circulating, he published his own in Frankfurt –
and made it longer, the one thing the pirates and forgers hadn't thought of. A
Parisian publisher, Le Prieur, was about to bring out his history of the War
of the Austrian Succession, the manuscript of which had been filched from
under Mme Denis's nose – or bed, since her lover, the marquis de Ximénès,

was probably to blame – while her uncle was in Prussia. But this was not the moment to bring out such a book: the Seven Years War was looming, and the parties to the earlier war had switched allies (with France now siding with Maria Theresa of Austria, and England with Frederick). The former Historiographer Royal, having researched the facts in the royal archives, had planned to end the work by eulogizing Louis XV as a peacemaker. Since the French monarch was about to go to war again, that would now look like acid sarcasm. So Voltaire compromised by agreeing to let Le Prieur publish if he could revise the manuscript. Too late. A different pirated edition appeared in Rouen, soon to be followed by a Dutch version and an English translation. Le Prieur's edition (already printed but about to be amended) was seized, together with the manuscript but without Le Prieur, and locked away in the Bastille. Disaster. Even Voltaire could see that a return to Paris was even less probable than before.

Events of this kind made it still more imperative that he publish his works in authentic, properly supervised editions. Just as Voltaire liked to have two homes in two separate jurisdictions, so also he found it expedient to employ two publishers – Lambert in Paris, the Cramers in Geneva – each of whom he kept carefully in the dark about the other. What one might call a belt-and-braces approach to the dissemination of the Voltairean Word. Except that the Cramers soon found out. They had to be pacified by having first call on all Voltaire's revisions and additions.

Towards the end of the year, as Voltaire continued to salvage what he could from the shipwreck of his ambitions at Potsdam and Versailles, news began to filter through of a much more momentous disaster: an earthquake at the western end of the Mediterranean. At around 10 a.m. on the morning of Sunday, 1 November 1755, it had struck the city of Lisbon while God's creatures were at Mass worshipping the Almighty who so loved the world . . . Some 30,000 men, women and children perished, crushed by collapsing masonry or burned to death in the ensuing fires. For every stove in the city had been stoked in preparation for a festive lunch. A tsunami overwhelmed Cadiz. The range of the Atlas Mountains in Morocco shook throughout its length: thousands died in Tangier, Meknès and Agadir. Associated tremors were felt as far away as Milan and Amsterdam. It took over three weeks for news of the disaster to reach Paris and Geneva; and when Voltaire heard it, he happened to be revising the proofs of his *Discours en vers sur l'homme*, his own version of Pope's verse *Essay on Man* and first published in 1738–9. How ridiculous the philosophy of Optimism now seemed, how hollow its shibboleths and saws: 'Whatever is, is Right'; 'All is well'; 'The best of all possible worlds' . . . In the absence of a knowledge of tectonic plates, and at a time when so many people trusted implicitly in the reality and wisdom of divine providence, such appalling loss of life must have seemed even more shockingly cruel and arbitrary than it can today. For a sceptical deist and lapsed Optimist like Voltaire such a disaster was not only an indictment of Pope and Leibniz, it also represented a tremendous challenge to the dogma and ritual of the Christian Church. That the earthquake should have struck Lisbon on All Saints' Day, during a religious service, seemed particularly ironic, not least because he had also been proof-reading those chapters of his world history that deal with the Spanish and Portuguese Inquisitions. The seeds of Chapter 6 of *Candide* were now planted: 'How they had a splendid *auto-da-fé* to prevent earthquakes and how Candide was flogged.' As for many people throughout Europe, the details of the disaster were such as to put Voltaire in mind of the Day of Judgment, but his own response was one of bitter and irreverent anger: 'All it lacked was a trumpet.'[14]

The earthquake reverberated throughout Europe for some time, literally and metaphorically. A month after the devastation of Portugal and Morocco, the town of Brigues in the Swiss canton of Valais was badly damaged by a further tremor, and even at Les Délices they felt a small shockwave, at twenty past two in the afternoon: a bottle of muscat wine tottered off Voltaire's table, and he felt 'honoured' to have witnessed the phenomenon. Some said even that the bells of St Peter's Cathedral in Geneva had rung unaided, but the master of Les Délices had heard nothing. Metaphorically, the consequences of the disaster continued to be felt. Initial reports from Lisbon had overestimated both the number of casualties (at 100,000) and the extent of the damage, but more precise information did little to attenuate the sense of disaster. For Voltaire, admittedly, the shock was mitigated by delight when he learnt that members of the Portuguese Inquisition had indeed perished on 1 November, just as they were about to carry out an *auto-da-fé* on some Jews – that is to say, to burn them publicly as heretics.

But nevertheless he felt so angered by the random injustice of the event that he wrote what is perhaps his bleakest, most pessimistic work: the *Poème sur le désastre de Lisbonne*. 'Evil is upon the earth,' he proclaims: 'You foolish philosophers who cried: "All is well", /Come and see these dreadful ruins.' Where is the divine justice? How can you possibly say that the dead have been fairly punished for their crimes? And why Lisbon? Why not London or Paris, those other cities of 'vice'? And why was God obliged to create a world that is subject to natural disasters? Was He not omnipotent? How can this appalling carnage possibly contribute to a 'greater good'? God *is* free, just and merciful. So why *do* such disasters occur? In our perplexity 'we need a God who will speak to the human race', and yet no such God is to be heard. We can but suffer in silence . . . Which is how Voltaire first thought of ending this heartfelt expression of human perplexity in the face of senseless human tragedy. But eventually he added: '. . . and hope'. The last six lines of the definitive version end by recalling a dying caliph's final prayer: ' "I bring you, one and only king, one and only infinite being, /Everything that you in your immensity do not have: faults, regrets, ills and ignorance." But he could have added: *hope*.' Voltaire was still an optimist, if not an Optimist.

CHAPTER FIFTEEN

From Earthquake to Book Launch:
Candide (1755–1759)

How an optimist wrote a masterpiece and bought a kingdom

O N 14 DECEMBER 1755 Voltaire and his niece-cum-nurse-cum-wife moved to their winter residence at Montriond, on the outskirts of Lausanne. They would have gone earlier except for the sudden and tragic death of their landlord, the young Monsieur de Giez, an event which had left Voltaire no more enamoured of the deity than had the wholesale slaughter of Lisbon. Once ensconced at Montriond Voltaire was not to be budged for several months, especially since his niece had now bought him another house-coat for Christmas, a sumptuous confection of ermine and velvet costing 432 *livres*. At last he was warm! And he looked like a king, much to the displeasure of the Calvinists, who considered the luxury in which he lived to be virtually a mortal sin. Six horses, four carriages, a coachman and postillion, two footmen, one valet, a French cook (male, as in all the best houses), an underchef, a secretary and assorted other slaves. How could he expect to pass through the eye of a needle with such a retinue?

But as the monarch of Montriond held court the world continued to flock to see him, beginning with the best of Lausanne society, whom he entertained in style. The food and conversation were sensational, and even close neighbours sought to prolong their stay for as many nights as they could. Friends came from Geneva, strangers from far afield. And strange strangers, like the 27-year-old Oliver Goldsmith, who was undertaking the Grand Tour on foot before going home to write *The Vicar of Wakefield*. As at Cirey, Voltaire would make his appearance only in the evening, after a long day's work; and his guests would listen, rapt, as he delivered himself of such opinions and witticisms as were then uppermost in his mind. Years spent dictating to his secretaries meant that he could hold forth effortlessly without hesitation or repetition, deviating nevertheless as the fancy or the conversation took him. Sometimes he would read them his poems or perform short extracts from his plays.

The poet-playwright holding court was also a preacher in his pulpit, and Voltaire now became increasingly and courageously vocal in the assertion of his own beliefs. He called his poem on the Lisbon earthquake a 'sermon', as he did also the *Poème sur la loi naturelle* – begun in Prussia five years earlier (as a refutation of La Mettrie's materialism) and then rewritten in 1753 in the intellectually invigorating company of the Duchess of Saxe-Gotha. He now published this dangerously frank profession of deist faith. At first he thought he had better bury it – like a time-bomb – in the supplement to a discreet volume of miscellany, but then he decided to bring it out with his other 'sermon' as a 'taster' for the 1756 Cramer edition of his complete works. Publicity mattered more than safety. And so did the truth. Lambert complained from Paris that the Cramers had an unfair advantage in being able to publish the most up-to-date versions of his works, but little did they know at what cost to the Cramers. Determined to get his texts just right – since this might, for all he knew, be the last edition to appear in his lifetime – their celebrity author would often demand that an entire page be reset to accommodate a single revision or correction. And demand not just once: sometimes two, three, or even four times over. Voltaire's mercurial mind was ill-suited to the full stop. But it thrived on the brevity and deadpan dogmatism of the encyclopedia entry, and he continued to supply Diderot and d'Alembert with contributions to their grand enterprise, which had now reached volume 5 and the letter E for Encyclopedia. F and G were next. Who better than Voltaire to write about 'Fire' and 'Frenchman'? And 'Fornica-tion'? He confessed to d'Alembert with regret that he was ill-qualified to say or do much on that subject. 'Flagellation' was abandoned because he did not have access to the authoritative book on the subject. And then H: 'History' might take him a while.

On 21 March 1756 Voltaire and his niece returned to their summer
residence at Les Délices. The Seven Years War was now imminent, though
of course no one knew it would last seven years. It would doubtless be over
by Christmas. Out of the Prussian blue Frederick wrote to Voltaire (via
another *encyclopédiste*, the abbé de Prades), informing him that he had just
adapted his *Mérope* as an opera and inviting him to the opening night. The
squeezed orange declined the kind offer and wrote instead to Countess
Bentinck, now in Vienna, praising France's new ally, the Empress of Austria,
and proclaiming the merits of the Danube over the Spree. For if he was
evicted from Switzerland, it was to his homeland that he hoped to run, and
Maria Theresa was Louis's new ally. For the moment, however, his system of
dual residence seemed to be working well, and he even thought of renting a
halfway-house between the two (at Rolle). To make sure of the Montriond
end he travelled to Bern (since Lausanne and the Canton de Vaud fell under
its control within the Helvetic Confederation) and there dined his friends
and sweet-talked his enemies, including a number of particularly prickly
pastors. Even his friends had been nervous about the visit, and there was
much talk in the city that he might sow the 'dire seeds of atheism' or inject
the 'venom of his unbelief'[1] into the local body politic. But of course they
had all forgotten what a charmer he could be: by the time he left, the whole
of Bern felt that it had been gloriously honoured.

This summer at Les Délices was as delightful as the last. The garden
paradise had now also become something of a menagerie, and the patriarch
lorded it over an eclectic array of pets: rabbits, a fox, an eagle, and a monkey
called Luc. Luc? In memory of Frederick and his 'cul à l'envers' . . . an arse
back to front, or Esra. So much for the man he had sometimes called the
Solomon of the North. M. de Giez's young widow had joined them, to keep
Mme Denis company while her uncle locked himself away like a hermit with
his books. And his accounts. Though no miser Voltaire was an attentive
manager of money, always alive to the latest investment opportunity and
never unaware of the cost of a trinket. At this stage in his long life he was
worth approximately a million *livres*. He had begun to reduce the risk element
in his investment portfolio, and after the purchase of Les Délices about a
third of his capital was now on deposit at 4 per cent with his banker, Jean-
Robert Tronchin, in Lyons. But he sought annuities where he safely could,

and purchased another from the spendthrift Elector Palatine, 'lending' him a further 130,000 *livres* at 10 per cent. The advancing years – and possibly earthquakes – had made him rather more inclined to prize security of income over long-term capital growth.

Usually working and often indisposed – whether because of his unreliable digestive system, or the many colds brought on by this lacustrine climate, or simply by way of polite excuse – Voltaire himself consumed little; but his family and guests expected the best, and he was ready to supply it. In the paradise and menagerie it was always open house, and an increasingly corpulent Mme Denis presided over the good life in energetically cheerful fashion. The meals were copious and on grand occasions ran to five or six courses. For each course a selection of dishes was placed on the table (again as in all the best houses), from which the host or guest would choose as preference, proximity or yesterday's menu dictated. *Potages* of every kind were followed by *entrées*: fish (often trout from the lake, and costing twice as much as meat, whatever the type) or poultry (mostly chicken and turkey). Then came the *rôtis*: roast game (pigeon, pheasant, partridge, thrush, quail, lark) or meat. Beef was the most prized, pork the least (except for suckling pig and ham, which were considered edible by gentlemen and their ladies). The roasts were followed by the *salades* and the *entremets* (literally, 'between dishes'), which might be sweet or savoury: offal, omelettes, fritters, and all manner of pie. And vegetable dishes: peas and beans, carrots and turnips (for Europeans had yet to encounter the eggplant or the marrow, or even a tomato). Cheese and fruit filled any remaining empty spaces: Roquefort or Parmesan, or perhaps something more local; not just apples, pears and peaches, but figs and dates and pomegranates. Melons sometimes, though they had long been thought inimical to a satisfactory digestion. Voltaire's favourite was the orange, so delicious and sought after that he liked to think it had been Eve's 'forbidden fruit'. And sometimes, as a special treat, the table was graced with the astonishing pineapple, recently introduced. The first two to be successfully grown and ripened in a French conservatory had been served up at a banquet by Louis XV in 1733.

Expensive white bread was preferred to the pauper's black. Wine was served from the sideboard, where the bottles were kept cool in buckets. Beaujolais was Mme Denis's favourite, but Voltaire preferred the best red burgundy, a Corton or a Chambertin, something with body. White wine did not agree with him, whether dry or sweet. He also liked his wine to have had a few years during which to mature. Not that this was always possible. In March 1758 he discovered that six of his eight casks of '56 had gone off. Moreover, wine did not always travel well: one year later he found that six casks of his Languedoc had not survived their journey. No wonder he was keen to make his own. And very proud of it he was, too.

Among the habitual guests at these feasts were the Cramers, including Gabriel's witty French wife, and the Tronchin tribe, including François, who was working on a new play, and Théodore, who continued to remain sanguine about the philosopher's health despite the latter's strident allegations. New faces included the painter and portrait-artist Jean Huber, to whom we owe so many images of Voltaire and his circle over the ensuing years; another senior judge at the Dijon *parlement*, Charles de Brosses, from whom the 'owner' of Les Délices would soon be buying a mansion; and a clutch of pastors – Jacob Vernet, Jacob Vernes, and others more individually named – who figure significantly in Voltaire's correspondence during this period.

On 8 June Voltaire's younger niece, Mme de Fontaine – as skeletal as her sister was not – arrived with her lover and future husband, the marquis de Florian. Through no fault of her own the visit was ill-starred. On the day of her arrival a maid chose this moment when Voltaire's secretary was particularly busy with domestic arrangements to enter his room and find a letter that Collini had written to a young woman of his acquaintance and in which he made disparaging and risqué comments about Mme Denis. For reasons of her own the maid showed it to her mistress, and Voltaire had no option but to dismiss Collini (nevertheless remaining in friendly correspondence with him for the rest of his life). Another secretary was found, but within three months young Wagnière had taken over this vital role (and become a key source for future biographers). Meanwhile Mme de Fontaine's constitution was proving unequal to the delights of Les Délices, and she fell so seriously ill that during the months of September and October her uncle despaired of her life. Théodore Tronchin now did have something to do, and the lady had recovered sufficiently to take her leave on 24 October. But not before her uncle had charged her lover with an important commission. In writing his histories Voltaire had conceived the idea for a new military weapon: a horse-drawn tank. He instructed the marquis de Florian on his return to Paris to show a model of it to the comte d'Argenson, still Minister of War, who in turn consulted Richelieu. Much as he cherished his friend, the new commander of the French army in Germany dismissed the idea as daft. So, too, fourteen years later, did Catherine the Great of Russia, who much preferred Voltaire's books.

A no less ill-starred visit was that of Jean d'Alembert, from 10–30 August. Diderot – not wholly persuaded of Voltaire's merits – had willingly ceded the challenging delight of meeting this influential contributor to their encyclopedia. And it would be a useful opportunity for his colleague to research his planned article on 'Geneva', especially as anyone who was anyone in the city was likely to be entertained at Les Délices in the course of the next three weeks. But the article would prove highly controversial when it was published the following year (1757), partly because it presented Calvinism as being really only a form of deism, and partly because its author called on the city to make good the absence of a municipal theatre. The influence of host on guest was plain to see, and to the advantage of neither in the eyes of the good people of Geneva. Nor in the eyes of Rousseau, who would later publish a stinging riposte to d'Alembert's views on 'spectacles'. For the moment, however, Jean-Jacques wrote a long letter in reply to Voltaire's two 'sermons': praising the *Poème sur la loi naturelle*, but refusing to accept the anti-providentialist thesis of the poem about the Lisbon earthquake. For Rousseau, God's beneficent hand is omnipresent: he can feel it.

As Voltaire was about to show in *Candide*, he himself was no longer at all so sure. Especially when the British, at the outset of the Seven Years War, proceeded to arrest Admiral John Byng for having lost Port Mahon on the island of Minorca – to a French fleet commanded by the versatile duc de Richelieu. Voltaire was pleased for his friend but upset for the admiral (whom he had met in London thirty years earlier). When Thomas Pitt, brother of the new British prime minister, William Pitt, visited Les Délices on 20 December, Voltaire told him that Richelieu thought Byng innocent of all charges of dereliction of duty or error of judgement; and he promised to write accordingly or, better still, to get Richelieu to write. It did no good: both Houses of Parliament approved the verdict of guilty handed down at the court martial, and the unfortunate admiral was executed on 14 March 1757. 'To encourage the others', as Voltaire later wrote in *Candide*. But he well knew that such cruel and disproportionate 'justice' has quite the opposite effect, and he was beginning to think that, with his wealth and relative independence of action, he might be able to play a much more active role in fighting such injustice. It was therefore important to preserve and enhance that independence. A renewed offer from Frederick, in June 1756, was refused, as was an invitation to visit the imperial court in Vienna. He would rather 'scold his gardeners than pay court to kings'.[2] For all that, he continued to harbour the vestigial illusion that he might yet find influence *and* independence at the French court, and he looked to Mme de Pompadour, Richelieu, and the duc de La Vallière, to advance his cause. But it was no use: the piqued and stubborn king had set his face permanently against such a return.

So the Swiss idyll continued. Having returned to Montriond for the winter of 1756–7, Voltaire and Mme Denis began to make use of a theatre they had located in Lausanne, which could seat 200 people and was available for use by amateur theatre companies. They had soon recruited enthusiastic participants from among the local aristocracy and gentry, and audiences flocked to see their productions: Voltaire's own works, of course, but also some opera buffa. Most of Europe might be at war, but Voltaire was temporarily at play – and certainly not minded to accept an invitation to the Russian court recently extended by the Tsarina Elisabeth. Why should he? 'After having lived with kings,' he later recalled, 'I made myself king in my own home.'[3] On the other hand he did accept Elisabeth's proposal that he write a history of her father, Peter the Great. Ever since his history of Charles XII of Sweden, he had wanted to set that particular record straight.

Though at play, Voltaire nevertheless observed the progress of European hostilities. Frederick – having started things by invading Saxony on 29 August – was having a bad war, opposed as he was by the French to the west, the Austrians to the south and east, and the Russians to the north and east. Not to mention the Swedes and sundry German principalities. Added to which, his British-cum-Hanoverian ally had been trounced by Richelieu at Klosterseven. 'Luc' now had his back to the wall: the French were seeking to cut off his retreat from Bohemia into Saxony, while the Russians had invaded Eastern Prussia. Following his recent overtures Voltaire had renewed his correspondence with Frederick, and he wrote to express sympathy and support for his former friend and his family. The King replied in his own hand, with tender gratitude. So, too, did the King's sister, Wilhelmine, who genuinely believed that her last hour had come. Indeed so did Frederick, who contemplated taking his own life – like Cato or Brutus – in the event of a permanent defeat. He subsequently changed his mind and resolved instead to die a glorious death on the battlefield. Dated 8 October 1757, this latest letter from Frederick reached Voltaire on 12 or 13 November, but unbeknownst to its recipient the Prussian king had just won a fabulous and defining victory over the French (under Soubise) at Rossbach one week earlier. Twenty thousand Prussians had defeated 60,000 Frenchmen by attacking them as they passed between two plateaus. The artillery fired down on them from above; then the advancing infantry shot at them; and lastly a series of cavalry charges put them to rout. In a very short time some 2–3,000 Frenchmen lost their lives, and 5,000 were taken prisoner. The remainder fled.

Voltaire no longer felt quite so sorry for Frederick, and the Frenchman in him smarted at this dishonourable defeat. However, his principal hope had been for peace. For a time he had thought fondly of engineering a settlement between France and Prussia by using his influence with Richelieu and Wilhelmine. But neither a rampant Prussian conqueror nor a shamed Louis would now be in a mood to parley. He almost despaired at this seemingly ineradicable propensity of his fellow human beings to go to war; but instead he sat down and began to write *Candide*. It was also time to move to Lausanne for the winter. Montriond had the disadvantage of being outside the city (on the road westwards to Ouchy), and it had been a major inconvenience for his guests to have to make their way up to the theatre at Monrepos, then down to Montriond and then back to the city over icy or snow-covered roads in the dead of night. So he rented a new home, called Le Grand-Chêne, in the centre and much closer to the theatre.

Like Les Délices, it offered spectacular views: just the right setting in which to compose a timeless, universal story about the human condition. A story that tells how innocent young Candide, of bastard origin, is kicked out of the most beautiful of castles for kissing the Baron's daughter, Cunégonde. How he wanders in the snow and is press-ganged into the Bulgar army just in time to take part in a wonderful war with the Abars:

Never was there anything so fine, so dashing, so glittering, or so well regulated as those two armies. The trumpets, the fifes, the hautboys, the drums and the cannon produced a harmony such as was never heard in hell. First the cannon felled about six thousand men on each side. Then the musketry removed from the best of all possible worlds nine or ten thousand ruffians who were polluting its surface. The bayonet, too, was the sufficient reason for the death of a few thousand. The sum total may well have come to about thirty thousand souls. Candide, who was trembling like a philosopher, hid himself as best he could during his heroic butchery.[4]

We learn how Candide escapes and meets up with his old tutor, Dr Pangloss, who 'taught metaphysico-cosmo-codology' and could 'prove wonderfully that there is no effect without a cause'. How they are shipwrecked outside the port of Lisbon and arrive in time for the earthquake. How Candide is flogged in an *auto-da-fé* and rescued by an old woman with only one buttock (the other having been eaten during a tummy-rumbling siege). How he is reunited with Cunégonde, only to have to leave her again and depart for South America with his servant Cacambo. How they are mistaken for Jesuits and nearly cooked by cannibals. How they find Eldorado – and leave it behind. How Candide returns to France with Martin, a Manichaean, before travelling to England and Venice. How everyone – Candide, Cunégonde, with her brother the new baron and her maid Paquette (and Paquette's boyfriend, Giroflée the monk), Pangloss, Martin, the old woman, and faithful Cacambo – are reunited at Constantinople. And how, variously battered and mutilated by the vicissitudes of existence, they all nevertheless cling to life and remain determined to make a go of things. ' "Let's get down to work and stop all this philosophizing," said Martin. "It's the only way to make life bearable." The little society fell in with this laudable plan.' Except for Pangloss. Once a philosopher, always a philosopher:

'All events form a chain in the best of all possible worlds. For in the end, if you had not been given a good kick up the backside and chased out of a beautiful castle for loving Miss Cunégonde, and if you hadn't been subjected to the Inquisition, and if you hadn't wandered about America on foot, and if you hadn't dealt the Baron a good blow with your sword, and if you hadn't lost all your sheep [laden with treasure] from that fine country of Eldorado, you wouldn't be here now eating candied citron and pistachio nuts.' – 'That is well said,' replied Candide, 'but we must get on with our gardening.'[5]

In the short space of a hundred pages, divided into thirty sprightly chapters, *Candide* is a pot-pourri of autobiography, pacifist and anti-clerical satire, anti-providentialist scepticism, and gloriously humane good humour and good sense. Look at the facts, and stop relying on philosophical systems (whether Leibnizian or Manichaean); think for yourself and discuss the matter, don't just mouth pre-packaged sound-bites; expect the unexpected; and keep smiling. For Voltaire had remembered a great truth. The French – and not only the French – were much more likely to condemn the horrors of war and religious intolerance if these were made to seem absurd. Don't rant and rail: just show people what's dumb. Horrors and injustices are always someone else's problem, but none of us wants to look foolish. As he told Damilaville, a fellow-*philosophe*, ten years later: 'I have only ever addressed one prayer to God, and it is very short: "My God, please make all our enemies ridiculous." God has granted my wish.'[6]

Begun at Le Grand-Chêne at the turn of the year 1757–8, *Candide* was composed intermittently over the following months, and largely at Les Délices (where Voltaire and Mme Denis returned in the middle of March). Its final chapter ('Conclusion') owed much to Voltaire's current circumstances. Like 'the little society' living just outside Constantinople, he had located himself on the outskirts of a major city, poised between west and east (Louis and Frederick). Of bastard origin and constantly on the run, he had settled down to do some literal and metaphorical gardening. Moreover, the extensive research he had undertaken for his histories had left him with a profound sense of the muddle of human destiny and yet the extraordinary resilience of the human spirit. As Candide travels in space, so Voltaire had travelled in both time and space, from epoch to epoch, from continent to continent; and the universal spectacle of man's inhumanity to man had made earthquakes seem like the least of our troubles. The student of Newton never lost his sense of awe at the orderliness of God's physical creation, and the student of Locke never lost his faith in reason. But unlike Rousseau he could not quite 'feel' the beneficent hand of God in the march of human affairs. As he approached his mid-sixties, he felt less and less inclined to trust in the 'conspiracy' of a divine providence and increasingly persuaded that history is a series of cock-ups. Witness, indeed, Pangloss's strange history of syphilis:

> 'Paquette was made a present of it by a very knowledgeable Franciscan who had traced it back to its source. For he had got it from an old countess, who had contracted it from a captain in the cavalry, who owed it to a marchioness, who had it from a page, who had caught it from a Jesuit, who, during his noviciate, had inherited it in a direct line from one of Christopher Columbus's shipmates.'[7]

Voltaire continued nevertheless to fear that both fate and man might conspire against *him*. While profoundly content at Les Délices, he was conscious all the same of treading a fine line between acceptable celebrity and dangerous, condemnable notoriety. Calvinist seriousness, however enlightened, was not the ideal climate for Voltairean polemic and wit. He was nervous. And so he began to think of abandoning Le Grand-Chêne (already) for some other 'second home'. He had exhausted the delights of Lausanne society, and in any case he was not sure that he wished to end his days on Swiss soil. For the moment his restlessness was assuaged by a visit to the Elector Palatine at Schwetzingen: his distinguished but possibly unreliable debtor was due to make him a payment. Having departed on 30 June with only Wagnière for company, Voltaire prospected for a possible home in Lorraine and was offered the Château de Craon near Lunéville (in which residence Saint-Lambert had spent some of his childhood in the company of the marquise de Boufflers). But when Stanislas consulted his son-in-law's minister, the abbé de Bernis, it was clear that Louis would not look favourably on such a move. So the unwanted Voltaire proceeded on to Schwetzingen, where he arrived on 16 July, and for the next three weeks he was able once again to enjoy lavish hospitality and entertainment in this best of all possible German castles. In return he treated his host to readings from his unfinished *Candide*. Meanwhile Mme Denis had remained at Les Délices with her sister (accompanied by her son, and of course the marquis de

Florian), and together they entertained Countess Bentinck as best they could without the Master. The Countess soon departed for Bern and later Montriond, but on Voltaire's return towards the end of August – after a leisurely journey via Strasbourg and Colmar – he invited her back. There was something he wanted to show her.

Now finally persuaded that Louis would never forgive his departure for Prussia and allow him back into the royal fold, Voltaire nevertheless refused to see himself as exiled from France. What better way to prove it than to live on French soil just across the border from Geneva? And he had found exactly the place, or rather two: at Fernex and Tournex – which, as a reformer of spelling, he promptly redesignated Ferney and Tourney. An offer of 130,000 *livres* for the former was accepted on 7 October 1758 by its owner, Jacob de Budé. The latter had only recently inherited it from his half-brother, Bernard de Budé, 'comte de Montréal, seigneur de Ferney et de Boisy', their family having owned it since 1674 (but having first settled in Geneva in 1549).[8] Although the transaction was not officially completed until 9 February the following year (our purchaser refused to pay the stamp duty), the new owner took possession at once and assumed immediate responsibility for paying the wages of the Ferney staff. Or at least until the following 22 February, on which date their pay was annually reviewed and when he himself could decide whether or not to keep them on. Thus did the patriarch become master to: Jandin, who drove the cart and looked after the horses (45 *livres* p.a.); two cowherds, Dutil and Jacques (48 *livres* and 30 *livres* respectively); Moïse (or Moses), a shepherd (60 *livres*), and his two assistants, young Charles (15 *livres*) and reliable old Merma (18 *livres*), a head-gardener (120 *livres*), assisted by the promising young Brillon (24 *livres*); Germond, probably the steward, who was entitled to 120 *livres* p.a. and a new set of clothes every two years; a gamekeeper (20 *livres* per month, plus some wood for his fire); Michon, the housekeeper (27 *livres*), who was assisted by two other women, Louise and Pernette (21 *livres* each), and Dunan, a nice but lazy footman (54 *livres*). In sum, an annual wage-bill of 843 *livres*, and a blatant case of sexual discrimination.[9]

What Voltaire had bought was more like a sixteen-bedroom fortress than a house, and he rebuilt it at a cost of 50,000 *livres* in the elegant, neo-classical style apparent today. As well as comprising a large quantity of land, the estate came with a boundary wall punctuated by four towers (complete with arrow-slits), a parish church, a worm-eaten gibbet, and various rights to tax the tenants and to sit in judgement over them (if not still to hang them). His 'subjects' – the inhabitants of the village of Ferney – were few in number, a hundred at most, and exceedingly poor: no birth nor marriage had been celebrated for the past seven years. In fact some were in prison, for trying to smuggle salt across the border from Geneva. Though the view was very fine across the lake and towards the Alps, some of the surrounding land was marshy and unproductive. The remainder had been badly farmed, and the whole place spoke of neglect and petty larceny. It occurred to Voltaire that he might do good.

The acquisition of Tourney was less straightforward. The owner, his friend Charles de Brosses, the Dijon judge, was a seasoned litigant and a mulish negotiator. In the end Voltaire bought a lease on the property for 35,000 *livres* (a price based on a highly inflated assessment of the estate's revenue) and agreed to spend 12,000 *livres* on repairs, it being provided that the whole estate (including all furniture and household effects) would revert to de Brosses on Voltaire's death (which the judge therefore had a motive to hasten with further litigation). In the event poor de Brosses got his comeuppance by dying first, but not before all manner of legal wrangling about his new tenant's husbandry of the woodlands. It was customary in such transactions to present the vendor's wife with a gift – by way of symbolically sealing the negotiations – and so, showing a due sense of rural charm, Voltaire proposed to offer Mme de Brosses a plough. Not just any old plough but the very latest in agricultural technology, a plough that tilled as it sowed as it harrowed. When de Brosses expressed the opinion that his wife was unlikely to find this implement of especial use in her boudoir, it was agreed that 500 *livres* in cash would do just fine.

Situated in the tiny region of France known as the Pays de Gex, itself bordered to north and west by the Jura Mountains, the two estates at Ferney and Tourney adjoined each other (with the two principal houses being just under three miles apart) and were so positioned on two frontiers that the combined property offered Voltaire a reassuring number of escape routes should the French authorities ever decide to come after him: immediately south (a mere four miles) to the city of Geneva, which was at that time wholly surrounded by French territory; directly on to the lake itself, for flight to independent Savoy; or immediately east into the Canton de Vaud and the jurisdiction of Bern. Only slightly further east lay Neuchâtel, which was under Prussian rule. So if the worst really did come to the worst . . . Moreover, the Pays de Gex was so remote from Paris that Voltaire could be sure to have advance news of any move to arrest him before the men in blue actually arrived on his doorstep. Indeed he would even have time to pack. And he was not being melodramatic: on 23 January 1759 the Paris *parlement* condemned the *Encyclopédie*, and in March the royal *privilège* was withdrawn. It was forbidden to distribute or reprint the seven volumes so far published. And to think that Voltaire had accused Diderot and d'Alembert of timidity.

With shrewdness and wealth Voltaire thus acquired a kingdom of his own, as free from outside interference as it was possible to be in eighteenth-century Europe. Accordingly he arranged to pay ceremonial visits to his new domains. In the late autumn of 1758 he arrived at Ferney with Mme Denis in a fairy-tale coach, he resplendent in crimson velvet edged with ermine, she spilling from her finest dress and twinkling with diamonds. As became a lord and lady of the manor, they attended Mass in the local church, though the new monarch's 'people' amounted only to a handful of scruffy peasants and his 'cardinal' was no more than the local priest. On Christmas Eve they travelled in similar state to Tourney, this time with Mme de Fontaine (also bejewelled). A cousin, dressed in the uniform of the King's Musketeers, rode grandly alongside the coach. The party was greeted on arrival by a respectable turnout of the local gentry, including the departing tenant, who was to entertain everyone to dinner. An expert on cannons had been brought from Geneva to mastermind a gun-salute. As to the local canon, he made a speech, and the new landlord replied by promising to bestow his bounty upon the parish. Thereafter he was presented with a beribboned basket of oranges, and the ladies with two bouquets of flowers. Wonderful. Especially as the lease entitled Voltaire to be called a count. Not quite 'King' perhaps, but better than plain François-Marie Arouet. By and by, the comte de Tourney took his gracious leave and returned to Geneva along a barely passable road that posed a threat to axle and digestion alike.

With all rat-runs now in place, the rat made bold. Just as he had secured the bolthole of Cirey before publishing the *Lettres philosophiques*, so now he was ready to publish *Candide*. And if the *Lettres* had been a bomb, his new philosophical tale was a nuclear device: he was determined that the fall-out should spread far and wide. This indeed had been one of the attractions of the Cramers: their pan-European network of distribution. At some point towards the end of 1758 Voltaire had closeted himself away with Wagnière for three days, revising and dictating a final version of *Candide*. (Mme Denis had become rather concerned: was her uncle quite well?) A manuscript version was dispatched to the duc and duchesse de La Vallière for their delectation and advice (and perhaps to other friends, but theirs is the only one that has survived to this day).

But still Voltaire sought to improve on perfection. A reading of Helvétius's *De l'esprit* (*On the Mind*) had suggested a new episode to him, in which he might condemn slavery and colonial exploitation (no matter that he himself had made a fortune out of the latter – though not the former). Travelling in Surinam, on his way back from Eldorado, Candide chances on a black slave lying half naked on the ground and missing his left leg and his right hand:

> 'My God!' said Candide in Dutch. 'What are you doing lying here, my friend, and in this dreadful state?' – 'I'm waiting for my master, Mr Van der Hartbargin, the well-known trader,' replied the Negro. – 'And is it Mr Van der Hartbargin,' said Candide, 'who has treated you like this?' – 'Yes, sir,' said the Negro, 'it is the custom. We are given one pair of short denim breeches twice a year, and that's all we have to wear. When we're working at the sugar-mill and catch our finger in the grinding-wheel, they cut off our hand. When we try to run away, they cut off a leg. I have been in both these situations. This is the price you pay for the sugar you eat in Europe.'[10]

The addition of this episode was clearly important since it is the event that changes Candide's mind: ' "O Pangloss!" [. . .] That does it. I shall finally have to renounce your Optimism. – "What's Optimism?" asked Cacambo. – "I'm afraid to say," said Candide, "that it's a mania for insisting all is well when things are going badly." ' Evidently Voltaire had been looking for the worst example of man's inhumanity to man that he could find. His choice is instructive. For in administering the estates of Ferney and Tourney he would be determined not to drive a hard bargain with his slaves. As to the sugar, this was still very much a luxury, and in France average annual consumption ran to no more than one kilogram per person. The price rose sharply during the Seven Years War, and Voltaire complained bitterly each summer when he had to purchase large quantities for the making of jam. (They had to do something with all that fruit.) He tried to reduce the cost, as usual, by avoiding payment of the duty.

With *Candide* now complete, the best of all possible authors was determined to pull off a major coup by publishing it more or less simultaneously in as many parts of Europe as he could manage. To this end, under conditions of great secrecy, unbound copies of the work (in pocket-book duodecimo format) were dispatched from Geneva on 15 and 16 January 1759: 1,000 to Robin, a bookseller, in Paris; 200 to Marc-Michel Rey in Amsterdam; and others to London and Liège. The Cramers meanwhile kept 2,000 copies back for local sale – the normal print run for a book that was expected to do well – and they waited for the large parcels to reach their appointed destinations. The element of surprise was central to the plan, and Voltaire was careful to make no reference to the book in his correspondence. On a prearranged date the book was 'published'. Was this date 20 February, Voltaire's unofficial sixty-fifth birthday? Perhaps. But we know only that on 22 February the police authorities in Paris reported that *Candide* was being circulated clandestinely by the duc de La Vallière and the comte d'Argental. On 23 February the Venerable Company of Pastors expressed their concern in Geneva. Other editions appeared like outbreaks of the plague at Lyons and Avignon. Several Parisian publishers – Lambert, Prault, Grangé – issued their own on the back of Robin's Cramer edition. Duly taken by surprise and quickly overwhelmed, the authorities seized what they could and smashed any press on which the book was being printed. But, like Soubise at the Battle of Rossbach, they were powerless to stem the tide. By 10 March Voltaire calculated that some 6,000 copies had already been sold, and it is likely that this had risen to 20,000 after a further fortnight.[11] Even Swift's hugely popular *Gulliver's Travels* (published on 28 October 1726) sold only half that number over a similar period. The first English translation of *Candide* appeared within six weeks of the original and sold at least 6,000. By

May the British reader could read *Candide* in French or in any one of three different English translations. Exactly three years later the book was finally and belatedly placed on the Vatican's Index of forbidden books. But by that time the damage had long since been done. The work had of course been published anonymously, and like a blank-faced schoolboy Voltaire denied all knowledge of it, let alone authorship. Nobody was fooled, but he was doing what he could to protect his publishers.

Voltaire's new bomb had worked a treat. The Paris *parlement* spluttered rage and denounced *Candide* as an attack on religion and public decency. The senior Genevan Pastor considered it to be 'full of vile things that were conducive to inhuman behaviour, contrary to good morals, and an insult to Providence'[12] – a view directly contrary in its particulars to that of most modern readers. Fréron thought the best form of attack was to accept Voltaire's disclaimers and thus rob him of the glory. Even the publisher Pierre Rousseau, who had printed an edition of it in Liège in March, wished that the author had been more respectful towards religion and its ministers. 'Let's eat Jesuit,' cry the cannibals of South America, mistaking Candide and Cacambo for missionaries. Voltaire, for his own part, was now on a mission to have the Church for breakfast.

CHAPTER SIXTEEN

The Vineyard of Truth (1759–1763)

In which our hero ploughs a straight furrow and roots out infamy

E VERY MISSION NEEDS a statement, and Voltaire's was simple: 'Ecrasez l'infâme!' (literally, 'Crush the infamous!'). Back in the days of those philosophical supper-parties at Sans Souci *l'infâme* had been shorthand for all that Frederick and his enlightened symposiasts abhorred: superstition, fanaticism, intolerance. Church and monarch were the targets in so far as religious faith or absolutist rule encouraged or depended upon this unholy trinity. Benighted unreason, whether personal or institutional, was the enemy. The Inquisition, the persecution of Protestants and Jews, the power struggle between Jesuits and Jansenists, the arbitrary rule of law . . . In Catholic Europe human beings were neither free to worship a God of their own choosing nor able to trust in their own innocence as a guarantee against criminal conviction. Such a state of affairs was itself intolerable.

Frederick was sceptical about Voltaire's commitment to the cause. On 18 May 1759 he told him: 'You will always caress the *Infâme* with one hand while scratching it with the other, which is just how you deal with me and everyone else.'[1] But Voltaire himself was more bullish: 'It needs only five or six *philosophes* of like mind,' he had assured d'Alembert two years earlier, 'and we can topple the colossus.' The agenda, of course, was not one of total revolution, nor indeed did it even include universal education, let alone an end to élitism, racism, sexism, ageism, and all the other antagonisms of twenty-first-century enlightenment. But the apparently limited goal was, in its insidious way, of far-reaching consequence: 'It's not a question of

The Château de Ferney, in an eighteenth-century engraving.

stopping our servants from going to church or chapel; it's a matter of freeing each family head (*père de famille*) from the tyranny of the impostors [i.e. Judaism, Christianity, Islam] and instilling the spirit of tolerance. This great mission has already had notable successes. The vine of truth has been well tended by men like d'Alembert, Diderot, Bolingbroke, Hume, etc.'[2] In essence the 'mission' was still that proposed a quarter of a century earlier in the *Lettres philosophiques*: the establishment of a religious, moral and social order founded on reason and conducive to personal liberty, prosperity and happiness. But now there were more *pères de famille* ready to heed the call, and Voltaire himself was at greater liberty to deliver it. Despots, whether of nations or the family hearth, would be enlightened. 'Never,' he told his friend Damilaville in January 1762, 'has there been a more opportune moment to toil in the vineyard of the Lord.'[3] 'Tend your vines,' he exhorted d'Alembert in February 1764: 'and crush the infamous.'[4]

The new domains at Ferney and Tourney became Voltaire's literal and metaphorical vineyard, and the 65-year-old martyr to his own entrails toiled with indefatigable zeal. His remaining hair might be white, and all his teeth gone, but it was as though he had taken out a new lease on life itself. The estates were united, tidied, and extended by further purchases of land. And they were transformed. Marshes were drained, long-fallow fields were cleared and ploughed and manured, vines were planted, all of which brought employment and much needed wages to the local peasantry. More horses were needed, so a stud farm was created and oats were sown. This forgotten corner of France (administratively part of Burgundy) still laboured under an iniquitous regime of feudal taxes, but a few letters to men in high places soon achieved their abolition and gave a further kick-start to its moribund economy. Various local disputes were addressed and resolved. Voltaire had never been happier. He attended to everything personally, tramping round stable and pasture in his new clogs, prodding this and patting that, a latter-day Virgil in a realm of pastoral delight. The mountain-locked Pays de Gex had become his very own 'kingdom of Kashmir',[5] and the sworn enemy of the *Infâme* poured out his new-found enthusiasm for agriculture in a verse epistle to Mme Denis, his unlikely Ceres: 'Thus can a man live in the shade of his trees, / At war with the fools but in himself at peace.' And he had marked off a special area near the house at Ferney. This was 'Monsieur de Voltaire's field', and here, like a Chinese emperor, he worked the land himself until well into his eighties.

The construction of the new house at Ferney was more or less complete by the autumn of 1759, although the fitting-out of the interior took another eighteen months. It would soon prove too small, however, and in 1765–6 the symmetrical château was extended by two two-storey wings, providing the extra width of a generous-sized room on each flank. Built on the foundations of the old fortress and designed by Voltaire himself (later assisted by the architect, Racle), it perched – and continues to perch – on the top of a gentle hillock, with the ground sloping away on all sides.[6] Approaching from the north-west (now from the east) and passing the church on the left (now on the right), one immediately entered a large courtyard. Then as now a flight of shallow steps led up from the courtyard to the double doors of the entrance and the hall beyond. To the left, an antechamber (for patient visitors) and then (after the addition of the wings) the dining-room, with French windows on to the courtyard; to the right of the entrance, Mme Denis's bedroom and *cabinet de toilette*. Straight ahead, the modestly-sized drawing-room, with French windows leading out on to a terrace. Oval in shape, this had been designed on the model of the principal reception room at Sans Souci, and the south-western façade thus had a bowed front at its centre. But the stonework was soft and porous, and the bow has since been replaced by a more weatherproof straight line.

Just before the entrance to the drawing-room there was a corridor that led off to the right, past a modest-sized billiards room, towards Mme Denis's own sitting-room (in the new wing). To the left the corridor led past Voltaire's small bedroom, his valet's room, and then (in the other new wing) the library, which somehow or other contained more than 7,000 books. Underneath was Wagnière's tiny office, from which the secretary could answer his master's bidding via a trap-door in the library floor. From the library Voltaire could step out through French windows on to the terrace, and then set off down his favourite tree-lined avenue. Leading south-west from the house, it afforded spectacular views of the Savoy Alps and the permanently snow-covered peak of Mont Blanc.

On the first floor, where the Master himself rarely ventured, were the guest rooms: a lavish suite for special guests, and other bedrooms. On the second, under the mansard roof, were ten small rooms for the servants. Not all had fireplaces. The basement contained a kitchen, laundry-room, wood-store, wine-cellar, fruit-store and two larders. The sanitary requirements of master, mistress and guests were met by the *chaise percée*, while bathing facilities seem to have been modest (and much less luxurious than at Cirey). Much later a small, separate stone-built pavilion was constructed outside, just beyond – and at an angle to – the library. Here water was heated in a boiler and delivered through lead piping to a tin bath lined with marble. In 1771 this was state-of-the-art, but thick dressing-gowns were still required. (The pavilion has since been demolished.) The formal gardens near the house were laid out with special care, and gave on to extensive parkland planted with oak, lime and poplar. Beneath one venerable lime-tree, underplanted with bushes, Voltaire contrived a summer retreat, a circular space with a bench and four entrance/exits through the screen of shrubbery. Here, in subsequent years, the elderly *philosophe* came to seek refuge from the madding crowd of visitors who had come to gawp and chat; here he could read and reflect, at one with the peace and beauty of nature that spoke to him of God the Creator, the first and foremost agriculturalist of them all. Man might cultivate his garden, but every garden was His.

The new house, even with its additions, was relatively modest in its proportions, though of course the smallness of the rooms and the lowness of the ceilings made for greater warmth in this mountain climate. When the biting north wind ('la bise') blew down from the Jura, many layers of clothing were necessary, and Voltaire's famous, full-length house-coats were an absolute must, especially for a man without an ounce of spare flesh on him and whose blood was thinning with the advancing years. A wig provided some extra warmth, but more generally he preferred a crown of at least five or six silk caps under a woollen hat to keep his brain from freezing over. It could be bitterly cold in paradise.

But the setting was magnificent, and the new owner sought to open up the perspectives to and from the house. Blocking the view most grievously was the local parish church, barely fifty metres from the house and itself in very great need of repair (as it once more is today, though parish needs are served elsewhere). As though symbolizing his own campaign against the monstrous intrusions of the Church into the everyday lives of civilized men and women,

Voltaire decided that the church must go. So, without consulting the local priest or his parishioners, he signed a contract for the offending edifice to be demolished and rebuilt – as far as possible with the same stones and to the same design – in a less obtrusive location. On 8 August 1760 he wrote to his old friend Thiriot:

> Yes, I am building a church. Please convey this consoling piece of news to the children of Israel, and may all the saints rejoice. Nasty people will no doubt say that I'm building this church [. . .] so that I can tear down the one that was spoiling a lovely view and put a grand avenue in its place. But the impious can say what they like, and I shall see to my own salvation.[7]

Soon, however, vociferous protests from various quarters stopped the builders from proceeding, and eventually, despite offering the local priest a new house and a pay-rise, Voltaire was obliged (by the local bishop and other authorities) to concede that the church would have to stay exactly where it was. But, if he wanted, he could indeed rebuild it at his own expense. Which – come the spring of 1761 – he did, throughout further, inevitable controversy. It had been agreed that he could replace the principal façade and entrance with something more splendid, but not everyone was aware of the agreement and there was uproar from local 'conservationists'. Then the builders moved a large wooden cross that stood in the church graveyard and which had been donated by local bigwigs. Voltaire wanted it out of the way (it would ruin the look of his new church), and he was alleged to have referred to it as 'those gallows' (in French, *potence*). Ever resourceful, he claimed that *potence* was a technical term for any architectural feature with a protruding cross-member . . .

The new façade was imposing. Two square bell-towers flanked it, each topped with a small dome, while the entrance itself was adorned with four pilasters and surmounted by a window. Above the window a pediment stretched from one dome to the other, complete with a cross and a weathervane (in the form of a cockerel rather too reminiscent of St Peter's denial of Christ). Gracing the pediment was an inscription, with its third word placed beneath the first two but in much larger letters: 'Deo erexit Voltaire'. No one – no saint, no member of the Holy Family, no Holy Spirit

— was allowed to come between a deist Voltaire and the Almighty. Many years later a waggish poet, the abbé Delille, would put an altogether different interpretation on this inscription: 'That's a fine word,' he said, 'between two great names.'[8] But this was not the last indignity to which it was subject. During the Revolution the church was partly demolished (the twin towers have gone) and entirely emptied of its contents: the inscription was removed. Decades later, in the middle of the nineteenth century, it was recovered from a Ferney tavern and replaced.

As to the interior of the church, Voltaire was keen to do what he could. A new baldachino, for example, was erected over the altar. But a proper church needs holy relics. So he wrote to the Pope, requesting something suitable, perhaps a bone or two. In return he received, somewhat to his disappointment, a hair shirt that had purportedly belonged to St Francis. A papal hint to the ostentatious François perhaps? Relic or no relic, Voltaire left it lying on his mantelpiece. And of course every (Catholic) church needs a crucifix — or at least a representation of Christ. So the deist philanthropist commissioned a Lyons sculptor, Perrache, to produce a life-size effigy of Our Lord in gilded wood (cost: 1,200 *livres*), which was placed upon the altar. Looking more like a Roman emperor or nobleman, this particular figure bore no trace of the Passion but expressed rather the Voltairean conception of Christ as a sage of antique wisdom. Despite its secular appearance it was removed during the Revolution and never recovered. And here in his refurbished church the new Lord of the Manor would attend Sunday Mass and even — on Easter Sunday 1761 — take communion. For he believed it essential, pending a broader enlightenment, that the 'people' should remain god-fearing (otherwise all hell might break loose). So the patriarch duly set an example of pious religious observance. And each time he left at the end of the service he would glance at the tomb he had had built for himself, outside the church and yet against its wall and beneath its overhanging roof: half in and half out, a place of deist compromise. But the tomb had the shape of a pyramid: the deist was also a pharaoh. Even in death Voltaire would be playing a part.

Indeed the theatre continued to occupy a central position in the living Voltaire's activities, and at first he used the house at Tourney for the purpose. Thus, when the duc de Villars visited in September 1760, he and other guests were given supper at Les Délices and then taken across the border to Tourney (just under a mile away) for the evening's performance of the theatricals that were now — since d'Alembert's article — even more controversial in Geneva. Some guests, unable to return to the city (where the gates would be shut), travelled on to spend the night at Ferney. The remainder returned to Les Délices, where the accommodation was still insufficient for large numbers. But the stage at Tourney was tiny, and conditions were hardly ideal. Moreover, once Voltaire and Mme Denis had moved in permanently to the château at Ferney it would be much better to have a theatre directly to hand.

Since he had been obliged to retain the church in its present position, Voltaire made a virtue of necessity and decided to create a theatre out of the large barn that stood at an angle between the house and the church and conveniently obscured all but the new façade (visible, sideways on, from the front of the house). The new building, finished in October 1761, could seat 300 people, and the stage was large enough for the spectacular sets that were now all the rage in Paris. The comte de Lauraguais had been responsible for the revolutionary step of banishing spectators from the stage of the Comédie-Française, and he was duly invited to be the guest of honour on Voltaire's own opening night. Some months later the duc de Villars returned with the duc de Richelieu, and together they were treated to a performance of one of Voltaire's latest plays, *Olympie* (*Olympia*), in which a large funeral pyre occupied centre stage — with real flames. Flames just like the three depicted in the Arouet coat-of-arms that now adorned the pediment of his new residence alongside Mme Denis's less combustible escutcheon.

Once established with his niece at Ferney, Voltaire found himself — willingly — at home to the world. The great and the good came to stay; performing artists took up temporary residence and sang or acted for their supper; refugees of sundry provenance and diverse merit were welcomed one and all under his newly restored roof, to be given shelter against persecution and injustice, against the *Infâme*. Secretaries took dictation, and letters were dispatched daily to all corners of the (European) world. This remote and barren corner of France had become an intellectual and cultural nerve-centre, a would-be miniature of Paris or Versailles, and all through the presence — and fortune — of one man: 'Messire François Marie Arouet de Voltaire, chevalier, gentilhomme ordinaire de la Chambre du roi, comte de Tourney, Prégny et Chambésy, seigneur de Ferney'. Or at least that's what it said on his contracts. Zozo had done well. And the parties were fabulously lavish. On 6 March 1762, for example, 300 people were invited to a performance of his new comedy, *Le Droit du seigneur* (the forerunner of Beaumarchais's much funnier *Marriage of Figaro*) and afterwards entertained to supper and a ball that lasted until dawn (and until the gates of Geneva were once again open). Voltaire's annual living costs had risen to some 35,000 *livres*, but why worry? At his age he might as well enjoy life while he could: 'I have decided to stop caring and to treat everything with a laugh. It's very good for my health.'[9] But of course he did still care. Nine months later he was writing to d'Alembert: 'I have realized that there is no point in half measures. They're just a trap. I must wage war and die a noble death, "with a pile of immolated bigots lying at my feet".'[10] Whether in pleasure or in battle the message was the same: he was rich, he was free, he was old, and he could do — he must do — exactly what he wanted.

And he wanted what he had always wanted: to write plays and to fight the good fight in the name of reason. In the case of *L'Ecossaise* (*The Scotswoman*) — the prose comedy with which he opened his new theatre — he did both. The latest theatrical success in Paris had been Charles Palissot's *Les Philosophes*, a satire that caricatured some of the leading figures of the French Enlightenment — notably Diderot and Rousseau — as being variously unprincipled, pompous or daft. Voltaire himself was spared (Palissot admired him), and so too was d'Alembert (for having resigned from his collaboration on the *Encyclopédie*). But the worst of it was the glee with which Voltaire's old enemy, the journalist Fréron, had greeted the new production (premiered on 2 May 1760) and exploited it to ridicule the *philosophes* further. Written partly in response to previous Fréron attacks and published by Cramer earlier in the year, *Le Caffé ou l'Ecossaise* (its original title) had featured an odious Frélon, a venial police-informer masquerading as a journalist (who witnesses the main action of this otherwise quaint romantic intrigue of love and revealed identity). Accordingly Voltaire now gave the play prominence, and the Comédie-Française eagerly rode the tide of Palissot's success by staging this reply on 26 July. Another triumph. And even Fréron, to his credit, took Frélon in his stride, reviewing the play with wit and suggesting that the 'sages' of the *Encyclopédie* would now celebrate their temporary victory by singing a *Te Voltarium*. For 'frelon' (without the accent) means 'hornet'; and Fréron had not lost his sting.

That Voltaire should have been 'spared' by Palissot was nevertheless symptomatic of the fact that he was no longer perceived as epitomizing the radical. And for conservatives like Fréron it was the atheists and materialists who now worried them most. Similarly, in the world of the theatre, Voltaire was beginning to seem old hat. Despite his apparent subservience to tradition and convention, Voltaire the playwright had always tried to innovate and to move the Comédie-Française on. Ancient Greece and Rome, and to a lesser extent the Bible, had provided the staple of Corneille and Racine and their lesser contemporaries. Voltaire, with the advantage of his historical researches, sought out new subjects and above all new settings, and then pushed for these to be lavishly reconstructed on stage. Far from offering the austere, timeless, placeless claustrophobia of, say, Racine's *Phèdre*, from which almost all physical action is banished, his plays were spectacles that promised unexpected delights and the shock of the new: the queen who poisons herself on stage in *Hérode et Mariamne*, the costumes for *Mahomet*, the backdrops for *Sémiramis*. Now that spectators no longer had to be accommodated on stage, he could experiment with more elaborate sets: the pyre in *Olympie*, for example, or the split stage in *L'Écossaise*, where the scene shifts from right to left between the coffee-house and the heroine's bedroom. Similarly, for his new tragedy *Tancrède* Voltaire wanted a split stage featuring the public square (in besieged eleventh-century Syracuse) and the interior of the governor's palace. The square would be filled with extras, decked in all manner of medieval Norman armour and weaponry, while various representatives of the Moorish enemy would provide further opportunity for exotic accoutrement.

One thinks of Shakespeare, and indeed Voltaire's theatre-going in Drury Lane in the 1720s had much to do with these innovations. But he would only go so far. As *Tancrède* (premiered on 3 September 1760) shows, the emphasis remains on the plot and the pathos of its intricate, if implausible knots (themselves reminiscent of *Zaïre*). Aménaïde, betrothed to Orbassan, secretly loves the gallant knight, Tancrède. Mistakenly thought to have betrayed the Normans out of love for Solamir, the Moorish leader, she is condemned to death. Tancrède, believing her guilty and unfaithful, nevertheless fights a duel

with Orbassan and saves her life before going off to fight the Moors —
successfully but at the cost of his own life. In the final, heart-wrenching scene
an innocent Aménaïde explains all to a dying Tancrède, and, upon his death,
flings herself across his body and dies ('I hear him calling me'). And so when
Mlle Clairon at the Comédie-Française suggested that a real scaffold be
installed on stage (thus as a backdrop to Tancrède's duel) and the stage hung
with black drapery, Voltaire objected robustly. In his view the words, the
situation, and an *immobile* spectacle were alone sufficient to move the audience
to tears (and weep they copiously did): but 'a tomb, a room draped in black, a
gallows, a ladder, people fighting on stage, dead bodies being carried off', it
all smacked of fairground theatricals. Mlle Clairon and her colleagues were in
danger of ruining French theatre by borrowing what was worst in the
theatrical practice of 'those barbarous English': 'the interest must derive from
what is said'.[11] The most popular playwright in eighteenth-century France
had drawn the line. They had come far enough since the days of Corneille.

As indeed he had particular reason to know. For he had just agreed to take
in a distant relative of the great playwright, the eighteen-year-old Marie-
Françoise, who was descended from Pierre Corneille's uncle. Her family had
fallen on hard times, and she owed her convent education to none other than
Fréron, who had got the Comédie-Française to perform her ancestor's
Rodogune and donate the takings towards conventual costs. But her schooldays
were over and she was in need of protection, so Voltaire the philanthropist
(and enemy of Fréron) stepped in. She herself arrived to take up residence in
late December 1760, shortly after Voltaire and Mme Denis had made the
definitive move from Les Délices. Here was the daughter they had never had.
Uncle and niece set about her education, determined to remedy the many
gaps left by a convent schooling. The pretty, snub-nosed pupil was willing
but not particularly intelligent, and a sense of the tragic was plainly quite
beyond her. Not that any of this prevented her new hosts from enrolling her
as an actress in their home productions.

There was also the question of a dowry. Voltaire decided to borrow
Fréron's idea of raising further money by publishing a luxury, subscription
edition of Corneille's plays. But he would go one better: he would write a
commentary on them also. He duly did so, and, as in the days of *La Henriade*,
mustered a most impressive list of subscribers: Louis XV himself, thanks to

the intervention of Mme de Pompadour and of Louis's new minister (and Voltaire's friend), the duc de Choiseul; Elisabeth of Russia and soon afterwards her successor Catherine II; the Empress Maria Theresa; etc., etc. By the time the first edition appeared in 1764, there were 1,176 of the grandest names, who between them had signed up for some 4,000 copies. The profits were all to go to young Marie-Françoise. Like some fairy godfather Voltaire had meanwhile identified a suitable match: a handsome 22-year-old dragoon of modest but independent means, called Pierre-Jacques-Claude Dupuits, who lived in the locality. The young couple fell hopelessly and conveniently in love and were married at midnight in the newly restored church at Ferney on 13–14 February 1763. Fortunately the bride's insufferably boorish father had been prevented from attending. Voltaire, who now doted on his ward, provided a handsome dowry out of his own resources, and the charming pair were invited to live at Ferney. Not so another member of the Corneille clan, an impecunious labourer and ex-soldier who turned up at the door in search of charity. A few *livres* secured his permanent departure. Would there be others? No. Except for Marie-Françoise's baby, born – like Voltaire's *Commentary* – the following year.

The presence of two tsarinas on the subscription list reflected Voltaire's recent engagement with Russian history. The first volume of his *Histoire de l'empire de Russie sous Pierre le Grand* (*History of the Russian Empire under Peter the Great*) appeared at the end of 1759, and the second in June 1763. Between volumes Elisabeth Petrovna had died (15 January 1762); Peter III had succeeded but become deeply unpopular through his support for Frederick of Prussia; and in July 1762, four days after he had been forced to abdicate, he was murdered at the behest of his wife. She, Catherine the Great, would rule Russia until her death in 1796. In receiving the original invitation to write a history of Peter the Great, Voltaire had been keen to take up the story where he had left off in his earlier history of Charles XII of Sweden. Although the Russians themselves expected – and desired – a simple panegyric, the Master of Ferney was minded to be more scholarly, and he faced great difficulties in securing the necessary documentation. In the end he produced an account that glorified Peter as a hero of the Enlightenment, bringing civilization to a barbaric land. Accordingly he pleased the new empress, with whom he sustained a personal correspondence that lasted until his own death. To do so, he had had to pull some punches – notably in his account of Peter's brutal role in the death of his son and heir Alexis – but the account is no whitewash. As Frederick himself would have put it, he scratched as he caressed. And he certainly continued to caress Catherine. For, as with Frederick, Voltaire saw here an opportunity to influence the course of European history 'from the top down'. If Catherine would act on her enlightened opinions, duly encouraged by her correspondent, then the darkness might yet be lifted from one further corner of the world. When she agreed to buy the impoverished Diderot's library for a large sum of money while yet granting him the use of it throughout his lifetime, Voltaire was persuaded of the genuineness of her commitment to learning and reason. Little could he know that she would later buy his own library.

But for the moment this library had now been transferred from Les Délices to Ferney, and it was much in use as Voltaire settled down to a concerted campaign against the *Infâme*. In particular he began once more to study the Bible, as he had almost thirty years earlier with Mme du Châtelet at Cirey. So much 'infamy' was justified by an appeal to biblical authority that one way to combat it was to demolish that authority. With the aid once more of Dom Calmet's commentary, and a battery of biblical exegesis, Voltaire hunted down the contradictions and absurdities to be found in Old and New Testaments alike. Gradually he accumulated a store of ammunition that would soon be fired off in his *Dictionnaire philosophique* and in sundry *contes* and pamphlets. How Aaron's rod became a serpent and frogs covered the land of Egypt (Exodus 7). Or the whoredoms of Aholah and Aholibah (Ezekiel 23). Or how the Lord permitted Ezekiel, as a very special favour, to bake his barley cakes with cow dung rather than the 'dung that cometh out of man' (Ezekiel 4). Etc., etc.

All good fun. But in the spring of 1762 he learnt of an event that had taken place just six months earlier, not century upon unimaginable century ago, and an event that had happened not somewhere in the Middle East but here in France, in the city of Toulouse. That event and his response to it was to prove Voltaire's most signal victory in his campaign against the *Infâme*. Indeed it was to define one of the images – perhaps *the* image – by which Voltaire has come to be known by posterity: the champion of human rights.

The Philosophes *at lunch: an engraving by Jean Huber of an imaginary symposium figuring Voltaire and some leading contemporary thinkers.*

CHAPTER SEVENTEEN

Jousting with Injustice:
Calas and Rousseau (1761–1765)

Wherein one man proclaims his innocence and another confesses

THE EVENT OCCURRED in Toulouse on 13 October 1761. Jean Calas was a cloth merchant who had managed the family business for the past forty years in the rue des Filatiers, one of the main Toulouse thoroughfares. He had been married since 1731 to Anne-Rose, and they had produced four sons and two daughters. They were Protestant. On the evening in question the two daughters, Rosine (20) and Nanette (19), were away in the country, picking grapes. The youngest son, Donat (22), was serving an apprenticeship in Nîmes, while Louis (25), the second-youngest, had left home after converting to Catholicism five years earlier – partly thanks to the efforts of Jeanne Viguière, the now elderly Catholic house-keeper who had served Jean and Anne-Rose for most of their married life. But the two eldest sons, Marc-Antoine (almost 29) and Pierre (28), were at home. Both worked in the family business, although Marc-Antoine – an intelligent, studious, rather private man – would like to have studied for the Bar. His religion prevented it.

The Calas family lived over the shop. Entry to their modest home was gained along a narrow hallway. Immediately to the left was the door to the shop, which had a window and door on to the street. Further along on the left was the storeroom, which was linked to the shop by double doors (wide enough for the rolls of cloth). Beyond that a spiral staircase rose to the first floor, where a corridor gave on to sitting-room, dining-room, kitchen and parental bedroom. The children and servant slept on the second floor. That evening the family had a guest: Gaubert Lavaysse, a young Protestant friend of nineteen, who had learnt a trade in the shipbuilding industry and was planning to emigrate soon to the West Indies. Some time shortly after seven they sat down for a supper of pigeon and chicken, followed by Roquefort and grapes, prepared and served by Jeanne. As the meal was ending, at about half past eight, Marc-Antoine — who had been characteristically silent — left the table and, they supposed, went out for his usual walk. Soon the others retired to the sitting-room, while Jeanne dozed in the kitchen. About an hour later, Pierre escorted their guest by candlelight down the stairs and towards the front door. As the two men passed the shop, they found the door unexpectedly open and explored inside — where they found Marc-Antoine, dead.

Interrogated by the police later that evening, Jean Calas and his son Pierre stated that they had found Marc-Antoine lying on the floor. Lavaysse was not questioned. Two days later all three men stated that they had actually found him hanging — from a wooden pole of the kind used in rolls of cloth, which had been placed across the half-open double doors between the shop and the storeroom. Having taken the corpse down and laid it out on the floor, they had then lied: suicides were forbidden a dignified, Christian burial. The police were suspicious: the rope marks on Marc-Antoine's neck could have been the result of a strangulation. It was also the case that money was missing from his pocket: had he been murdered during a robbery? Or had he lost it gambling (of which he was fond) and incurred shaming debts? But the authorities did not follow up these lines of enquiry, for they wanted to believe only one, highly improbable story: that Jean Calas, with the assistance of his son and guest, and in the presence of his wife, had murdered Marc-Antoine to prevent him from converting to Catholicism like his younger brother. This theory had rapidly gained currency among the neighbours and rubbernecks who had gathered outside the house on the night of the incident, and to whom the investigating magistrate, David de Beaudrigue, had been only too willing to listen. Beaudrigue was bigotry incarnate, and to him the 'truth' was so plain that he omitted entirely to search either the corpse or the house itself for evidence that might account for this death. Instead he took every member of the household into custody, together with another

Protestant, called Cazeing, in whose house the murder was alleged to have been planned.

According to the procedures of the day, Beaudrigue constructed an account of the incident as he understood it to have occurred – a murder by strangulation or hanging – and this was then read out three times in every Toulouse parish over the following three Sundays (18 October – 8 November). The faithful were required, on pain of excommunication, to supply what relevant testimony they could to confirm or deny the account. (Thus did Church and *parlement* together rule.) After considerable and necrobiotically problematic delay Marc-Antoine was finally laid to rest on 8 November, having been given a martyr's funeral with all the pomp that the Roman Catholic Church could muster. But no evidence was forthcoming either of the involvement of Cazeing or of Marc-Antoine's desire to convert. It is true that he had often attended Roman Catholic services but he had done so, it seems, from a love of music (which, for a man of his position and means, could not easily be otherwise satisfied); and Jeanne Viguière herself testified that she had never heard him speak of such an intention. But the authorities were determined to prove their case, and the interrogation of the alleged culprits became more intense. At a formal hearing on 18 November Jean Calas continued to protest his innocence, but inevitably he made a poor impression: public speaking was not his forte, and by his own admission he had lied. The public prosecutor demanded the maximum sentences: Jean, Anne-Rose and Pierre Calas to be hanged, their bodies publicly burned, and their ashes scattered to the four winds; Lavaysse to be sent to the galleys for life; and Jeanne Viguière to be imprisoned for five years. But the presiding judges preferred for the moment to resort to torture in order to extract confessions.

The case was now taken up by the section of the Toulouse *parlement* that dealt with capital crimes. As was customary before the Revolution, all judicial proceedings took place behind closed doors, and the magistrates responsible for reaching a verdict deliberated long and hard. A death sentence required a majority of two, and, after ten sittings of the court, it was decided by the narrowest of votes on 9 March that Jean Calas be broken on the wheel and then strangled, after which his body was to be publicly burned. But not before some preliminary torture. On 10 March ropes were attached to Jean Calas's arms and legs, and, as the gaolers pulled,

an increasingly nervous Beaudrigue waited eagerly for the confession that
would exonerate his actions. But despite the excruciating pain Calas would
make no such confession. He was innocent – and in any case a confession
would condemn the rest of his family to death. Next came the water torture:
and he was twice made to drink ten jugs of water straight off. Still no
confession. Then they walked this somewhat frail man of sixty-two through
the streets of Toulouse, barefoot, with a noose round his neck, to the
scaffold – and the wheel. He was roped to the (perpendicular) wheel, his
arms and legs were broken with an iron bar, and there he hung: semi-
conscious, in agony, gazing up to heaven for two hours in the consoling
presence of a Roman Catholic priest and generally presenting an edifying
spectacle to the assembled crowd. With such strength as was left to him, he
continued to protest his innocence. Since – in the minds of the credulous
onlookers – mendacity at this critical moment would have meant certain
consignment to the fires of Hell, everyone was impressed. But it mattered
little: Jean Calas was publicly strangled and burned. The Toulouse magistrates were thoroughly dismayed at this lack of a confession, particularly as
Versailles had now taken a keen interest in the affair. So they tried to wrap
things up quickly by merely banishing Pierre Calas from the city and quietly
dropping all the charges against Mme Calas, Lavaysse, Jeanne Viguière, and
Cazeing. It was time, they felt, to move on.

   Voltaire first learnt of the matter about ten days later, from visitors to
Ferney who brought the latest gossip from the Dijon *parlement*. His first
informants assured him of the straightforwardness of the case: Calas had
murdered his would-be Catholic of a son. 'We may not be very estimable
ourselves,' Voltaire wrote to De Bault, a lawyer at the Dijon *parlement*, 'but the
Huguenots are worse, and what's more they denounce the theatre.'[1] But
within the next few days further information soon persuaded him of Calas's
innocence, and by 4 April he had determined to do something about it.
Needless to say, Geneva was in a state of outrage at this treatment of an
innocent Protestant, and even more so when Donat Calas fled there from
Nîmes. (His two grape-picking sisters had been arrested and sent to separate
Catholic convents.) At once Voltaire invited him to Ferney to hear his
account of these terrible events, and he was struck by the young man's
gentleness and lack of guile. Could such a son have murderers for parents?

Why, they had never so much as smacked him. Voltaire was soon weeping —
and angrily plotting his campaign.

The first thing was to get the legal proceedings made public. Exceptionally
this had occurred in the case of Damiens, the man who had tried to
assassinate Louis XV and who had been executed in 1757. So there was a
precedent. 'If there is one thing that can stay the hand of fanatical rage, it is
publicity.'[2] The second thing was to keep it simple. There was no point
demanding a new investigation, or raising the question of robbery and
possible murder by an unknown third party. Better to stick to the suicide
theory, even if, as the Toulouse magistrates had concluded after a number of
attempted reconstructions, a man of Marc-Antoine's height would have
found it very difficult to hang himself in the manner alleged. And better to
emphasize the sheer implausibility of the official story: that this family and
their guest could all sit down to a nice supper together and then calmly
murder the eldest son by strangling him in cold blood. But taking this
strategy forward was not a simple matter. Many people were only too ready
to believe the worst of the Huguenots (as Voltaire had himself at first).
Others, predictably, thought it best not to rock the boat. And others could
simply not be bothered to care about some obscure cloth merchant from
Toulouse. But all this simply strengthened Voltaire's resolve: if no one else
was going to intervene, then it were best he did. Especially as he was well
placed to do so. He had the money and he had the influence, not least in the
Protestant circles that he now sought to mobilize in Germany and England,
as well as in France and Switzerland.

He also needed the support of Mme Calas, who had taken refuge in
Montauban and was destitute (her husband's estate having been confiscated).
Accordingly he made arrangements for her to be taken to Paris and looked
after by the d'Argentals and other friends. Lavaysse went to join her. But she
was to keep a low profile for the moment as he endeavoured — by
correspondence and a wide network of intermediaries — to gain the support
of those in high places: Mme de Pompadour, who was said to be deeply
affected by the account of Calas's courageous death and to have shared her
feelings with the King; the duc de Choiseul, the King's most influential
minister, who believed Calas innocent but did not wish to confront the
Toulouse *parlement*; Saint-Florentin, the minister charged with overseeing

Protestant affairs; the ministers and officials at the Treasury, who needed Protestant assistance if they were to replenish coffers depleted by the Seven Years War; and anyone else he could think of who might conceivably bring pressure to bear in this campaign to have the Calas verdict overturned and the dead man's innocence posthumously declared. Writing in Mme Calas's name, and in that of her son Donat (whom he asked to vet the result), he composed 'their' first-hand accounts of the events in the form of two letters (from mother to son, and the son's reply), and published these as pamphlets intended for wide circulation in Paris and throughout Europe. With half a century of experience behind him, the tragedian tugged skilfully at the heart-strings as he evoked the defenceless innocence of this worthy family and depicted each stage in their terrible drama. The effect of pathos was stronger than any argument. He then drafted Donat's official requests, to the Chancellor (Maurepas) and to the royal council, that His Majesty order the Toulouse *parlement* to account officially for its proceedings in the case. A further memorandum from Donat and a statement from Pierre, both similarly ghost-written and both highlighting the iniquity of current legal procedures, were written and published soon afterwards.

At the same time Voltaire wrote and distributed an anonymous pamphlet about the case of one Elizabeth Canning, an English girl who alleged that she had been abducted and held against her will in a brothel – for which nine people were sentenced to death. But because capital sentences required royal approval (which took time) and because all court proceedings were published, it had been possible to expose the truth – the unmarried Elizabeth, with the aid of an aunt, had been trying to conceal a pregnancy – before innocent people were wrongly executed. In Toulouse, by contrast, Calas had been executed the day after sentence was passed; and so secret were the proceedings that even his wife and family had neither read nor heard the sentence before it was carried out.

Voltaire's campaign gathered pace, and opinion began to turn in his favour. On 8 October Maurepas gave orders for the Calas girls to be freed from their convents and allowed to rejoin their mother in Paris. The case itself duly came before the royal council on 7 March 1763, approximately eleven months after Voltaire had first taken an interest. According to the procedures Mme Calas, her son, her maid, and Gaubert Lavaysse had all been obliged to commit themselves voluntarily to prison, but this in practice meant being entertained to dinner at the Versailles gaol (along with her two daughters and supportive friends). At the palace itself the meeting – of some 100 council members – lasted three hours, at the end of which it was unanimously decided to order the Toulouse *parlement* to account to the King for the trial and execution of Jean Calas. The King himself approved the decision. Nanette Calas fainted twice.

This was a significant victory against the *Infâme*, and Voltaire stood ready to capitalize on it. Towards the end of the previous year Voltaire had written his celebrated *Traité sur la tolérance (Treatise on Tolerance)* and had it printed by Gabriel Cramer. But he had held back from publication lest it should confuse the issue and harm the Calas cause. Now, emboldened by the royal council's verdict, he began to distribute printed copies privately. The text begins by narrating the Calas affair, with particular emphasis on the way in which prejudice and fanatical hatred had taken the place of evidence and hard fact. But Voltaire then broadens the perspective, drawing on all the material with which he had once again been made familiar by his work on a revised edition of the *Essai sur les mœurs*. His message is clear: religious diversity and religious tolerance are economically and socially beneficial. One has only to look at the history of the Ottoman empire or Peter the Great's Russia, of India and Persia, of China and Japan. And the work ends with a 'Prayer to God'. Let not difference be a source of hatred and persecution: 'May all men remember that they are brothers!' Of course, it was really a prayer to the government: Have faith in human reason, trust the King's subjects not to abuse the privileges of religious and civil liberty.

As to Protestants in particular, Voltaire chose this moment to propose a programme of reform in his *Traité*. Since the Revocation of the Edict of Nantes by Louis XIV in 1685 it had been illegal in France to participate in Protestant worship or to give shelter or assistance to Protestant ministers – for men, on pain of a life sentence in the galleys; for women, on pain of life imprisonment. All personal property was also confiscated in such cases. Anyone who professed to be a Protestant minister or was found conducting a Protestant service was himself liable to the death penalty – like Rochette, who had recently been hanged on the orders of the Toulouse *parlement* on 19 February 1762. All Protestants were required to baptize their children into the Roman Catholic Church within twenty-four hours and to bring them up as Catholics. Marriage was legal only if celebrated in a Roman Catholic church. Entry into the liberal professions depended on having been certified by a Catholic priest as a regular communicant member of the Church. French Protestants, mostly concentrated in the Languedoc, accommodated themselves to these rules as best they could, outwardly complying while inwardly practising their own reformed version of the Christian religion (and sometimes participating in clandestine worship). Such accommodations were nevertheless perilous and unpalatable.

Voltaire's programme was modest, and he was careful to present it on the utilitarian basis of encouraging Huguenot émigrés to return to France so that they might restore their talents, enterprise and wealth to its body politic. For their sake at least, Protestants should be allowed the possibility of legitimate marriage outside the Catholic Church, and their children should be entitled to be brought up as Protestants and to inherit. He stopped short of demanding freedom of worship. But even this programme was too incendiary, and the *Traité* was quickly perceived as a dangerous work with which it was ill-advised to be associated. The duc de La Vallière warned Voltaire from Paris that the ice was once again thin. Choiseul, though a friend and sympathizer, begged not to be sent a copy for fear of being incriminated. And now it seemed that the council's verdict of 7 March 1763 might not necessarily lead to the exoneration of Calas: the Toulouse *parlement* was dragging its feet and putting up some mean-spirited resistance. Symptomatic of their strategy was the demand that Mme Calas, destitute or not, pay 1,500 *livres* towards the costs of the report ordered by the King. Voltaire and others paid on her behalf. But he need not have worried. On 4 June 1764 the royal council unanimously threw out the verdict of the Toulouse *parlement* and ordered a retrial – by a group of the council's own members. And this body of men duly cleared the name of Jean Calas on 12 March 1765. The four co-accused – Mme Calas, her son Pierre, Gaubert Lavaysse and Jeanne Viguière – were acquitted of all charges and given leave to claim damages against the Toulouse *parlement*. Since, for a variety of reasons, they were unlikely to succeed in this claim, each participant in the events received a royal grant: 12,000 *livres* for Mme Calas, 6,000 each for her two daughters, 3,000 for each son and for Jeanne Viguière, plus 6,000 to cover legal expenses. Donat Calas

Members of the Calas family learning of their acquittal, as depicted by Carmontelle.

was with Voltaire at Ferney when the news came, and the two men wept once more, with joy and relief.

Following this verdict, for which the accused had once again been required to accept temporary incarceration at Versailles, a leading engraver, Carmontelle, depicted the prison scene. Mme Calas is seated slightly to the right, calm and dignified, beside one of her two pretty daughters, also seated. Behind them stands the other daughter, while their kindly-looking and rather stout maid, Jeanne Viguière, looks on from the centre of the picture. The four women listen attentively as, to the left, a handsome Gaubert Lavaysse reads from a document announcing the decision, with his smiling friend Pierre Calas puckishly reading the text over his shoulder. Voltaire quickly ordered twelve copies and made sure that all his friends bought some too. The proceeds were to go to the Calas family, but it was also important that this powerful image of noble and vindicated innocence be seen and distributed as widely as possible. Like famous newspaper photographs of the modern era, it would serve as a powerful icon with which to mobilize public opinion. Meanwhile he hung one of the prints above his bed.

The triumph was total: the son of François Voltaire, *conseiller du Roi*, had very publicly beaten the lawyers of the *parlement* at their own game. Moreover the Jansenists' defeat was also the Calvinists' victory, and the troublesome playwright was now the toast of Geneva. In Paris the *philosophes* were beside themselves with delight, and even Diderot – who always had his suspicions about Voltaire's radical credentials – was moved to inform his mistress, Sophie Volland, that 'if there really were a Christ, I can assure you that Voltaire would be saved'.[3] One person who was not so sure, however, was Jean-Jacques Rousseau. For relations between the two men had soured dramatically, and the fundamental divide between their personalities and their moral attitudes had been laid bare by circumstance. The author of the *Discourse on Inequality* had not taken kindly to Voltaire's comment about wanting to walk on all fours, and he strongly resented the manner in which Voltaire (among others) was wilfully misreading his argument about man's natural goodness as a simplistic call to abandon reason and return to the forest. (In *Les Philosophes* Palissot had depicted him eating lettuce leaves.) Furthermore, as a citizen of Geneva, Rousseau felt strangely dispossessed by this cuckoo in the Calvinist nest, and – in the absence of first-hand knowledge – increasingly convinced that Voltaire alone was responsible for what certain axe-grinding correspondents depicted to him as the moral decline of the city of his birth. But he was also increasingly out of touch, so that his impassioned denunciation of the theatre in response to d'Alembert's article on Geneva in the *Encyclopédie* struck even some Genevan traditionalists as coming from another age. Their city had changed over the years, and it was perhaps time to compromise on this vexatious issue. Which, of course, only made Rousseau blame Voltaire the playwright all the more.

On 17 June 1760 Rousseau wrote the celebrated, not to say infamous, letter to Voltaire in which he roundly declared that he hated him. Three years earlier he had undergone a crisis in his most treasured relationships – with Mme d'Epinay, his protectress, with Grimm, their mutual friend, and with Diderot, his closest friend and philosophical ally. At the time of the letter in question, he was living in solitude, with his common-law wife Thérèse Levasseur, in a cottage beside the forest of Montmorency (just north of Paris) and under the patronage of the maréchal de Luxembourg. Here he wrote not only the *Lettre à d'Alembert sur les spectacles* (1758) but the bestselling novel *Julie ou la Nouvelle Héloïse* (1761), his radical thesis on education, *Émile* (1762), and his blueprint for a better society, *Du contrat social* (1762). Evidently, having now broken with the *encyclopédistes*, he had been brewing for a showdown with the man he still regarded as the leader of the *philosophes*, and he did not mince his words:

> I do not like you, sir. You have chosen to wrong me in the ways that would cause me the most grievous hurt, and I your disciple and enthusiastic admirer. You have brought ruin on Geneva, as your reward for the asylum you received there; you have alienated my fellow citizens from me as your reward for the plaudits that I helped them to heap upon you; it is you who have made it intolerable for me to live in my own native land; it is because of you that I shall die in a foreign country, deprived of all the consolations due to a dying man and accorded the honour of being flung into a common grave, while in my own country, whether in life or death, you will everywhere be granted all the honours to which a man may aspire. In a word, I hate you – just as you intended I should. But I hate you as one who could more worthily have loved you, had you but wished it.[4]

Unversed in the finer points of Rousseau's prickly sensibility, Voltaire quite simply thought the man had lost his mind. Sharing his astonishment by letter with d'Alembert, he recommended soothing baths and a diet of restorative broth. And how could Rousseau choose this particular moment for his declaration of hatred when he, Voltaire, had just been trying to defend the *philosophes* from Palissot's caricatures and Fréron's razor-edged glee? Voltaire was dismayed, and disappointed. A valuable ally had been lost to the cause: St Paul had turned out to be Judas. He never forgave him, and the hapless Rousseau became the butt of some of his most vindictive satire. He lost no opportunity to savage *La Nouvelle Héloïse*, which he dismissed as 'silly, middle-class, dirty-minded, and boring'.[5] The champion of natural virtue was no more than a vicarious lecher, while his message to the French nation was plain: 'his principal suggestion is that we all kill ourselves'.[6] This allusion to the novel's famous passage on suicide was particularly ungenerous since in a letter to d'Argental Voltaire had earlier expressed his (unironic) approval: 'an admirable piece . . . it makes one want to die'.[7] As to the even more famous letter in which the hero, Saint-Preux, describes his visit to a Parisian brothel, Voltaire found it at once distasteful and dull. So, as he happened to be preparing a new edition of *Candide*, he inserted a brief and witty episode in which Candide is seduced – and relieved of a few Eldoradan diamonds – by a leading Parisian courtesan whose establishment appears for all the world like a literary salon. It was not just the rule book that Voltaire liked to rewrite.

The relationship worsened in the following year. After the publication of *Du contrat social* and *Émile* in April and May 1762, the Paris *parlement* issued a warrant for Rousseau's arrest, and he was forced to flee. Worse still, the Genevan authorities condemned the two works, ordered all copies to be shredded and burned, and threatened to arrest this citizen of their city should he dare to enter its gates. Needless to say, Rousseau held Voltaire especially to blame for this hostility, but in reality he had more enemies in Geneva than he realized. Its pastors, for example, were particularly keen to put clear water between their Calvinism and Rousseau's deism (as expressed in *Émile* in the section entitled 'Profession de foi du vicaire savoyard' ('Profession of faith by the Savoyard vicar')). And the city fathers were uncomfortable at being cited in *Du contrat social* as a model of latter-day Athenian democracy (as they had been before in the *Discourse on Inequality*) when the polemical purpose of this encomium was the denigration and reform of French absolutism. For France was a powerful, bellicose and unpredictable neighbour.

Voltaire himself pleaded plausibly innocent. What reason had he to persecute Rousseau? Indeed he had even offered him shelter at Tourney, but the man had been too proud to accept.[8] And moreover – though he hated to say so – he admired the 'Profession de foi': 'forty of the boldest pages ever written against Christianity'.[9] The pedagogical theories of *Émile* might bear every resemblance to 'the gobbledygook of some foolish nurse', and the programme set out in *Du contrat social* was seriously 'unsocial'.[10] Even the 'Profession' was not without its internal contradictions, especially as its author seemed remarkably ambivalent – in action as in word – about whether he was a deist or a Christian. But this was simply a further sign that Rousseau was off his head. Lapsed or not, he was still an ally against the *Infâme*.

The said ally, rejected by Geneva and Bern, now spent the next three years sheltering on Prussian soil just outside Neuchâtel. From here, in 1764, he wrote his *Lettres écrites de la montagne* (*Letters written from the Mountain*), nine letters of closely argued self-explanation in response to the Genevan public prosecutor, Jean-Robert Tronchin (not to be confused with Voltaire's banker of the same name), whose *Lettres écrites de la campagne* (*Letters written from the Countryside*) had set out the case against him. This, too, was condemned by the Paris *parlement*, and when the pastors of Neuchâtel called time, he briefly sought refuge on the Île de Saint-Pierre in the Lac de Bienne before fleeing to England in 1766 and into the welcoming arms of David Hume. In the *Lettres écrites de la montagne* Rousseau not only defended himself but attacked those he believed to be his enemies, notably Voltaire, whom he denounced as the author of the anonymous *Sermon des cinquante* (*Sermon of the Fifty*) and accused of atheism. And this at the very moment when the judges appointed by the royal council were deliberating over the posthumous fate of Jean Calas. That these were the same men who had already voted for a retrial did not necessarily mean that a favourable outcome was assured (although, as we shall see, Voltaire was sufficiently optimistic at this point to publish his own *Dictionnaire philosophique* in July). How *could* Rousseau put his own vendettas before the fate of an innocent man? How *could* he bite the philosophical hand that once had fed him? How *could* he thus endanger a fellow-*philosophe* by exposing his authorship of such a violently anti-Christian pamphlet as the *Sermon*? (To this last question the answer was plain: Rousseau had made a point of publishing his own incendiary works under his own name, because – with some naïvety – he regarded the practice of anonymous authorship as a hypocritical and cowardly fiction.)

So Voltaire launched his most vitriolic counter-blast, calling on the Genevan authorities to exercise the full severity of their laws against this 'seditious blasphemer', this 'scoundrel'.[11] But, worst of all, he delivered the devastating piece of ammunition that had been in his possession since June 1762, a secret known only to a handful of Rousseau's most intimate friends and associates. In an anonymous eight-page pamphlet entitled *Sentiment des citoyens* (*How Citizens Feel*) – for Rousseau was a 'Citizen of Geneva', and his whole philosophy was based on the primacy of feeling over reason – Voltaire told the world how Rousseau, the champion of virtue and the author of a book on how to educate the young, had abandoned all five of his own children on the steps of an orphanage and never set eyes on them again. Oddly, Rousseau never realized who the real author of *Sentiment des citoyens* was, and he continued to blame the Genevan pastor, Jacob Vernes. In his public reply he denied having 'abandoned' his children (for indeed he had registered them with all due formality), but this economical use of the truth was a mere stop-gap. The time had come to explain to the world just who he was and what he stood for. And thus do we have Voltaire to thank not only for clearing the name of Jean Calas but for being the catalyst of Rousseau's *Confessions*, one of the world's great autobiographies.

CHAPTER EIGHTEEN

D for Dictionary, D for Danger
(1764–1768)

On the convenience and inconvenience of pocket-books

THE BUZZWORD OF the *Infâme* had been coined at the supper-table of Frederick of Prussia, and so too (in September 1752) was the idea of a subversive dictionary to rival the *Encyclopédie*. Subtitled the *Dictionnaire raisonné des sciences, des arts et des métiers* (*Analytical Dictionary of the Sciences, Crafts and Trades*), the brainchild of d'Alembert and Diderot contained many an impious and insubordinate thought. If you knew where to find them. (The article on cannibalism, for example, ends with a cross-reference to 'Holy Communion'.) But the *Encyclopédie* was long, expensive, and – for Voltaire's taste – rather too timorously oblique. Moreover it would take many years to complete. (Another twenty, to be precise.) The possibility of something shorter, cheaper and more populist had appealed to Voltaire greatly at the outset, but the project of a work by divers hands – itself a major innovation of the *Encyclopédie* – had fallen foul of the bitchiness of Potsdam.

In less subversive circles the desire to popularize was commonplace. Samuel Johnson's *Dictionary of the English Language*, published in London in 1755 in two lavish folio volumes, was soon abridged and reissued in a two-volume octavo format for 'common readers', to whose pockets it was well adapted in both size and affordability. Its purpose (as stated in the preface) was to provide a 'vocabulary of daily use' for those who 'know not of any other use of a dictionary than that of adjusting orthography, and explaining terms of science or words of infrequent occurrence'. Two years earlier John Wesley, the founder of Methodism, had published *The Complete English Dictionary*, also in pocket-book format, which was specifically designed to offer less formally educated readers some access to the cultural heritage of their society. Similarly in France at least thirty 'portable dictionaries' had been published in the preceding twenty-five years, many of a theological nature.

As to subversion, it was the Huguenot refugee Pierre Bayle who had set the standard with his *Dictionnaire historique et critique* (1697), an alphabetically arranged anthology of cross-referenced articles that gave eloquent voice to its author's probing scepticism. But it, too, came in weighty folio volumes. As Voltaire remarked (of the *Encyclopédie*): 'I would like to know what harm can come of a book that costs a hundred *écus* [300 *livres*]. Twenty folio volumes will never start a revolution; it's the pocket-books at thirty *sous* that represent the real threat. If the Gospels had cost 1,200 [Roman] *sestertia*, the Christian religion would never have established itself.'[1] But affordability was not the only issue. So also, in the fast-moving modern world, was time: 'I think that from now on we ought to put everything in dictionaries. Life is too short for reading so many fat tomes one after another. Woe to long dissertations!'[2]

On returning to the project, Voltaire appears at first to have envisaged his new dictionary as a kind of testament in which he took stock of his beliefs and opinions before handing them down to posterity. Montaigne's *Essais* were an explicit model. Thus, to Mme du Deffand on 18 February 1760: 'I rarely have the honour to write to you, Madame, but my poor health and my plough are not the sole reasons. I am engrossed in accounting to myself, in alphabetical order, for all that I should think about this world and the next, an account intended for my own use and perhaps, after my death, for that of decent people.'[3]

But by the time the work was published anonymously in Geneva in July 1764 by Gabriel Grasset under the title *Dictionnaire philosophique portatif* – in octavo and numbering 344 pages – the intention had clearly changed. For the result is quite other. The alphabet is mere camouflage for a hilarious and savage – and, of course, totally unfair – debunking of the Christian religion, and particularly the Bible. (Which is why Voltaire chose Grasset rather than Cramer, who was now widely known as his publisher: with this dangerous dictionary clandestine circulation was essential.) Some of the entries-cum-articles contain serious statements of Voltaire's own deist position (for example, those on 'Atheism' and 'Religion'), but many resemble the chapters of a joke-book designed for after-dinner speakers at an anti-clerical banquet. Take Amos, for example (in the article 'Prophets'):

> It is believed that King Amasias gave orders to remove the prophet Amos's teeth to prevent him from speaking. It's not that you can't speak at all if you have no teeth — there's many a toothless crone that can talk till the cows come home — it's just that a prophecy needs to be enunciated clearly, and people simply won't listen to a toothless prophet with the due degree of respect.

Unless, of course, he is called Voltaire.

Material of this kind had been compiled over many years, and the *Dictionnaire philosophique portatif* is a patchwork quilt stitched from a work-box of hard-earned erudition, 'an Ali Baba's cave of intertextuality'.[4] However, rather than hectoring his readers or even professing soberly to inform them, the author constantly calls on them to put two and two together, to think for themselves, to 'dare to know'. For, as Voltaire wrote in the 1765 preface: 'The most useful books are those where half the work is done by the reader.' The Bible was a book you read as an authority not to be questioned. The New Testament, indeed, was the 'gospel truth'. But 'enlightenment' meant getting people to think for themselves, to see through the nonsense that held them in thrall. 'Reader, you must reflect. Develop this truth: draw your own conclusions' (from 'Morality'); 'How much there is to say on this subject! Reader, it is for you to say it yourself' ('Priest'); 'What should we conclude? You who are reading and thinking, you conclude' ('Sensation'). In Voltaire's view 'books rule the world',[5] so that writing is therefore the most effective form of political action. The reader-friendly brevity and variety of the entries, together with the author's licence to switch topics and targets at the drop of a full stop, produced a marvellous medium for versatile Voltairean wit. To the cavalry charge of the pamphlet and the fifth-column seductions of the *conte* was now added the lightning guerrilla raid of the dictionary definition.

Voltaire's new work was designed above all to inculcate an attitude of mind, and the result was a vade-mecum for budding *philosophes*, an

Enlightenment psalter enabling all enemies of the *Infâme* to sing in tune but from a hymn-sheet of their own choosing. And there were more hymns and psalms to come. Over the next five years Voltaire brought out five new editions, adding further articles and supplementing existing ones as he went. By 1769, when the work was re-entitled *La Raison par alphabet* (*The ABC of Reason*), it contained 118 entries – of which just over half are devoted to the letters A–F! – and the whole of human knowledge is contained between 'abbé' and 'virtue' . . . That is to say, not quite an A to Z but more an instructive route-map from low-grade Christianity to 'pagan' virtue and the high moral ground of deist rationality, good sense and clean living.

Critics of the seventy-year-old Voltaire see evidence of anecdotage in his increasing fondness for the short form and in his seemingly inexhaustible relish for mocking the same, naughty biblical event over and over again. His preference for scatology over eschatology was unswerving. Perhaps more seriously he is charged with being increasingly yesterday's man: lampooning the Church when the battle had already more or less been won, and now lagging well behind the intellectual cutting-edge of Paris where enlightened agnosticism, and even materialist atheism, were considerably more respectable than they had been when last he was there. And it is certainly true that, just as in the theatre where he now so firmly resisted innovation, Voltaire may have begun to sense that he was being outflanked, even overrun, by a new generation. Hence his delight in 1765 when he learnt that the Italian scientist Lazzaro Spallanzani had disproved the microscopist John Needham's alleged observations of spontaneous generation – or rather regeneration – among chopped-up eels. (Which phenomenon, if duly attested, would have meant that God the Creator was no longer required.) But this middle-aged resentment that the world might be passing him by came admirably late to this subversive, and he still had some subverting to do. For him the battle against the *Infâme* was far from over – indeed might never be over.

Best of all, his words were still considered dangerous. In Geneva the *Dictionnaire philosophique portatif* was shredded and burned by the public executioner in late September 1764, as it was in Bern and Holland just over two months later. It was similarly condemned by the Paris *parlement* on 19 March 1765. As usual, of course, Voltaire played dumb – and enjoyed himself hugely as he denied authorship in letters designed to be read by the police.

Thus to d'Alembert (slyly protecting him also): 'Well, indeed, I have read this diabolical dictionary. It appalled me, as it did you, but what pains me most grievously is the thought that there are Christians sufficiently unworthy of that fine name as to be able to suspect me of being the author of such an anti-Christian work.'[6] To him, and also to Damilaville, he described it with gusto as an 'abominable little dictionary', 'smacking of heresy', 'the work of Satan'.[7] As he knew from long experience, a colourful denial is one of the best publicity techniques. Not that his pocket-book needed much publicity. The first edition quickly sold out, and copies changed hands for large sums. Reprints were numerous, and various unauthorized editions appeared in Lyons, Liège, Amsterdam, The Hague . . . As with *Candide* the epidemic spread quickly, and the police – seize what they might – were powerless to inhibit the contagion.

But his words were also dangerous in a way that genuinely grieved him. As witness the terrible fate that befell the young aristocrat, Jean-François Lefebvre, chevalier de La Barre. Born in 1745 and subsequently orphaned, he had been brought up in Abbeville by his aunt, the delightful and broad-minded abbess of the local convent. During the night of 8–9 August 1765 a wooden crucifix on the Pont Neuf in the middle of the town was defiled: the body of Christ had been slashed with a sword or knife. A day or so later the figure of Christ in the cemetery had been smeared with filth. The devout were appalled, and suspicion soon fell on a group of well-to-do young men who sought relief from the boredom of their provincial lives in acts of impious tomfoolery. Three young men in particular stood out: La Barre, and his friends d'Étallonde and Moisnel. For they were often to be heard singing rude songs and loudly discussing the latest pornographic novel. Moreover during a Corpus Christi procession through the streets of Abbeville they had made a point of rushing past, as though in a hurry, and omitting to doff their hats.

Two people had a particular grudge against La Barre's aunt: Belleval, a fifty-year-old lawyer and tax official whose amorous attentions she had repelled, and Duval de Soicourt, another lawyer, who had hoped to marry his son to one of the abbess's richest convent pupils – before she married Belleval's son instead. And it was Duval who was appointed to investigate the incidents. D'Étallonde, though four years younger than La Barre, was by all accounts a more seasoned blasphemer. But his father was a senior judge. When more and more people started remembering how he loved to beat the crucifix on the Pont Neuf with his cane as he passed, he was quietly encouraged to make himself scarce. La Barre, meanwhile, was able to establish a solid alibi for the night of 8–9 August. But the unrequited Belleval whipped up local opinion against the abbess's nephew by publishing a list of all the impious remarks and actions for which he was allegedly responsible. Even if he hadn't slashed the crucifix, he might have done . . . A formal hearing began on 13 September. On 27 September orders were given to arrest the three men, but only La Barre and Moisnel were apprehended. Whereupon Belleval had no difficulty in terrifying the young and impressionable Moisnel into confirming the impious behaviour of his friends (though not their responsibility for the two incidents in question). The police then searched La Barre's room at the convent. Amongst a choice selection of erotic literature they found a copy of the *Dictionnaire philosophique portatif*. Ah ha!

Eventually Duval constituted a magistrates' tribune consisting of himself, an elderly local grandee of failing wits, and a part-time lawyer and pig merchant of vanished reputation. At the end of the trial, on 27 February 1766, the public prosecutor demanded that d'Étallonde have his hand cut off, then his head, and that his body be subsequently burned. As to La Barre he recommended merely that he be condemned to hard labour for life. But on 28 February the bench – in effect Duval – pronounced sentence: d'Étallonde was to have his tongue cut out before his hand was sliced off, and he was then to be burned alive. (But since he was absent, this was all blessedly notional.) As to La Barre, he was to have his tongue cut out, and he was then to be beheaded and burned. He was of course to be tortured first, in order to extract a confession. Moreover a copy of the *Dictionnaire philosophique portatif* was to be thrown on to the funeral pyre at the same time as his severed head and corpse. Moisnel received a suspended sentence. The magistrates cited no legal article in support of their decisions.

The sentences had to be confirmed by the Paris *parlement*, and so La Barre and Moisnel were transferred to the Conciergerie (the prison serving the Palais de Justice on the Île de la Cité), where they were held for the next three months. On 4 June La Barre appeared, without defence counsel, before a court of twenty-five judges — and, as usual, behind closed doors. The case was heard quickly — they had many to get through — and no one seemed particularly interested, except for one rather bovine and irascible *conseiller* who made a long speech laying the blame for the sacrilegious events at Abbeville firmly at the feet of the *philosophes*, and particularly Voltaire's. By a vote of fifteen to ten it was agreed to let Duval's sentences stand. Next day some of the fifteen began to have misgivings, but only a royal pardon could now save La Barre. His aunt used what influence she could to secure it, but to no avail. The papal nuncio and the Bishop of Amiens (in whose diocese Abbeville fell) similarly tried and failed.

The sentence was carried out in Abbeville on 1 July. Having been tortured (unsuccessfully) for an hour, the condemned man ate a hearty meal — in the company of the priest appointed to direct his conscience during these final hours — after which he enjoyed a cup of coffee. In the circumstances, he remarked, it was unlikely to keep him awake. After lunch he was taken to the scaffold in a cart, in his shirtsleeves, with a noose round his neck and a notice hanging down his back that proclaimed him guilty of impiety, blasphemy and heinous sacrilege. It was raining hard, but the crowds were undeterred: it wasn't every day you saw a gentleman executed. And especially not one who just laughed when his sentence was read out. And who laughed even louder when he turned round and saw a piece of paper dangling at the end of a rope. It was standing in — or rather hanging — for the absent d'Étallonde. The seven executioners appointed to effect La Barre's demise then simulated the removal of his tongue — what mercy! — after which the young man placed his head on the block. Aware that the executioner holding the axe was the one who had recently needed two goes to dispatch his victim, La Barre enquired whether his neck was suitably positioned. The answer was categoric. A delighted crowd applauded madly. These young rascals needed to be taught a lesson, especially this fellow who had shown not a whit of repentance. And they applauded again as the executioner held the head aloft, its lips and eyelids twitching. When he placed it on the ground, they watched him prod it with his foot until its features were still. Then he threw it on to the bonfire, along with the body to which it had so recently belonged — and a copy of Voltaire's dictionary, the work of the devil incarnate. The flames of righteousness burned long into the night.

Voltaire first heard of the case on the very day that La Barre was executed. Even he had thought that the Paris *parlement* could not possibly uphold such a flawed sentence, and so he was appalled to learn the truth on 7 July. Not only did he feel some measure of personal responsibility, he was also seriously alarmed by the fact that the *parlement* had clearly wanted to punish the *philosophes* in the person of this harmless – and courageous – young nobody. Had the unpardoning king adopted a new hardline policy? Were the *philosophes* to be rounded up? Did the Bastille beckon once again? Just to be on the safe side (of the border), Voltaire departed one week later to take the waters at Rolle, in the jurisdiction of Bern, and there he remained for the next three weeks, occasionally returning to Ferney but still nervous about being arrested on French soil. He wondered if it might not be best to set up a little colony of *philosophes* somewhere safer – say, Cleves, in the now Prussian-controlled Rhineland – where some of them (Damilaville, d'Alembert, Diderot, maybe even d'Holbach and a few others) could set up their own publishing house and get on with attacking the *Infâme* in peace. It might take no more than two or three years to achieve 'a great revolution' in the way people thought. But his fellow-*philosophes* remained unpersuaded of the attractions of Cleves, and anyway Frederick had started laying down too many conditions. It was not a serious possibility.

'Revolution' for Voltaire was always about shaping the way people thought. Indeed the role of 'opinion' had gradually become central to his own historical writings. In 1761, in a new edition of his works, he had brought out a revised edition of his *Essai sur les mœurs*, having added chapters on medieval Europe and the colonization of South America. Originally he had thought of calling this book the *Histoire de l'esprit humain*, which – since *esprit* means both mind and spirit – combines our more recent historiographical concepts of *mentalité* (mentality, or mind-set) and *Zeitgeist* (spirit of the age). In its full title the book became an *Essai sur l'histoire générale et sur les mœurs et l'esprit des nations depuis Charlemagne jusqu'à nos jours* (*An Essay on General History and on the Manners and Mind/Spirit of the Nations from Charlemagne to the Present*). At first Voltaire's principal intention as a 'philosophical' historian had been to reject all the myths, legends and fables that passed for 'history' (both ancient and modern). At the same time he had wanted to move the emphasis away from kings and courts to the broader picture of everyday life: 'the history of human beings'.[8] How did individual nations go about things? What had been the strengths and weaknesses of their policies and actions? In particular, how had they conducted their commercial activity (for that impinged hugely on the everyday lives of the people)? Above all, he wanted to identify the causes and effects of *change*: of the changes in human behaviour and the changes in the laws by which they governed that behaviour.

But increasingly Voltaire had become interested in the way people's thinking changed. And in 1763, in some *Remarques pour servir de supplément à l'Essai sur les mœurs* (*Remarks Intended to Serve as a Supplement to the Essay on Manners*) he had focused on what he called the 'collective mentality' (*mental collectif*). What he should have written, he said, was a 'history of opinion'. For the moment he illustrated this in negative terms: the Crusades and the rise of Islam, for example, were the result of 'opinion': that is, religious prejudice and intolerance. And so the opposite of 'opinion' was Reason. Essentially the history of a nation was like the life of a person: a progression from fond beliefs (for example, in witches) to a lucid, rational state of enlightenment. But it was a short step from this to the idea of 'opinion' as positive and to our modern notion of influencing government through the orchestration of public opinion. For this in effect was what the campaign against the *Infâme* was all about. And in 1768 Voltaire published his *Précis du siècle de Louis XV* (*Short History of the Age of Louis XV*) in which he sought to demonstrate just how far 'opinion' had come since 1714.[9] In the last chapter he itemized the 'progress made by the human mind': the fact that enlightened thinking and a broader cultural awareness had penetrated deep into the French provinces; the banning of the Jesuits and the consequent removal of a major obstacle to the intellectual development of French children; commercial advance, in the form of cheaper textiles, greater agricultural efficiency, less regulated grain markets; improved living conditions, like the provision of running water in Parisian houses (at last); and the invention of a clock that would allow the accurate calculation of degrees of longitude on long sea voyages.

In the case of La Barre, rational opinion quickly formed in the victim's favour. Duval was dismissed, and the other defendants acquitted. Like its counterpart in Toulouse, the Paris *parlement* was keen to move on, and the fact that La Barre had been executed in Abbeville and not Paris would mean that this terrible injustice would soon be conveniently forgotten. Which is why

Voltaire published his own 24-page account of the affair. Lest we forget . . . Skilfully he exposed the petty jealousies and small-town prejudice that had motivated the legal protagonists of the story, and he ended by placing particular emphasis on the details of the execution and the terrible and extraordinary disparity between the crime and the punishment. That a young man should lose his life because he sang a few songs and omitted to doff his hat?

Momentarily unnerved by the Paris *parlement*'s attack on the *philosophes*, Voltaire nevertheless resumed his campaign against the *Infâme*. One essential precondition of a successful publicity campaign is not to bore the intended target. And he himself was aware of the dangers of repetition and anecdotage. Writing with a copious facility that derived in part from the belief that he might die at any moment, Voltaire poured out a series of works in which he adopted all manner of personae and voices. Not least this made it look as if the *Infâme* had a whole host of new enemies. The biblical criticism continued, and he imagined himself as a young, newly appointed theology professor at the University of Salamanca who suddenly finds he is having difficulty with his biblical text. Sixty-seven difficulties to be precise, hence his *Questions de Zapata* (March 1767), soon to be followed by an equally disparate set of *Lettres sur les miracles* eight months later. Back in 1761–2 Voltaire had adopted the voice of an imaginary rabbi Akib to denounce the Inquisition in Portugal and its execution of the Jesuit priest Malagrida (aided and abetted by the supposedly enlightened marques de Pombal). Now he adopted the voice of an English clergyman and preached the gospel of deism as a moderate 'third way' between the irrational superstitions of established religion and the social dangers of atheism. Published in May 1767, these *Homélies prononcées à Londres en 1765* extol the benefits of rational enquiry and promote the advantages of getting men and women to believe in a God who rewards the good and punishes the bad. For if you remove the notion of a just God, then – as Dostoevsky later announced – everything is permitted. And of course that would be bad for social stability, not to mention business.

Similarly, and continuing the habit of a lifetime, Voltaire would rewrite the works of real people. (Just think how many of Crébillon's plays he had reworked.) Thus Jean Meslier, a Roman Catholic priest, had left behind a testamentary statement in which he regretted having spent his lifetime teaching the 'errors' of Christianity, and in which he now professed a form of materialist atheism and advocated a radical reform of the social system. This had been circulating in manuscript since Meslier's death in 1729, and Voltaire had known of its existence since at least the mid-1740s. But now that it was being given prominence by d'Holbach and his fellow-atheists, Voltaire decided to issue his own bowdlerized version in the form of 'extracts' from Meslier's testament, thus turning him into a relatively harmless fellow-plaintiff against the obscurantism and intolerance of the Church.[10]

Voltaire's former friend and mentor, Viscount Bolingbroke, had died in 1751, and his *Philosophical Works* had appeared in five volumes in 1754. Five excessively long and badly written volumes in Voltaire's view. So he composed his *Examen important de milord Bolingbroke*, merging his own thoughts with those of the enlightened English aristocrat and propounding the gospel of deism in his own more eloquent voice. This he published in 1766 in a so-called *Recueil nécessaire* (*A Necessary Collection*), an anthology of ten anti-Christian works that included eight of his own (including the *Catéchisme de l'honnête homme*, the *Sermon des cinquante*, etc.), an extract from Rousseau's 'Profession de foi du vicaire savoyard', and an anonymous *Analyse de la religion chrétienne* (attributed to Dumarsais, a contributor to the *Encyclopédie*). Like the *Dictionnaire philosophique* this collection was a deist kit – like a 'necessary' or lady's work-box – for freethinking enemies of the *Infâme*.

A kind of ventriloquism was at work here, which can also be seen in Voltaire's 'dialogues of the dead' written about this time. Borrowing a format previously popularized by Fontenelle and others, he created imaginary discussions between men such as Erasmus and Rabelais. In some cases, as in the 1768 *conte*, *L'Homme aux quarante écus* (*Mr Average*), he would feature as one of the participants himself – here in the guise of the venerable sage whose time may be past but whose wisdom is eternal (and who knows better than to trust fancy economic theories). Just like the religious sceptic of *Le Philosophe ignorant* (1766–7), who voices his doubts in a series of fifty-six fragments (reminiscent of Pascal's *Pensées*) while nevertheless professing his faith in God the watchmaker and in the existence of a single moral code universally shared by humanity. And it was but a short step from this pseudo-autobiography to the imaginary world of *contes* like *L'Ingénu* (1767) and *La Princesse de Babylone*

(1768) in which he could give expression to his Enlightenment attitudes through the mouths of handsome and perceptive young men. It was all a form of armchair theatre.

Or fairground fun. In the *Contes de Guillaume Vadé* (1764) Voltaire invented the character Guillaume by way of allusion to Jean-Joseph Vadé, who was famous for having introduced the risqué language and action of fairground theatricals (and puppet shows) into the more genteel world of musical comedy (performed at the Opéra Comique, formerly known as the Comédie-Italienne). This collection of *contes* – in verse and prose – is introduced by Guillaume's equally non-existent relative Catherine as if they were her late cousin's work. The verse tales, of a comic and scabrous kind, mark Voltaire's return to the genre associated with his probable biological father, the chevalier de Rochebrune, while those in prose are irreverent parodies of the oriental tale (in *Le Blanc et le noir* (*The White and the Black*)) and the newly fashionable moral tale (*Jeannot et Colin*). The polemical thrust of the whole collection is made explicit by the inclusion of a 'Discours aux Welches' ('An Address to the "Welches" ') – the 'Welches' being Voltaire's latest nickname for his compatriots (and derived from German usage). By 'Welches' he meant 'the enemies of reason and merit, the fanatics, the stupid, the intolerant, the persecutors and the calumniators'. As opposed to the real 'Français', by which he meant 'the *philosophes*, good company, real writers, artists, in fact anyone who is nice'.[11]

But by 'Welches' he meant especially 'Jansenists', on whom this address – like the whole collection – is an attack. Now in the political ascendant – especially since the Jesuits had been relieved of their pedagogical functions (1761) and successively banned from the regions of France (1762–4)[12] – the Jansenists were the party of earnestness and moral austerity, the enemies of fun. Hence Voltaire's ventriloquial insistence throughout the collection on the delights of both popular and ancient culture (in which the Jansenists would have found evidence of pagan immorality), and the recurrent theme of education – but education of a resolutely unorthodox and unsolemn kind. In short, the 'Welches' were the 'Français' who had forgotten how to laugh, who had forgotten their Rabelais. Unlike the Prior whom we meet in the first chapter of *L'Ingénu*:

The Prior, who was already getting on in years, was a most excellent cleric, beloved by his neighbours as once he had been beloved by his neighbours' wives. What had led him above all to be held in high regard was that he was the only local incumbent who did not have to be carried to bed when he had supped with his colleagues. He had a reasonable grasp of theology, and when he was tired of reading St Augustine, he would read Rabelais for fun. Consequently everyone had a good word to say for him.

He might be a priest, but he was 'good company'. Rather like Father Adam, the lapsed Jesuit who had become a permanent house-guest at Ferney since January 1763 and had a mistress in the village. For it was the Jansenists who never tired of reading St Augustine.

L'Ingénu was – and remains – Voltaire's most successful *conte* after *Candide*. Begun in the autumn of 1766 (and perhaps even earlier, in 1764), it was written mainly in the following spring and summer, and published by Cramer towards the end of July 1767. A Parisian edition appeared with 'tacit' permission on 3 September, and some 3,500 copies were sold within four or five days. Permission to publish was withdrawn a fortnight later, but by the end of the year the *conte* had appeared in at least nine editions. It was the subject of countless imitations, 'sequels' by other writers, and theatrical adaptations. By 1785 the work itself had gone through no less than thirty-nine editions.

It tells the story of a young and handsome Huron. A native of French-occupied Canada, he arrives one day on a Breton beach in the company of English traders. The local prior and his good sister, Mlle de Kerkabon – 'who had never married, though she much wanted to' – believe that he is their long-lost nephew: that is, a Frenchman who has been denied a decent education. So they see at once to his conversion. Having read the Bible, the intelligently literal-minded Huron – the Ingénu – believes that baptism must take place in a river, and he is soon to be found naked in the Rance, awaiting the ceremony. (The Prior has only just finished persuading this conscientious Bible-reader that there is no need for him to be circumcised.) Only the fair Saint-Yves – 'a young girl of Lower Breton pedigree, who was extremely pretty and very well bred' – is able to persuade him, having sized up the situation, that a church would be better. Where she becomes his godmother

— and thus makes herself ineligible to marry the newly christened 'Hercules'. When the perplexed Huron tries to 'marry' her anyway, she is locked away in a convent for the better protection of her maidenhood.

Hercules now repels some English raiders and is sent off to claim a royal reward in Versailles, but finds himself arrested on suspicion of having Huguenot sympathies and is then imprisoned in the Bastille in the same cell as a Jansenist rather improbably named Gordon. What could be worse? Except that he has a lot of time for reading and educates himself with a Voltairean syllabus of philosophy, history and literature. Meanwhile the resourceful Saint-Yves makes her way to Versailles, secures the Ingénu's release by sleeping (on a Jesuit's advice) with the influential minister, the marquis de Saint-Pouange, and dies of shame. Despite the fact that everyone tells her how virtuous she has been. Since 'time is a great healer', the grief-stricken Huron — an Ingénu no longer — duly becomes an excellent officer in the French army and 'an intrepid philosopher'. As to 'good Gordon', he abandons Jansenism in favour of the motto: 'It's an ill wind that blows nobody any good.' Which prompts the sardonic narrator to conclude: 'How many decent men and women in the world have been able to say: "An ill wind blows nobody any good." '

Voltaire the ventriloquist had on this occasion chosen to attribute his allegedly 'true' story to none other than Pasquier Quesnel, the leading Jansenist, who is thus the narrator who here corrects Gordon, the lapsed Jansenist (who has discovered a heart and learnt to cry). At one level such an unflattering portrait of the Jesuits makes this attribution entirely appropriate; but a rather risqué *conte* about uncircumcised Hurons and resourceful maidens is, of course, the last thing the austere Jansenist might have written. Which all added to the fun.

The popularity of *L'Ingénu* derived partly from its wittily irreverent take on a number of topical issues (several of which had been foregrounded by Rousseau, who is thus implicitly satirized): the 'noble savage', the ongoing debate about education following the expulsion of the Jesuits, the persecution of the Huguenots and the practice of arbitrary arrest, the growing influence of the Jansenists, etc. But it also appealed to the contemporary taste for the sentimental novel, so much so that to this day many readers remain moved by the tragic death of Saint-Yves. But should we take the sentimentality at face value? Certainly the pathos of her situation may move us to outrage at the abuse of ministerial office for sexual gratification. But need she have died? Samuel Richardson's Clarissa Harlowe had – at very considerable length – died of shame after being raped, and Rousseau's Julie had met her death (following a boating accident) with extraordinary selflessness and calm. In Voltaire's view these depictions of virtue are perniciously implausible, so ludicrously high-minded that they leave the rest of us feeling wholly and unjustifiably unworthy. Saint-Yves – as her name suggests and like an earlier Voltairean heroine – is a Cosi Sancta, a quasi-saint. But she has been so brainwashed by sentimental fiction (she spends her convent days reading novels) that she does not realize the true nature of her heroism. And that indeed is a tragedy.

As Voltaire's pseudo-real or overtly fictional personae multiplied, so too did the number of his enemies. One such was Father Claude-François Nonnotte, who in 1762 had published *Les Erreurs de Voltaire* (*Voltaire's Errors*). In this boldly entitled work – published in two duodecimo volumes that would fit easily into a pocket – the (now-banned) Jesuit priest had attacked Voltaire's *Essai sur les mœurs*, mainly on the doctrinal level but also regarding some matters of fact. Not all his corrections were accurate, which led Voltaire to amend the title of his own copy to *Les Erreurs de Nonnotte*. But the attack was well mounted (the book went through fifteen impressions up until 1823), and it threatened to be damaging. In particular it took France's leading historian to task for never giving references. (The said historian thereafter quietly changed his practice.) Nonnotte's editor offered to sell Voltaire the entire run of the first edition – 1,500 copies for 3,000 *livres* – but our hero was no coward. And no spendthrift. He refused the offer, alleging a fear that he might be excommunicated for suppressing such a useful book . . . Instead he wrote his own pamphlet, the *Sottises de Nonnotte* (*Not-So-Clever Nonnotte*) in which he duly took issue with thirty-three 'sottises' (literally, foolish mistakes). Now, in April 1767, under the title *Honnêtés littéraires* (*Literary Decencies*), Voltaire returned to the fray. Here, chapter by chapter, he attacked all his old favourites, from Desfontaines and Fréron to Rousseau and the Genevan theology professor Jacob Vernet. And also poor Nonnotte, upon whose priestly chastity he now cast unfounded and unworthy aspersions.

Other new enemies included the abbé Riballier, headmaster of the Collège Mazarin in Paris, and his colleague, the abbé Coger, who had both taken issue with Voltaire's defence of Marmontel's *Bélisaire* (about the Emperor Justinian's general of that name and a call for religious toleration on the grounds that one does not need to be Christian to be virtuous). Then there was Pierre-Henri Larcher, a distinguished Greek scholar and translator of Herodotus. Contacted by the abbé Mercier de Saint-Léger, an editor of the Jesuit *Journal de Trévoux*, Larcher had been persuaded into print in March 1767 to criticize Voltaire's latest historical work, his *Philosophie de l'histoire* (1765). Here, far from professing any proto-Hegelian theory of history, Voltaire had traced the history of the world from earliest times until Charlemagne. This was obviously dangerous ground, not least because his principal objective was to discredit the origins of Christianity as set out in the Old Testament (which meant also ridiculing the Jews' claim to be God's chosen people). Larcher had been irritated by the errors perpetrated by Voltaire (whose knowledge of Ancient Greek was shaky; and of Hebrew, non-existent). Although Larcher was a man of enlightened views and a friend of the *encyclopédistes* his sense of professional integrity overruled any reservations he might have had about becoming the tool of the reactionaries. Though Lemercier de Saint-Léger and/or his associates prefaced the work with a stinging personal attack on Voltaire, Larcher himself would seem to have had no quarrel with the thrust of Voltaire's polemic, and his critique rather took the form of detailed textual commentary designed to set Voltaire straight on matters of fact.

Or rather to set the late abbé Bazin straight. For it was in the name of this fictitious personage that Voltaire's dangerous *Philosophie* had been published (and introduced by the abbé's no less fictitious nephew). Once again Voltaire quietly made the corrections suggested (when he used the *Philosophie* as an introduction to his next revised edition of the *Essai sur les mœurs* in 1769), but that did not stop him also launching a counter-attack on Larcher, publishing it as *La Défense de mon oncle* (*In My Uncle's Defence*) as though it had been written by Bazin's outraged nephew. Using the Ancient Greek word for 'archer' (cf. Larcher/'l'archer'), he attacked Monsieur Toxotès, transforming the respectable Hellenist into a figure of almost total fantasy: a libidinous pedant who dreamed of taking his sexual pleasure with woman or beast as he studied the civilizations of ancient Egypt and Babylon. Whereas the abbé Bazin, of course, was a scholar and a gentleman, a model of erudition and pious sobriety and . . . not wholly dissimilar from the Patriarch of Ferney. Voltaire did enjoy his polemic. For him this kind of pamphlet war was a game of disguise and pseudonymic striptease every bit as satisfying as his stage performances in the role of Lusignan. And the danger only added to the excitement.

The danger, however – as the La Barre case had recently demonstrated – could be very real. As indeed Voltaire was reminded soon afterwards. For some time now he had been in the habit of smuggling forbidden books out of Geneva (whether printed by the well-known Cramer or on the more clandestine presses of Grasset) among the personal effects of his visitors. In November 1766 his friends the d'Argentals had arranged for Mme Lejeune, wife of a Parisian bookseller, to travel to Geneva disguised as the wife of one of their servants. Having taken possession of a plentiful supply of illicit material, she then proceeded to Ferney across an unprob-lematic border. There, in looseleaf form, the books were carefully packed into three trunks, hidden beneath old theatrical costumes. These were then loaded on to Mme Denis's carriage, commandeered for the purpose, and off went Mme Lejeune back to Paris. For this return journey she was accompanied by a customs official called Janin, on whom Voltaire believed he could count. But when they reached the border at Collonge, about thirteen miles away, Janin revealed his treacherous hand and the trunks were searched. It had been expected that the customs officials at this frontier with the Pays de Gex would simply give the trunks the lead seal of their approval in the normal way and wave Mme Lejeune through.

Among the books discovered were eighty copies of the *Recueil nécessaire*, Voltaire's deist anthology for freethinkers. D for dynamite! The customs officers seized the books and impounded the carriage and horses. Terrified of what might happen to her, Mme Lejeune simply ran away. It was winter, and the fields were covered in snow. A couple of days later she turned up at Ferney, in the middle of the night, desperate for help. Next day she was taken to Geneva, from where she made her way surreptitiously back to Paris. No doubt she decided not to take a book for the journey (though, perhaps to protect her, Voltaire claimed that she could not read).[13] But the situation was serious. The customs men would have sent a report to their superiors, and this would certainly reach Versailles, perhaps even the King. Voltaire was furious, so furious in fact that he succumbed to a fit of 'apoplexy' and lost consciousness for fifteen minutes. But after three hours in bed he was as right as rain and maniacally dictating messages to the d'Argentals and others. By way of displaying their innocence, Voltaire and his niece immediately lodged an official complaint and demanded the return of their carriage. It was paramount that Maupeou, second-in-command to Chancellor Maurepas (effectively the Minister of Justice), be persuaded to defuse the situation. And he did. For he was sympathetic to the *philosophes* and their cause. At the end of January Voltaire learnt that nothing further would be said about the matter. Now that *was* progress!

Apoplectic or no, Voltaire was not being melodramatic. The political situation in Geneva had grown particularly tense at this time, so tense in fact that in 1765 he sold his interest in Les Délices and vacated it on 2 April. (With the money he could begin the new wings at Ferney.) The struggle between traditionalists and modernizers was reaching crisis point. The city's populace fell into four categories: 'inhabitants' (foreigners with the right to reside); 'natives' (the children of inhabitants or natives); the 'bourgeois' (natives or naturalized inhabitants who had been able to afford to purchase the necessary accreditation); and 'citizens' (the children of citizens or bourgeois). Only the citizens or bourgeois enjoyed full political rights (which in turn permitted certain financial privileges), and yet they numbered less than half the total Genevan population of 20–25,000 at this period. Increasingly the natives felt unfairly excluded by their status from access to the liberal professions and from opportunities to enjoy the full economic benefits of their work. The ruling authorities were trying to keep the lid on their increasingly vociferous demands for a greater degree of democracy. Meanwhile an absolutist France looked on with increasing concern, and when attempts at reaching a compromise failed in December 1766 it sent troops to blockade the city. They took up position in January. Had the King decided to teach his Gentleman in Ordinary a lesson, he would certainly have had the means. The Pays de Gex was no longer the back of beyond.

The King did not so decide. And soon Voltaire was inviting the military to Ferney, entertaining the senior officers to dinner and inviting everyone to his theatre. He even wrote a three-act verse comedy for them, *Charlot ou la comtesse de Givry*, set in the days of Henri IV. He enjoyed the men's company, and it was better to have them as friends. But his days as indefatigable host were coming to an end. If he had been a tourist attraction at Les Délices, at Ferney his home had become something of a World Heritage Centre. A visit to the Patriarch was a must. These visitors came from all over the world – from France, Germany, Great Britain and Ireland, Italy, Russia, North America, India – but a significant majority were English or Scottish, and often young gentlemen engaged upon their Grand Tour (especially once the Seven Years War was over). For Ferney was so conveniently situated on the route from Calais to Florence. It has been calculated that some 150 Englishmen visited Voltaire during the 1760s, though the host himself guessed at well over twice that number: 'for fourteen years now I have been the innkeeper of Europe', he simultaneously complained and boasted.[14] But generally he enjoyed these visits, and his English was still good, particularly his command of increasingly dated expletives. He even suggested to Casanova that he would quite like to have been an Englishman himself.[15] Some visitors came more than once, like Lord Palmerston and Adam Smith, author of *The Wealth of Nations*. Some reminded him of the past, like Lord Hervey, Earl of Bristol and Anglican Bishop of Derry. (His father, to whom Voltaire had once addressed his love in English verse, had died in 1746.) As he greeted the Bishop on the front steps of his château, Voltaire gestured towards his church and theatre. 'And which of these buildings stages the greater farce?' he asked his guest. 'It rather depends on who has written it,' came the unfazed reply.[16] And other visitors were picturesque, like the tall Quaker, Claude Gay, who arrived in full Quaker fig and declined most of the food and wine he was offered before taking a rather frosty leave and returning to Geneva on humble foot.

Voltaire himself, of course, was also picturesque. For special guests he would dress formally in a shirt and jabot, a decorative flared waistcoat that reached to mid-thigh, a longer frock-coat, elegant breeches rolled at the knee, stockings, and shoes with buckles of gold or silver. On his head he would wear a wig whose elaborate and dusted curls had long gone out of fashion. But mostly he preferred something casual. A Major W. Broom reports being received by him (on 16 March 1765) 'dressed in a robe-de-chambre of blue sattan and gold spots on it, with a sort of sattan cap and blue tassle of gold'. (He also notes that his host 'is tall and very thin, has a very piercing eye, and a look singularly vivacious'.)[17] The 24-year-old Boswell – future biographer of Dr Johnson and visiting at Christmas-time in 1764 – describes a mixture of the formal and informal: 'a slate-blue fine frieze greatcoat nightgown and a three-knotted wig'.[18] The informality extended to Voltaire's behaviour, and during a visit he would be quite capable of talking to his guests while continuing to play chess (for he hated losing). His usual opponent was the ex-Jesuit Father Adam – whom he was wont to introduce with the comment: 'This is Father Adam, but he is not first among men.'[19]

Many visitors simply came for the afternoon, but several – like the fortunate if somewhat star-struck Boswell – were invited to stay for a night or two. As at Cirey, Voltaire spent the morning working before having 'dinner' at about 2 p.m. Thereafter he would take his guests for a walk in his elegant gardens. And of course, come the evening at supper, he was usually on top conversational form. Sometimes, with new guests, it took time to break the ice. 'He received me with dignity,' Boswell reports, 'and that air of the world which a Frenchman acquires in such perfection. [. . .] He sat erect upon his chair, and simpered when he spoke. He was not in spirits, nor I neither. All I presented was the "foolish face of wondering praise".' But things began to improve when the conversation turned to Glasgow:

> I said, 'An Academy of painting was also established there, but it did not succeed. Our Scotland is no country for that.' He replied with a keen archness, 'No; to paint well it is necessary to have warm feet. It is hard to paint when your feet are cold.' Another would have given a long dissertation on the coldness of our climate. Monsieur de Voltaire gave the very essence of raillery in half a dozen words.

When Boswell then asked Voltaire if he still spoke English, he replied: 'No. To speak English one must place the tongue between the teeth, and I have lost my teeth.' Not that this piece of information has ever stopped the dentate French from saying teet'. Nor indeed Voltaire: Major Broom reported three months later that 'he spoke English all the time'.

Many witnesses seem to have been so transfixed by the spectacle of their host that they quite forgot to note their surroundings (and indeed, as he sadly reflected, ever to send him a thank-you letter). But two observant Americans on their way back from Italy – John Morgan and Samuel Powell – recorded that Voltaire's drawing-room was dominated by a painting depicting Mars leaving the bed of Venus. Plainly the uncle of Mme Denis cast his net wide in his search for role models. They also noted that his snuff-box bore a portrait of Frederick the Great (from whom it had doubtless been a gift). Perhaps the chamberlain's fond memories had come to outweigh his bitter recollections of oranges and Frankfurters. And, as they left, the travellers from the New World made sure to catch another glimpse of the now-notorious inscription on the church façade that proclaimed their host's direct line to God.

One visitor caused history to repeat itself. At Cirey Mme de Graffigny had got herself into considerable trouble over the leaking of some of Voltaire's comic verses (from *La Pucelle*). At Ferney it was the turn of the young actor and dramatist, Jean-François de La Harpe, whose subsequent course of professorial lectures on ancient and modern literature made him into a late-eighteenth-century Boileau. In his case the poem in question was an irreverent satire called *La Guerre civile de Genève* (*Geneva's Civil War*). Voltaire's own career as a playwright was flagging. *Olympie*, first staged in Paris on 10 March 1764, had closed after ten performances. *Le Triumvirat* had opened and flopped soon afterwards on 5 July. His latest tragedy, a barely concealed account of the Swiss entitled *Les Scythes*, had been reluctantly staged by the Comédie-Française on 26 March 1767, but it closed after four performances. (Which was odd, he thought: the soldiers had seemed to enjoy it at Ferney.) Had he lost his touch? Or was French theatre simply going to the dogs? But one ray of hope was offered by La Harpe, who had achieved success at the age of twenty-four with his *Warwick* (1763), a tragedy of the old school. Perhaps it was still possible to stem the tide of bourgeois drama and pseudo-Shakespearean melodrama.

So Voltaire invited La Harpe to stay, and he arrived to spend the spring and summer of 1765 in the Master's company. And in that of the legendary Mlle Clairon, whose three-week visit in July provided a good excuse for Voltaire to reprise his role as Lusignan in *Zaïre* (and to defer his plan to dismantle the theatre in order to create more rooms). It was a special occasion: he had not seen the famous actress for seventeen years. She, too, was delighted. But the building works were tiresome, and she preferred to sleep not at Ferney but at Tourney, where the house had been let to Gabriel Cramer. There, also, the parties were excellent.

The author of *Zaïre* soon formed a close, quasi-paternal bond with his new protégé, a man of short stature and exalted theatrical ambition. La Harpe returned the following autumn with his new wife, Marie Marthe, whose unexpected pregnancy had hastened their marriage. No less unexpected was the revelation of her hitherto hidden talents as an actress, which were themselves a match for those of her new husband. These talents were much appreciated in the Pays de Gex. As were those of another young protégé and playwright, Chabanon, who had arrived earlier in the year. With Mme Denis, Mme Dupuits (née Corneille), and the husband-and-wife team of the Constant d'Hermenches (old faithfuls since the days of Monrepos at Lausanne) to call on also, the 1767 season at the Théâtre de Ferney was a triumph. Even *Les Scythes* had everyone in tears. On 4 October, the feast of St Francis and Voltaire's name-day, two of his comedies were performed – *Charlot* and *La Femme qui a raison* (*The Woman Who Is Right*); Chabanon's commemorative verses were recited; the leading ladies sang madrigals in the Patriarch's honour; and the evening ended with fireworks, supper and a ball. Surrounded by men in uniform and as many young women as the region could muster, the elderly hero of the Enlightenment danced until two in the morning.

After the party, the hangover. Some weeks later Voltaire learnt that copies of extracts from his Genevan satire were circulating among his Calvinist neighbours. In the privacy of a manuscript he had indulged himself in mocking several local dignitaries who had been making his life difficult. Now they would be even more awkward: he was furious. And immediately he suspected La Harpe. His young protégé was in Paris, where he had also given copies to Dupuits. On his return La Harpe eventually confessed to his foolishness, but Voltaire was in no mood to forgive him. He might be seventy-four but he could still feel jealous. For the probable fact of the matter was that Mme Denis was once again responsible. Back in 1755 she had – knowingly or unknowingly – allowed her lover, the marquis de Ximénès, to make off with one of Voltaire's manuscripts, his controversial account of the War of the Austrian Succession. This time, it seemed, her amorous interest in the diminutive but vigorous La Harpe had enabled – and perhaps encouraged – a similar theft.

Uncle and niece engaged in some spectacular rows, witnessed by Wagnière, as Mme Denis tried to defend La Harpe's innocence and Voltaire realized why she did so. For him the leaking of such a document was a very serious matter. If he could trust neither his niece nor a young man to whom he had offered nothing but hospitality and support, how could he ever be safe? And the betrayals hurt. In his anger Mme Denis's long-acknowledged failings became intolerable crimes: her profligacy, her vulgarity, her superficiality. Suddenly weary, Voltaire blamed her for filling his house with people and noise at every hour of the day and night. How was he supposed to work? Was he to spend his days hiding in the bushes under a lime-tree? Was he never to have a house he could call his own? On 28 February 1768 he asked Mme Denis to leave. Next morning she did. D for domestic, D for departure.

ENDINGS
(1768–1778)

From Garden to Grave

CHAPTER NINETEEN

April Foolery (1768–1769)

Wherein a deist continues the struggle and prepares the ground

A T N O O N O N 1 March 1768 the Master of Ferney found himself alone. Mme Denis had left in high dudgeon without saying goodbye, and she had taken Mme Dupuits, née Corneille, as her companion. It had in fact been agreed for some time that she should visit Paris, and arrangements for the journey were already well in hand when the dispute occurred. Which simply gave the theatrical Mme Denis a golden opportunity to indulge herself with this dramatic gesture. She loved rows, and had a sharp tongue. If her uncle was determined to make himself so thoroughly unpleasant, then she would show him just how much *she* cared!

When Voltaire learnt the news from Wagnière, he was so astonished that he nearly hit the man. How could his secretary have concealed this from him? He hadn't meant his niece to leave quite so immediately. Despite the presence of Wagnière, Father Adam, thirteen household servants, and twenty-three gardeners and farmhands,[1] the place felt suddenly empty. After a miserable lunch Voltaire wrote to his niece at once, voicing his hurt. By the end of the day he had dictated fifteen letters to diverse recipients: frenetic correspondence had long been his palliative against feelings of exclusion. One week later he wrote again to his niece: he would sell Ferney and join her wherever she chose to be. He had not forgotten that the estate was registered in her name: as the daughter and widow of public servants, she was exempt from certain taxes. But Voltaire was also well aware of her increasing antipathy to the Pays de Gex and her great desire to be in Paris. As to

Tourney, he would keep it and go there in the summer. A further week later he confided in Chabanon by letter that he intended to return to Paris and to die in Mme Denis's arms.

But as spring arrived and his garden began to cheer up, so did Voltaire. He was enjoying the peace and quiet. He could go to bed early. Like swallows, the first English visitors began to arrive, but he refused to see them. And, for that matter, anybody else who called. At meal-times he filled the silence by having his secretaries read to him: from good books rather than the Good Book, but for all the world as if he were a monk. Had he not always told his niece that the monastic life suited him? Apropos, an inspection of his domestic accounts revealed that Mme Denis had left a mountain of unpaid bills, and of course now he would have to pay for her living expenses in Paris – which were unlikely to be modest. Perhaps 20,000 *livres* a year. Admittedly he was owed about 160,000 *livres* – half of this by the incorrigible Duke of Württemberg – but how could he get his debtors to pay? The neighbours were told that Mme Denis had gone to Paris to persuade them (and to have treatment to her gums).

Mme du Châtelet had used to worry about leaving her dear François to his own devices. There was no knowing what he might get up to. And Mme Denis felt the same: 'I shudder to think of [him] being all alone.'[2] Both women had good reason. As Holy Week approached, the Lord of the Manor decided that he would take communion on Easter Sunday. It was time that he set an example to his parishioners again, and with Mme Denis absent someone had to go. It was also advisable to be in good standing with the Lord above – or more especially His Church below – just in case he should die. After all, he didn't want to be dumped in an unmarked grave like a mere actor. His local priest, Father Gros, was an amenable sort, and so too was a local Carmelite prior whom he summoned to hear his 'confession'. Absolution was granted in the twinkling of an eye. Now duly penitent, the Patriarch processed to his church on the morning of Easter Sunday (3 April). His two gamekeepers, shotguns slung across their chests, preceded him like some royal bodyguard, while a retinue of servants followed on behind. Once inside, and with his 'people' so conveniently gathered together in one place, he could not resist a desire to address them – and rose to speak as the priest himself was beginning his sermon. Just a few words: to bid the congregation pray for the Queen, who was seriously ill, and to ask whoever was responsible for a recent theft if they would kindly own up. The communion itself was delicious, for Voltaire had donated some excellent brioche for the occasion.

News of Voltaire's performance spread rapidly. The Bishop of Annecy, Monseigneur Biord, was particularly vexed since Ferney fell within his diocese, and he wrote to his troublesome brother-in-Christ to demand that he demonstrate the sincerity of his penitence by publicly disavowing all his previous attacks on Christianity. After some inconclusive epistolary fencing, Biord then wrote – from the safety of independent Savoy – to Saint-Florentin, Louis's minister. The King was notified of his subject's latest prank, and – for form's sake – Voltaire was duly cautioned. But his friends were astonished. Surely Father Adam, his freethinking version of a private chaplain, had not managed to convert him over a game of chess? O they of little faith! In June the suspected convert published a *Profession de foi des théistes* (*The Theists' Profession of Faith*) in which the anonymous author goes much further than Rousseau's Savoyard vicar. Communion itself is an absurd ritual: 'imitating God, who created man, by in turn creating God with a few words and a handful of flour'.[3] The wise theist (or deist) can but observe this nonsense in silent amazement and pray to God on behalf of those who perpetrate it. Even supposing that our prayers have any effect on the Almighty whatsoever.

Silence, of course, was not Voltaire's forte. Pamphlets continued to pour from the ventriloquist's pen, ridiculing Christian apologists, defending his fellow-*philosophes*, and dispensing advice to all and sundry – including the rulers of Poland and Russia. One antagonist, the abbé de La Bletterie, wondered wearily if Voltaire had simply forgotten to die.[4] Needham's experiments with eels had clearly left their mark, for our natural philosopher now conducted his own on some slugs and snails – cutting their heads off to see if they would grow back. Which some did (for perfectly good, unmiraculous reasons), leading him to publish a short pamphlet on that subject also. But he was less good on sea-shells, like those which had been found – in fossilized form – on top of the highest mountains. Horrified that such evidence might lend credence to the story of the Flood, he stoutly maintained the theory that such shells had been dropped along the way by pilgrims. In the Pyrenees perhaps, for the scallop shell is associated with St

James of Compostela. But in the Alps? Well, yes, he replied, by pilgrims on their way to the Holy Land. But the Caucasus . . . ? Mmm. And what about the reindeer and hippopotamus fossils found at Étampes just south of Paris? A collector must have mislaid them. What is singular about Voltaire's *Singularités de la nature* is the sudden closedness of his mind. Scientific research was opening up new vistas with which he was simply too old to cope – or rather which he found it impossible immediately to incorporate within his deist conception of God the perfect watchmaker. Pending a solution, he crudely papered over the cracks in his own polemic.

For, even though Voltaire had now dropped his campaign slogan of 'Écrasez l'infâme', he was still very much involved in the promotion of deism as the humane alternative to the intolerance fostered by organized religion (not to mention the sexual depravity of monks as depicted in his latest *conte*, the *Lettres d'Amabed* (1769) – with its suggestive Anglo-French title). And he was also still very much involved in the pursuit of justice. As the case of the ungrateful abbé Desfontaines testifies, the Calas affair was far from having been the first judicial wrong that he had sought to redress on behalf of others. But it had brought his name to new prominence as what was later called a 'champion of human rights', and the victims of intolerance soon turned to Calas's defender in their plight. People like Pierre Paul Sirven, an expert in feudal tax law who lived in Castres, east of Toulouse, in the Languedoc. He, his wife, and their three daughters – Marianne, Elisabeth and Jeanne – were all Protestant, though the couple had perforce gone through the motions of Catholic marriage and baptisms. On 6 March 1760 the 23-year-old Elisabeth, having already shown signs of mental instability, ran away from home and told the local bishop that she wished to convert to Catholicism. He accordingly entrusted her to the care of some nuns. In the convent her behaviour became even more disturbed. Claiming to have been guided by angels, she would remove her clothes and demand to be whipped. After seven months the nuns returned the young woman to her parents. Wishing for a fresh start, they moved to a village near Mazamet, south-east of Castres. Just over a year later, on the night of 15–16 December 1761, Elisabeth disappeared. Her body was discovered nearly three weeks later at the bottom of a well, into which she had either fallen or (more probably) thrown herself.

In this strongly Protestant area the local (Catholic) authorities were keen to show their muscle. To them this seemed like a classic case of Protestant parents murdering their offspring to prevent a conversion, a bloodthirsty fantasy that sprang from the notoriety of the Calas case, which was just then being judged in the Toulouse *parlement*. And when two incompetent – or unscrupulous – doctors inferred from a post-mortem examination that the woman had been dead before she fell down the well, these authorities issued orders on 20 January 1762 for the arrest of Sirven, his wife, and their two remaining daughters. The four of them at once resolved to escape on foot into the nearby mountains – at some physical risk to Mme Sirven, who, at sixty-three, was eleven years older than her husband, and to Marianne, who was three months pregnant. At first they waited to see how the Calas case would turn out, but once Marianne's husband Ramond learnt of the merchant's execution (10 March) he urged them to flee. They headed for Switzerland: Sirven directly for Geneva and then Lausanne, his wife and daughters indirectly through the Cévennes to Nîmes. Aided by the Protestant 'resistance', they finally arrived in Lausanne.

Meanwhile, as in the Calas case, an official report of the Sirvens' alleged crime was read out in local churches, and the Sirvens' property was confiscated. A long delay ensued: the Toulouse *parlement* was in dispute with the King over the raising of taxes, and such due legal process as existed was more or less suspended. But on 20 March 1764 three local magistrates sitting in Mazamet finally pronounced sentence: M. and Mme Sirven to be hanged (unlike the chevalier de La Barre, they did not enjoy the aristocratic privilege of being beheaded), and their daughters to be banished (after they had witnessed the execution of their parents). In the absence of all four culprits the sentence was carried out on 11 September 1764: a picture of Elisabeth's parents was hung from the gallows instead.

Voltaire learnt of the case in February 1762, but he does not appear to have met the family until 5 April 1765, when they travelled from Lausanne to Ferney to provide him with signed statements. Mme Sirven, too ill to accompany her husband and daughters, died a few days later. By the time Sirven and his daughter Marianne visited Voltaire again on 18 May 1766, he had succeeded in clearing Calas's name. It was now the turn of the Sirvens to benefit from his well-oiled procedures: the publication of a pamphlet setting out the facts of the matter while again calling for religious toleration, and the dispatch of innumerable letters to enlightened and well-placed allies (Catherine of Russia, Frederick, the duchesse de Saxe-Gotha, etc.) who would contribute to the legal expenses and thus proclaim their devotion to the cause of French justice!

At least the remaining Sirvens were safe – unlike La Barre, executed on 1 July 1766 – and for the moment their case was relegated to Voltaire's pending tray. Where it had more or less remained until 7 March 1768, a week after Mme Denis's precipitate departure. Voltaire now learnt that the royal council had refused his application for the sentence to be set aside. Since Sirven was a fugitive from justice (*sic*) and had been tried and executed *in absentia*, the only way in which he could establish his innocence was to submit himself for retrial (by the same magistrates). And to do that he would have to return to the Languedoc and give himself up. The legal deadline was 11 September 1769. This was plainly a risky and unwelcome prospect, but eventually – on Voltaire's advice and with his very substantial support – Sirven duly did so, lodging at a hotel in Mazamet on 31 August 1769 for the duration of his new trial. This lasted some two and a half months, during which Sirven was repeatedly subjected to gruelling and intimidating interrogation. At the end the public prosecutor demanded ten years' banishment and a fine of 1,000 *livres*, but the bench decided to drop the case in the absence of conclusive evidence. Though not therefore acquitted, Sirven was nevertheless granted his freedom and given back his confiscated property – and required to pay costs of 224 *livres* in respect of the earlier trial *in absentia*. He appealed against the verdict. The Toulouse *parlement* – chastened after the Calas affair and, like all *parlements*, temporarily reformed by the new chancellor Maupeou – subsequently cleared Sirven and his family of all wrongdoing on 25 November 1771.

Maupeou's reforms were substantial. Above all he had abolished the practice whereby the office of magistrate in a *parlement* could be bought or bequeathed. Instead all magistrates were now to be appointed by the King and paid a salary by the state. Throughout the century the power of the *parlements* had been growing, and they had increasingly refused to do the King's bidding. The famous 'revolt' of the *parlement* in Rennes in 1764–6 was symptomatic. Voltaire had always been an implacable opponent of the *parlements*, not least because of their strong Jansenist leanings, and his history of the Paris *parlement*, begun in January 1768 and published in 1769 (under a pseudonym, in Geneva and Amsterdam) was his contribution to the increasingly strident debate about their future. Though Voltaire had no cause to love Louis XV, he did believe – passionately – in the institution of the monarchy as the surest guarantee of political stability and national prosperity. Certainly he wished to see the French monarchy reformed, with a king at once less beholden to the Church and more subject to a framework of fair and just laws. Such a ruler was Frederick of Prussia, and – he hoped rather than believed – Catherine the Great. But the *parlements* as currently constituted could not provide the safeguards against absolutist (but potentially enlightened) rule that were to be found most notably in Great Britain. Rather they were a self-serving and self-perpetuating oligarchy, a poisonous presence corrupting the body politic. As evidenced by the conviction of La Barre. But Maupeou's reforms were later reversed by Louis XVI on 12 November 1774, six months after his grandfather and predecessor had died of smallpox at the age of sixty-four.

But for the moment Voltaire was more concerned about his own future – and the possible lack of it. He was particularly saddened to learn of the death, on 13 December 1768, of Étienne Noël Damilaville, who had succumbed to throat cancer at the age of forty-five. Having served in the Royal Guards, an élite cavalry regiment, and fought in the War of the Austrian Succession, he had trained as a lawyer and then become a tax administrator. He was an unflamboyant but sterling supporter of the *philosophes*, and numbered Diderot and d'Alembert among his close friends. He had first written to Voltaire in 1760 at the height of the furore surrounding Palissot's satirical play, *Les Philosophes*, and from then on had been an invaluable servant to Voltaire in Paris, displaying all manner of unsung diligence during the Calas and Sirven affairs and circulating clandestine works (notably the *Dictionnaire philosophique*) to well-chosen recipients in the capital. Voltaire only met him the once, when Damilaville visited Ferney for five weeks in the early autumn of 1765, but he had treasured his friendship and selfless loyalty to the cause: 'Écrasez l'infâme!'

Although his own health had never been wholly reliable, Voltaire recognized that he had lived a long life and could hardly complain. Indeed it was with some pride that each year he attested formally to the continuance of his existence so that his agents and lawyers could demand the payment of his various annuities. His longevity had turned these into golden investments. While his eyesight was poor – snow-blindness had been a constant problem since he moved to this mountainous region – and while he would soon lose all hearing in one ear, he was nevertheless in reasonably good fettle. He retained considerable mobility, albeit increasingly with the aid of a stick, and of course there was still all that energy. While he might have lost his teeth, he had not lost his bite. Nor his sense of humour. When Mme Cramer came to stay at snow-bound Ferney for a few days in February 1769, she reported that her host had been 'lively and communicative' and that 'we nearly choked with laughter as we talked about death'.[5]

Perhaps he had told her of his latest cunning plan. For he had resolved once more to take Easter communion. But this time it would not be so easy. The Bishop of Annecy had drawn up new lines of defence. The abbé Gros, the parish priest of Ferney, was expressly informed of the new conditions that his celebrated parishioner would now have to fulfil if he were to be granted absolution. An oral disavowal of his anti-Christian writings would no longer suffice: the Bishop wanted a written statement, signed before witnesses and duly registered by a notary. And the freethinking Father Adam was henceforth forbidden to say Mass.

Voltaire relished the challenge. Rather than take communion in church, he decided that he would feign terminal illness and secure it – in the form of the last rites – at his own bedside. As Palm Sunday drew near, Voltaire requested Gros to administer the last rites. The priest duly required him to disown the 'bad things' he had written, to which their author retorted with injured innocence that they weren't 'bad': he had been slandered and libelled by his enemies. On Palm Sunday Voltaire attended Mass in his own church but without taking communion. On Tuesday he summoned Gros again: his fever is high, the end is near. Wearily Gros attended him and found a not notably feverish writer even less inclined than before to recant. Stalemate. Easter being a busy time of year in the confessional, Gros was being temporarily assisted by a local Capuchin (Franciscan) monk, Father Claude Joseph. Ever resourceful, Voltaire told Wagnière to summon this monk and then placed a shiny new *écu* on his bedside table. On being requested to hear the dying man's 'confession', Father Joseph accepted the proffered coin but then expressed his regrets: he had people to see in the church, he would return in a day or so. Voltaire had lost a piece. So he summoned a doctor, who took his pulse and found no trace of fever. On being summarily charged with incompetence and invited to reconsider, the doctor quickly discovered the fever in question – which discovery he was then requested to communicate to Gros forthwith. As Voltaire knew, the dying were dispensed from confession before receiving the last rites if the circumstances were sufficiently urgent. The laws of the land defined urgency as three consecutive bouts of high fever. 'Monsieur de Voltaire has had eight,' he informed Gros in a note on Good Friday, 'of very high fever.'

Gros, caught between the Bishop and his terrestrial master, showed spirit. He too was ill, he responded, indeed terminally ill. (He would in fact die within the year.) So now, if Voltaire would just kindly produce that written statement . . . Easter Sunday (26 March) came and went. On Tuesday Gros negotiated with Voltaire, and both men saw Father Joseph as the key to a satisfactory outcome. So Gros wrote out what purported to be Voltaire's statement of orthodox Christian belief and his rejection of all heresies and false readings of the Scriptures. The handwriting was his own, and the spelling and syntax not at all up to Voltairean standards, but he hoped it would persuade the monk to hear Voltaire's confession. The signature could be obtained later, somehow. At 1 a.m. the following Thursday morning Voltaire roused his household with the claim that he was at death's door. Gros must be summoned at once. But Gros preferred to stay in bed. So at 10 a.m. Voltaire sent him a signed statement, witnessed by Wagnière and another secretary, Bigex, professing his membership of the Roman Catholic Church and his readiness to do all that was required in order to be allowed to take communion. That afternoon, in the presence of a notary, Raffo, he dictated a statement claiming that his works had been libelled and misrepresented by ill-intentioned enemies (like Nonnotte); that

he owes it to the truth, to his honour and to his piety to declare that he has never ceased to respect and practise the religion professed throughout the kingdom; that he pardons his detractors; that, if ever he should have let slip any indiscretions that were prejudicial to the religion of the State, he begs forgiveness of God and the State; that he has lived and wishes to die in the observance of all the laws of the kingdom, and in the Catholic religion, itself closely bound to the law [*étroitement unie à la loi*].[6]

In other words, he was declaring himself to be a French subject who wished to conform with the law of the land, but he was not saying he believed in the Christian religion. And how could anyone deny him eternal salvation (i.e. a decent burial) over a few, unwitting indiscretions.

Gros thought he was getting somewhere. He and Joseph visited Voltaire the following Saturday morning (1 April), and, as arranged, the monk went in to hear the 'dying man's' confession. Having carefully left the door ajar, Wagnière listened to the proceedings – and recorded them for posterity. His master began by pleading a faulty memory. If Father Joseph would be kind enough to recite the appropriate words – the Creed, the Lord's Prayer, 'Forgive me, Father, for I have sinned', that kind of thing – he would do his best to recite them after him. Which he did, though the monk was so nervous and so faulty in his own delivery that the resultant recitations barely qualified as authentic text. When Father Joseph mentioned the 'bad works' and tried to get Voltaire to sign the requisite statement of orthodox belief and recantation, his adversary motioned the piece of paper away. Why bother with such formality when he had just recited the Creed? Then, with all the skills of a tragedian, he treated Father Joseph to a long and moving speech about how he forgave his enemies the evil of their slander and asked only for mercy and tolerance. At the moment of maximum pathos he peremptorily instructed a rather weepy Father Joseph to grant him absolution. And it was done. Whereupon Voltaire summoned Gros to administer the sacraments and Raffo, the notary, to record the occasion. At the very moment of taking communion, Voltaire declared aloud: 'With my God in my mouth I declare that I sincerely forgive all those who have made false accusations against me to the King and who have failed in their evil intent.'[7] This declaration was written down, signed by Voltaire and Raffo, and witnessed by Wagnière and Bigex. In a few words he had ridiculed the Eucharist and outmanoeuvred a bishop. In the end it was he who had done the absolving. Check and mate.

Now feeling considerably better, the Patriarch rose from his bed and went for a walk in his garden with Wagnière. He seemed to have no need of a stick. Gros, meanwhile, was asking Joseph for Voltaire's signed statement. He hadn't signed? Disaster! What *would* the Bishop say? So a fortnight later Gros, Joseph, and a handful of co-operative friends (several of whom had not even been present at the requisite time and place) collected in Raffo's office and co-signed a declaration to the effect that they had heard Voltaire recite the words of the unsigned statement (prepared by Gros) before he received the sacraments, and that Voltaire had himself told them that he had earlier recited the same words when Father Joseph had heard his confession. This document was then sent to the Bishop of Annecy. Voltaire did nothing to stop them from covering their backs in this way. Moreover, whether out of gratitude or a bad conscience, he used his influence to secure a state subsidy for the local Franciscan friars (fifty *livres* for each of the twelve members of the monastery). Soon afterwards he received a letter from the head of the Order in Rome, thanking him for his help and appointing him a lay member of the Order. François was now an honorary Franciscan. He could not resist writing to Cardinal de Bernis, the King's ambassador to the Holy See, to inform him of this signal achievement. He signed himself, 'Brother Voltaire, your unworthy Capuchin'.[8] Needless to say, there had been a slip-up. The Father General of the Order had been away in Corsica: a secretary had mistakenly sent Voltaire the standard letter of thanks addressed to bene-factors. The honorary membership was quickly withdrawn.

And the Bishop tried one last move. In a long letter Biord sought once more to place Voltaire in a dilemma: either he was sincere, in which case he would now publicly disown his anti-Christian writings, or he was a hypocrite, lacking all sense of honour and probity. When Voltaire replied, under the alias of a fictitious relative, that the Bishop's letter must surely be a forgery (i.e. the real bishop would never have doubted his word), Biord published the two letters, together with his correspondence from the year before with Saint-Florentin. But without the latter's permission (and certainly not Voltaire's). Louis's minister was far from pleased. He com-plained to Biord and warned him firmly: in such cases it was always better to presume the penitent's sincerity. Did it matter what Voltaire really thought? Appearances were all. But once again Voltaire's Parisian friends were aghast. Did this not indeed smack of hypocrisy?

What they had perhaps forgotten was how much Voltaire loved playing

games. He might be in his mid-seventies, but he was still the child who loved
to be naughty, the competitor who liked to win. And in this case, as we shall
see, the game had been a dress-rehearsal for the rather more serious drama of
his death. In April 1776 he would lament to a visiting Englishman, Martin
Sherlock (as reported by him): 'Ah! Sir, you are happy, you may do any thing
(*sic*); we are born in slavery, and we die in slavery; we cannot even die as we
will, we must have a priest.'[9] But Voltaire was determined to die a free man.

CHAPTER TWENTY

The Watchmakers (1769–1773)

Of silkworms and high priests, of statues and serpents

MME DENIS WAS now more worried than ever about her incorrigible uncle. He seemed to attract trouble, like the newly invented lightning-conductor he was soon to have installed in the grounds at Ferney. Nevertheless she was reluctant to give up the rediscovered delights of Paris. Perhaps he might join her there? Or take separate lodgings? For Voltaire the capital had lost none of its allure, but Louis XV was implacable. Choiseul conveyed to his friend that he could return on condition that he ceased to write. He might as well have asked Voltaire to stop breathing. In June 1769 Mme Denis began to resign herself once more to the prospect of the Pays de Gex. But she would need a maid, a footman, a coachman and a two-horse carriage. And she had one or two outstanding bills . . . Her uncle refused to pay them, pleading poverty and uncooperative debtors. Moreover he was not sure that she ought to return. Ferney could be very cold and isolated during the winter months. Perhaps they might spend them in the south – in Toulouse, for example – where he was the talk of the town and where Lekain, star of the Comédie-Française, was performing to packed houses in some of his best-known plays. Or would she like to tour? To see Hyères and Montpellier? He has arranged for a carriage to be specially fitted out for extra comfort – a 'dormeuse', he calls it, meaning a 'sleeping-car' or mini-caravan: 'and we would be followed by a good waggon containing everything we need.'[1]

But these placatory suggestions came to nought, and Mme Denis returned to Ferney towards the end of October, having left her brother-in-law, the marquis de Florian, to sort out her affairs – and her debts. Voltaire had missed her badly: he would not send her away again. Nevertheless he demanded some changes, on the real or spurious grounds of needing to make economies. (He had just lost a small consignment of diamonds to some Tunisian pirates, he said.) No more grand parties, and no more plays. The theatre was turned into a silkworm factory. Responding to the new ambience, the robustly corpulent Mme Denis went on a diet. The couple now dined alone (Voltaire ate scrambled egg to lend moral support), but food was provided separately – and still lavishly – for passing guests and visitors. Voltaire would lock himself away in his room for fifteen hours a day, studying and writing, but many people still came, from far and wide, in the hope of meeting the great man. And some would get a sighting, as of a rare bird – an analogy reinforced by his beak-like nose and the eccentricity of his dress. Extravagantly obsolete wigs and gaily coloured breeches alternated with opulent house-coats and multiple silk caps. But the old eagle proved resolutely elusive. His time was precious. He had books to write and battles to fight.

Voltaire now presented himself as the high priest of deism, and he lost no opportunity to argue and reargue his case: most notably in *Dieu et les hommes* (*God and Men*) (1769), a treatise with forty-four chapters, and in *Dieu, réponse au Système de la nature* (*God, a Reply to the System of Nature*) (1770). This 56-page pamphlet was his immediate riposte to baron d'Holbach, whose bold profession of atheist materialism had been published earlier that year. And he continued to reply to d'Holbach, notably in the *Questions sur l'Encyclopédie*. This, Voltaire's last great work, was a successor to the *Dictionnaire philosophique*. Although he incorporated fifty entries from the latter in the *Questions*, the new 'dictionary' was a distinct entity, more ambitious in scope and less urgently polemical than its predecessor. It was as if Voltaire were writing his own *Encyclopédie*, and he wrote entry after entry as the alphabet moved him. Or rather as his intellectual fancy took him. The first three volumes – for A, B and C – were printed by Cramer during the summer of 1770 and published in December. In order to expand the print run, and to keep all parties on their commercial toes, Voltaire had the *Questions* simultaneously produced by the Société Typographique of Neuchâtel. By the following December he had finished a further six volumes. There is nothing like a long-term project for keeping a person alive. And there he sat, mostly in bed, studying and dictating to three secretaries: Wagnière, Father Adam, and Durey de Marsan, a man with a neat hand and a colourful past, who needed the money and acted as go-between for the printers in Neuchâtel. And each day Voltaire would dictate article after article like some omniscient Scheherazade, deferring Z for Zoroaster just as long as he possibly could. The Bible, world religions, history both ancient and modern, literature of every age and genre, science and technology . . . all was grist to his ceaseless mill as he ground out the cereal of a lifetime's learning and reflection. In prose.

Or verse. For he was simultaneously pouring out a stream of epistles and satires on any topic that caught his eye. The rhyming couplet, like the encyclopedia article, still came as easily as a breath. In 1768 a shipbuilder in Nantes had named his latest construction *Jean-Jacques*. So his main commercial rival, not to be outdone, christened his new vessel *Le Voltaire* — and informed the honorand at once. Reminded of a famous Horatian ode, Voltaire then wrote his own, satirical pastiche, complete with passing sallies at Rousseau, Nonnotte, Fréron and divers favourite enemies. And nobly he addressed the newly launched *Voltaire* from the poop-deck of his advancing years: 'May you, as I have, prove equal to the storms ahead.'

In the same year he had read a work entitled *Traité des trois imposteurs* (*Treatise on the Three Impostors*), based on a manuscript about Spinoza first printed in 1719. Spinoza's quasi-pantheistic philosophy denies the existence of a transcendental God, which led antagonists to equate it with atheism. Hence the comment attributed to him by Voltaire in his verse satire on metaphysics, *Les Systèmes* (*Systems*) (1771), where Spinoza confides to the Deity: 'Strictly between ourselves, I think that you do not exist.' Thus the anonymous author of the *Traité* condemns Moses, Jesus Christ and Mohammed as impostors, mere anthropomorphic representations of God who lack any supernatural status that might justify reverence or worship. To which Voltaire replied (in *A l'auteur du livre des Trois Imposteurs* (*To the author of the Trois Imposteurs*) (1769)) that there was a fourth impostor: the purveyor of this dangerous nonsense. Because God *does* exist, and a belief in His existence ensures moral order and social stability. Thus:

If the heavens, stripped bare of his august mark,

Could ever cease to manifest his presence,

If God did not exist, it would be necessary to invent him.[2]

But for Voltaire there was no need to invent God. Evidence of the intricate, intelligent workings of His creations was everywhere to be seen.

And now, as though he too were impersonating God, Voltaire became a watchmaker himself. In Geneva the political struggle between conservatives and progressives had reached an impasse, and disenfranchised artisans were voting with their feet by emigrating to France in large numbers. At that time French territory extended to the shores of Lake Geneva just north of the city, so that the small fishing village of Versoix fell under the rule of Louis XV. Geneva itself had capitalized on its prime geographical position at the crossroads of global trade routes (from Scandinavia to Italy and Africa, from the Atlantic Ocean to the Levant and the East Indies), and since the days of Cardinal Richelieu its powerful neighbour had envied both the position and the consequent wealth. So why not set up a rival trading centre? In Versoix. The recent blockade of Geneva had hurt the French far more than the Genevans, for the latter continued to be supplied across the lake while the former discovered that they had unwittingly but severely disrupted the trade routes connecting Lyons and Marseilles with countries to the east. If Versoix were established as a commercial centre and trading port, it would greatly enhance France's leverage with Geneva.

Voltaire had reason to be keen on the idea, for the blockade (begun in January 1767) had hurt the economy of the Pays de Gex particularly badly. And his own money was increasingly invested in the area. So, as early as February 1767, he had begun to write to men in high places, notably Choiseul, detailing the plan and promoting its benefits. Choiseul was persuaded, and a road was built by the military, connecting Versoix via the Franche-Comté with the main French highways. But transforming Versoix into a major port was a rather larger enterprise, as was the construction of hundreds of houses to accommodate the expected influx of Genevan migrants. The attendant cost required a royal edict — of which, at the beginning of February 1770, there was still no sign. French finances were in poor order, and the Versoix project was top of nobody's list of priorities. Not least because many of the refugees were former French Huguenots, who would thus be reimporting their Protestantism into the Gallican fold. Terray, the new minister in charge of the public purse, began his term of office by reneging on a Treasury bond issue, unilaterally deferring repayment to an unspecified later date and at an unspecified rate of interest. Voltaire had 200,000 *livres* invested in these bonds: they might as well have been plundered by North African corsairs! So he proposed that he be repaid part or all of this sum on condition that he invest it in the Versoix project. Terray was not interested.

Voltaire's motives were not solely financial. He welcomed this influx of Protestants into the Pays de Gex, and at Versoix he dreamed of establishing a new model city of religious toleration. Needless to say, Monseigneur Biord spotted the strategy and inveighed against it, thus encouraging Louis XV to stay his hand further. The resultant political uncertainty left the refugees disheartened, so that the tide of migration began once more to flow in the opposite direction. Voltaire therefore decided to substitute Ferney for Versoix: like William Penn he would found a colony on the principles of liberty, hard work and god-fearing morality. Indeed he had already begun, creating employment for the local (largely Catholic) population by helping – with advice and capital – to set up new businesses. (Pierre Sirven himself opened a shop there.) What had been an ailing and almost exclusively rural economy ten years ago had now been transformed by the advent of light industry: tanning, tile-making and the manufacture of silk. Voltaire's ancestors would have been proud of him. The heir to several centuries of textile merchants was now producing silk stockings for the luxury market.

And soon pocket-watches. Many of the fugitive 'natives' from Geneva had learnt this trade. So Voltaire began by investing 60,000 *livres* in equipping the necessary workshops and by inviting fifty workers (belonging to twenty families) to Ferney. He built houses for them, at a cost of 100,000 *livres*, lent them a further 100,000 interest-free, and appointed himself unofficial sales manager. This meant sending a box of samples to Choiseul and asking him to distribute them at the forthcoming marriage of the Dauphin to the young Austrian princess, Marie-Antoinette. Another friend, the duc de Praslin (in charge of foreign affairs), agreed to send Voltaire's watches to French consulates for distribution as gifts. This in turn prompted Voltaire to write a circular letter to His Majesty's ambassadors asking each one to help him find outlets for his wares. He particularly enjoyed writing to Cardinal de Bernis in Rome again. Huguenot horology in the Holy See!

The Versoix project lapsed finally when Choiseul fell from power in December 1770, and his removal represented a major setback to Voltaire's watchmaking. The duc de Praslin had also been replaced, by the duc d'Aiguillon, an expert in the art of promising everything and delivering nothing. Moreover, times were hard. A poor harvest had once again led to a steep rise in the price of bread, and Voltaire's workers were suffering. With characteristic practicality he devised a form of potato bread, mixing two parts' cereal flour with one part potato, and sent the recipe to the Lieutenant of Police in Paris – in case it might help alleviate the unrest. (Since potato bread has long been popular in Ireland, it did not follow that it necessarily would.) Like his design for a horse-drawn tank, however, the seeds of this remarkable culinary advance fell on stony ground. (Marie-Antoinette's later suggestion of brioche, of course, fared even worse.) By December 1771 three of the new watchmaking businesses were on the verge of bankruptcy, and Voltaire had to bail them out by drawing on 80,000 *livres* of his own capital. Not only was the competition from Geneva fierce, but Paris retailers insisted on cripplingly high profit margins. Choiseul had allowed the watches to be imported to Paris via Lyons tax-free (French regions and cities could levy duty on goods transported through them), but this privilege now looked as if it might be withdrawn. Furthermore, the general economy of the Pays de Gex continued to suffer from the area's anomalous situation: its closest market, Geneva, was a foreign country, so that all imports and exports were taxed. Voltaire began to address himself to this anomaly.

Meanwhile the high-priest-cum-sales-manager was being turned into a statue. His admirers had long been itching for the moment of his apotheosis, the day when he would die and they could turn him into a god for all eternity. But he kept on living, so they lost patience and acclaimed him anyway. The prime mover was Jacques Necker, the Genevan banker, who had now established himself in Paris and become an extremely wealthy man. His wife, the daughter of a Genevan pastor, presided over a salon that regularly welcomed the leading *philosophes* of the day. The couple were both staunch Protestants and, like their wide circle of influential Protestant friends, also great admirers of Voltaire – because of what he had done for Calas and

Sirven, but also because of his dogged attempts to bring religious toleration to the Pays de Gex. On 17 April 1770 Mme Necker invited seventeen *philosophes* to dinner, among them Diderot, Grimm, Marmontel, d'Alembert, Saint-Lambert (Émilie's former lover), Helvétius, and the abbé Raynal, whose voluminous and controversial history of European colonization, the *Histoire des deux Indes* (*The History of the Two Indies*), was published that year. It was agreed to raise money towards a statue of Voltaire. On the pedestal would be inscribed: 'To the living Voltaire, from his compatriots in the Republic of Letters' ('par les gens de lettres ses compatriotes'). Pigalle, perhaps the most celebrated French sculptor of his day, was chosen – Raynal went to fetch him from the next room, where he had been awaiting this foregone conclusion – and he showed them a model of what he had in mind.

There was temporary disagreement about the subscriptions. Some suggested two *louis* each (i.e. forty-eight *livres*), and from 'men and women of letters' only. But others wanted to include potential contributors like Richelieu and Choiseul, whose prestige would be as welcome as their money. The latter course was chosen, and a figure of 12–15,000 *livres* was decided upon as the target. Pigalle would receive 10,000 for his work. But where would it be displayed? The Comédie-Française was the obvious place, but the company was currently without a permanent home. Perhaps the royal library (later the Bibliothèque nationale)? Raising the money was easy, and the target had been reached by the end of July. Frederick of Prussia was quick to give, and to send a eulogy: 'Should the French language ever cease to exist, Voltaire will surely be translated into whatever replaces it.'[3] Voltaire's friend and faithful correspondent, Mme du Deffand, declined to contribute. Though she was a celebrated and distinguished salon hostess and sympathized with the less radical *philosophes* (the *encyclopédistes* worried her), she offered Voltaire the elegant but implausible explanation that she had refused 'out of humility'.[4] Less parsimonious by far was Jean-Jacques Rousseau, who wished to add his two *louis* to the kitty – 'having already paid quite dearly for the honour of doing so'.[5] The statue's model was outraged, and ordered d'Alembert to return the money at once. But wise counsels prevailed, and thus did the author of the *Confessions* pay tribute to his Genevan cuckoo.

Pigalle now had the rather hazardous task of sculpting from life, and he visited Ferney for the purpose from 17–25 June 1770. He had decided to represent Voltaire in the nude, like some hero of antiquity. But the visit to Ferney concerned only the head: for the remainder he would spare the Patriarch's blushes by using an old soldier in the Invalides as his model. The Patriarch himself protested modestly that even his face was hardly worth sculpting these days. When Pigalle got out his equipment, the more ignorant witnesses to the scene believed – with a modicum of glee – that he had come to perform some essential medical operation. Voltaire himself, of course, was not given to sitting still for any longer than five seconds, and so Pigalle had some difficulty in capturing his likeness. His model, however, put the sitting to good educational use and interrogated Pigalle about his art. He was busy writing an article for the *Questions* on 'Metal Casting' ('Fonte'), whereby he meant to ridicule the episode in Exodus where Moses melts down the Golden Calf within the space of a night. So he wanted to know how long it would really have taken him. Several months, came the reply. Whereupon Voltaire ordered Wagnière to bring Pigalle pen and paper 'so that I can have a signed statement from him to that effect, and show Moses what a fool he was'.[6]

It was an episode that had troubled Zapata, too, Voltaire's young theology professor in Salamanca. 'And [Moses] took the calf which they had made, and burnt it in the fire, and ground it to powder, and strawed (*sic*) it upon the water, and made the children of Israel drink of it' (Exodus 32: 20). If the Golden Calf was seen and worshipped by an entire people, it must have been big. So how could he melt it down so fast? And 'ground it to powder'? Ah, decided the young Spaniard: these must be miracles.[7] But Pigalle's finished statue was rather less miraculous. While the bust from life (in clay) seems to have met with Voltaire's approval and to have represented a decent likeness, once copied in marble it looked nothing like him, and the overall effect was monstrous. The statue remained in Pigalle's studio before being left to Voltaire's great-nephew, Dompierre d'Hornoy, who donated it to the Académie Française in 1806. From there, unregretted, it has passed into the safe-keeping of the Louvre.

The Necker subscription was symptomatic of the gradual deification of Voltaire. The Comédie-Française was particularly aware of their debt to France's greatest living playwright, and in September 1772 Mlle Clairon organized a ceremony of homage at her home in the rue du Bac. A bust of

Voltaire was placed on a pedestal, and the famous actress, dressed as a priestess of Apollo, crowned it with a laurel wreath. Then, before a distinguished assembly, she addressed it in the words of a celebratory ode by Marmontel. In the art of tragedy this great writer had surpassed even Corneille and Racine. When informed of the compliment Voltaire quickly returned it, likewise in verse, attributing the success of his plays to the skills of the acting profession. It was Mlle Clairon who had grown the laurels. Much as he would like to have replaced the lifeless bust with his own rather more animate presence, Voltaire nevertheless drew comfort from the tribute. His recent plays had not fared well. *Les Guèbres* (*The Parsees*), written in 1768 and published in 1769, was never publicly performed. A familiar story of intolerant priests and persecuted minorities in the last days of the Roman empire ends in the triumph of tolerance and forgiveness. But pathos and dramatic intensity were missing. In *Le Dépositaire* (*In Trust*), a five-act comedy in alexandrines, he had given centre stage to Ninon de Lenclos, the fabled courtesan to whom he had once been introduced as a child. Of fading beauty and lost reputation, the lady is guardian to her former lover's two sons and outwits the unscrupulous churchwarden who holds their inheritance in trust. Virtue is as virtue does. But several longueurs made it less than comic, while its overt anti-clerical message made it unacceptable to the censor, even in the more enlightened Paris of 1770. And the third play never to be publicly staged was *Les Lois de Minos* (*The Laws of Minos*), a tragedy written in 1772 as a thinly veiled commentary on the contemporary politics of Poland. Voltaire thought that the topicality would draw the crowds, but shrewder opinion at the Comédie-Française soon identified the play's capacity to send its audience to sleep. So, too, presumably did the comtesse du Barry, the King's new mistress (Mme de Pompadour having died in 1764), to whom he also sent a manuscript copy. For she was otherwise well disposed to him.

But if his latest plays were flops, his former successes continued to add lustre to his name. While theatre was still banned in Geneva, the Genevans were becoming increasingly enthusiastic theatre-goers. The converted barn at Ferney remained full of silkworms, but a local impresario, Saint-Gérand, had opened an establishment at Châtelaine. The street on which it stood was itself the Franco-Genevan border, and Calvinists had barely a mile to walk from the city centre in pursuit of their illicit pleasure. Performances began at

4 p.m., leaving just enough time for this particular section of the audience to return home before the city gates were shut. In the event of a delayed start, resourceful contingency plans were cheerfully adopted. Voltaire attended regularly, having his own private box on the left of the stage. Old habits die hard, and he would often interrupt the proceedings by offering advice on the interpretation of a scene or about a particular actor's technique. Whether or not he had written the play himself. He brought Lekain down from Paris in September 1772 to perform in some of his best-known plays: *Adélaïde du Guesclin, Mahomet, Sémiramis*. In the case of *Mahomet* he spent the whole day at Châtelaine directing the cast. When the amateur actor playing Séïde proved unequal to the task, Voltaire acted the scene out himself to show him – with a verve that left onlookers astonished by his momentary rejuvenation. On 19 September, despite bad weather, the theatre was already full by 11.30 in the morning. Everyone, including the most sober pastors that Geneva could muster, was determined to see Lekain in *Sémiramis*. The author himself had taken up position in the wings, just off-stage but in full view of the audience. And, like the audience, he wept. Beside himself with enthusiastic approval, he tapped his stick repeatedly on the floor; and at the moment of highest drama his stooped and skeletal frame careered across the stage to shake Lekain by the hand. He just had to congratulate him there and then on his extra-ordinary talent.

But, alas, even the extraordinary talent of France's greatest living actor could not rescue Voltaire's next creation, *Sophonisbe*. The subject, like the title, belonged to the play (written by Jean Mairet) generally recognized to have been the first 'proper' classical tragedy performed in France (in 1634). As with the plays of Sophocles and Crébillon, Voltaire was still determined, literally and metaphorically, to rewrite theatrical history. But he was more especially determined to return to Paris, and his fond hope was that a successful new play would provide the pretext and at last cause the King to relent. And as usual he sought to mobilize his friends in high places. But d'Argental was powerless, and Richelieu was ruthless. Though still in charge of court entertainment, Voltaire's old friend knew what the King liked, and the list of forthcoming plays to be performed at Fontainebleau did not include Voltaire's. Nevertheless, and no doubt for old times' sake, *Sophonisbe* was eventually performed there before the King at the end of October 1773. But when Lekain opened in the play at the Comédie-Française on 15 January 1774, the response was poor. Another flop.

Much more successful was Voltaire's latest *conte*, *Le Taureau blanc* (*The White Bull*). Begun in 1771, if not earlier, it was completed in 1773 and published in three instalments in Grimm's manuscript periodical, the *Correspondance littéraire*, from November to January (1774). It tells the tale of Nebuchadnezzar, King of Babylon, who had the misfortune to be turned into a bull for seven long years. Or at least that's how the mischievous reader of the Old Testament interpreted Daniel 4: 32: 'and they shall drive thee from men, and thy dwelling shall be with the beasts of the field: they shall make thee to eat grass as oxen, and seven times shall pass over thee'. The Voltairean imagination runs riot as we find ourselves transported to the banks of the Nile, where the hapless bull is grazing under the watchful eye of the Witch of Endor. Helping her to guard the bull are Baal's ass, Tobias's dog, a scapegoat, and the serpent who beguiled Eve. Jonah's whale wallows nearby, ready to serve. Elijah's raven and Noah's dove flutter aloft.

Along comes the beautiful Amasida, daughter of the King of Tanis. For nearly seven heartbreaking years she has not set eyes on her beloved Nebu . . . But her guardian, Mambres, stops her. She has been forbidden by her father, on pain of being beheaded, even to speak the name of the man who conquered Egypt. Mambres is a mere 1,300 years old. Formerly a eunuch and prophet to the pharaohs, he is now a high priest of wisdom and sound common sense. When Amasida promptly falls for the handsome white bull, Mambres trades professional advice with the Witch before devising a plan to save his ward. Apis, the bull-god, has died (for some gods do): and the high priest of Memphis is seeking a replacement . . . While the good people of Memphis are travelling to Tanis to fetch their new god, Mambres has time for a sumptuous dinner with Daniel, Ezechiel and Jeremiah. The carp's-tongue tart is delicious, and of course not a hint of beef on the menu. Meanwhile the serpent is deep in conversation with Amasida, who in a weaker moment reveals a love that dares to speak its name. Has she lost her head? Not quite. Four thousand priests have arrived from Memphis with a motley crew of demigods (Phoebe's cat, Arsinoe's crocodile, etc.) and 'an enormous basket filled with sacred onions, which were not quite gods but looked very much as if they might have been'.[8] And just as everyone acclaims the white bull as the new Apis, he turns into a man 'and married the fair Amasida there and then'. Rather as the Ingénu had wished to 'marry' the fair Saint-Yves before the forces of Breton reaction insisted on the foreplay of a church service.

For Voltaire the great thing about a *conte* was that he could play several parts. In this case, of course, he is the elderly magus who was once emasculated by Louis the Pharaoh, and he takes pleasure in sending up his own elderliness. Long periods of apparently wise cogitation look suspiciously like 'senior moments' of total vacancy, and the reader may wonder if Mambres has lost his own plot. 'My advanced age has meant some reduction in my lights and powers,' he confesses; 'good old Mambres thought harder than ever,' the narrator assures us.[9] But, no less obviously, Voltaire is the serpent too: 'Time was when I could have helped you while away many a happy hour [he tells Amasida]. But latterly my imagination and my memory have not been quite what they were. Alas, where are the days when I used to entertain the girls? Still, let's see if I can remember some moral tale to please you.'

And the fair Amasida has already told him what will please her: 'I prefer [a story] to be neither trivial nor far-fetched. I particularly like the ones which, from beneath the veil of the plot, reveal to the experienced eye some subtle truth that will escape the common herd.'[10] Readers are like animals perhaps, a bovine herd in their dumb passivity; and yet all of us have the ability to be transformed into human beings by the subtle and devilish art of story-telling. If we will but laugh at totems and break the silence of taboo, we can find our happy ending and rule supreme in our own domain.

Including kings. For the veiled truth of this story is not simply that the Old Testament contains implausible episodes no less unreal than the metamorphoses of Ovid. That emerges as a naked fact. But why does *Le Taureau blanc* end with the words: 'Long live our great King who is no longer dumb!' ('qui n'est plus bœuf!')? A contemporary reader would have wondered about the significance of the seven years during which Nebuchadnezzar had remained silent. Might this be the equivalent of the seven years that had elapsed between 1764, when the Rennes *parlement* refused to levy the royal tax known as the *corvée*, and 1771, when Maupeou reformed the *parlements* – and when Louis XV took the unusual step of making a public statement of his support (the so-called *lit de justice* of 13 April 1771)? The royal ox had found its tongue. And it would not have escaped the 'experienced eye' of a contemporary that white was the colour of Bourbon royalty. The story was a compliment to Louis, but it is doubtful if he took the point. In any case he was about to undergo his own, terminal metamorphosis.

Voltaire resembled his magus of common sense in one further way: 'Mambres [. . .] no longer enjoyed quite the influence he once had.'[11] Or at least that is what this terrestrial watchmaker wryly feared. Through his wealth, influence and indefatigable letter-writing he had sought to make Ferney not only a model township of religious toleration and economic prosperity but also a hub of international affairs. The wheels within wheels of political action held an endless fascination for this student of history, and he still loved to oil them or to arrest their complex movement with a well-directed spoke. Nothing pained him more than being left out. Sometimes his distance from the real centres of French power (Paris and Versailles) rendered his interventions clumsy or misunderstood. Choiseul, for one, felt bitter at Voltaire's apparent support for his much more conservative successor, Maupeou. And the distance could cause Voltaire himself to misjudge or idealize situations. There was no question that he had an impressive network of influential contacts and correspondents who were sympathetic to the *philosophes*: the Empress of Russia, the King of Denmark, the King of Prussia, and his sister the Queen of Sweden. (Her young son, Gustaf, succeeded to the throne on 12 February 1771 while pursuing his enlightened studies in Paris, but nevertheless remained there a further six weeks to complete them.) And there was no question that he had the measure of their limitations. He had reason to know Frederick's, and he told d'Alembert in 1773 that he thought Catherine 'the most despotic ruler on earth'.[12] For he was well aware of the horrors of Russian serfdom. Nevertheless progress was progress, however slow. 'The rays of your light cannot shine everywhere at once,' he told her the following year with soothing, pragmatic diplomacy.[13]

But Voltaire could get carried away. Self-interested territorial ambition began to look like an enlightenment crusade. In 1770, as Catherine pushed south into the Crimea and began to erode Ottoman supremacy in the region, he could see her being crowned in Constantinople,[14] an Empress of Reason driving back the darkness of Turkish Islam. Even less plausibly, he called on Frederick, her ally, to head south and dispose of the Pope.[15] Two 'impostors' gone! But in the real world the King of Prussia was seeking as usual to hold the balance of European power, limiting Catherine's advance through a *rapprochement* with Austria and her French ally. And so Voltaire was deeply shocked two years later when Catherine, Frederick, and Maria Theresa of Austria calmly divided Poland between them. Each gained valuable territory, and for Frederick in particular this meant the unification of his kingdom, hitherto split between Brandenburg and East Prussia. Catherine and Frederick pretended to Voltaire, in the age-old way, that annexation was a form of liberation: the Poles would now enjoy religious and civil freedom. And Voltaire tried to believe them, not least because it would be counterproductive to offend them. But the reality became plainer to him as time passed. In 1775 he told Frederick: 'You kings [. . .] are like the gods of Homer. You use human beings for your own purposes, and the poor things don't realize it.'[16] The crowned heads of Europe were the real watchmakers.

CHAPTER TWENTY-ONE

A Fight to the Finish (1773–1776)

Wherein the mind proves superior to matter

'LIFE IS A STRUGGLE to the last.' When Voltaire wrote these words to the maréchal de Richelieu on 30 March 1775,[1] he knew exactly what he was talking about. Since the beginning of February 1773 he had been suffering from what can retrospectively be diagnosed as cancer of the prostate. One night he rose from his bed to work and caught a chill on his bladder. His former doctor, the celebrated Théodore Tronchin, had moved to Paris in 1766, and since then Voltaire had more or less dispensed with all doctors. A healthy scepticism born of experience and reading Molière? Or perhaps a shrewd, elderly view that now that something might really be wrong he would rather not know. At any rate he suffered his chill in silence. Four days passed, and his condition quickly deteriorated. He was running a high fever, he had great difficulty in passing urine, and his legs were swollen with fluid. At the time they called this 'dropsy', the condition from which his probable biological father was thought to have died in 1719. A doctor, François-David Cabanis, was summoned and promptly prescribed a cold bath. After four hours the swelling had scarcely abated, and the pain was intense. Everyone feared the worst, not least the patient.

But Voltaire was not yet done. Very gradually, and much to his own surprise, he began to recover. Somewhat. Three months later the swelling had still not disappeared. 'I can see death at the end of my nose,' he informed d'Alembert on 8 May.[2] High fevers were frequent, and he experienced significant periods of unconsciousness. Micturation was problematic. At his age, of course, he was more than used to the frailty of his body. Over recent years he had often taken to his bed: with a cold, after a fall, or simply for the warmth. Admittedly there had been a touch of 'wolf, wolf' in his behaviour, and he had been fond of proclaiming the imminence of his demise whether by letter or by appearing before visitors like a rather melodramatic ghost. And on other occasions his very real frailty had led to misunderstandings. In December 1772 he had not been well enough to attend a dinner-party organized by Mme Denis, and he was served a simple meal in his room. But it was his custom on such occasions to invite his favourite guests for private bedside conversation. One such favourite was Judith de Saussure, the exceedingly attractive, 28-year-old sister of the distinguished Genevan physicist, Horace-Bénédict de Saussure (who had installed Voltaire's 100-foot lightning-conductor for him the previous year and would later climb Mont Blanc with several crates of scientific equipment in 1787). During his tête-à-tête with Mlle de Saussure, Voltaire passed out twice. On the third occasion Mme Denis herself came to investigate what was going on. Tongues soon wagged, particularly as the fair Judith had something of a reputation (or rather was on the way to losing it). But at the age of seventy-eight? Surely not . . . As the rumours spread (even to the King), the story lost nothing in the telling. Hercules was mentioned. Protesting his genuine innocence to his old friend Richelieu – a connoisseur in such matters – Voltaire nevertheless slyly fostered the myth: he had fainted from 'nervousness' and 'respect' for his guest.[3] It pleased him that people might think he had risen again.

As spring gave way to summer in 1773, Voltaire regained some of his strength and adapted to his new condition. Work continued. In August he welcomed a very special house-guest: the Duchess of Württemberg, who was on her way back from consulting the distinguished Dr Tissot in Lausanne. Not only was she the wife of his least co-operative debtor, she was the daughter of one of his favourite people: the late Wilhelmine, Margrave of Bayreuth, and sister of Frederick of Prussia. The Duchess resembled her mother closely, and Voltaire remembered them both from his days in Potsdam and Bayreuth. It was a fond and tearful reunion. Two days later, after dinner with François Tronchin at Les Délices, she was about to depart for Paris when Voltaire arrived in a carriage. He had been invited to join them but, whether from illness or emotion, had wondered whether to go.

Their farewells were now so affecting that the Duchess delayed her departure and accompanied her rediscovered friend back to Ferney. But it had all been too much. The following night he fell seriously ill once more, and summoned Dr Tissot.

Voltaire's life began to seem like borrowed time, and when the crisis of February 1773 was repeated on 21 March 1774 the octogenarian was left in no doubt: 'I have been given notice to pack my bags and leave.'[4] Which of course just made him even more determined to stay. Especially as the alternative was so unattractive. While it might serve social stability that the majority of people believed in an after-life of hell-fire or heavenly reward, he himself was under no such illusions. Back in 1772, at the time of the death of the duchesse d'Aiguillon, he had told Richelieu frankly: 'Everything passes, and then it is one's own turn to pass on towards nothingness, or at least towards something that bears no relation to us ["qui n'a nul rapport avec nous"] and which is therefore for us the equivalent of nothingness.'[5]

'Everything passes': and so it seemed. Damilaville had gone in December 1768, and then other friends: Thiriot, the Duchess of Saxe-Gotha, both in 1772. Worst of all his younger niece, Elisabeth, marquise de Florian (formerly Mme de Fontaine, née Mignot) died of tuberculosis at the beginning of May 1774. He had built a pretty new house for her and her husband in Ferney – a residence called 'Bijou' – but she had not been able to enjoy it for long. Less distressingly, Louis XV died shortly after her on 10 May, of smallpox. News of the momentous event reached Ferney six days later. Within a fortnight Voltaire had sent Cramer two short pamphlets to publish: a eulogy of the deceased sovereign principally designed to recommend its author to the new king, Louis XVI, and his queen, Marie-Antoinette; and another defence of inoculation as the best means of combating the terrible disease that had just carried off the French sovereign at the age of sixty-four.

Louis's death would mean change. The late king (Louis XVI's grandfather) had become deeply unpopular towards the end of his reign, not least because of his relationship with Mme du Barry and the extravagance of court life at a time of national economic difficulty. He had categorically ceased to be 'le bien-aimé'. The new king and queen were very young, nineteen and seventeen respectively. Might their youth herald a new dawn? Perhaps.

Voltaire learnt that Louis had allowed himself to be inoculated against smallpox on 18 June. But they would need good advice. To whom would they turn? The duc de Choiseul perhaps? But instead the new king chose as his chief minister Maurepas, now seventy-four, who had been out of the political limelight for over thirty years. He had the merit of being a man of no party, and he then displayed the even greater merit of promoting the able and forward-looking Turgot to replace Terray as Controller-General of Finance. Turgot had made his name as the financial administrator of the region round Limoges, bringing increased prosperity to this backward area and introducing a range of measures specifically designed to help the peasant and labouring classes. He was a friend of the *philosophes*, and his liberal economic principles were music to Voltaire's merchant ears. Especially when he deregulated the corn trade on 13 September and later abolished a whole range of obsolete fiscal measures.

But even as the French economy was moving forward, its judicial system was slipping back into the past. On 12 November 1774 Maurepas reversed Maupeou's reforms of the *parlements*: the old order was reinstated. The young king had become a little white bull. Nevertheless Voltaire took heart from the fact that momentum was building behind the *philosophes'* programme of social and economic reform. Some important symbolic bastions were now administered by key allies: d'Alembert at the Académie Française, Antoine-Nicolas de Condorcet at the Académie des Sciences. Just turned thirty, this brilliant mathematician had also been taken on as an adviser by Turgot. Together they sought to stimulate French economic life and to repair some of the damage done by endless war and expensive royal philandering. So the time was ripe for a renewed attempt to boost the finances of the Pays de Gex. The major obstacle to its development had always been its commercial dependence on Geneva, for the routes into French markets across the Jura were hazardous in all seasons. And of course the tax barrier between the Pays de Gex and Geneva boosted the cost of imports while making exported goods less competitive. Why not move the tax border so that it fell between the Pays de Gex and the rest of France? The idea was not new, and the Président de Brosses, owner of Tourney, had tried unsuccessfully to bring about a version of it. But surely Turgot would approve?

He did. The general principle was accepted. However, the local tax-farmers had to be compensated in some way, especially in respect of the salt tax: this had been a major source of their income. Voltaire offered 20,000 *livres* a year, and then promptly lowered his offer by 25 per cent – alleging his 'discovery' that they only actually got 7,000 at present. His art of bargaining was always to create the impression that he might reduce rather than raise his bids. The tax-farmers wanted 60,000. Turgot split the difference at 30,000. But the new arrangements would have to be ratified by a special meeting of the local authorities in Gex, a kind of mini-parliament consisting of representatives of the nobility, the clergy and the 'third estate'. So on 12 December 1775 Voltaire mustered what strength he still possessed and travelled to Gex. Whenever he needed to impress high-ranking visitors to Ferney he had been in the habit of mobilizing a ceremonial militia, a small detachment of dragoons each decked out in a handsome uniform at his expense. The proceedings at Gex clearly called for some pomp and circumstance, so he took twelve dragoons with him and proudly stationed them in the square outside the assembly rooms. All went well. Voltaire recommended the proposals to the meeting in an eloquent but barely audible speech, and they were unanimously accepted. A protocol was signed by each party. Whereupon Voltaire rose to his feet, flung open the window on to the square, and shouted, 'Liberté!' The dragoons saluted with their sabres. A large crowd had gathered, and with great whoops of joy they began to decorate Voltaire's horses with cockades and to strew his carriage with laurel. Further crowds acclaimed the 'liberator' along the road to Ferney, where his own 'subjects' lined the route and cheered him to the echo. It was as if a king had carried out a revolution.

But who was going to pay the 30,000 *livres* a year? Turgot thought that the burden should fall on landowners, but – as Voltaire had pointed out in *L'Homme aux quarante écus* seven years earlier – that was surely unfair. Merchants and manufacturers were often just as rich, and the disincentive effect of the proposed tax would be ruinous to the agricultural economy. So he summoned all interested parties to Ferney for another meeting, in the spring of 1775, but negotiations proved tortuous. One participant had been trying to manipulate the salt market – a vital commodity in the days when it provided the principal means of preserving food – and the consequent turmoil was unconducive to a harmonious outcome. But even as these negotiations dragged on throughout the year, the local economy quickly showed the benefits of the new tax regime.

Ferney itself had now grown from a tiny impoverished hamlet into a prosperous community of some 800–1000 inhabitants. It boasted over eighty houses, most of them built with Voltaire's money and then let. The watchmaking industry was thriving, with an annual turnover of half a million *livres* and rich export markets in Spain and the Levant. And now there was further cause for celebration. Mme Denis herself had been very seriously ill, and her recovery in the spring of 1775 offered a splendid pretext for some no less serious festivity. On 18 May the proceedings began with a High Mass, itself an excuse for some excellent music (as well as being a helpful contribution to Voltaire's campaign to be allowed a decent burial). Then there was a military parade: Marie-Louise evidently felt well enough to review some handsome soldiers. Her uncle's local militia was unequal to this task, and so the French army – cavalry as well as infantry – was invited to

Voltaire takes breakfast in bed on 4 July 1775, in the company of his friends (contemporary engraving).

oblige. There followed an open-air banquet for 200 guests. The spectacle was so lavish that all of Ferney turned out to watch, and indeed a significant section of the population of Geneva. Voltaire estimated that there must have been about 4,000 people present.[6] Another grand party was held on 25 August, St Louis's Day. St Louis having been the patron saint of a succession of French kings, this day had become the occasion of an annual national celebration, the eighteenth-century equivalent of 14 July. And then, of course, there was 4 October – St Francis's Day – which meant more pomp and circumstance in honour of the local ruler: a military parade, followed by a grand dinner and a ball. All Ferney was ablaze with torches and candles, an illuminated colony of enlightenment.

Voltaire's daily routine was recorded by a visitor in December 1774.[7] In the morning he worked, now usually in bed: reading, dictating the latest pamphlet, letter or dictionary entry to his team of secretaries. Then he would rise and dress at noon. A clean shirt and underwear were brought by his favourite servant, a stout woman by the name of Barbera (or Barberat), who mothered him with brusque affection and a singular lack of awe. It was beyond her, she said, how anyone in their right mind could think there was an ounce of common sense in his: and he loved her for it.[8] Now more or less presentable, he would receive visitors or else simply continue to work. He no longer took the midday meal, preferring the simple sustenance of coffee or chocolate. Between 2 and 4 p.m. he would go out in his carriage, accompanied by Wagnière, and survey some corner of his domain to make sure that all was proceeding as it should. Then he worked until eight o'clock, when he would join Mme Denis and others for supper. Health permitting, that is, and as long as there were no pretty young women to keep him bedridden.

Out of an annual income of approximately 150,000 *livres*, about a third went on the upkeep of his châteaux and grounds (and Mme Denis), while the remainder was invested in the expansion of his 'colony'. He would give instructions for a new house to be built (the same visitor commented) as though he were merely ordering an extra pair of shoes. Voltaire's 'work' was thus a mixture of writing and administration. In short, he loved to manage: his own estates, the wider business community of Ferney, the affairs of nations, and – above all – European public opinion. As he told Richelieu in

April 1775, he still considered it his 'duty' to combat injustice,[9] and the fulfilment of this duty was what kept him alive. And he did love a battle. It had long since scandalized him, for example, that the feudal institution of serfdom remained in force in the Franche-Comté, just across the Jura Mountains. On acquiring this territory from Spain in 1678, France had enshrined the rights of property enjoyed by local landowners (notably the monasteries), and all servants (including their work and their own 'possessions') were property. One such, a Mme Aberjou, arrived on his doorstep in October 1773, exhausted, destitute, and with a long tale of abuse and exploitation at the hands of her 'owner', a member of the *parlement* in Besançon called Brody. Voltaire gave her house-room for a few days while he arranged alternative accommodation and provided her with financial support. Then he took up her case with the royal council in Paris. Though she died in the following January, he pursued her case and the general issue of serfdom none the less. But he, too, died before it was finally resolved – by the French Revolution.

There were many other causes to occupy the ailing campaigner, most notably the case of Thomas Arthur, an Irish Jacobite and servant of the French crown. Better known as the Baron of Tollendal and comte de Lally, this gentleman was a brilliant soldier who had distinguished himself during the French victory at Fontenoy in 1745. Voltaire had met him when his friends the d'Argenson brothers (as Foreign Minister and Minister of War) were about to send Lally off to assist Charles Edward Stuart, the Young Pretender, in Scotland. In 1755, at the beginning of the Seven Years War, Lally was dispatched to India to defend French interests against the British. This time Voltaire had been alarmed: these French interests were earning him personally an annual income of 20,000 *livres*, and he was not at all sure that this 'mad Irishman' ('une diable de tête irlandaise')[10] could be trusted to look after his money. And he was right. After some mixed military fortunes Lally eventually surrendered at Pondicherry in 1761. On being brought to London as a prisoner of war, Lally learnt that in Paris he was being accused of treason. Having secured permission from the British Admiralty to return 'home' to defend his honour – promising to come back to London when he had – Lally then travelled to France and loudly proclaimed his innocence. On 3 November 1762 he was arrested and imprisoned in the Bastille: his trial did not begin until April 1764. As Voltaire wrote at the time: 'In France we always like to start by putting a man in prison for three or four years, and then we try him.'[11] On 6 May 1766 Lally was found guilty of abusing his position and betraying French interests in India: i.e. treason. On 9 May he learnt that there was to be no royal pardon: he would be beheaded that day. Having tried to take his own life with a geometric compass, he was quickly bundled into a cart and taken to the Place de Grève outside the Hôtel de Ville. There, on a rickety, hastily erected scaffold, his head was placed on the block. The executioner duly severed the 'diable de tête irlandaise' – at the second attempt. And to loud applause. The applause that was also to be heard two months later when the same executioner managed to dispatch the chevalier de La Barre at the first attempt.

Voltaire had followed the case and was shocked by its terrible denouement ('which does not seem to me to have been foreshadowed in any of the previous acts').[12] Essentially Lally's colourful, rather high-handed character had created many enemies, several of whom testified against him. But being hateful was not a capital offence. And it was more or less the Irishman's only offence, as Voltaire then demonstrated in Chapter 34 of his *Précis du siècle de Louis XV*. But there the matter rested until Lally's nineteen-year-old son wrote to him in the summer of 1770. Although he did not explicitly ask for Voltaire's assistance, he informed him of his own intention to clear his father's name, and set out his case for the defence (confirming with his own evidence most of what Voltaire had written on the subject). Being illegitimate (like his father before him indeed), the younger Lally was legally prevented from petitioning the King on his father's behalf, and he now proceeded to rectify the situation as best he could – mainly by securing the right to use the Irish title of Tollendal (by which he had been registered on his birth certificate).

In April 1773 Lally's son wrote again to Voltaire, this time expressly asking for his help. Though very seriously ill, the defender of Calas and Sirven agreed and initiated a campaign of pamphlet and letter. Here was an excellent opportunity to remind people of the iniquities of the Paris *parlement* before Maupeou's recent reforms. And as usual his campaign was effective: the image of a traitor was replaced in the public mind by that of an innocent victim of injustice. Despite the reinstatement of the old *parlement* in 1774,

Voltaire continued to pursue the case, in concert with Lally's son. As in the Calas case, he applied to the royal council (on 5 December 1776) to have the verdict on Lally overturned, and the council once again responded (21 April 1777) by demanding an official report. As Voltaire later lay dying, he heard (26 May 1778) that on the previous day the council had thrown out the sentence on Lally and ordered a retrial. In fact that retrial never took place, but to all intents and purposes the Irishman's name had been cleared.

And then there was Gaillard d'Étallonde, the probable culprit in the La Barre case. Having fled Abbeville, he had become an officer in the Prussian army and lived under the shadow of the death sentence pronounced *in absentia* in 1766. Voltaire had written to him at the time, encouraging him to believe that he might hope for justice as time passed. Now that his mother was dead and his father gravely ill, d'Étallonde was keen to be pardoned so that he could legally inherit (along with his elder brother), and he appealed to Voltaire for help in November 1772. After considerable delay Frederick granted his friend's protégé a year's leave from the army, and d'Étallonde came to shelter at Ferney in April 1774, where he remained for the next sixteen months. The blasphemer and troublemaker turned out to be a modest and polite young man, and Voltaire warmed to him immediately. At first he went along with d'Étallonde's intention to seek a pardon, thinking that Maupeou might persuade the King to this outcome as a way of distancing himself from the former, discredited Paris *parlement*. But when Louis XV died and Maupeou's reforms were reversed, it seemed more expedient – and indeed appropriate – to seek a retrial. For there was nothing to 'pardon'. And Frederick, for all his scepticism about the possibility of success, was proving an accommodating and influential ally in this cause. So in July 1775, on the occasion of Louis XVI's coronation, Voltaire published *Le Cri du sang innocent* (*The Cry of Innocent Blood*), a ghosted account of the events at Abbeville as related by d'Étallonde. But the appeal for justice fell on deaf ears, and d'Étallonde had reluctantly to return to Potsdam on 31 August. Only in 1787 was the sentence finally quashed, and only after d'Étallonde had signed a statement decrying all blasphemers and opponents of the 'one true Religion'. He had recovered his inheritance by denouncing his erstwhile host and protector – and when the dead man could no longer defend himself.

Voltaire's final causes were also his first causes: religious intolerance, the existence of God, and the future of the French theatre. His subversion of the Old and New Testaments culminated in the resoundingly entitled *La Bible enfin expliquée* (*The Bible Explained at Last*), which appeared in 1776. This time he was rewriting Dom Calmet's *Commentaire littéral*, borrowing his method – a biblical quotation followed by commentary – but substituting for the Benedictine monk's learned discussion his own sceptical irreverence and a literal-mindedness that bordered on the wilfully childish. In the *Histoire de l'établissement du christianisme* (*History of the Founding of Christianity*), begun in 1776 but published posthumously, Voltaire ends by asking what is the point of such a book 'if it doesn't cure at least a small number of readers of the gangrene of fanaticism'. Our purpose here below is 'to worship God, to cultivate the earth that he has given us, and to help each other as we live out our short lives'. Such a philosophy stands to reason: for reason 'tells us that the world cannot have organized itself, and that societies cannot exist without virtue'. The history of Christianity is the history of the corruption of these plain and simple truths.[13]

But by now atheism was an even greater 'corruption'. Following the publication of d'Holbach's *Système de la nature*, the Creator had been having a hard time of it, and the self-appointed apostle of deism spent many of his precious remaining hours writing in His defence. God was too important to be left to the theologians. One well-known story bears eloquent testimony at this period both to the strength of Voltaire's belief in God and the enduring implacability of his opposition to Christianity. One day in May (probably in 1776, perhaps in 1775) he woke his house-guest, the marquis de La Tour Du Pin Gouvernet, at three o'clock in the morning. Voltaire was off to see the sun rise. He had been rereading Rousseau's 'Profession de foi du vicaire savoyard', in which the vicar demonstrates the splendours of God's creation by taking his pupil to the top of a mountain at dawn. 'Let's see if Rousseau was right,' he exhorted the sleepy marquis. Voltaire had put on his best clothes for the expedition, pale grey breeches, and a coat and waistcoat of sunrise-gold. He might have been the Sun King himself. After a lantern-lit journey of some two hours they reached a small valley just as the dawn was beginning to break. Aided by his guide and the young marquis, Voltaire climbed to the top of a hill, from where the three men beheld a glorious sight. The Jura Mountains rose before them, the dark green tips of their trees etched against the pale blue light of morning, while below their feet a landscape of meadow and stream began to emerge from the crespuscular blur. And there, on the far horizon, among the pine-clad peaks, the sun rose in a vast semicircle of purple fire. Resplendent. Incontrovertible.

Voltaire removed his hat and prostrated himself on the ground. Thus prone, as though in prayer before the altar of a great cathedral, he improvised a quasi-poetic chant of worship. 'I believe, I believe in You,' he repeated with apparently unironic fervour; 'Almighty God, I believe!' Whereupon he got to his feet, replaced his hat, and dusted the dirt from his elegant breeches. Then, with his now-customary stooped posture, he eyed the heavens with that look which Collini had once seen on his face when he took communion in Strasbourg, and added: 'As for Monsieur, the son, and Madame, his mother, that is quite another matter.'

The implausibility of Voltaire's ability to undertake a long walk and a steep climb suggests either that the story is false or that the men must have travelled by carriage for the better part of the journey. But the various elements of the narrative ring wholly true: the empiricist's desire to see for himself; the theatrical performance and the automatic recourse to verse at moments of high drama; and the parting shot of witty irreverence whereby Voltaire Almighty reasserts his terrestrial independence. He would believe in that which it was rational to believe in, but he would not be duped.

Probably begun in earnest in December 1774 and completed in April 1775, *L'Histoire de Jenni* (*The Story of Jenni*) bears the subtitle 'The Wise Man and the Atheist' and consists in large part of a dialogue between John Freind, an Anglican, and Birton, an adept of d'Holbach's materialism. Freind is a fictional amalgam of two real people: John Freind (1675–1728), one of the leading physicians of his day, who became Professor of Chemistry at Oxford, then doctor to the Earl of Peterborough during the War of the Spanish Succession, and finally Member of Parliament for Launceston; and his brother, Robert Freind (b.1667), an Anglican clergyman and headmaster of Westminster School. The fictional Freind is Voltaire's mouthpiece, a stalwart if rather humourless deist of great good sense and exemplary moral rectitude.

The action turns on the exploits of Freind's nice but accident-prone son, the improbably named Jenni (*sic* for Johnny?). At Barcelona young Jenni is wounded and taken prisoner, where he falls prey to wrong-headed Catholics and the fond attentions of Doña Boca Vermeja and Doña Las Nalgas – in whose names the hispanophone reader will have identified the vermilion mouth and the buttocks that were the instruments of his fall. But Father comes to the rescue, converts a few graduates from the University of Salamanca (perhaps former pupils of the perplexed Professor Zapata), and takes his son back to the safety of England – and the prospect of conjugal bliss with sweet Miss Primerose (sic). Alas, young Jenni, having tasted of the fruits, now falls in with some bad company, notably Birton and his mistress, the irredeemably promiscuous Mrs Clive-Hart. For all atheists are immoral debauchees who will cleave your heart – and more. Having poisoned her elderly husband and (it seems) Miss Primerose too, la Clive-Hart absconds to the New World with Birton and a gullible Jenni. There they roam and rampage through the Blue Mountains before the scarlet woman is captured and eaten by Red Indians. When Freind senior catches up with them, it transpires conveniently that he is also the grandson of William Penn (1644–1718). For the native Americans revere this Quaker founder of Pennsylvania. The rampaging atheists are allowed to leave in peace.

On the sea voyage back down Chesapeake Bay, Freind and Birton debate the existence of God in the presence of Birton's friends and the remainder of the ship's company. In the mouths of his protagonists Voltaire recapitulates all the arguments that he and his own opponents had rehearsed over many, many decades, and in the end Birton is persuaded of the merits of deism. Persuaded not by metaphysical argument but by evidence. For Freind has two trump cards: the starry firmament above, which finally convinces Birton of the existence of an intelligent Creator; and his own moral example, which demonstrates to the atheist the social utility of religious faith. Having followed the debate as though it were a battle in which the outcome remained uncertain to the last, Birton and his fellow-atheists fall at Freind's knees: 'Yes,' said Birton, 'I believe in God and in you.' Miss Primerose has recovered from her poisoning, and on his return to England a grateful and penitent Jenni marries and lives happily ever after. The narrator of the story concludes: 'You will agree that a wise man may cure a madman of his folly.' For Voltaire considered that he had spent a lifetime trying to do just that.

One such madman was Shakespeare. Just as Birton represented the forces of darkness, so now also did the English playwright from whom Voltaire had once learnt so much. For him Shakespeare had been an unruly genius, his plays a sprinkling of rough diamonds buried in the mud. But now this 'Gilles-Shakespeare' – as he called him, meaning that Will Shakepeare was a clown – had come to epitomize all that was wrong with the modern French stage: all mud and no diamonds. Voltaire's enthusiasm for the medium itself, of course, remained undimmed. He had missed having his own theatre at Ferney, and the journey to Châtelaine nearly five miles away was becoming a chore. So in 1776 he commissioned a public theatre in the village of Ferney – in fact a large, refurbished shop (and today the tourist office of a renamed Ferney-Voltaire)[14] – and persuaded the impresario Saint-Gérand to have his troupe alternate their performances between Châtelaine and Ferney. Then he secured the services of Lekain to come and perform once more to packed houses. Voltaire's 'colony' now had its own version of the Comédie-Française, though Marie-Antoinette was keen to have her favourite actor back in Paris as soon as possible. For the Comédie-Française, founded in 1680 by Louis XIV, was still entirely beholden to the crown.

But in Paris all the talk was of Le Tourneur's new translations of Shakespeare, which, although first advertised in 1772, had only just begun to appear – under the full panoply of royal approval. On 14 March 1776 the first two volumes had been ceremonially presented to Louis XVI, to whom the complete edition was dedicated. Le Tourneur's prefatory material represented a direct attack on the conventions of classical French theatre in its eulogy of Shakespeare's unfettered genius and the powerful imagination that was evident in his plays. Voltaire was appalled. For him Shakespeare was responsible for the present sorry state of French theatre: the emphasis on intellectually undemanding spectacle and stage action, the dilution of the tragic into mere sentimentality, the terrible slide towards the banal and the prosaic. For his opponents, of course, Shakespeare represented the way forward, salvation from the empty, repetitive formulas of traditional dramaturgy. For had not Voltaire himself, the great heir to Corneille and Racine, quite plainly run out of theatrical ideas and inspiration?

The blindness and intransigence of Voltaire's last-gasp opposition to Shakespeare is testament to the importance he attached to this area of his own reputation – and to the pain he felt at being overtaken in this of all domains. So he fought back by writing an open letter to the French

Academy, staunch bulwark of the literary glory of France – and of the glory that France's new king had just thrown out of the window. Voltaire's intention was that the letter be read out at the Academy's meeting on 25 August, St Louis's Day. To achieve his polemical aim he was obliged to traduce his target, emphasizing and distorting the crudity of language and comedy to be found in Shakespeare's plays (and which Le Tourneur had discreetly bowdlerized). And then he set this crudity beside the timeless perfection of Corneille and Racine . . . It was as if, he said, some scruffy jester had been let loose in the gilded galleries of Versailles.

As secretary of the Academy, d'Alembert duly read out Voltaire's formal letter on St Louis's Day. Since this meeting was traditionally open to the public, there was a sizeable and distinguished audience, including the British ambassador. And d'Alembert did justice to his friend's polemic, quoting the coarse words of Shakespeare's porters and grave-diggers with a theatrical reluctance that spoke eloquently of his distaste and then revelling in the prosodic jewels of Corneille and Racine, allowing them to hang gorgeously on the air. A triumph. But also a Pyrrhic victory. The Academy had done right by one of its Immortals, but the wider public was unconcerned. Moreover the King was displeased at this slight to his own patronage, and the Academy was forbidden to publish Voltaire's letter. (Needless to say, he published it himself anyway.) Worse still, Voltaire's friends were embarrassed. For he had travestied himself much more than the supposedly vulgar Clown of Avon. Even La Harpe (whom Voltaire had long since forgiven) held his tongue, when he of all people might have been expected to defend their shared aesthetic ideals. But the author of *Zaïre* and *Mahomet* now seemed no better than a ranting conservative who was completely out of touch – and who had lost his touch. If only he could come to Paris and show people what he really stood for.

CHAPTER TWENTY-TWO

The Last Act (1776–1778)

Our hero is bled, absolved and crowned

I N THE SUMMER OF 1776 it was just over a quarter of a century since Voltaire had last set foot in Paris. His name had remained in the public mind, but the complex reality of the man had been gradually superseded by the simple adorability – or detestability – of an idol. He was the champion of Calas and Sirven. For many Parisians and most of the French, he was a distant, fabulous figure even more remote than the King. In fact almost a god, whose almighty hand periodically intervened in the affairs of men and wrought miracles of justice. It was an agreeable way to be regarded, and Voltaire did nothing to dispel the myth in his fifty-page autobiography, the *Commentaire historique sur les œuvres de l'auteur de la Henriade (Historical Commentary on the Works of the Author of La Henriade)*, published anonymously towards the end of the summer. It had to be anonymous – and repeatedly disowned by its author – for it offered an extensive and detailed account of his greatness: not so much the greatness of his published works as the importance of his connections and the influence he had enjoyed in the highest places throughout a long and distinguished life. Above all, it portrayed a benefactor of humanity and a stout friend of the oppressed.

As the principal agent of his own apotheosis – and by way of assisting his future biographers – Voltaire was determined that his life should end with a rousing climax. The only proper stage for that climax was the city of his birth, and the best pretext for travelling to Paris was a new play. These terminal circumstances called for a tragedy in the grand and traditional manner. Surely the young King would not prevent his return for such a purpose? The very public attack on Shakespeare had had the satisfactory result of placing Voltaire's name on the lips of all Parisian theatre-goers: and the advanced publicity of the autobiography, together with all the reports of Lekain's performances at Ferney, ensured that it never left them. Although he had upset the King, he was still counting on the support of Marie-Antoinette, who had allowed Lekain to go to Ferney. So all he needed was the new play.

But his recent efforts had not augured well. *Sophonisbe* (1774) had been taken off after four performances at the Comédie-Française; *Les Pélopides*, another rewriting of Crébillon, had been rejected, as had *Don Pèdre*, begun in 1761 and resuscitated in 1774. But in the autumn of 1776 the King's brother invited Voltaire at very short notice to write something for a celebration he was arranging in honour of the Queen. The resulting concoction of verse, music and dance – on an Austrian theme and improvised in two days – was a great success, and encouraged Voltaire to work even harder on his new tragedy, *Alexis Comnène* (eventually to be entitled *Irène*). Set in eleventh-century Byzantium, this new play centred on the deposing of the Emperor Nicephorus by the brilliant young general, Prince Alexis. But this historical fact was a mere pretext for the invented predicament of Irène, married to the Emperor but in love with the Prince. Alas, Voltaire saw only too well that his new plot might better serve a comedy: 'I'm afraid that people may laugh at a woman who takes her own life rather than sleep with the man who has conquered and murdered her husband – when she doesn't love the husband and absolutely adores the murderer [. . .] You won't find a woman in Paris who would kill herself rather than be raped.'[1] And so far the script had only three acts. It needed five.

The stress began to tell. There was no lavish party on St Francis's Day that year: François preferred to play the grumpy recluse. Father Adam, now aged seventy-one, was told to leave in November. No more chess: he hadn't the time. The Pays de Gex still had to raise its 30,000 *livres*, and a solution was no nearer. The previous year Turgot had suggested a compromise: 20,000 to be paid by the landowners, the rest by the merchants and manufacturers. Much better, except that Voltaire was now liable for about half the 20,000. Turgot's national economic reforms having proved too radical for his own political good, he had now been replaced by Jacques Necker. A Genevan Protestant in charge of the French economy? Times were changing. So Voltaire appealed to the man whose wife had honoured him with a statue. The threat of a heavy tax burden was causing panic among the watchmakers of Ferney, who were beginning to leave. A judiciously temporizing letter from Necker saved the day, acknowledging their current tax-free status while refusing to enshrine it in legislation. This was one less problem to worry about, but only one. Voltaire's debtors continued to prove uncooperative, and his liabilities were growing in step with the developing economy of his colony. Above all, he did not wish to erode his capital. One particular sum of 300,000 *livres*, held in Paris, was earmarked as a legacy to be divided equally between Mme Denis, her brother the abbé Mignot, and her nephew Dompierre d'Hornoy. Though Voltaire pleaded poverty he was still as rich as Croesus.

Winter at Ferney could be unforgiving, and Voltaire's health suffered further from the rigour of the climate. So, too, did that of Mme Denis, who once more fell ill: the cold and damp played havoc with her chest. She had begun to hate the place. But Voltaire was proving remarkably resilient: a minor stroke, or fit of 'apoplexy', laid him temporarily low in March 1777, but there were no lasting consequences. Indeed he had now completed the fourth and fifth acts of *Irène* – and begun another tragedy. Just in case. Entitled *Agathocle*, it was to be set in ancient Sicily. Meanwhile he had agreed to contribute five articles to the periodical of which La Harpe had recently become editor, the *Journal de politique et de littérature*. In the first of these he slated Sterne's *Tristram Shandy* as the work of a charlatan: the author promises to tell you a story and never does. (Six years earlier, when the novel first appeared in French, he had taken a much less curmudgeonly view.) At the same time he was conducting his campaign in favour of legal reform by publishing a commentary on Montesquieu's *De l'esprit des lois* (*On the Spirit of the Law*) and entering for a competition recently launched by the Economic Society of Bern, which invited contestants to describe their ideal criminal justice system.

For Voltaire this was easy. Unlike the laws of nature (and therefore God), the laws of man are mutable and flawed. Often devised by the strong as the means of oppressing the weak, they should be reformed to protect the weak and inhibit the strong. In the France of 1777 the elements of such reform were plain: cease arbitrary imprisonment (the infamous *lettre de cachet* that lands the Ingénu in the Bastille, and indeed that his own father had once obtained with a view to his son's arrest); abolish interrogation under torture; open trial proceedings to the public; secure the rights of the defendant to a fair trial, including proper cross-questioning; conduct a thorough investigation of motive (instead of assuming all Protestants want to murder their children); punish in due proportion to the crime; improve prison conditions; end the death penalty; seek to prevent crime by more efficient deterrents and by eliminating the conditions that foster it (for example, begging and vagrancy); make punishment beneficial to the punished and to society at large; reward virtue. In other words, rather less tough on crime, and a whole lot tougher on the causes of crime.

It was a wonderful programme, and Voltaire ended his essay by reflecting how much greater a chance of implementation it stood than fifty years ago:

Look how almost every monarch in Europe now pays homage to a way of thinking that fifty years ago it would have been thought impossible even to suggest to them. Today there isn't a single province where some wise person is not trying to make men less wicked and less wretched. Wherever one looks, new organizations are being set up to encourage work, and hence virtue; wherever one looks, reason is making progress. Even the fanatics are worried. The only real discord is in North America, whereas Europe's monarchs are divided merely in their views as to what will do most good. Take advantage of this moment, for it may not last long.[2]

The North American discord, of course, was the War of Independence, carried out in the name of principles that Voltaire had espoused for three-quarters of a century. As to the European realm of sweetness and light, it was a heartwarming but implausible dream.

Voltaire published his essay with Grasset under the ambiguous title *Le Prix de la justice et de l'humanité* (*The Prize/Price of Justice and Humanity*). But it was such a good topic that instead of competing for the prize he doubled it by contributing his own fifty *louis* (1,200 *livres*) and called on his most influential correspondents (Frederick, Catherine, all the usual suspects) to follow his lead. No doubt he would also have asked Marie-Antoinette's brother, the recently crowned Emperor Joseph II of Austria, if this enlightened monarch had called to see him on his way back from Paris to Vienna. But much to Voltaire's disappointment he did not. On 13 July the Patriarch of Ferney had put on his finest wig and assembled various dignitaries — not to mention a large contingent of dragoons — to witness this auspicious encounter. He had no doubt that the studious and unstuffy young man who had been pursuing his love of science under the name of Graf von Falkenstein for the past three months would want to meet him. But the imperial carriage drove straight on to Versoix, despite being stopped by two intoxicated Ferney watchmakers who asked the occupant whether he had lost his way. Unfortunately they claimed to have been sent by Voltaire, which only confirmed the Emperor in the wisdom of his route-planning — and of his mother Maria Theresa's advice. The King of the Pays de Gex removed his wig and cleaned the egg from his face.

This was also a taste of his own medicine. For he had himself become as elusive as royalty. The man who had once held open house to the world now skulked in the bushes of his garden retreat. Worse, he would unceremonially evict important visitors for trespassing on his time. Of course he still loved being a celebrity, so he devised a thoroughly regal procedure. At a pre-announced hour he would emerge from his drawing-room to take a walk in his garden, and appropriately qualified persons were allowed to come and line his route. Carriage after carriage would enter the courtyard and deposit well-to-do sightseers while the 'people' pressed their noses to the iron gates and excitedly pointed him out at the climactic moment of his eventual appearance. But this year on St Francis's Day — his last — he made an exception and reinstated the tradition of public festivity. In the morning he took up position at the entrance to the château and there received the homage of his 'subjects'. Then he reviewed a parade of dragoons in the company of his special guest, the Landgrave von Hesse-Kassel (erstwhile supplier of asparagus plants). The parade was followed by a procession of shepherds and shepherdesses — some real ones, some pretend — who brought offerings of eggs and milk, fruit and flowers. It was like a harvest festival. As usual there was a grand dinner (only 200 guests this time), followed by fireworks and much singing and dancing. And as usual the grumpy old recluse turned into the life and soul of the party, surrounded by well-wishers and radiating energetic joy. At one point he was seen tossing his hat in the air out of sheer delight.

But there was one sorry moment. During the pastoral procession a demure young woman of twenty had blushingly presented Voltaire with two white doves, which she had tamed and nurtured herself. That evening he learnt that they had been cooked and eaten. They were pets, not food. And he felt especially sorry on behalf of the donor. For she was a new favourite of his. Born Reine Philiberte Rouph de Varicourt in 1757, she belonged to a noble but impoverished family of the locality. As did her eight brothers and one elder sister. She was tall, good-looking, intelligent and kind – but without a dowry. Rather than see her consigned to a convent at the age of eighteen, Voltaire had therefore invited her to become Mme Denis's companion. He had also nicknamed her 'Belle et Bonne', for she was both beautiful and good. And he proceeded to dote on her with a grandfatherly affection that did not entirely preclude a quite evident susceptibility to her charms. But these charms were reserved for another, a soon-to-be-reformed bounder called Charles Michel, marquis de Villette. And he too was a favourite. Together this couple were about to play a key role in Voltaire's last days – and beyond.

The marquis de Villette, now forty-two, was the son of an extremely rich parvenu who had only recently acquired his title (in 1763). After a period of spectacular youthful dissipation Charles Michel embarked on an undistinguished military career that included being wounded at the Battle of Minden in 1759 and eventually ended in scandal. Imprisoned and then released, he was banished from Paris for a period of two years, which gave him the idea of visiting Voltaire – that other 'exile' – in February 1765. Voltaire had known his mother back in 1734 when her reputation was such as to allow her son much later to spread the (probably unfounded) rumour that he was Voltaire's son. Born on 1 December 1734, the boy's conception would indeed have occurred at a moment when Voltaire's relationship with Mme du Châtelet had temporarily founded on the rock of her affair with Maupertuis. But the putative lover was then quite ill, and subsequently he never gave any hint of his paternity. Yet the marquis de Villette was, if nothing else, a symbolic son of Voltaire and grandson of the chevalier de Rochebrune. For he was a born poet and performer. He was very widely read, could recite innumerable poems by heart and write good ones of his own, told wonderful stories, and did impressions of people that rivalled the younger Voltaire's in their wit and accuracy. And he was an intelligent freethinker. His smitten host harboured high hopes of his capacities as a warrior against the *Infâme*.

But Villette had less worthy pastimes. Having inherited his father's wealth and title in April 1765, he proceeded to contract a host of new debts even as he paid off the old ones. He thrived on controversy, not least if it concerned the nature of his uncertain sexual orientation, and he was given to insulting women. His abuse of Sophie Arnould, the leading opera singer of the moment, led to a duel with her lover and the subsequent imprisonment of both men. Obscene verses attacking a lesbian actress, Mlle Raucourt, almost led to a third incarceration. Another incident in Paris during the summer of 1777 – when he slapped a dancer and avoided a duel with her lover – had prompted this latest visit to Ferney, where he arrived at the end of September. And then he met Belle et Bonne. The dastardly marquis fell in love at once and proposed to her – in verse – on the very evening of St Francis's Day. Strongly encouraged by Voltaire and despite what she may have known about her suitor, Reine de Varicourt accepted. She believed Villette to be sincere in his affections, and for a man of such wealth (and title) to propose to her when she had no dowry was an opportunity not to be missed. The couple were married at midnight on 19–20 November in Ferney church. As the bride was preparing herself for the wedding, Voltaire came and presented her with a magnificent diamond necklace, which he fastened round her neck. Then he gave her an empty ledger, bound in morocco leather, and advised her to keep a daily record of her income and expenses. If she made sure to balance this book, she would be rich and happy. Gilt-edged advice to go with its gilt-edged pages – and no doubt obliquely intended for the bridegroom.

Among the many estates and residences that Villette had inherited and not yet managed to squander was a magnificent town house in Paris, at the corner of the rue de Beaune and the quai des Théatins (now the quai Voltaire) – the very place where Voltaire had lived over half a century ago, in 1722, when it had belonged to the marquis de Bernières and when the marquise had been his mistress. Villette had transformed the place, creating imposing entrances, adding a fourth floor, and letting out the second to a homosexual friend,

Thibouville. He himself lived in luxurious apartments on the first floor, and it was to these that he now intended to take his new bride. And Voltaire, too, if he wished to join them.

He did, very much. But it still all depended on the play. And on the Comédie-Française. On 2 January 1778 the company listened to a reading of *Irène* – in the absence of Lekain, who was unwell – and agreed to perform it, more out of gratitude towards its author (who had brought them so much artistic and financial success in the past) than out of any enthusiasm for the play itself. When Lekain refused the leading role, however, on the genuine grounds of ill health, Voltaire took it as a slight and ordered the company to suspend all preparations for the play. He would come and supervise this production himself.

But when? Ever the master of timing, Voltaire now carefully prepared and delayed his entrance. As the days went by, more and more people in Paris asked not if but when he was coming. Louis XVI bid his ministers search for the documentation that might support the ban his grandfather had imposed, but there was nothing to be found, not even a trace of the *lettre de cachet* that had once been issued after the publication of the *Lettres philosophiques*. In any case Louis's ministers saw no objection to Voltaire's return. The world had moved on, and many influential people actively welcomed it. But the young King was nervous – about this as about so much else – and his nervousness expressed itself as reactionary opposition to change. Nevertheless there was very little he could do, as Voltaire realized. Once the celebrity had arrived in Paris, it would be very difficult to send him away. And so, on the morning of Tuesday, 3 February, a carriage left Ferney, containing Mme Denis and the marquis and marquise de Villette (and her unborn baby). Two days later Voltaire departed from Ferney in the company of his secretary and his cook. He imagined that he would be absent for about six weeks, but nevertheless there were long and tearful farewells. His 'subjects' were distressed to see him leave, for given his age it was not certain that he would return. And indeed he would not.

The journey was long but not uncomfortable. The carriage itself was the 'dormeuse', especially designed and built for long journeys, and complete with a stove to warm its occupants. The exterior was painted blue and sprinkled with stars, as though telling of the Almighty's presence inside. Sometimes Voltaire would read, or ask Wagnière to read to him. Sometimes he would tell stories that left his secretary (our witness) quite helpless with laughter. Especially after Voltaire had pressed him to another drink: rather than play 'I spy', the great man had decided to relieve the tedium of the journey by getting his strait-laced secretary drunk. At each staging post their cosy intimacy was replaced by boisterous public acclamation. In Nantua (between Geneva and Bourg) the whole town turned out to welcome this famous man and then again the next morning to cheer him on his way. In Dijon sundry grandees assembled to greet him, and some even disguised themselves as servants so that they could attend a Voltairean supper. He had planned to spend some days here on legal business, but the crowds made him cut short his stay. After spending the next night at Joigny he was heading for Moret when the axle broke: the equivalent of today's puncture, though rather less quickly mended. But Villette had been coming to meet him, and he now brought Voltaire and his two companions safely to their intended inn. Next day (10 February) they left for Paris, and reached the customs barrier at about 3.30 in the afternoon. When the officials asked if they were carrying anything 'contrary to the King's orders', Voltaire replied: 'I rather think the only contraband is me.' At which point one of the officials realized who he was dealing with: 'By God, it's Monsieur de Voltaire!' The search was suspended at once, and the carriage proceeded on its way, leaving a number of awestruck customs men wondering what they had just seen. A gentleman, a ghost, a god?

   Voltaire now entered Paris. How different from the last time he had been there . . .

As soon as Voltaire arrived at the Villette residence, he set off again at once for the reunion that he cared about above all: with the comte d'Argental, who had remained such a loyal and judicious friend throughout the long years of his absence. His guardian 'angel', as he called him, lived close by on the quai d'Orsay, and so Voltaire walked. It was good to smell the river and the dung-strewn streets, to hear the bustle and clatter of the world's second-largest city, and to take in all the familiar sights: the bridges staggering across the Seine to the Île de la Cité under the weight of their houses, the spire of the Sainte-Chapelle and the sprawl of the Palais de Justice, the twin towers of Notre-Dame in the distance. And he, too, was a sight. It was carnival time, and passers-by laughed at this clown in his thick fur coat, at his old-fashioned wig and his extraordinary red bonnet that resembled nothing more than a plump tea cosy. Gilles-Voltaire had arrived, and nobody recognized him. Street urchins jeered. At this historic moment it transpired that the 'angel' was out, but d'Argental hurried round soon afterwards to the rue de Beaune for their long-awaited embrace. And he came with shocking news: Lekain had died two days earlier, at the age of forty-eight. They had buried him that very morning in the church at Saint-Sulpice (for with his last performance the great actor had secured religious absolution from the mortal sin of his profession). Voltaire was heartbroken – and dismayed. 'I am neither prejudiced nor superstitious,' he is reported to have said, 'but if the actor is dead, the author will not go far.'[3]

In the days which followed, *le tout Paris* came to visit. The marquis de Villette and his wife, together with Mme Denis, did the honours while Voltaire made brief appearances to be introduced to – or reunited with – especially significant callers. He wanted as much time as he could decently reserve for the improvement of *Irène*. Mme du Deffand – she who had declined to contribute to the cost of his statue – informed him with her usual affectionate wit that she would look forward to meeting him again in a day or two, when the rush was over. Unless of course he had died in the meantime. The rush included Necker and Turgot (who thought Voltaire unchanged from when he had last met him eighteen years earlier), and several well-disposed members of the Academy, who came at d'Alembert's suggestion to bid their fellow-academician ceremonial welcome. (Needless to say, the ecclesiastical Immortals found that they had other engagements.) On Friday 13 February Théodore Tronchin, his former doctor, called at Voltaire's behest. The journey and the change of routine had quite put paid to his 'regularity', and the laxative he was accustomed to using three times a week was no longer working. This was important: for as one of Voltaire's characters had pointed out in his penultimate *conte*, *Les Oreilles du comte de Chesterfield* (*The Earl of Chesterfield's Ears*) – and in mock-materialist vein – the key determinant of human behaviour is neither sex nor ambition nor money but the commode (*la chaise percée*). Bowel movements make the world go round. Unpersuaded of the fundamental importance of his patient's complaint, the eminent Tronchin prescribed an alternative and departed. But he would soon be back: the reluctant doctor to a man he had never liked and who always thought he could diagnose himself better.

On Saturday it was the turn of the Comédie-Française to pay an official visit and to share their grief at Lekain's untimely death. Discussion turned to *Irène*, on which Voltaire was spending every spare waking moment. He wanted it premiered before Easter, and it was time to distribute the roles. Perhaps they could have a preliminary run-through tomorrow (Sunday? These actors *were* godless). But Voltaire's legs had now started to swell again, and Tronchin forbade him to go out. So the troupe returned to the rue de Beaune and read through the play in the presence of Voltaire and his old friend Richelieu. The two elderly gentlemen had celebrated their reunion by having a row, with Voltaire complaining that the maréchal never answered his letters and the maréchal complaining that the great writer had stopped sending him free copies of his books. But the pair had now made up, and Richelieu was ready to bring to bear on the proceedings all the experience he had acquired after many decades of organizing royal entertainments. The roles were duly distributed.

Next day it was the turn of Benjamin Franklin to visit. He had come to Paris as the representative of the American Congress in order to sign the treaty (6 February) that now made France the friend and supporter of the new republic. Franklin had been an enthusiastic reader of Voltaire for the past forty-five years, while Voltaire admired the American as an eminent scientist and the 'inventor of electricity'. Theirs was an enormously symbolic meeting, especially when Franklin ushered his eight-year-old grandson Benjamin forward to ask for the Patriarch's blessing. Voltaire placed his elderly hands on the young boy's head and duly blessed him in the name of 'God and Liberty'. It was a public-relations triumph, for both parties. Voltaire had associated himself with republicanism and the new, while the word 'Liberty' secured for Franklin the repeatable evidence that the champion of Calas supported American independence. When Lord Stormont, the British ambassador, called an hour later to pay his respects to France's most eminent anglophile, he had perforce to display the stiff upper lip that had served him so well on the occasion of Voltaire's previous diatribe against Shakespeare in the Academy.

And so it went. The star was in excellent spirits, buoyed up by the excitement of his return and the extraordinary public acclaim. In salon and newspaper, in coffee-house and tavern, he was – Franklin apart – the exclusive centre of attention. But his health was clearly deteriorating. His prostate and bladder were now both in the advanced stages of cancer (as a post-mortem examination was soon to reveal), and he was passing and excreting pus in an alarming way. Tronchin, unable to dissect his patient, simply diagnosed old age and overwork. He ordered him to rest. And would have instructed Voltaire's hosts to ensure this rest, except that they were temporarily absent. So he left a peremptory note:

> I would very much have liked to tell M. le marquis de Villette in person that, ever since his arrival in Paris, M. de Voltaire has been spending the capital of his strength and energy; and that all his real friends surely wish him to live on the income only. Moreover, the way things are going, this capital will soon be used up, and we shall all soon be witnesses, if not accomplices, to the death of M. de Voltaire.[4]

Then, just for good measure, Tronchin sent a copy of this note to the *Journal de Paris*, who published it a day or so later.

Voltaire was himself keenly aware of his perilous physical state, and he worried about the consequences of dying in Paris. The Villette residence was in the parish of Saint-Sulpice, which was precisely where the body of Adrienne Lecouvreur had been refused a Christian burial all those years ago and ignominiously buried like a bag of rubbish. Lekain, of course, had fared better, but Voltaire was not going to renounce his sinful past for anyone. The clergy themselves were no less apprehensive. A recantation would be wonderful, but the likelihood was that Monsieur de Voltaire would once again play them false. The curate of Saint-Sulpice, M. de Tersac, had particular reason to be anxious and had been trying unsuccessfully for some days to secure a meeting with his illustrious new parishioner.

On 20 February Voltaire's (unofficial) eighty-fourth birthday was marked by a visit from Mme du Barry, the now-redundant royal mistress, and the receipt of a letter from a local priest, the abbé Gaultier (who had seen Tronchin's note in the paper). The letter was an especially welcome birthday present for it suggested to its recipient that here was somebody with whom he might be able to do satisfactory confessional business. A preliminary meeting the next day confirmed the judgement: Gaultier was a 'kind fool'.[5] Which was just as well, because Voltaire's condition now assumed an alarming new dimension. Just after noon on Wednesday, 25 February, he was sitting in bed dictating to Wagnière when a coughing fit caused a bronchial artery to burst and blood started pouring from his mouth and nose. Tronchin was summoned and duly bled him further. The patient was forbidden to speak, to be spoken to, or to have visitors. Though he continued to spit blood for the next three weeks, the said patient defied his doctor with his incurable loquacity. For a wordless Voltaire might as well be dead. And of course he would need to speak if he was to confess . . . Gaultier was summoned, but the curate of Saint-Sulpice arrived instead. He was summarily dismissed by Mme Denis: her uncle wished only for the abbé Gaultier.

The latter, duly authorized by the Archbishop of Paris, Christophe de Beaumont, arrived on Monday, 2 March. He was greeted at Voltaire's bedside by Wagnière, the marquis de Villevielle (a relative of Villette's), and Mme Denis's brother, the abbé Mignot. They politely withdrew, but the ever-faithful Wagnière performed his usual service of leaving the door ajar and standing guard – ready to intervene if his master should be tricked into some dishonourable recantation, and poised to record what transpired. Voltaire had prepared his own written 'confession': 'I die worshipping God, loving my friends, not hating my enemies, and detesting superstition.'[6] But the Church, of course, had a rather longer text in mind. So Wagnière was ordered to fetch pen and paper, and Voltaire wrote out the following statement in his own rather shaky hand:

> I, the undersigned, hereby declare that at the age of eighty-four, having vomited blood for the past four days and being unable to get as far as the church, and Monsieur le curé de Saint-Sulpice having been kind enough to add to the number of his good works that of sending me a priest, Monsieur l'abbé Gaultier, I have said my confession to him; and that if God disposes of me, I shall die in the holy Catholic religion into which I was born, hoping that God in His divine mercy will deign to forgive me all my errors; and that if I have offended the Church I beg forgiveness of God and of it.[7]

Not a word about faith, not a word about sin. But it was enough for his 'kind fool', who realized its inadequacies but nevertheless absolved the penitent deist. On receiving Voltaire's signed 'confession', together with 600 *livres* to be spent on the poor of his parish, the abbé Gaultier then asked the three witnesses to sign. Villevielle and Mignot agreed, but Wagnière refused on the grounds that he was a Protestant. His employer was astonished. When Gaultier then proposed that Voltaire take communion, the sick man rather blasphemously refused: 'Monsieur l'abbé, I would remind you that I am constantly spitting blood. We really must avoid getting the Almighty's blood mixed up with mine.'[8] The priest was then shown the door – and refused admittance every time he subsequently called. As Voltaire's friends and fellow-*philosophes* realized, the deist had done the very minimum in order to observe the niceties: 'If I were living on the banks of the Ganges I would very happily die with a cow's tail in my hand.'[9] But he was mistaken if he thought he had done enough to secure a Christian burial.

There were now two weeks to go until the first night of *Irène*, and Voltaire began to recover his strength a little. Tronchin continued in vain to forbid him to speak, and the players of the Comédie-Française came to his bedside to rehearse. Voltaire was disappointed to discover that a visit to Versailles was out of the question. Though the Queen was well disposed, and indeed interested to meet the playwright if not the *philosophe*, her husband regarded him as the devil incarnate. But soon a rumour began to circulate that the Queen intended to attend the first night, which indeed she did. On Monday, 16 March she and her retinue – along with 1,185 Parisian theatre-goers – arrived at the large hall in the Tuileries palace that was now the Comédie-Française's temporary home. *Le tout Paris* again was there, apart from the King – and apart from Voltaire. He was too ill to attend. The play triumphed, less because of its intrinsic merits (which were few) than because everyone was determined to celebrate the return of 'Sophocles' to the city of his birth. It was a question of national prestige, and there was even talk that the authorities had forbidden all adverse criticism in the press. Bad reviews of Voltaire censored? Times *had* changed. For the man himself it was all very gratifying, suggesting even that good taste had not irretrievably vanished from the world of Parisian theatre. He was even more gratified when the company displayed his bust in its foyer alongside that of Corneille. For it had been their unswerving tradition never thus to honour a living writer.

On 21 March Voltaire was well enough to venture out for a carriage ride, his first since returning to Paris nearly six weeks earlier. He wanted to visit the newly created Place Louis XV (now the Place de la Concorde) and to see the work being carried out on the tree-lined promenades that were then being laid out across the Champs-Élysées, leading to the new bridge across the Seine at Neuilly. The city moat prevented further exploration.[10] But through the trees he could just make out the Hôtel d'Évreux, completed in the early 1720s and later acquired for Mme de Pompadour in the 1740s as her Paris residence. She had found it convenient for her shopping trips along the rue Saint-Honoré. (The elegant mansion was later renamed the Élysée palace, and since 1871 has been the official residence of presidents of the French Republic.)[11] Soon Voltaire was surrounded by a throng all straining to catch a glimpse of this living legend.

With each performance of *Irène* it was rumoured that 'Sophocles' would at last be well enough to attend in person, which of course did wonders for the ticket-sales. But on Monday, 30 March Voltaire did at last attend. It was his day of triumph. Early in the afternoon, enveloped in a sable coat lined with crimson velvet, he set off in his star-spangled carriage for the Louvre, where he was to be welcomed by the Academy. Here, in another break with tradition (and no doubt at d'Alembert's suggestion), some twenty of a possible forty Immortals gathered in the entrance hall to greet Voltaire before accompanying him into their meeting-room. Here they invited him to preside – another honour, since this function was usually filled by lot – and he addressed them with warm gratitude. Including two abbés who, unlike the immortal bishops, had risked damnation to attend. Then d'Alembert read out a eulogy in which he compared his friend's poetic skills with those of Boileau and Racine, for it was principally as a verse dramatist that Voltaire had been elected in April 1746. From the Louvre Voltaire proceeded in his carriage to the nearby Tuileries, acclaimed on all sides by the crowd. The play was to begin at 5.30 p.m. As he entered the theatre there was a huge roar of greeting from the expectant audience, and everyone strained for a view as he shed his voluminous fur and took up position in his box. Situated on the second tier, immediately to the left of the stage, this was the box reserved for Gentlemen of the Royal Bedchamber, and in the usual way he bid his ladies – Mme Denis and the marquise de Villette – take their place in the front two seats. But he was soon obliged to join them there by a clamorous audience determined to get a good view of this extraordinary phenomenon. He had once quipped to d'Argental that he worried about appearing in person 'in case he was mistaken for one of Shakespeare's ghosts',[12] but to the assembled company he was finally – most wonderfully and unexpectedly – alive.

And then he was crowned. Brizard, the elder statesman of the Comédie-Française, entered his box holding a laurel wreath and invited the marquise de Villette – Voltaire's favourite Belle et Bonne – to place it on the great man's head. There it remained for a few minutes, but, whether out of modesty or for fear of looking ridiculous, Voltaire preferred to watch *Irène* uncrowned. Twenty tumultuous minutes later the play began. The actors excelled themselves in their roles, but their efforts were wasted: the audience had come not to weep but to cheer, and cheer they did, at almost every line. At the end the author rose to acknowledge their enthusiasm. Then the curtain rose unexpectedly once more. Voltaire's bust had been brought from the foyer and set on a pedestal, where it was now surrounded by all the members of the Comédie-Française holding garlands and wreaths. Mme Vestris, who had performed in the leading role, recited some verse, including the lines: 'No, you have no need to reach that black shore / In order to enjoy the honours of immortality'; and then each player came forward and crowned the bust with a wreath or garland. And to round the evening off, they now performed a comedy – his own *Nanine*.

At the end of the performance the cheering was even more tumultuous. Voltaire – pale, exhausted, his eyes wet with tears – waved and took his leave. Outside the theatre another crowd awaited: the people of Paris, from fat merchant to bedraggled vagrant, from streetwise stallholder to dust-covered mason, from slender flower-girl to bustling mother-of-five. They called for torches the better to see their new idol, and they shouted their approval: 'Long live the defender of Calas'. The more intrepid climbed on to his carriage in the hope of shaking his hand: even the hem of his garment would have done. The atmosphere was one of sentimental joy. The detail of Voltaire's achievements was known to few who participated in the scene, but they had come to marvel at a frail, elderly man who – they sensed – had triumphed against the odds. There was no pre-revolutionary anger in their cheering. Rather Voltaire had, by his very presence, united the highly disparate members of this throng and given them hope in the midst of their individual fears and tribulations. He was an icon – a hero, a saint, a god – and he was here fulfilling the role usually played by the monarch. Yet the King and Queen were conspicuous by their absence. And by this very absence the royal couple foolishly displayed their growing irrelevance to the life of the French nation.

ANECDOTE TÉATRALE DE L'HOMME UNIQUE A TOUT AGE

Crowning of Voltaire at the Théâtre Français (Comédie-Française) in 1778 (engraving).

CHAPTER TWENTY-THREE

Out Like a Candle (March–May 1778)

Wherein we learn how to bury an infidel and to keep the flame burning

V OLTAIRE NOW HAD six weeks to live. But he behaved as if he were indestructible. He had intended to return to Ferney for Easter, but he was enjoying himself so much in the capital that he began to think of settling there. Mme Denis was delighted and went house-hunting at once. Various attractive properties were to let, but there was one for sale – in the rue de Richelieu, leading north from the Palais-Royal and the Louvre – which would be just right. Choiseul lived opposite (so the neighbourhood was smart), while other friends and entertaining salon hostesses lived conveniently close. It would also be handy for the Tuileries. The contract was signed on 30 April. Unfortunately the house was more or less unbuilt: four walls and a magnificent staircase alone gave substance to the splendour of the plans. Voltaire's optimism temporarily failed as he threw himself into Wagnière's arms on the way home from the notary's and exclaimed: 'Ah, my friend, I have bought a house, but all I have acquired is my tomb.'[1]

Although he was still the object of disapproval at Versailles, and of course in high ecclesiastical circles, it was now clear that no official steps would be taken to banish him. 'After 30 years of absence and 60 years of persecution',[2] he had earned the right to stay. In any case he had become a folk hero: all manner of sketches and engravings were in circulation, whether caricature or from life, depicting him in every possible pose and garb. More lastingly the up-and-coming sculptor Houdon now immortalized both himself and his subject by creating the famous bust that has come down to posterity as the most expressive and beautiful likeness of the ageing *philosophe*. Voltaire had become an institution whom now only God could remove from the scene.

It was customary for theatres to close for three weeks at Easter, and at the Comédie-Française tradition demanded that the honour of the last perfor-mance before the recess be accorded to a play of recent or time-honoured note. And so on Saturday, 4 April Voltaire returned to the Tuileries to watch *Irène* and to listen to Molé – Lekain's successor as the male lead – bore the audience with an end-of-term speech about the season's highlights. It was an anticlimax after the heady atmosphere of the previous Monday. More exciting were the many visits that he continued to receive, not least from his fellow-*philosophe*, Diderot. The editor of the *Encyclopédie* had his reservations about Voltaire – about his combative personality, about his deism, about his new antipathy to Shakespeare – and he later commented that it was like meeting a ruined fairy castle: 'but you soon realized that an old sorcerer still lived inside'.[3] As to the sorcerer, he found his guest rather talkative, and he could hardly get a word in. (A month earlier Tronchin would have considered Diderot the ideal visitor.) Unused to this experience, Voltaire subsequently observed that the man lacked one essential talent: the art of conversation. And this of a writer subsequently recognized as a master of the philosophical dialogue. Plainly the two men were ill-equipped for their meeting, for each of them liked to play all the parts.

Voltaire was now well enough to visit as well as be visited. And off he went to see some leading ladies: Sophie Arnould, the diva whom Villette had insulted; Mme du Deffand, to return the compliment of her own visit; and Suzanne de Livry, his old flame from sixty years before. Voltaire had written to her some three years earlier, at the time of her husband's death, and he was eager to see her again. On Tuesday, 7 April, Suzanne – now the marquise de La Tour Du Pin Gouvernet – received him fondly, and as they sat in her drawing-room they gazed at the portrait of the young Voltaire painted all those years ago by Largillière. How he had changed! And to think of all that had happened since! After he left she gave orders for the painting to be taken round to the rue de Beaune. It was a present, in memory of their past love. The recipient, meanwhile, had other visits to make. He now proceeded to the masonic lodge of the Nine Sisters, in the rue du Pot-de-fer – in a building formerly occupied by the Jesuits – and was there admitted as a freemason. Contrary to rumour he had never before belonged to a masonic order, and indeed had ridiculed masonic practices. But recent reforms had included the foundation of this particular lodge, whose members were sympathetic to the 'new ideas'. They had ceremonially welcomed Voltaire upon his arrival in Paris, and here again he wished to return the compliment.

And there were plays to go to. The Comédie-Française might be closed, but at the Palais-Royal the duc d'Orléans and his morganatic wife, Mme de Montesson, had a theatre of their own. Louis-Philippe, duc d'Orléans, was the grandson of the Regent who had twice put Voltaire in the Bastille. Rather as the duc and duchesse du Maine had once sought to rival Versailles, so the duc d'Orléans presided over a liberal and cultivated court that far outshone that of his cousin, Louis XVI. When the Revolution came, his son – Louis-Philippe-Joseph, duc de Chartres – supported its activists from the start, took the name of Philippe-Égalité on being elected to the Convention in 1792, voted for the execution of his cousin in 1793, and died on the scaffold himself in the same year. His grandson, also Louis-Philippe, would become king following the revolution of 1830. The present duc d'Orléans and his wife were enthusiastic theatre-lovers, and on the evening of 7 April they welcomed Voltaire and his fellow-masons (plus some 250 other guests) to a performance of *Nanine*. Two days later he returned for a performance of Mme de Montesson's own comedy, *L'Amant romanesque* (*The Romantic Lover*), when her son, the future Philippe-Égalité – then in his late twenties – took every opportunity to engage him in conversation. On 11 April Voltaire visited again in order to meet the young duke's children and was greeted by the duc and duchesse de Chartres with a lack of formality that left the former courtier thoroughly astonished at the genuineness and warmth of the royal couple. At the end of his life Voltaire had met a young prince who was considerably more radical then himself. And he may even have dandled his son, the future king of France, on his bony knee.

The Comédie-Française would soon be open again, and Voltaire was hoping that they might take on *Agathocle*. He must do some work on it. And wouldn't it be better if they called themselves the Théâtre Français instead? Wasn't it silly to be known as 'comédiens' when they mainly performed tragedies? (Four years later the name was changed, only later to revert.) But above all there was the Academy to think of. Having been invited to be its president – by men who no doubt foresaw a brief and honorific term of office – Voltaire decided to galvanize his fellow-Immortals into action. The Academy had been founded (by Cardinal Richelieu in 1637) with the specific aim of 'perfecting' the French language, and its principal *raison d'être* was the compilation of a dictionary. The first edition appeared in the year of Voltaire's birth, and there had been three since. But this dictionary was prescriptive and exclusive rather than descriptive and comprehensive, a stern guide to polite usage rather than a compendious treasury of verbal riches. Which is what Voltaire now proposed. In short, a linguistic revolution. All words were to be admitted, whatever their origin and class. Those with a dubious past were to be rescued from obscurity in the full glory of contextual quotation. Everything that had been purified out of the language was to be restored, warts and all, to the corporate memory of the nation. It was an ambition that Voltaire had cherished since the 1760s, and on 7 May he harangued the academicians with an account of its virtues. They would eventually see the light.

But for Voltaire the light was beginning to fade. Towards the end of April his health gave renewed cause for concern. He complained to Tronchin of excruciating pain in his lower abdomen and sought relief in wine and quinine. Having decided that in future he would spend most of the year in Paris, he still intended to travel back to Ferney for the summer. And Tronchin told him that he was well enough to do so. But through Villette's friend Thibouville he now heard from well-placed sources that Louis XVI was intending to prevent his return to the capital. So he decided against the journey and dispatched a reluctant Wagnière on 1 May to deal with the backlog of business affairs on his behalf (with full powers of attorney). Anyway he was still having too much fun to leave. Four days earlier, he had attended the opening night of the new season at the Comédie-Française, for which the company had wisely decided to ignore *Irène* in favour of an old favourite, *Alzire*. In order not to steal the limelight, its author abandoned his usual box for that of an acquaintance, sitting as far back in its darkness as he could. But he could not escape the roving lorgnette. The performance was interrupted for forty-five minutes as this particular audience paid its adoring tribute. On 29 April it was the turn of the Académie des Sciences, where he was seated beside Benjamin Franklin. Sophocles and Solon, said the amateurs of classical reference: two distinguished men who had each in his own way changed the course of history.

On Saturday, 9 May Voltaire was due to attend another meeting of the Academy, with a view to pushing through his plan for a new dictionary. Too exhausted to attend but anxious that his absence would allow opponents of the project to prevail, he sat up half the night – sustained by copious amounts of coffee – to write a speech for the next meeting, to be held on Monday. But on Sunday afternoon he felt particularly unwell, and after a short walk in pursuit of some fresh air he returned home to bed. His temperature rose, and the pain was acute. Tronchin prescribed opium – in small doses – which the patient subsequently consumed to considerable excess. He was clearly desperate for relief and unwilling to take his doctor's advice that small doses would procure it in sufficient measure. A servant was sent out to the apothecary several times that night. The result was inevitable: a prolonged period of delirium. After this the pain was even more excruciating, and it was almost impossible for Voltaire to urinate. He was not a model patient. He shouted and screamed, writhed and groaned, blamed everyone for murdering him, whether doctor or friend, and heartily wished he had never come back to Paris in the first place. But that was his way of coping. Thanks to the soothing effects of laudanum he continued to work: by corresponding with Wagnière about Ferney business, by pursuing the battle over his latest dictionary, by receiving members of the Comédie-Française to discuss their forthcoming productions. His body might be failing, but his mind was as sharp as ever.

Voltaire had begun life by refusing to die, and he had no intention of giving up now. But his bowels had different ideas. They ceased to move. And with them his world. Come Saturday, 23 May the end was clearly nigh, and on Monday Mme Denis wrote to Wagnière in Ferney to summon him back. She had always resented his centrality in Voltaire's life, and he had always suspected her of wishing only for a speedy inheritance. Now he retro-spectively accused her of neglecting his master, whereas she had more probably been playing down Voltaire's latest illness in order to keep Wagnière at Ferney. Which was where her uncle badly needed him to be. As to 'neglect', Voltaire had been at death's door ever since she had lived with him: it was very difficult to believe that this was really it. But it was. He had now virtually stopped eating. Worse, he had virtually stopped talking. On 26 May he learnt that the royal council had thrown out the sentence handed down by the Paris *parlement* on the innocent Lally. It was his last victory, and it occasioned his last written words (dictated to a secretary), a brief letter of congratulation to Lally's son: 'The dying man revives on hearing this great news: he embraces M. Lally most tenderly; he sees that the King is a defender of justice: he will die happy.' And he ordered the news to be pinned on a piece of drapery where he could look at it: 'On 26 May the legal murder carried out by Pasquier [the judge who had presided in the Lally case – and in that of La Barre] on the person of Lally has been avenged by the royal council.'

The clergy now circled like vultures. Voltaire's 'recantation' of 2 March would not suffice, and the abbé Gaultier had been sidelined. At the instigation of the Archbishop the young firebrand curate of Saint-Sulpice, M. de Tersac, had tried once again to gain access to his notorious parishioner and was threatening to refuse him a Christian burial. The matter was becoming one of national importance, and there was extensive debate about the legality of such a refusal. Condorcet in particular was eloquent in his objections to the curate's threat. But both Mignot – Voltaire's nephew was only nominally an abbé – and Dompierre d'Hornoy (his grand-nephew) were lawyers, and they doubted if a legal appeal to the *parlement* would meet with success. The King washed his hands of the affair, regarding it as an exclusively ecclesiastical question. The Church itself was divided, and many clergymen were opposed to the zealous curate's line. Several felt that it would have been much wiser not to make an issue of it. For what might the people of Paris not do if they saw their hero thus treated? Quickly the Archbishop came to see the benefits of a fudge, and both Lenoir, Lieutenant of Police, and Amelot, the minister in charge of law and order, were keen to achieve it. Lenoir and Mignot met and planned a compromise: upon Voltaire's death the body would be transported to Ferney as though he were still alive. The point was to remove him from Paris before the public realized he was dead, but at Maurepas's sensible suggestion it was further agreed that the cortège might stop some seven or eight miles beyond the city walls so that the body could be embalmed in preparation for its long journey. To aid the fiction,

Amelot gave Dompierre d'Hornoy an official letter approving Voltaire's passage across France in the event of his dying *en route* to his home at Ferney.

This was Wednesday, 27 May. The dying man had now entered a period of terminal calm. He barely spoke. Occasionally he took some orange jelly or sucked on small lumps of ice to soothe his fever. Close friends and relatives awaited the inevitable: Mme Denis, Belle et Bonne and her husband Villette, Mignot, Dompierre d'Hornoy, Wagnière, Villevielle, Richelieu, d'Argental . . . Lenoir had ordered a media blackout, so the people of Paris were unaware how close the end now was. But the abbé Gaultier knew, and he wrote to Voltaire, urging him once more to confess. Dated and received on Saturday, 30 May, the letter prompted Mignot to fetch Gaultier at once. But the abbé insisted on being accompanied by de Tersac. The two priests arrived towards the end of the afternoon, still hoping to get Voltaire to sign a recantation. Eye-witnesses later tallied in their account of what ensued. First, de Tersac asked Voltaire if he believed in the divinity of Jesus Christ. The dying man did not hear – or pretended not to hear. Believing the former to be true, the marquis de Villevielle then shouted in Voltaire's ear: 'Monsieur l'abbé Gaultier is here. Your confessor.' To everyone's astonishment there came a reply: 'Monsieur l'abbé Gaultier? My confessor? Then be sure to give him my compliments.' M. de Tersac was presented in a similar manner and hesitantly repeated his question: 'Monsieur, do you recognize the divinity of Jesus Christ?' Voltaire then reached out a hand and shoved the priest away. 'Let me die in peace,' he said and turned over on his side, his back stubbornly turned on the persistent priest.

The two clerics insisted no further and departed, consoling themselves with the belief that their would-be penitent was no longer in his right mind. But it had never been righter. Some ten minutes before his death he grasped the hand of his valet, Morand, and said: 'Adieu, my dear Morand, I am dying.' A few minutes later he took his own pulse and shook his head. No one knows what his last, mumbled words were, but it seems that his last thoughts were for Mme Denis. Everyone was to take good care of her.

Shortly after 11 p.m. on Saturday, 30 May 1778 Voltaire died.

And now where would he go? Despite his April foolery with the Bishop of Annecy ten years earlier, Voltaire had realized that a Christian burial at

Ferney was out of the question. The pyramid he had built would have to remain empty of its pharaoh. Instead he had envisaged being taken from Ferney at the eleventh hour to a rented house on the Swiss side of the border. There he could die on Protestant soil, untroubled by any need for absolution and the last rites. Subsequently his body was to be brought back to Ferney and entombed in the bathhouse. This small pavilion, adjacent to his library and his favourite garden walk, would make a splendid mausoleum.

But Ferney was a long way from Paris, and the techniques of mummification were not what they were in ancient Egypt. He would have to be buried somewhere closer to Paris. The abbé Mignot had planned for the moment meticulously. Shortly before Voltaire's death he had obtained from the abbé Gaultier a simple signed statement: 'I declare that I was called to hear M. de Voltaire's confession, and that I found him unable to make himself heard and unable to think clearly' ('sans connaissance'). From M. de Tersac he had obtained an equally terse statement: 'I consent to M. de Voltaire's body being removed without ceremony, and I hereby relinquish all curial rights in his regard.' Unable to find the original of Voltaire's signed 'confession' of 2 March, Mignot had a fresh copy prepared and encountered no difficulty in persuading de Tersac to sign it as being faithful to the original. Equipped with these documents, Voltaire's nephew bided his time.

On Sunday, 31 May a post-mortem examination was carried out on Voltaire's body to determine the cause of death. A local apothecary, Mitouard, came to embalm the corpse and was allowed to retain Voltaire's brain, which he placed in a jar. The marquis de Villette took possession of Voltaire's heart in a similar manner (and subsequently transported it back to Ferney). That evening after dark a brainless, heartless Voltaire was dressed and seated upright in his star-spangled carriage, carefully tied to the framework so that he should maintain this convincing posture throughout the journey. At about 11 p.m. the carriage moved off into the night, followed by another containing Dompierre d'Hornoy and two of his influential cousins: an army officer and a member of the King's household. They were headed for Champagne. As was Mignot, who had gone on ahead. For the abbé was the nominal abbot of a Cistercian monastery at Scellières, not far from Troyes: that is to say, he drew an income from the monastery's land but left the religion to the local prior. And this prior, Dom Potherat de

Corbierres, had been somewhat surprised to open his door at seven o'clock that evening and find his landlord standing on the step.

Mignot explained his predicament. His uncle had expressed a dying wish to be buried at Ferney, but it had become clear that the body, though embalmed, was not quite up to the journey. Would the prior mind if they buried him here at Scellières? At least until they could think of a way of getting him back to the Pays de Gex. The prior had little option but to agree, and the three documents that Mignot now produced would no doubt protect him when the poor monk later had to explain himself to the Bishop of Troyes.

The abbey of Scellières was not the grandest of resting-places. Lost amidst marsh and woodland, the monastery comprised only one other monk, Dom Meunier. The abbot's residence was in ruins, while the priory itself was modest. The chapel was in a poor state of repair and most resembled a barn. Still, Voltaire was unlikely to mind. When his body arrived late the following afternoon, it was placed in a simple deal coffin and then escorted into the chapel by the abbé Mignot, in full ecclesiastical garb, accompanied by Dompierre d'Hornoy and his two cousins respectfully dressed in mourning. The coffin was placed on trestles at the far end – in the equivalent of a chancel – amongst a forest of candles: funeral vespers were sung. Then dom Meunier and some lay assistants kept vigil throughout the night.

The following morning (Tuesday, 2 June) a requiem Mass was celebrated by the prior, six priests of the locality, a deacon, a subdeacon, a beadle, choristers (but no musicians), sundry bell-ringers, and some rather Shakespearean grave-diggers. Each priest had been able to rustle up some parishioners, and so there was even a congregation (of about sixty). It was not quite Notre-Dame, and some people distinctly remembered being distracted by the sound of frogs croaking in the marsh. Moreover, it was unnerving to have to look at the large hole that had been dug in the middle of the chapel floor. But soon the hole was filled, and the abbot and his cousins returned to Paris with their duty done. Leaving dom Potherat to face his superiors.

The Bishop of Troyes happened to be visiting Versailles at the time, and when the Archbishop of Paris informed him of what was afoot, he wrote at once to dom Potherat, forbidding him to grant Voltaire a Christian burial. The letter arrived too late. Mignot – this abbot who was a lawyer – had helpfully provided his prior with a reply, in which he defended his actions by quoting canon law and arguing that it had been perfectly in order to bury Voltaire since he was not officially excommunicate. As a worthy heir to his uncle, Mignot now published both letters in Grimm's *Correspondance littéraire* – to mobilize opinion and prevent undue punishment being meted out to Potherat. In the event the prior was temporarily relieved of his post and recalled to Cistercian headquarters.

The Church felt cheated of its prey and sought posthumous revenge. Thus, despite d'Alembert's best efforts, the Academy was forbidden to hold its customary memorial service. But Voltaire's friends fought back. Frederick of Prussia gave orders for a requiem Mass to be celebrated in the Roman Catholic cathedral in Berlin. On 26 November he delivered his own eulogy of Voltaire at a special session of the Berlin Academy. Two days later the members of the masonic lodge of the Nine Sisters held a memorial meeting to which, quite exceptionally (because they were women), Mme Denis and the marquise de Villette were invited. And the Academy replied to the ban on its own commemorative ceremony by making 'A Eulogy of Voltaire' the subject of its poetry prize for 1779.

Unworthy Christians seized on certain malicious rumours that had begun to circulate about the nature of Voltaire's death. Reports of the pain he had suffered were transformed into lurid, minatory tales about the agony of the damned. He was said to have writhed dementedly in an attempt to avoid hell-fire, at once screaming for Christ to save him and denouncing his companions for their impiety. And he had died, they said, consuming the contents of his own chamberpot. Among the enemies of the *philosophes* such fables would be told and retold for over half a century. But the simple truth was as Mme Denis described it: her uncle had died 'in great pain, except for the last four days, when he went out like a candle'.[4]

Now a very rich woman, Mme Denis soon took a husband, a retired dragoon called Duvivier who had become a regular visitor since her return to Paris. His Christian name was François. And she immediately disposed of the Ferney estate to the marquis de Villette – apart from her uncle's library, which was sold to Catherine the Great and carefully transported to St Petersburg under the supervision of Wagnière.[5] The Ferney estate was valued at 180,000 *livres*, and she swapped it with the marquis for a Parisian town house (in the rue du Mail) and an annual income of 3,200 *livres*.[6] Voltaire's niece had no intention of exiling herself from Paris again, and nor did she wish to become an estates manager. Belle et Bonne, however, rather took to the idea of being the lady of Ferney, at least during the warm summer months. But it was not to be. Her husband soon discovered that his new acquisition was actually costing him a lot of money: Voltaire's 'colony' had been heavily subsidized from his other income. Having at first let the château, the marquis was then obliged to sell the whole estate and finally found a buyer in 1785: namely, the 27-year-old Jacques-Louis de Budé, a member of the old Genevan family who had previously owned it. (It was recently acquired by the French state and has become a museum.) Budé paid the full 180,000 *livres*, plus a further 30,000 for the contents.[7] Villette died in 1793, of natural causes, while his wife lived out a troubled and financially insecure widowhood until 1823. Four years before her death she helped to found a masonic lodge in Voltaire's memory, and addressed its opening meeting with a moving, eloquent speech about the man who had transformed her life – and the lives of many.

As to Voltaire's heart, his former architect Léopold Racle had designed a small cenotaph for it in the drawing-room at Ferney, opposite the stove, and inscribed it with these simple words: 'Son esprit est partout et son cœur est ici' ('His spirit is everywhere and his heart is here'). The cenotaph and inscription are still there, but after the sale of the estate the heart was transferred back to Paris in a silver-gilt casket and is said now to reside in the Bibliothèque Nationale de France.[8]

The Comédie-Française kept the flame burning also. *Agathocle* was premiered on the first anniversary of Voltaire's death, to polite applause. Ten days later they revived *Rome sauvée* and performed his comedy *Le Droit du seigneur*, which had first been staged at Ferney in 1762. But the three performances of this double bill were poorly attended. Simultaneously, at the Opéra Comique – the theatre that Voltaire had never liked – the loyal d'Argental had engineered a production of *Charlot* (retitled *La Comtesse de Givry*), the comedy that had gone down so well with the military at Ferney in

1767. But here too the response was poor. The theatre-going public were now interested only in Voltaire's classics – and his legend.

But the reading public continued to read him. During his last years Voltaire had been attending energetically to the publication of his 'collected works': in the quarto edition (30 vols, 1768–74) and Cramer's so-called 'édition encadrée' (1775) that ran to 40 octavo volumes. Now the task fell to others. Charles Palissot, author of *Les Philosophes* and enemy of the *encyclopédistes*, demonstrated his continuing approval of Voltaire by publishing a 'selected works' in 55 octavo volumes (1792–1802). But what was really needed was a 'Complete Works' – if that were possible. Hence the so-called Kehl edition (1784–9). This project had begun as the brainchild of the leading publisher and press baron, Charles-Joseph Panckoucke (1736–98), who had discussed it with Cramer and with Voltaire himself during two recent visits (in 1775 and 1777). In August or September 1778 Mme Denis authorized him to return to Ferney and take possession of all Voltaire's manuscripts, carefully tidied and arranged by Wagnière. (Fortunately Louis XVI had dropped his original plan to search Voltaire's house immediately after his death and confiscate his work.)[9] Those manuscripts that had been brought to Paris (or originated there) were similarly entrusted. As well as the manuscripts, Panckoucke was also given Voltaire's correspondence – for the 'Complete Works' were to include his letters.

Panckoucke assembled an editorial team under his overall supervision. It included his brother-in-law, Jean-Baptiste Suard; Condorcet, who was working on a life of Voltaire and found himself appointed to deal with the plays; La Harpe; Wagnière; and a man called Decroix. During the winter of 1778–9 the methodical and omniscient Wagnière proved invaluable to the team's work, and he was dearly missed when he left Paris at the beginning of June to go and install Voltaire's library in St Petersburg (where he remained until February 1780). Decroix, however, tried to fill the gap. A native of Lille, he worked as a financial administrator in Flanders. He had accompanied Panckoucke (also a native of Lille) on his visit to Ferney in 1777, and it had become his dream to produce the most complete of complete editions of the great man's work. Voltaire's poetry was his particular interest and love, and to this he devoted himself especially. But his zeal, his scrupulousness, and the efficiency of his editorial methods informed the project as a whole.

Unfortunately he also later embellished Longchamp's memoirs, thus tempting future biographers of Voltaire with many an unreliable tale.

Panckoucke got cold feet. The scale of the project was immense, and so were the estimated costs. Over half the works in question were banned in France. And as to the letters . . . Many of the correspondents were still alive, and some were the crowned heads of Europe. One of them, Catherine, now suggested that he produce and publish the edition in St Petersburg. But Panckoucke's feet remained cold, and he preferred to pass the project over to a brilliantly successful 46-year-old businessman: Pierre-Augustin Caron de Beaumarchais, the author of *Le Barbier de Séville* (1775) and future author of *Le Mariage de Figaro* (1784). He was busy funding the rebels in the American War of Independence, but he would no doubt be able to fit this minor matter into his hectic schedule.

Beaumarchais bought the rights to the 'Complete Works' for 300,000 *livres* on 25 February 1779. He then rented a disused fort at Kehl, on the east bank of the Rhine near Strasbourg (and in the margravate of Baden); installed twenty-four printing presses; bought three paper-mills in the Vosges to supply them; and imported a font (the so-called Baskerville type) from England. A subscription was launched in January 1781, and sales were both inhibited and stimulated when the Archbishops of Amiens and Vienna firmly warned their flocks that purchase would constitute a mortal sin. In 1785 the Archbishop of Paris said much the same thing in his Lenten Address, this time including *The Marriage of Figaro* among his list of forbidden fruits. When Beaumarchais ridiculed him in verse, Louis XVI made *himself* look ridiculous by throwing the playwright temporarily in prison. In June a royal decree ordered the Kehl edition to be 'suppressed'. It was just like old times. But thirty volumes had already been published (the first in 1783), and by 1790 Beaumarchais had produced two complete editions: 70 volumes in octavo, 92 volumes in duodecimo. The editorial problems were as predicted, and the correspondence had perforce to contain gaps, but it was a major – if imperfect – achievement.

The final volume included two works of particular interest. One was the *Mémoires pour servir à la vie de M. de Voltaire* (*Memoirs to Serve for a Life of M. de Voltaire*). Written by Voltaire himself in 1758–9 and essentially an attack on Frederick the Great, these memoirs had remained unpublished within their author's lifetime. Pirated editions had begun to appear from 1784, but the

Prussian king's death in 1786 had allowed Beaumarchais to complete his project with the definitive version. To complete it, and to count the cost. He had managed to sell only 2,000 subscriptions, and he had produced 15,000 copies. Many of these were found lying in his cellars when his Parisian mansion was ransacked by revolutionaries in August 1792. Like all attempts to produce the Complete Works of Voltaire – then as now – it had been a noble, nightmarish and extremely expensive undertaking.[10]

The other work of particular interest was Condorcet's *Vie de Voltaire* (*A Life of Voltaire*). The long process of retrospective assessment had begun.

'*Le Flambeau de l'Univers*' (*The Torch of the Universe*):
a late-eighteenth-century stipple engraving depicting Voltaire, Rousseau and Franklin.

CHAPTER TWENTY-FOUR

Conclusion

The Author considers his Subject

W HO WAS VOLTAIRE? What sort of a person was he? In himself, in his dealings with others, in his writings. What was his place in history? It is difficult enough to answer such questions in respect of any living person, even the humblest mortal whose deeds may be of little consequence to the life of nations and who seldom writes more than a cheque. But in the case of a hyperactive polymath who lived till he was eighty-four, died over 200 years ago, and seldom kept a straight face, it is virtually impossible. Nevertheless, as Dr Pangloss would remind us, there is no effect without a cause. So the Author must try to make sense of his extraordinary Subject.

Voltaire's two 'autobiographies' are unhelpful. The *Mémoires pour servir à la vie de M. de Voltaire* (1758–9; published in 1790) is largely an attack on Frederick the Great, while the *Commentaire historique sur les œuvres de l'auteur de la Henriade* (1776) is a rather disjointed piece of self-advertisement. In any case Voltaire would have regarded it as ill-bred to talk openly about himself, and certainly not at length, still less in print. Ill-bred, and perhaps ill-advised: for a bared soul is a soul exposed to the dangers of ridicule and misrepresentation. Moreover, he might not have told us the truth. As his doctor, Théodore Tronchin observed in 1756 when writing to Jean-Jacques Rousseau: 'Of all men living, the one he knows the least is himself.'[1]

Perhaps such 'truth' is unavailable. Ever since Rousseau's *Confessions* a great deal of 'life-writing' — whether biography or autobiography, whether of real or imaginary persons – has wittingly or unwittingly demonstrated the dangers of aiming for such a 'truth'. For how does one summarize or 'essentialize' a life? Indeed should one even try? Are we born or made? Is the child father to the man? What is the relative weight to be attached to sexual, financial, intellectual, moral, spiritual, familial, social and political imperatives? How far does it matter whether obedience to these imperatives is conscious or unconscious? What of free will? Is a life constructed, undergone or simply survived? Conspiracy or cock-up? And what of the act of narrative itself? With its silent, inbuilt assumptions about causation and 'character', a story can launch a thousand lies. Does the passage of time imply change or repetition? *Plus ça change* . . . ? Are we getting somewhere or going nowhere? Do lives have 'shape', or are they a tangle of contradictory impulses and random exploits that we comb illusorily into a tidy curriculum vitae? A Biography, or just a biological blip in the vast panorama of eternity?

Voltaire would have shared these concerns but hated their formulation. 'Systems' – even systematic scepticism – made him very nervous. Which is why it is fundamentally wrong to see him (and his fellow-*philosophes*) as forefathers of the Final Solution. Though Voltaire and his like-minded contemporaries championed reason, they used it not to construct 'perfect' answers – like ethnic cleansing – but to posit provisional ones in the pragmatic game of achieving human happiness. 'As far as I possibly can,' Voltaire told Frederick in 1737, 'I bring the metaphysical back to the moral. Human beings are what interest me.'[2] And when it came to finding historical explanations, he was wary of overarching theories: all talk of hidden currents and irresistible trends had the potential to distort the evidence in the name of a false precision. For his own polemical reasons he presented the history of the world as the history of human progress, a gradual process of enlightenment, culminating in the imminent triumph of Reason. But privately he took a much less sanguine view of the muddle and mess of human affairs. History was a hit-and-miss story, a long accretion of happy and unhappy accident. 'I rather share the opinion of the Englishman,' he once wrote, 'who said that all origins, all laws, all institutions, are like a plum pudding: the first person put in the flour, the next added the eggs, a third the sugar, a fourth the raisins; and so we have plum pudding.'[3] In the case of Voltaire's own history, time was the cook, and the proof of the biographical pudding must be in the eating. That is to say, a matter of personal taste, an interpretation.

At five foot nine or ten Voltaire was quite tall for his day. Not exactly one of the seven-footers that Frederick the Great's father used to collect for his army, but tall none the less. And he was certainly thin, an ectomorph who became positively skeletal many years before his death and decomposition. Mere skin and bone. But, despite the fact that he was the runt of the litter and nearly died at birth, he was resilient and robust. Two siblings, after all, had perished in infancy. And he did survive a near-fatal attack of smallpox. Though he endlessly complained of his health and frequently took to his bed, there was rarely anything seriously wrong with him. As his doctor kept telling him. Except for his digestive system. Diet was a constant problem, and stomach ulcers would seem to have been the bane of his physical existence (as Rousseau's urinary difficulties were his). For the last twenty-five years of his life the behaviour of his bowels – and indeed those of his niece – became an obsession: laxatives and enemas were his weekly sacraments (usually on a Wednesday).

Voltaire's digestive system cannot have been helped by the fact that he lived on his nerves. Endowed with extraordinary energy, even up until the very last days of his long life, he was a driven man. Constantly planning and plotting and performing and play-acting; thinking and doing and writing; ambitious, determined, stubborn, often foolishly pig-headed. But also spontaneous, generous, impetuous. Inconsistent. And often naïve. He lived on the edge. Of the possible, of the permissible. On the edge of the royal court or of France itself, of Geneva and Prussia, of England and Russia. In all but the last case he experienced the centre at first hand but preferred – or was obliged – to live at one remove from its realities: a remove that was bridged by consummate networking and the most voluminous and diverse correspondence of any writer that ever lived. On the edge, but always at the leading edge: of dramatic art, science (whether playing with fire or cutting up slugs), biblical studies, historiography, philosophy, literature. And always on the perilous cliff-edge of the forbidden. Sometimes he fell into the abyss – early exile in the Loire, imprisonment in the Bastille, financial skulduggery in England, ignominious shenanigans at Frankfurt – but mostly he managed to teeter safely on the brink of perdition. And at the utmost limits of his own manifold and protean capacities.

It is tempting indeed to think that the child was father to the man: that the bastard produced the rebel. Being a bastard could, of course, be perfectly respectable: the duc du Maine was a royal one, the maréchal de Richelieu a highly successful one. But whether or not he really was illegitimate, Voltaire believed that he was — and believed that it mattered. He spent his life at once craving acceptance and flamboyantly disdaining it, desperately wanting to belong and desperately wanting not to care. (Witness his experience at the French court during the mid-1740s.) The recurrent hypochondria and the valetudinarian impatience with his physical limitations were no doubt a form of attention-seeking. He was deeply insecure: he needed to be cared for, to be loved and protected. (As Mme du Châtelet saw much more clearly than Mme Denis.) And if there was one thing Zozo-François hated, it was not being the focus of attention. He lived on the edge but he longed to be at the centre of everyone's world.

As the last and belated addition to the Arouet family he had had to compete and clamour for this attention. At school he won it through his intelligence and poetic talent. On leaving school he sought it by satirizing the Regent and ingratiating himself at the court of his rival. Soon he moved — literally and metaphorically — centre-stage: with his plays, with his controversial epic on the Wars of Religion, with his *Lettres philosophiques*. And there he remained for as long as he possibly could. Writing play after play, *conte* after *conte*, book after book. The man who had refused to be a lawyer spent many happy hours pursuing lawsuits when he could: on his own behalf and on behalf of others, of the wronged and the persecuted — of those who had been illegitimately treated. The runt of the litter was always trying to prove he was right. He refused to let things go for fear that someone might think him a dupe. There is no doubt that his endless fights — with Desfontaines and Jean-Baptiste Rousseau, with Fréron and Nonnotte, and (least admirably of all) with Jean-Jacques — were demeaning and usually a waste of his valuable time. Sometimes the campaigner was simply courting publicity (of the kind that is never bad), and sometimes the champion of reason and truth was simply outraged by the lies and the distortions and wanted to set the record straight. And sometimes he was just defending his name. For he had to be careful. His wafer-thin immunity from being formally exiled or even returned to the Bastille depended in large measure on his reputation; and if too much mud were to stick, he could end up offering the King and the Church just the excuse they needed to 'disappear' him. But if the child was father to the man, that man also remained a child: wilful, self-obsessed, resistant to compromise, and unwilling to forgo the pleasure of his tantrums. A child who wanted to be seen *and* heard.

Voltaire's sex life, like most sex lives, is poorly documented: discretion, decorum and prejudice have substituted the penumbra of the closet for the limelight of the world stage. But sexual passion does not seem to have been a major motivating force in his life. Predominantly heterosexual, he may have had homosexual leanings and/or active relationships. With Thiriot perhaps (the one-time associate of Desfontaines), quite possibly with the effeminately handsome Lord Hervey, but probably not with the abbé Linant (as Nancy Mitford suggests) and probably not with Frederick – for whom nevertheless he entertained strong feelings (of love or anger, admiration or disgust, depending on the moment) and with whom he conducted a correspondence that does indeed often read like the communing of lovers. He plainly delighted in the company of women, especially actresses; he had several (well-born) mistresses – vivacious debutantes like Suzanne de Livry, beautiful blondes like the marquise de Bernières or golden redheads like the comtesse de Rupelmonde; and he found in the raven-haired Émilie du Châtelet the greatest love of his life. A woman every bit his intellectual equal (while in some respects his superior), and a bed-partner who very nearly ruined his health. His relationship with her thrived as a companionship of intelligence, of common interests passionately shared, and it was built on a strong foundation of gratitude. Even as she led him by the nose from Cirey to Lunéville to Versailles and back to Lunéville, before eventually throwing herself into the arms of Saint-Lambert, Voltaire remained loyal. (Just as he remained deeply loyal to male friends like d'Argental and Richelieu.) In arranging for him to live at Cirey and then forsaking Paris to join him in this unlikeliest of paradise retreats, Émilie had revolutionized his life and placed him under an obligation that he never forgot. Nor would have forgotten had she lived to a proper age. Nor would ever have wanted to forget. Though she nagged and bossed, he knew it was all meant for his own good. And she was enormous fun: quick-witted, irreverent, and energetic. A great actress and a great singer. A great 'wife'. And a great mind. No wonder so many women, like Mme de Graffigny, came to hate her.

Whereas Marie-Louise Denis was at best a companion. At the outset the uncle and niece enjoyed themselves in bed, but their relationship soon became one of fondness and convenience. For her he represented wealth, security and celebrity – at the price of those dreadful Genevan winters. For him she represented lively company and a useful châtelaine – at the price of her vulgarity and her profligacy. She was much less good at everything than the divine Émilie, except perhaps housekeeping, but she had a kind and cheerful heart. Aristocratic and/or intellectual women tended to be catty about this *bonne bourgeoise*, notably Mme d'Epinay (friend of Rousseau and Diderot) who thought her a hoot and in 1757 described her to her own lover, Melchior Grimm, as 'a short, fat woman, completely round, of about fifty [she was forty-five], and an implausible representative of her sex' ('femme comme on ne l'est point').[4] But such women underestimated the fact that Marie-Louise's transparency and lack of guile were both reassuring and refreshing to a man beset by spies and potential enemies. And her soft spot for a uniform – or an attractive young dramatist – was easily tolerated. Just as long as she did not allow them access to her uncle's manuscripts.

She was expensive, of course, but fortunately her uncle was a highly successful businessman. His networking ensured that he was well informed, and his practical intelligence allowed him to profit from his knowledge. From the lottery coup onwards he was a man of ever more substantial means. The periodic complaints about his financial health were no less plangent but no more convincing than those about his physical health. Voltaire was a master of the balanced investment portfolio and a shrewd judge of risk. His involvement in colonial trade – about which we still know very little – seems to have paid off handsomely. Meanwhile his activities as a private banker ensured a steady income stream. Men like Richelieu and the Duke of Württemberg could put up impressive collateral, but they were always strapped for cash. This made them triple A for creditworthiness and yet so eager for funds that they paid excellent rates of interest. True, they could be bad payers, but then that was why one employed lawyers.

Voltaire was generous with his riches. He was a lavish and unstinting host – though, if he were cross with someone or engaged on one of his periodic economy drives, the fare could suddenly be very meagre. He was fond of good wine and sparkled on champagne; and during his time at Cirey Émilie had sometimes felt obliged to ration him. For his own good, of course, and the good of his troublesome gut. Voltaire's physiology prevented him from being much of a *bon viveur*: when it came to eating, he was generally moderate, and later abstemious, in his patterns of consumption. Material luxury mattered relatively little to this cerebral man, though since he had rarely gone without (as he briefly did in the late 1720s), he may simply have taken this luxury for granted. But others — especially the ladies — could have what they wanted: food, wine, money, clothes, carriages, the latest furnishings, countless diamonds. By the 1740s, if not earlier, he had stopped taking royalties for his plays and books. Hence in part the continuing loyalty and eventual public gratitude of the Comédie-Française, whose solvency had depended largely on his successes. As to the innumerable books, he wanted not profits but readers. He drove his publishers mad: demanding endless revisions, keeping each in the dark about his dealings with their competitors. But they always knew that they were on to a good thing.

Was he lovable? Unquestionably he was never dull. A committed conversationalist, he was always in the know, never short of an opinion, and effortlessly witty. He was a fine public speaker, a charismatic performer, a brilliant mimic with an impish facetiousness and a breathtaking irreverence bordering on the cruel. Almost all who met him commented on the extraordinary vivacity that shone from his piercing eyes. He was a showman and an unrepentant egotist. But he was also capable of great altruism (long before Calas, Sirven and the others) — altruism that could be carefully concerted (towards Mlle de Corneille) or born of spontaneous impulse and affection (Belle et Bonne). He was always helping people. Indeed was that not why he never understood or forgave Desfontaines, whom he saved from prison and quite possibly death? He had innumerable protégés, especially young (male) writers, and his expensive experiment with the colony of Ferney became increasingly fuelled by a genuine love for its inhabitants, all of whom he must have known more or less personally. As on the occasion of his departure from Cirey, so too when he left Ferney to go to Paris, the gratitude and affection of those he had known, helped and entertained was deeply felt and openly displayed.

Some have considered him cynical and unfeeling, but he was neither. He was a profoundly emotional man — which is one reason why he so mistrusted emotion and promoted reason. He was variously choleric or bilious, optimistic perhaps but rarely sanguine in the sense of being calm and even-tempered. Generally he leapt before he looked — only then to stand back and take the ironic view. His success as a dramatist sprang from his unquestionable talent for creating pathos and for depicting human beings writhing in the clutches of impossible dilemmas. Alas, the theatrical tradition in which these depictions were able to ring true has been more or less lost to us, and Voltaire's genius as a playwright is almost impossible to retrieve from the rigor mortis of the page and the quaintness of the verse. But ring true they did, and the theatre-goers of France loved him for it throughout the course of a century. And he himself was at his happiest during an evening of amateur (or semi-professional) theatricals, at Cirey or Ferney, when he could perform in one of his own plays with his mistress and close friends. He would sometimes spend the entire day in costume, inwardly rehearsing and preparing himself for the display of his talent — and the display of his heart.

As to the cynicism, that was a carapace that is wholly typical of the sensitive and the insecure. Certainly he saw through hypocrisy and cant with a penetrating, unforgiving eye, and he was the first to doubt a person's motives. A lifelong study of human history had left him with few illusions: 'nothing more than a tableau of crime and misfortune'.[5] And as he grew older he doubted more and more whether it was ever possible to change things — human nature least of all. But what cynic bestirs himself as Voltaire did? Writing and scheming and campaigning long after his own personal position was more or less secure. Because it boosted his ego, one might say, and that was certainly part of it. But one major ingredient in his emotional make-up consisted in a deep-seated aversion to physical violence. War repulsed him. The monstrous detail of the torture and barbaric executions meted out to Calas and La Barre would have revolted him even had they been guilty. Frequently in his letters he refers to the physical horror — the 'atrocity' — of these and other public deaths, and on one occasion even suggests that they cause him nightmares.[6] For a time he thought that the chevalier de La Barre actually had had his hand cut off and his tongue ripped out, and the image stayed with him. More than three years after the event he told Turgot: 'I can still see that square in Abbeville even now.'[7]

And here we come to the core of Monsieur de Voltaire, manifest from his earliest years: a profound sense of revolt against the 'authority' – religious, royal, legal – that legitimates such inhumanity, and that legitimates it in the name of preposterous fibs. Hence his image of the plum pudding. Human institutions are not god-given and immutable. They are reformable: we can improve the recipe. If François-Marie Arouet openly and even cheerfully affirmed a filiation to the chevalier de Rochebrune (risqué poet and celebrity socialite), that was because he hated the fake legitimate: such as the po-faced, life-denying orderliness of his Jansenist father and brother, who had sold their souls to the status quo. As a school-leaver – at an age when young men can be surprisingly puritanical even as they recover from their latest hangover – he was genuinely shocked by the behaviour of the Regent and his court. As to the monarchy in general, he never ceased to be frustrated – and more frequently outraged – by the unholy alliance between the Crown and the Church, the one invoking the other as the source of its inalienable power. The tiny Île de la Cité – the ancient heart of Paris, with its Palais de Justice flanked by the Sainte-Chapelle and the cathedral of Notre-Dame – was for him a symbolic rotten core at the centre of the city and of the nation. The divine right of kings seemed such a sham when the kings were as ineffectual as Louis XV and when the 'divinity', in the form of the Catholic Church, was such a travesty of humanity and good sense.

Of course there was a God: a simple glance at a flower or the splendours of the night sky proved as much. And Newton had demonstrated His laws. So let us worship Him and the astonishing beauty and complexity of His creation. And yes, of course, we must love our neighbour as ourselves. If we cannot see the utilitarian logic of that, then indeed we must have our minds concentrated by the fond belief that a fairy-tale God will reward or punish us according to our just deserts. And yes, of course, there should be a king: there has to be a central, unifying source of political order and stability. But we do not require the infantilizing paraphernalia of miracles and resurrections. Or of newly crowned kings going about their kingdom engaged in the laying-on of hands as if they had the supernatural power to heal (a tradition that Louis XV had followed). On the contrary, all the mumbo-jumbo of the Bible and

Christian doctrine is one enormous act of obfuscation: smoke and mirrors —
or rather incense and confessionals — designed to trick the ovine majority
into obeying the mighty minority here on earth. And an insult to that most
precious of human gifts: reason.

It is easy to romanticize and misunderstand the nature of the divide
separating Voltaire from the various representatives of authority in eighteenth-
century France. He was born into the upper bourgeoisie and shared its
outlook, including its social ambitions. In declaring himself the son of the
chevalier de Rochebrune, he was claiming to be an aristocrat. And, like his
official father before him, this was what he always wanted to be. Hence the
ennobling 'de' added to his pseudonym. Hence the recurrent ambition to be a
courtier. Hence the lifestyles at Cirey and Ferney, where the servants danced
attendance. And he shared other attitudes that may shock us in their élitist
nature. For almost every educated person in France — at least up until the 1760s
— 'enlightenment' was a top-down affair. The supposed 'popularizer', Fontenelle, was alleged to have said at the beginning of the century: 'If my hand were
full of truths I would not open it for the people.' Others had taken up the
image and talked of slowly spreading the fingers to let grains of truth slip
through to those beneath.[8] D'Alembert for one accepted this view of things.
Voltaire did not contest the assumption that for the masses a little learning
might be a dangerous thing. And perhaps even a superfluous thing. When La
Chalotais argued for a state education system in 1763 (following the expulsion
of the Jesuits), the Patriarch of Ferney wrote to compliment him and noted
with particular gratitude that La Chalotais had not proposed anything that
might prevent his own gardeners from getting on with their job.[9] 'Enlightenment' for Voltaire did not include a whole range of aspirations that we
might now assume retrospectively to have been part of a radical agenda:
universal suffrage (or even just male suffrage), mass education, provision for
the poor and infirm. Nor did they for most progressives of the day. Even the
radical Rousseau had his doubts about democracy, while Diderot warned
against the consequences of sending the children of workers and peasants to
secondary school. Education was not a human right but a matter of broad
social utility.

Voltaire's contribution to the process of social and political change that
culminated in the French Revolution and the Declaration of the Rights of

Man was of a different order. From the day he left school the two principal targets of his hatred and venom were religious intolerance and absolutist government. It is somehow symbolic that the school-prize he received in his penultimate year at Louis-le-Grand was a history of the Wars of Religion. He may have pawned it but he never forgot its lesson. And this lesson underpinned everything he subsequently did and wrote. The Catholic massacre of Protestants on St Bartholomew's Day 1572 was a terrible demonstration of the violence and inhumanity to which the pacific teachings of Jesus can lead. The description of that massacre provides the most compelling, least formulaic passage of La Henriade, and the event itself seems to have haunted Voltaire for the rest of his life. He regularly notes the anniversary (24 August) in his correspondence, and sometimes complains of acute physical discomfort at its memory.[10]

Voltaire's hatred of religious intolerance and his objections to Bourbon autocracy were standard in the libertine circles of Le Temple during the last years of the seventeenth century and the first decades of the eighteenth. So, too, was the deism expressed in the 'Epître à Uranie', and from which Voltaire scarcely wavered throughout his long life. But to this aristocratic 'liberalism' Voltaire brought the bourgeois liberalism of the merchant and lawyer class. England showed him what he knew already: that the persecution of the Huguenots was not just morally unacceptable but also economically disastrous. Freedom and tolerance were good for business, and prosperity meant a better living standard for everyone, including the poor. While colonial conquest could bring great rewards, war itself was bad for business, and from the start of Louis XV's reign Voltaire was keen to deter the new king from bellicose adventure by eulogizing his predecessor not as the all-conquering Sun King but as an enlightened patron of the arts and sciences. Economic growth enabled by peace and tolerance, fostered by technological progress, and graced with (money-spinning) luxury and culture: that was Voltaire's agenda. It was the agenda he advocated in the Lettres philosophiques, and it was the agenda he pursued when he obtained a kingdom of his own at Ferney.

When Voltaire was young, and even in his middle age, this liberalism counted as progressive – within France. In one sense all he was trying to do was drag his country into the eighteenth century. This deeply conservative Catholic nation continued to bask complacently in the sunshine of Louis

XIV's former glories while the storm clouds of national bankruptcy gathered and the 'deluge' of popular revolt (famously foreseen by Mme de Pompadour) threatened. The Huguenots needed to be brought home, along with their money and skills, and the dead hand of the Catholic Church needed to be removed from the tiller of the ship of state. The king should govern within a set of rationally conceived legal constraints, not with the arbitrary whimsy of an ersatz god, still less as his Jesuit confessor might chance to opine. As Voltaire attempted to propagate this agenda in his twenties and thirties, he experienced and understood at first hand the full machinery of religious and political oppression. His programme was fairly moderate in its progressiveness, but opposition to it served to radicalize him. The publication of the *Lettres philosophiques* and the flight to Cirey was a pivotal moment. He had thrown down the gauntlet to a regime that was beginning to look *ancien*.

So why the sycophantic courtier of the 1740s? The one single, overriding issue for Voltaire throughout his life was the freedom to communicate. Freedom of speech, he believed, was 'the basis for all other freedoms; it is how we enlighten each other'.[11] 'Is there anything more tyrannical,' he asked, 'than removing the freedom of the press? How can a country say it is free when it is not allowed to write what it thinks?'[12] In his own particular case this issue was not so much moral or political as practical. How could he combine frankness with personal safety in the expression of his views? What was the right balance between full-frontal assault and cautious obliquity? His first period of imprisonment in the Bastille and the fate of others (notably Jean-Baptiste Rousseau) had shown him the dangers of going too far: he could so easily be condemned to silence and a futile, terminal marginality. And he so much wanted to be heard. The fig leaf of allegory and the nudge-and-a-wink of veiled allusion were helpful in every medium, be it a classical ode or a play set in Babylon. Which is why, of course, he was forever having such trouble with the censors. But his own physical security was always on the line. During those early years he could at any time have been arrested, thrown in prison without trial and left there to die. That was why Cirey was such a godsend: a private enclave offering ready flight to Lorraine or Prussia.

But in time it proved just slightly too marginal. Try as they might to bring the world to Cirey, Voltaire and Mme du Châtelet began to feel like small children who have been sent to bed early while the adults have the real fun. And at this point (reached in the late 1730s) Voltaire had really only two options: to accept Frederick's invitation to Berlin or to make a go of things at Versailles. Had it not been for Émilie he would probably have chosen the former. But she did everything she could to facilitate the latter. It was the only way she could keep him. And he duly played the game. But it was an inglorious period in his life: public honours piled up as his contestatory influence declined. The retreat to Lunéville helped, but at the price of a return to the margins. Following Émilie's untimely death he then had a chance to see what the other route was like: the Prussian court. But it, too, demonstrated very forcibly that rulers ruled alone. And if he himself was to hold sway he would have to do it from an independent base. The geography of Geneva and its environs constituted a brilliant solution to his lifelong problem: finding a place from where to speak.

Once Voltaire found such a place, his personal crusade for freedom and tolerance could become a much more public one. The showmanship of his publicity campaigns and the post-revolutionary transformation of this quasi-aristocratic liberal into a radical hero have led some to see these efforts as specious or meretricious, the feel-good pastimes of a vain and spectacularly rich busybody. But in the cases of Calas and Sirven (and several others) his interventions were crucial: to the families concerned, and to the wider cause of legal reform. And those interventions cost him not only money but time, effort, and a not inconsiderable quantity of emotional stress. If we are able to take the principles (if not necessarily the reality) of freedom, tolerance and justice more or less for granted in modern Western society, it is because people like Voltaire proclaimed their value when the very expression of those views was neither free nor tolerated and was likely to result in unjust punishment. And within eighteenth-century France – indeed within the entire known world of that time – no one proclaimed them louder or longer than Voltaire. With conviction but, for the most part, without self-importance: 'I am somewhat the Don Quixote of the poor and wretched,' he observed wryly in 1769.[13]

Voltaire was not an original thinker. Even his championing of Newton came increasingly to seem like a conservative move, the work of a deist defending God against the perceived atheism of Spinoza and his followers.[14]

But he was a great and tireless communicator. Words were what he loved best: music and the visual arts, for example, held little interest for him. Many of his 'communications' speak to us in a format or a language that can seem irretrievably *passé*, and it can be arduous to discern a modern relevance in their tentacular topicality. Indeed it is sometimes difficult to convey or reproduce Voltaire's famous wit because it is so highly contextual and (generally speaking) quite unlike the aphoristic one-liners of Oscar Wilde or Dorothy Parker. Imagine reading today's *Private Eye* or *Le Canard enchaîné* two centuries hence. And this despite the fact that Voltaire wrote so much in verse, a brief and memorable medium that is ideally suited to the sound-bite. But any one of his writings, however steeped in the preoccupations of its day, still displays the lightness of his touch, the quickness of his mind, and the urbane charm with which he makes his own point of view seem so seductively true.

If, of all his works, the philosophical tales have survived best and continue to command the widest readership, that is because – at least in some of them – these qualities shine through despite the need for explanatory footnotes. And because the issues are timeless. *Micromégas* is still a brilliant parable about our precarious human status, poised – cosmically, scientifically, morally, daily – between the micro and the mega. *Zadig* is an instructively silly story about the most fundamental questions: what is destiny? How can we be happy? *L'Ingénu* remains a clever and delightful comedy about the devastating power of asking the obvious question. And *Candide* . . . Mirthful and wise, the best of all possible stories, an allegory of life and living that does the work of a hundred bibles and a thousand moral tracts. And does not tell us what to do. For that above all was the objective of Voltaire Almighty: to confer freedom on his readers, the freedom to think and to feel and to speak as *we* consider fit. By the light of human reason.

Voltaire valued freedom above all else. In the short memoirs he wrote in 1758–9 he commented: 'I hear much talk about freedom, but I do not think that there has ever been a private individual in Europe who has achieved the kind of freedom I have. May those who have the will and the means follow my example.'[15] Perhaps this remark may stand, if not as his lesson to us (since we cannot all win the lottery), then as his epitaph. For it was above all by his example that he contributed to a sea-change in eighteenth-century European opinion. Rich, insubordinate, articulate, shrewd, cussed and courageous, François-Marie Arouet endeavoured to say and do as he himself – by the light of reason – deemed fit. And he strove to enable others to do the same. He managed both.

Voltaire never did say: 'I disapprove of what you say, but I will defend to the death your right to say it.'[16] But he did tell Frederick of Prussia: 'I am a tolerant man, and I consider it a very good thing if people think differently from me.'[17] In that respect the Author resembles his Subject.

Voltaire, in a sketch by Saint-Ours.

*Voltaire's Triumph on 11 July 1791. Early nineteenth-century etching,
after a contemporary drawing by Jean-Louis Prieur (1759–1795).
The procession is depicted turning right over the Pont Royal.*

Curtain Call

Zozo enters the temple of the gods

O
N 9 MAY 1791 Voltaire was exhumed: his skeleton was required for one last performance. His final resting-place continued to be a matter of controversy. Even though Mignot had never seriously considered removing the body to Ferney, this possibility disappeared with the sale of the estate. When the loyal nephew then attempted to replace the simple funerary flagstone in the chapel at Scellières with an elaborate carved tomb, the religious authorities objected. In December 1779 Villette had launched a public campaign to secure Voltaire a more dignified setting for his eternal rest, but this too had failed. The *philosophe* remained distinctly *corpus non gratus*.

The Revolution of 1789 changed all that. Church property was confiscated by the state and in many cases put up for sale. What would happen when the abbey at Scellières was sold? Was Voltaire's grave to fall into private and perhaps unreliable hands? The prospect was unthinkable now that the grave's occupant was a major star in the Revolutionary firmament. Responding to the mood of the moment, the Comédie-Française had revived *Brutus*, Voltaire's play of 1730 in which Roman republicans successfully prevent the restoration of Tarquin, their tyrannical king. Though France had finished with the absolutism of the *ancien régime*, it still had a king. When the first night of *Brutus* (17 November 1790) was attended by Mirabeau, the controversial Revolutionary leader who had come to dominate the newly created Assemblée Nationale, the atmosphere was heavily charged. Voltaire's republican lines were cheered to the echo and seemed to herald the end of the monarchy. The fact that both Voltaire and Mirabeau believed in a constitutional monarchy was irrelevant.

The new régime was heartily supported by men like Villette. The former marquis had dropped his title and abolished all residual feudal practices on his estates. He wrote articles advocating reform in the *Chronique de Paris* and saw himself as the guardian of Voltaire's memory. After all, the great man had died in his house. Unilaterally Villette had renamed the quai des Théatins (so called after a monastic order) the quai Voltaire — by simply replacing the street-sign with one of his own manufacture. On 9 November 1790 he attended a meeting of the Club des Jacobins, the political assembly that was as yet moderate in its views but would later become the focus for the more radical policies of men like Robespierre. Villette persuaded his fellow-citizens to agree a motion demanding the return of Voltaire's remains to Paris. On 19 November he leapt on to the stage during the third performance of *Brutus* and made the same proposal. If he were alive today, Villette proclaimed, the man who had written this play would be 'the foremost champion of the people'. Needless to say, the scene was reported in the *Chronique de Paris* the next day. Villette also proposed that Voltaire's coffin be laid to rest in the new Basilica of Sainte-Geneviève, which was currently being built on the site of the old Église Sainte-Geneviève (just across the square from the Collège Louis-le-Grand). The English had Westminster Abbey, and it was time the French had somewhere to bury their (non-royal) heroes. In short, a pantheon: a temple of all the gods. The idea caught on.

Scellières was put up for sale on 3 May 1791. On 8 May the Assemblée Nationale agreed to consider the proposal in committee and decreed in the meantime that Voltaire's coffin be taken from Scellières to the nearby parish church at Romilly. On 30 May, the anniversary of his death, it finally voted to transfer Voltaire's mortal remains from Romilly to the 'church of Sainte-Geneviève' in Paris. In fact this unfinished building had yet to be consecrated and was thus fortuitously a secular temple. In the middle of the fierce debate about its future use, Mirabeau had chosen that moment to die — on 2 April — and two days later the Assembly agreed the proposal originally mooted by Villette on behalf of Voltaire: that the 'building' of Sainte-Geneviève be reserved for the remains of great men. Pending its completion, Mirabeau's coffin was to be accommodated next to Descartes's in the crypt of the former church of Sainte-Geneviève: i.e. underneath the new Panthéon. Voltaire was the second Frenchman after Mirabeau to be thus honoured. Since Mirabeau was later removed, he is now the *primus inter pares* of all French gods. Chronologically at least.

When Voltaire's coffin was opened at Scellières on 9 May, there was some relief amongst the assembled dignitaries. He was intact. (There had been rumours that the grave might have been defiled.) The citizen-soldiers of the Garde Nationale rolled their drums and fired a salute. A piece of heel-bone disappeared . . . The open coffin was now taken in procession to Romilly church, and along the way mothers held up their children to kiss it as it passed. Once everyone had had a chance to view the skeleton, the coffin was sealed and kept in the church pending its transfer to Paris. On 6 July the final journey began. Thirteen years earlier the coffin had reached Scellières in under twenty-four hours, but the return could be more leisurely. It took four days, with overnight stops at Provins, Nangis, Guignes, and Brie-Comte-Robert. At each staging-post full municipal honours were paid to the departed, and a Mass was said in Voltaire's honour. Whether he liked it or not.

On the evening of Sunday, 10 July 1791 the cortège finally reached the gates of Paris, where it was met by the Mayor and other officials. Proceeded by a squad of cavalry and a small detachment of infantry, the hearse then made its way to the Place de la Bastille. A crowd watched as the coffin was lifted on to a platform that had been erected on top of a pile of rubble. It was famous rubble: the remains of the Bastille itself, which had been so memorably stormed on 14 July 1789. And the stones bore an inscription:

> Here in this place where despotism held you in chains,
> Voltaire, receive these honours at your country's hand.

And there the former inmate of this notorious prison awaited the spectacular events of the morrow, when his mortal remains were to be paraded through the streets of Paris, across the river, and then up the hill to the Panthéon, opposite his old school and near the Palais du Luxembourg.

Next morning it poured with rain, and there was talk of postponing the ceremony. But the clouds parted, and at around 2 p.m. the proceedings began. They had been carefully choreographed. At the head of the procession, the military: cavalry, drummers and riflemen. Then groups of children and students, followed by representatives of the political clubs, each with its own banner. Then portraits: Voltaire, Rousseau, Mirabeau. For this was a celebration of the Revolution, a civic festival to replace the religious processions of old. Next came a model of the Bastille, surrounded by a group of those who had stormed it and led by a *citoyenne* on horseback, dressed in the uniform of the Garde Nationale. She had been a heroine on that great day. The Bastille was followed by the theatre, in the form of representatives from the Comédie-Française. Then came Voltaire again, this time in the form of a gilded statue (copied from Houdon's), crowned with laurels and borne by students from the Académie des Beaux-Arts. They were all dressed in antique costume. Then, accompanied by members of the Academy and other writers, came the seventy volumes of the Kehl Complete Works . . . although, fearful of the rain, Beaumarchais had sent the real ones straight on to the national library and substituted a mock-up. (As a dramatist he was used to staging illusions.) After the Works, the musicians: they performed a sequence of funeral hymns.

And then came Voltaire the skeleton: inside his coffin, inside a sculpted porphyry tomb, on top of which the occupant was depicted lying peacefully on his deathbed. On the bed, an inscription: 'He avenged Calas, La Barre, Sirven and Monbailli.[1] Poet, philosopher, historian, he made the human mind to soar and prepared us to be free.' The sarcophagus was drawn by twelve greys (two of them reportedly lent by the Queen) in teams of four. Behind it came other groups of representatives: from the Assemblée Nationale, the regions, the city of Paris, the courts. More cavalry brought up the rear.

As in a religious procession there were 'stations', and the holy trinity of Voltaire the portrait, Voltaire the gilded statue, and Voltaire the marble sleeper was greeted at each one. First the procession headed north-west to the Opéra (then located near the Porte Saint-Martin), where the chorus sang and an actress kissed the marmoreal librettist. Then it continued south-west to the Place Louis XV before heading back east along the right bank of the Seine. Here it passed the Tuileries, the royal palace, where Louis XVI and

Marie-Antoinette were believed to be nervously watching from behind the shutters. For they were in serious trouble. Towards the end of June the King had foolishly decided to make a run for it, disguised as one of the Queen's servants as though he were in a comedy by Marivaux. He had headed for the north-eastern border and the protection of Austrian troops, but on 22 June he had been captured by 'patriots' at Varennes (in Lorraine, about fifty miles north of Cirey) and brought back to Paris on 25 June. He was a deserter and traitor: jeers and – worse – stony silence greeted him. Had the monarchy just died? Almost. Louis XVI was guillotined on 21 January 1793; his wife, on 12 October in the same year.

As the doomed couple looked on, the procession bore the new god across the river via the Pont Royal, from the Tuileries to the rue de Beaune, and reached the magnificent home of Monsieur and Madame Villette on the newly named quai Voltaire. Here the ex-marquis had created an arbour over the street, made by pulling four tall poplars together at the top and hanging a huge wreath of roses from the apex. The sarcophagus halted directly beneath it. To one side, on a makeshift semicircular stand, were fifty young girls in white dresses, each with a blue sash round her waist, a ringlet of roses on her head, and a laurel wreath in her hand. In the middle was Belle et Bonne, the former marquise de Villette, standing with her four-year-old daughter Charlotte – and the two daughters of the late Jean Calas, Rosine and Nanette. In harmony with an occasion that had been 'themed' by the painter David to evoke the ancient republic of Rome, Belle et Bonne wore a simple silk dress decorated with Etruscan motifs. Round her waist was a white sash that featured at its centre an image in black of the hearse and sarcophagus standing before her. Holding Charlotte by the hand, she stepped forward and bowed tearfully. She kissed Voltaire's marble likeness and crowned him with her laurel wreath. Then she held her daughter up so that the young girl might get a close view of this extraordinary man who had helped to turn Paris – and the world – upside-down.

After the choir had sung a specially commissioned ode, Belle et Bonne, her daughter, and the two Mlles Calas took up position in front of the hearse. Villette and La Harpe, who had been watching from a balcony, came down to walk behind them. And now the procession set off again, pausing briefly at the rue des Fossés Saint-Germain (the former home of the Comédie-

Française, now the rue de l'Ancienne Comédie) where a bust of Voltaire bore the inscription: 'At the age of 17 he wrote *Œdipe*.' The next station, very close by, was the new home of the Comédie-Française, the Théâtre de la Nation – now the Théâtre de l'Odéon, on the other side of the present-day Boulevard St Germain. Here an inscription read: 'He wrote *Irène* at the age of 83.' Thirty-two medallions recorded the titles of all his plays, and members of the company were dressed in the costumes of his most famous roles. Beneath menacing clouds a choir began to sing an aria from Voltaire's opera, *Samson*:

> Awake, ye people, and break your chains.
> Freedom is calling you.

Whereupon the heavens opened and everybody got soaked. A fire was lit inside the theatre to enable the more distinguished ladies to dry their clothes, but the disarray was general. Surely it was never like this in ancient Rome? When the rain abated, it was decided to proceed at once up the hill to the Panthéon and to complete the ceremony with dispatch.

And thus at dusk on Monday, 11 July 1791, Voltaire was delivered into the temple of all the gods. There was not a priest in sight. Corpus Voltarii Day was over, and Paris had substituted the son of a lawyer for a sixth-century shepherdess. Now, surely, the man could rest in peace.

But not quite. Thanks to the shifting tides of political fortune in nineteenth-century France, the status of the Panthéon altered around him. Following the restoration of the Bourbon monarchy in 1815, the 'temple' became a church. After the revolution of 1830 Louis-Philippe (duc d'Orléans and son of Philippe-Égalité) came to the throne as 'King of the French' and reversed the decision – which was re-reversed by Louis-Napoleon in 1851, and re-re-reversed in 1885 under the Third Republic. By which time nobody was really certain if Voltaire's remains were still in his tomb. It had long been rumoured that following the fall of Napoleon in 1814 a group of royalist fanatics had broken into the building, made off with Voltaire's bones – and those of Rousseau, who had become a god in 1794 – and buried the lot Heaven knew where. Under Louis-Napoleon it suited the Church to lend credence to this rumour – and to support it by pretending that a private inspection had revealed Voltaire's tomb to be empty. So in 1897 it was

decided to take a look. On Saturday, 18 December, before an invited audience
of a hundred people, the tomb was opened.

And there he was: his skull – which had been sawn in half during the post-
mortem – and his bones. They were in something of a jumble after all that
processing, but there could be no question: Voltaire was dead and well and
recumbent in Paris. Except for that missing piece of heel-bone. Rousseau,
too, was where he should have been. And together the two men now lie,
facing each other across the vaulted room, engaged in the most silent of
philosophical dialogues. And people visit. But it may not be quite what
Voltaire wanted. In 1772 he had commented to his biographer, the abbé
Duvernet, that people rarely receive the burial they desire: 'Those who would
be quite happy in an urn sitting on a friend's mantelpiece are obliged to go
and rot in a cemetery or its equivalent.'[2] Had he perhaps once envisaged
ending up in that urn which sits on top of his empty pyramidal tomb at
Ferney? Possibly. But it was his fate never to burn in the flames depicted on
the Arouet coat-of-arms, be they the flames of Hell or a crematorium. His
remains remain. For every age needs its relics and its gods.

Voltaire enters the Panthéon. Oil painting by Pierre-Antoine Demachy (1723–1807).

Notes

A note on sources and references

THE BIOGRAPHY OF Voltaire has become a palimpsest, each new version being written over the many that have gone before. This account of his life owes a substantial debt to *Voltaire en son temps*, the comprehensive study written and overseen by the great Voltaire authority, René Pomeau, in collaboration with other distinguished scholars. Originally published in five volumes by the Voltaire Foundation at Oxford (1985–94), this now standard work was reissued in a revised, two-volume edition in 1995, co-published with Fayard in Paris. I have supplemented its findings where necessary from more recent research, notably from the latest volumes of the Complete Works currently being edited by the Voltaire Foundation.

Voltaire en son temps is itself descended from a long and respectable lineage, beginning with the lives of Voltaire published by the abbé Duvernet and by Condorcet in 1786 and 1790 respectively. Both men had known their subject personally, as had his secretaries Sébastien Longchamp, Cosimo Collini and Jean-Louis Wagnière whose published and unpublished memoirs provided ample material for the monumental nineteenth-century biography produced by Gustave Desnoiresterres, *Voltaire et la société au XVIIIe siècle* (8 vols, Paris: Didier, 1867–76). Between Desnoiresterres and Pomeau came the no less authoritative accounts of Gustave Lanson (1906), André Bellesort (1925), Raymond Naves (1942) and André Delattre (1957). Pomeau's own epoch-making study, *La Religion de Voltaire*, first published in 1956 and revised in 1969, remains the finest intellectual biography of his subject.

In English an important biography has been Theodore Besterman's *Voltaire*, first published in 1969, then revised in 1970 and 1976. This work had several notable antecedents: by John Morley (1872), S.G. Tallentyre (1903), Norman L. Torrey (1938) and Nancy Mitford (1957). Peter Gay's *Voltaire's Politics* (1959) and Ira O. Wade's *The Intellectual Development of Voltaire* (1969) remain classics. Other anglophone writers have continued the line: John Hearsey (1976), Haydn Mason (1981), A.J. Ayer (1986) and Ian Davidson (2004).

My policy has been to provide an account of Voltaire's life that is based on well-attested and carefully weighed evidence as it is presented by Pomeau and others. Much of this now has the status of established truth, and so I have been able to use references sparingly. In the following notes I give sources for quotations and for research that post-dates Pomeau's biography. The four commonest types of reference are:

(i) *CW* followed by a volume and page number: indicating *The Complete Works of Voltaire* (Geneva, Banbury and Oxford: Voltaire Foundation, 1968–);

(ii) D followed by a document number: the conventionally accepted style of reference to Theodore Besterman's 'definitive' edition of Voltaire's correspondence in *The Complete Works*, vols 85–135;

(iii) Moland followed by a volume and page number: indicating Voltaire, *Œuvres complètes*, edited by Louis Moland (52 vols, Paris: Garnier frères, 1877–85). Pending completion of the Voltaire Foundation's edition, Moland's remains the standard work of reference;

(iv) Pomeau followed by a volume and page number: indicating the two-volume edition of *Voltaire en son temps* (1995).

All translations in the main text and in the notes are my own.

Curtain Rise

1 See Colin Jones, *Paris. Biography of a City* (London, 2004), p. 157. I am grateful to this excellent history of the French capital for several details in my evocation of late-seventeenth-century Paris. I have also drawn on other sources, notably Louis-Sébastien Mercier's twelve-volume *Tableau de Paris*. Though published in the 1780s, this describes many features of Parisian life that dated back at least a century.

2 Jones, *Paris. Biography of a City*, p. 159.

Chapter 1 Of Uncertain Birth

1 D8154 (3 March 1759). The remark about freedom that serves as an epigraph to this book is taken from the short memoirs that Voltaire wrote in 1758–9, which principally concern his relationship with Frederick of Prussia and were thus not published in his lifetime. See Moland, i. 39.

2 D6968 (15 Aug. 1756).

3 Her son, the subsequent duc de Saint-Simon (1675–1755), would later become famous as the author of voluminous, well-observed memoirs detailing life under Louis XIV and the subsequent Regency (1715–23) but which were not finally published until the nineteenth century.

4 *La Défense de mon oncle*, in *CW*, lxiv. 212. A church baptism was the only way in which a birth could be officially registered and the child thus given legal status.

5 D9981 (31 Aug. 1761).

6 D14117 (*c.*15 April 1767).

7 See Jean Orieux, *Voltaire* (Paris: Flammarion, 1999; first published 1966), p. 59. The story was originally circulated by L. Paillet de Warcy in his *Histoire de la vie et des ouvrages de Voltaire* (2 vols, Paris: 1824), i. 21–2.

8 *La Défense de mon oncle*, in *CW*, lxiv. 212.

Chapter 2 Of Priests and Poets

1 Pomeau, i. 27.

2 Jones, *Paris. Biography of a City*, p. 197.

3 Pomeau, i. 32.

4 *CW*, i (b), 4–5.

5 *CW*, i (b), 10.

6 Pomeau, i. 33.

7 Moland, vi. 393–4.

8 D5 (23 July 1711).

9 Pomeau, i. 34.

Chapter 3 White Nights and Early Nights

1 D2054 (28 July 1739).
2 D6347 (22 July 1755).
3 D37 [summer 1716].
4 Two visitors to Ferney (John Morgan and Samuel Powell) estimated the elderly Voltaire's height at 5′ 10″ in his shoes, while another (Major W. Broom) described him as 'tall'. See Sir Gavin de Beer and André-Michel Rousseau, *Voltaire's British Visitors, Studies in Voltaire and the Eighteenth Century*, 48 (1966), pp. 74 and 93.
5 Pomeau, i. 70.
6 Long thought to have been painted in 1718 and thus to depict Voltaire at the age of twenty-four, this portrait is now considered (following the work of Dominique Brême) to date from 1724–5 and thus to capture him at the height of his success at court. See *CW*, iii (a), p. xvii, and the exhibition catalogue, *Nicolas de Largillière (1656–1746)* (Paris, 2003), p. 164.
7 Moland, x. 245–6.

Chapter 4 Back to the Bastille

1 *Pace* Pomeau, i. 53. See Nicholas Cronk's introduction, in *CW*, i (b), 21–36.
2 Pomeau, i. 86.
3 Theodore Besterman, *Voltaire* (rev. edn, London: 1976), p. 86.
4 D128 (7 Oct. 1722).
5 Pomeau, i. 161.
6 D271 (*c*.20 April 1726).
7 De Beer and Rousseau, *Voltaire's British Visitors*, p. 73.

Chapter 5 England, 'Land of Liberty'

1 D299 (12 Aug. 1726).
2 See Nicholas Cronk, 'Voltaire rencontre Monsieur le Spectateur. Addison et la genèse des *Lettres anglaises*', in Michel Delon and Catriona Seth (eds), *Voltaire en Europe. Hommage à Christiane Mervaud* (Oxford, 2000), 13–21 (18).
3 *CW*, lxxxi. 51.
4 André-Michel Rousseau, *L'Angleterre et Voltaire* (3 vols), in *Studies in Voltaire and the Eighteenth Century*, nos. 145–7 (1966), i [145]. 118.
5 Rousseau, *L'Angleterre et Voltaire*, i [145]. 46, note 17.
6 'To the Queen': 'YOUR MAJESTY will find in this Book, bold impartial Truths, Morality unstained with Superstition, a Spirit of Liberty, equally abhorrent of Rebellion and of Tiranny (*sic*), the Rights of Kings always asserted, and those of Mankind never laid aside.' Quoted in Voltaire, *Letters concerning the English Nation*, ed. Nicholas Cronk (Oxford World's Classic) (Oxford: 1994), p. xiii.

7 See Nicholas Cronk's comments in *CW*, iii (a). 304–9.
8 *Letters philosophiques*, letter 11.
9 See *CW*, ii. 75, and Rousseau, *L'Angleterre et Voltaire*, i [145]. 154.
10 Rousseau, *L'Angleterre et Voltaire*, i [145]. 153.
11 D342 (14/25 Nov. 1728).

Chapter 6 From Bonanza to Bombshell

1 Moland, i. 44.
2 D638 (27 July 1733).
3 D303 (26 Oct. 1726: in Voltaire's English).
4 D330 (11 April 1728: in Voltaire's English).
5 See J. Patrick Lee, 'The Unexamined Premise: Voltaire, John Lockman and the myth of the *English letters*', *SVEC* [formerly *Studies on Voltaire and the Eighteenth Century*], 2001: 10, pp. 240–70; and Nicholas Cronk, 'The *Letters concerning the English Nation* as an English work: reconsidering the Harcourt Brown thesis', *SVEC*, 2001: 10, pp. 226–39.
6 D439 (21 Nov. 1731).
7 D488 (13 May 1732: in Voltaire's English).
8 *Lettres philosophiques*, letter 13.
9 *Lettres philosophiques*, letter 6.

Chapter 7 Sex in Blue Stockings

1 D3918 (2 May 1749).
2 D646 (*c.*15 Aug. 1733).
3 D766 (1 July 1734).
4 D779 (? Aug. 1734).
5 D793 (Oct. 1734).
6 D800 (*c.*1 Nov. 1734).
7 D876 (*c.*15 June 1735).
8 D881 (*c.*20 June 1735).

Chapter 8 A Marriage of True Minds

1 D885 (26 June 1735).
2 D935 (3 Nov. 1735).
3 D943 (? Nov. 1735).

4 *CW*, viii. 363.
5 'I too have composed my own little manual of metaphysics, for after all a man needs to be clear in his mind what he thinks about the things of this world' (D935 (3 Nov. 1735)).
6 D799 (*c*.1 Nov. 1734).
7 *CW*, xvi. 303 (l.129).
8 *CW*, xiv. 117–18.
9 *CW*, xiv. 123.
10 First published only in the following century, it appeared under this title in Voltaire, *Œuvres complètes* (Paris: Lequien, 1820–6).
11 *Essay on Man*, Epistle i. 285–94. Cf. Epistle iv. 113–16: 'God sends not ill; if rightly understood,/Or partial Ill is universal Good,/Or Change admits, or Nature lets it fall,/Short and but rare, 'till Man improv'd it all.'
12 Élisabeth Badinter, *Les Passions intellectuelles* (2 vols, Paris: Fayard, 1999–2002), vol. 1 (*Désirs de gloire (1735–1751)*), p. 22.
13 D1216 (1 Dec. 1736).
14 D1548 (7 July 1738).

Chapter 9 Worms in the Apple

1 The classic study of this relationship and correspondence is Christiane Mervaud, *Voltaire et Frédéric II: une dramaturgie des lumières 1736–1778*, in *Studies on Voltaire and the Eighteenth Century*, no. 234 (Oxford: Voltaire Foundation, 1985).
2 D1232 (21 Dec. 1736).
3 D915 (20 Sept. 1735).
4 D1107 (1 July 1736).
5 D1207 (24 Nov. 1736).
6 D1221 (9 Dec. 1736).
7 D1286 (18 Feb. 1737).
8 D1255 (*c*.15 Jan. 1737).
9 D1265 (22 Jan. 1737).
10 *Correspondance de Madame de Graffigny*, ed. English Showalter (Oxford: 1985–), i. 209.

Chapter 10 Court Proceedings: Berlin or Paris?

1 D2015 (15 May 1739).
2 D2526 (10 Aug. 1741).
3 D2178 (10 March 1740).
4 D2225 (6 June 1740).
5 D2227 (10 June 1740).
6 D2250 (27 June 1740).
7 Ibid.

8 Moland, i. 46.
9 D2310 (12 Sept. 1740).
10 D2368 (26 Nov. 1740).
11 D2365 (23 Nov. 1740).
12 D2370 (28 Nov. 1740).
13 D2377 (*c*.1 Dec. 1740).
14 D2399 (1 Jan. 1741).
15 D2477 (5 May 1741).
16 *Essai sur les mœurs*, ed. René Pomeau (2 vols, Paris: 1963), i. 195.
17 D2623 (30 June 1742).
18 D2649 (1 Sept. 1742).
19 D2723 (Feb. 1743).
20 D2771 (*c*.15 June 1743).
21 D3073 (31 Jan. 1745).

Chapter 11 The Way of the World

1 D3086 (?17 March 1745). The marquise, whom he had adored in 1718, had now become a devout Catholic.
2 Moland, i. 89.
3 D3093 (3 April 1745).
4 D3269 (11 Dec. 1745).
5 D1514 (5 June 1738).
6 D1498 (10 May 1738).
7 D2974 (14 May 1744).
8 D3015 (13 Aug. 1744).
9 D3348 (*c*.1 April 1744).
10 Pomeau, i. 493.
11 D3450 (19 Aug. 1746).
12 D3566 (*c*.25 Aug. 1747: written in Italian).
13 D3576 (Sept./Oct. 1747).
14 D3581 (20 Oct. 1747).

Chapter 12 Death of a Lover

1 D3651 (22 May 1748: in Italian).
2 D3723 (19 July 1748).
3 D3724 (19 July 1748).
4 D3856 (26 Jan. 1749).
5 Pomeau, i. 582.
6 D3851 (18 Jan. 1749).
7 D3952 (29 June 1749).

8 D4005 (4 Sept. 1749).
9 Pomeau, i. 607.
10 Ibid.
11 D4015 (10 Sept. 1749).
12 Pomeau, i. 608.
13 D4024 (23 Sept. 1749).
14 *Discours sur le bonheur*, ed. Robert Mauzi (Paris: 1961), p. 32.
15 Pomeau, i. 607. (The words were recorded by Longchamp.)

Chapter 13 Hello and Goodbye to Berlin

1 Throughout the following chapters I am indebted to Christiane Mervaud, *Voltaire à table* (Paris: Éditions Desjonquères, 1998) for information about eighteenth-century gastronomy.
2 D4025 (23 Sept. 1749).
3 Pomeau, i. 619.
4 D4166 (26 June 1750), note 1.
5 D4195 (23 Aug. 1750).
6 D5005 (5 Sept. 1752).
7 D4564 (2 Sept. 1751). In fact this letter belongs with Voltaire's epistolary narrative now commonly known as *Paméla* (see next chapter). In his *Mémoires pour servir à la vie de M. de Voltaire* he gives a slightly different version: 'One squeezes the orange, and one throws it away after drinking the juice' (Moland, i. 38).
8 Moland, i. 38.
9 D4755 (*c.*1 Jan. 1752).
10 D2488 (27 May 1741).
11 D5096 (*c.*5 Dec. 1752).
12 Pomeau, i. 703.
13 D5097 (*c.*5 Dec. 1752).
14 D5159 (16 Jan. 1753).

Chapter 14 A Niece for a Wife, or House-Hunting in the 1750s

1 D5441 (22 July 1753).
2 On the title of this work see Jonathan Mallinson's article, 'What's in a name? Reflections on Voltaire's *Paméla*', *Eighteenth-Century Fiction* 18: 2 (Jan. 2006).
3 D5640 (28 Jan. 1754).
4 Pomeau, i. 768.
5 D5836 (6 June 1754).
6 D5968 (27 Oct. 1754).
7 D6068 (5 Jan. 1755).

8 The house is now the Institut et Musée Voltaire, founded by Theodore Besterman in the early 1950s. It belongs to the City of Geneva and is open to the public. It may be visited online at http://www.ville-ge.ch/bpu/imv. The house itself has been substantially remodelled over the intervening centuries, but the layout of a small number of rooms has been carefully recreated. In the winter drawing-room the original panelling, fireplace and overmantel have been beautifully restored, while in another room the original flooring has been recreated. The house is now surrounded by urban Geneva: the gardens have been swallowed up, the views blocked. The 'long gallery' or wing currently houses the research library.

9 D6235 (5 April 1755).
10 D6214 (24 March 1755).
11 D7636 (? Feb. 1758).
12 D6229 (2 April 1755), D6231 (2 April 1755).
13 D6451 (30 Aug. 1755).
14 D6608 (1 Dec. 1755).

Chapter 15 From Earthquake to Book Launch: *Candide*

1 Pomeau, i. 836, and commentary to D6868 (19 May 1756).
2 D6965 (9 Aug. 1756).
3 Moland. i. 45.
4 *Candide*, Chapter 3.
5 *Candide*, end of the 'Conclusion'.
6 D14181 (16 May 1767).
7 *Candide*, Chapter 4.
8 Garry Apgar et al., *Voltaire chez lui. Ferney 1758–1778* (Yens sur Morges (Switzerland) and Saint-Gingolph (France): Éditions Cabédita, 1999), p. 14.
9 See *Bulletin d'information* (Fondation Voltaire à Ferney), no. 7 (September 2004), p. 2. The information is derived from manuscripts at the Institut et Musée Voltaire: Fonds Gerlier – Manuscrits Ferney. Ms FG 1, and FG 2, and dossier Wagnière, F14.
10 *Candide*, Chapter 19.
11 René Pomeau suggests a figure of 20,000 for the whole year (see i. 906), but this would appear to be a significant underestimate.
12 Pomeau, i. 905.

Chapter 16 The Vineyard of Truth

1 D8304 (18 May 1759).
2 D7499 (6 Dec. 1757).
3 D10284 (26 Jan. 1762).
4 D11695 (13 Feb. 1764).
5 D8871 (23 April 1760).

6 For a photograph of the Château de Ferney, visit www.ferney-voltaire.net.
7 D9124 (8 Aug. 1760).
8 D20719 (July 1777).
9 D8998 (20 June 1760).
10 D9743 (20 April 1761). The source of Voltaire's quotation has not been identified.
11 D9472 (16 Dec. 1760).

Chapter 17 Jousting with Injustice: Calas and Rousseau

1 D10382 (22 March 1762).
2 D10414 (15 April 1762).
3 Pomeau, ii. 132.
4 *Correspondance complète de Jean-Jacques Rousseau*, ed. R.A. Leigh (52 vols, Geneva: 1965–95), viii, letter 1019.
5 D9575 (26 Feb. 1761).
6 Moland, xxiv, 175.
7 D9575 (26 Jan. 1761).
8 D10705 (15 Sept. 1762), and note 6. Voltaire's claim remains unsubstantiated by any other source.
9 D10507 (14 June 1762).
10 D10507 and D10527 (25 June 1762).
11 D12262 (*c.*25 Dec. 1764).

Chapter 18 D for Dictionary, D for Danger

1 D13235 (5 April 1766).
2 D10894 (9 Jan. 1763).
3 D8764.
4 Christiane Mervaud, in *CW*, xxxv. 94.
5 *CW*, lxii. 461.
6 D12073 (7 Sept. 1764).
7 D11978 (9 July 1764), D11987 (16 July 1764).
8 *Œuvres historiques*, ed. René Pomeau (Paris: 1957), p. 48.
9 A new, enlarged version was published in 1769, and another in 1775.
10 See Roland Desné, in *CW*, lvi (a). 55–8.
11 Moland, xxv. 250.
12 In August 1761 the Paris *parlement* ordered all pupils in Jesuit schools and seminaries to leave them before the beginning of October. After intervention by the King, the deadline was deferred until 1 April 1762. In August 1762 the Paris *parlement* outlawed the Society in France and confiscated its property. Over the next two years most provincial *parlements* followed suit. When in 1764 the Paris *parlement* sought to exile all Jesuits from France, the King intervened again, accepting the dissolution of the

Society but permitting its members to remain in France and quashing all legal proceedings against them.

13 D13762 (23 Nov. 1766).
14 D14897 (30 March 1768).
15 Pomeau, ii. 286.
16 De Beer and Rousseau, *Voltaire's British Visitors*, p. 97.
17 Ibid., p. 93.
18 Ibid., p. 85.
19 Ibid., p. 66.

Chapter 19 April Foolery

1 *Voltaire chez lui*, p. 23.
2 D15134 (9 July 1768).
3 Moland, xxvii, 60.
4 Reported by d'Alembert in D14972 (20 April 1768). In D15178 (19 Aug. 1768) Voltaire remarks that in the matter of death he is quite happy to cede precedence to the abbé.
5 D15478 (*c*. Feb. 1769).
6 D.app.300, in *CW* cxvii. 486–7.
7 D.app.300, in *CW*, cxvii. 487.
8 D16141 (9 Feb. 1770).
9 De Beer and Rousseau, *Voltaire's British Visitors*, p. 185.

Chapter 20 The Watchmakers

1 D15828 (16 Aug. 1769).
2 Moland, x. 403.
3 D16552 (28 July 1770).
4 D16337 (8 May 1770).
5 *Correspondance complète*, ed. Leigh, xxxviii. 26 (letter 6723).
6 Commentary to D16485 (*c*.1 July 1770).
7 *CW*, lxvi. 389.
8 *Candide and Other Stories*, trans. and ed. Roger Pearson (Oxford World's Classics) (Oxford: 1990), p. 309.
9 Ibid., pp. 279 and 301.
10 Ibid., pp. 305 and 304.
11 Ibid., p. 290.
12 D18438 (26 June 1773).
13 D18831 (2 March 1774).
14 D16616 (28 Aug. 1770).
15 D16397 (8 June 1770).
16 D19340 (15 Feb. 1775).

Chapter 21 A Fight to the Finish

1 D19393.
2 D18356 (8 May 1773).
3 D18098 (21 Dec. 1772). The letter is signed by 'The sick old man of Ferney who is unduly honoured'.
4 D18863 (21 March 1774).
5 D17811 (4 July 1772).
6 D19484 (18 May 1775) and D19486 (19 May 1775).
7 D19217 (8 Dec. 1774).
8 Pomeau, ii. 456.
9 D19443 (27 April 1775).
10 D8757 (15 Feb. 1760).
11 D12002 (21 July 1764).
12 D13324 (29 May 1766).
13 Moland, xxxi. 107, 108–9, 115.
14 Ferney was known unofficially as Ferney-Voltaire as early as 1780, but the name was officially changed only in 1878, to mark the centenary of Voltaire's death. See D19658, note.

Chapter 22 The Last Act

1 D20471 (15 Dec. 1776).
2 Moland, xxx. 586.
3 Pomeau, ii. 567.
4 D21054 (*c.*18 Feb. 1778).
5 Pomeau, ii. 579.
6 Pomeau, ii, 582.
7 Pomeau, ii. 583.
8 Ibid.
9 Pomeau, ii. 585.
10 Jones, *Paris. Biography of a City*, 209.
11 Ibid., 212.
12 D20493 (1 Jan. 1777).

Chapter 23 Out Like a Candle

1 Pomeau, ii. 611.
2 D21129 (30 March 1778).
3 Pomeau, ii. 601.
4 Pomeau, ii. 635.
5 With the exception of all books in English, which Voltaire had bequeathed to his friend Henri Rieu (1721–87). A former naval captain and then Governor of the French part of the Île Saint-Martin in the Lesser Antilles, Rieu had returned to live at Ferney. Voltaire referred to him as 'mon cher corsaire'.
6 *Voltaire chez lui*, p. 42.
7 Ibid., pp. 43–4.
8 Ibid., p. 57, note 136.
9 See Pomeau, ii. 438.
10 The table of contents for the Complete Works currently being edited by the Voltaire Foundation runs to 118 pages

Chapter 24 Conclusion

1 D6985 (1 Sept. 1756).
2 D1376 (*c.*15 Oct. 1737).
3 D10580 (11 July 1762). The identity of the Englishman is unknown.
4 D7480 (25 Nov. 1757).
5 From *L'Ingénu*, Chapter 10.
6 D15855 (30 Aug. 1769). Cf. D13394, 13420, 13448 (all from July 1766).
7 D16091 (12 Jan. 1770).
8 See D11418 (15 Sept. 1763) and 13355 (15 June 1766). For a comprehensive account of this issue, see Harvey Chisick, *The Limits of Reform in the Enlightenment: Attitudes toward the Education of the Lower Classes in Eighteenth-Century France* (Princeton, NJ, 1981).
9 D11051 (28 Feb. 1763).
10 D15855; D16091.
11 Moland, xxv, 418.
12 D12938 (16 Oct. 1765).
13 D15903 (18 Sept. 1769).
14 See Jonathan Israel, *Radical Enlightenment. Philosophy and the Making of Modernity 1650–1750* (Oxford: 2001), pp. 522–7.
15 Moland, i. 55.
16 The phrase originates in S.G. Tallentyre, *The Friends of Voltaire* (London: 1907), p. 199, not as a quotation but explicitly as a paraphrase of Voltaire's attitude in defence of Helvétius's *De l'esprit* (*On the Mind*) when it was banned in 1758.
17 D1375 (*c.*12 Oct. 1737): 'Je suis tolérant, je trouve très bon qu'on pense autrement que moi.' Voltaire is here referring to Christian Wolff, whose Leibnizianism he rejected.

Curtain Call

1 This innocent man, executed on 19 November 1770, had been charged, together with his wife, with the murder of her mother (who had died of a stroke, or 'apoplexy'). His name was subsequently cleared – and his wife acquitted – thanks to Voltaire's efforts.
2 D17727 (4 May 1772).

Select Bibliography

(*SVEC* denotes both *Studies in Voltaire and the Eighteenth Century* (published by the Voltaire Foundation, Oxford) and its successor, *SVEC*.)

Collected Works by Voltaire

Œuvres complètes, ed. Louis Moland (52 vols, Paris: 1877–85).
Les Œuvres complètes de Voltaire. The Complete Works of Voltaire, ed. Theodore Besterman, W.H. Barber, Ulla Kölving, Haydn Mason, and Nicholas Cronk (Geneva, Banbury and Oxford, 1968–).
Œuvres historiques, ed. René Pomeau (Paris: 1957).
Romans et contes, ed. Frédéric Deloffre and Jacques Van den Heuvel (Paris: 1979).
Romans et contes, ed. Édouard Guitton (La Pochothèque) (Paris: 1994).

Selected Works

Essai sur les mœurs, ed. René Pomeau (2 vols, Paris: 1963).
Lettres philosophiques, ed. Frédéric Deloffre (Paris: 1986).
Traité sur la tolérance, ed. John Renwick (Oxford: 1999).

Works by Voltaire in English translation

Candide, trans. Theo Cuffe (Penguin Classics) (London: 2005).
Candide and Other Stories, trans. and ed. Roger Pearson (Oxford World's Classics) (Oxford: 1990; second edn, 2006).
Letters concerning the English Nation, ed. Nicholas Cronk (Oxford World's Classics) (Oxford: 1994).

Micromégas and Other Short Stories, trans. Theo Cuffe, ed. Haydn Mason (Penguin Classics) (London: 2002).

Philosophical Dictionary, trans. Theodore Besterman (Penguin Classics) (London: 1972; reissued 2004).

Political Writings, trans. and ed. David Williams (Cambridge: 1994).

Treatise on Tolerance, trans. Brian Masters, ed. Simon Harvey (Cambridge: 2000).

Voltaire. Selections, ed. Paul Edwards (New York: 1989).

Biographies of Voltaire

IN FRENCH

Collini, Cosimo Alessandro, *Mon séjour auprès de Voltaire* (Paris: 1807).

Condorcet, marquis de, *Vie de Voltaire*, ed. Élisabeth Badinter (Paris: 1994). Also to be found in Moland, i.

Desnoiresterres, Gustave, *Voltaire et la société au XVIIIe siècle* (8 vols, Paris: 1867–76).

Duvernet, Théophile, *La Vie de Voltaire* (Geneva: 1786).

Lanson, Gustave, *Voltaire* (Paris: 1906; reprinted, ed. René Pomeau, 1960).

Lepape, Pierre, *Voltaire le conquérant* (Paris: 1994).

Longchamp [Sébastien], et Wagnière [Jean-Louis], *Mémoires sur Voltaire* (2 vols, Paris: 1826).

Naves, Raymond, *Voltaire* (Paris: 1942).

Orieux, Jean, *Voltaire ou la Royauté de l'esprit* (Paris: 1966).

Pomeau, René et al., *Voltaire en son temps* (5 vols, Oxford: 1985–94; rev. edn, 2 vols, Oxford and Paris: 1995).

IN ENGLISH

Ayer, A.J., *Voltaire* (London: 1988).

Besterman, Theodore, *Voltaire* (rev. edn, London: 1976).

Davidson, Ian, *Voltaire in Exile* (London: 2004).

Hearsey, John E.N., *Voltaire* (London: 1976).

Mason, Haydn, *Voltaire. A Biography* (London: 1981).

Mitford, Nancy, *Voltaire in Love* (London: 1957).

Morley, John, *Voltaire* (London: 1885).

Tallentyre, S.G. (pseudonym of Evelyn Beatrice Hall), *The Life of Voltaire* (2 vols, London: 1903).

Studies of Voltaire

IN FRENCH

Apgar, Garry et al., *Voltaire chez lui. Ferney 1758–1778* (Yens sur Morges, Switzerland, and Saint-Gingolph, France: 1999).

Barthes, Roland, 'Le Dernier des écrivains heureux', in *Essais critiques* (Paris: 1964), 94–100.

Belaval, Yvon, 'L'Esprit de Voltaire', *SVEC* 24 (1963).

Bellesort, André, *Essai sur Voltaire* (Paris: 1925).

Delattre, André, *Voltaire l'impétueux* (Paris: 1957).

Donvez, Jacques, *De quoi vivait Voltaire?* (Paris: 1949).

Menant, Sylvain, *L'Esthétique de Voltaire* (Paris: 1995).

Mervaud, Christiane, *Voltaire et Frédéric II. Une dramaturgie des Lumières, SVEC*, no. 234 (1985).

———— *Voltaire en toutes lettres* (Paris: 1991).

———— *Le 'Dictionnaire philosophique' de Voltaire* (Oxford: 1994).

———— *Voltaire à table* (Paris: 1998).

Pomeau, René, *Voltaire par lui-même* (Paris: n.d. [1959]).

———— *La Religion de Voltaire* (rev. edn, Paris: 1969).

Rousseau, André-Michel, *L'Angleterre et Voltaire* (3 vols, Oxford: 1976).

Sareil, Jean, *Essai sur 'Candide'* (Geneva: 1967).

Van den Heuvel, Jacques, *Voltaire dans ses contes* (Paris: 1967).

IN ENGLISH

Barber, W.H., *Leibniz in France from Arnauld to Voltaire. A Study in French Reactions to Leibnizianism, 1670–1760* (Oxford: 1955).

Brumfitt, J.H., *Voltaire Historian* (Oxford: 1958).

De Beer, Gavin, and Rousseau, André-Michel, *Voltaire's British Visitors*, in *SVEC*, no. 49 (1967).

Gay, Peter, *Voltaire's Politics. The Poet as Realist* (2nd edn, New Haven, Conn., and London: 1988).

Howell, Robin, *Disabled Powers. A Reading of Voltaire's Contes* (Amsterdam and Atlanta: 1993).

Mason, Haydn, *Voltaire* (London: 1975).

———— *'Candide': Optimism Demolished* (New York: 1992).

Pearson, Roger, *The Fables of Reason. A Study of Voltaire's 'contes philosophiques'* (Oxford: 1993).

Wade, Ira O., *The Intellectual Development of Voltaire* (Princeton, NJ: 1969).

Other Works

Badinter, Élisabeth, *Émilie, Émilie. L'Ambition féminine au XVIIIe siècle* (Paris: 1983).
――― *Les Passions intellectuelles* (2 vols, Paris: 1999–2002).
Cassirer, Ernst, *The Philosophy of the Enlightenment*, trans. Fritz C.A. Koelln and James P. Pettegrove (Princeton, NJ: 1951).
Chisick, Harvey, *The Limits of Reform in the Enlightenment: Attitudes toward the Education of the Lower Classes in Eighteenth-Century France* (Princeton, NJ: 1981).
Israel, Jonathan, *Radical Enlightenment. Philosophy and the Making of Modernity 1650–1750* (Oxford: 2001).
Jones, Colin, *The Great Nation. France from Louis XV to Napoleon* (London: 2002).
――― *Paris. Biography of a City* (London: 2004).
Mauzi, Robert, *L'Idée du bonheur dans la littérature et la pensée françaises au XVIIIe siècle* (Paris: 1960).
Mortier, Roland, *Clartés et ombres du Siècle des Lumières* (Geneva: 1969).
Porter, Roy, *The Enlightenment* (London: 1990).
Roche, Daniel, *La France des Lumières* (Paris: 1993).

List of Illustrations

Plate Section

Acknowledgements

I SHOULD LIKE TO THANK the Provost and Fellows of the Queen's College, Oxford for granting me an exceptional period of leave to enable me to write this book. I am also indebted, as always, to the staff of the Taylorian Institution Library at Oxford for their outstanding service. I owe a particular debt to my agent, Catherine Clarke of Felicity Bryan, without whose intervention this project would never have found me, and to Rosemary Davidson, my editor, for her faith in its possibilities, the warmth of her encouragement, and the shrewdness of her guidance. I owe much also to the learning and expertise of many Voltaire scholars, notably the late René Pomeau and the distinguished co-authors of *Voltaire en son temps*. The work of Professor Christiane Mervaud in particular has shone as a beacon of excellence. I am similarly grateful to M. François Jacob and Mme Catherine Walser for their cordial welcome and assistance at the Institue et Musée Voltaire in Geneva. But my greatest debt is owed to Dr Nicholas Cronk, General Editor of the *Complete Works of Voltaire* and Director of the Voltaire Foundation in Oxford. Throughout the gestation of this book he has been unfailingly generous in sharing his extensive and up-to-the-minute knowledge of Voltaire and Voltaire studies. All remaining errors, nevertheless, are strictly my own.

Index